T0345286

Swarm Intelligence
Trends and Applications

Editors

Wellington Pinheiro dos Santos
Federal University of Pernambuco
Brazil

Juliana Carneiro Gomes
University of Pernambuco
Brazil

Valter Augusto de Freitas Barbosa
Federal Rural University of Pernambuco
Brazil

CRC Press
Taylor & Francis Group
Boca Raton London New York

CRC Press is an imprint of the
Taylor & Francis Group, an **informa** business

A SCIENCE PUBLISHERS BOOK

First edition published 2023
by CRC Press
6000 Broken Sound Parkway NW, Suite 300, Boca Raton, FL 33487-2742

and by CRC Press
4 Park Square, Milton Park, Abingdon, Oxon, OX14 4RN

Library of Congress Cataloging-in-Publication Data (applied for)

ISBN 978-1-032-03995-4 (hbk)
ISBN 978-1-032-03996-1 (pbk)
ISBN 978-1-003-19014-1 (ebk)

DOI: 10.1201/9781003190141

Typeset in Times New Roman
by Radiant Productions

Preface

Artificial Intelligence is based on three fundamental paradigms: the connectionist paradigm, the statistical paradigm and the symbolic paradigm. Connectionist Intelligence is marked by Artificial Neural Networks, which is intelligent models built from inspiration of the human brain. This area has gained new interest with the advent of deep neural networks, both in the domain of representing objects of interest, especially images, through convolutional networks, and in solving classification and regression problems. With the IV Industrial Revolution, marked by the advancement of Artificial Intelligence, Biotechnology, Digital Health, and the Internet of Things, the importance of Connectionist Intelligence methods increases more and more, mainly from the Covid-19 pandemic, which served as a catalyst for the digital transformation of health and information and communication technologies as a whole.

Symbolic Artificial Intelligence is based on modeling the solution of problems such as search and optimization. Initially marked by statistical methods and Mathematical Programming, Symbolic Artificial Intelligence takes an evolutionary leap with meta-heuristics. From the inspiration in nature, with the advent of the Particle Swarm Optimization algorithm, Swarm Intelligence emerges. According to this paradigm, Artificial Intelligence is now understood as collective intelligence: intelligent agents capable of simple operations are able to solve complex problems through collective mechanisms of population evolution and with the modeling of adequate social relations, which promote both the individual as well as the collective. Ants, bees, birds, wolves and other collective animals, such as humans themselves, are a constant source of inspiration for the construction and improvement of new collective intelligence algorithms. Through Swarm Intelligence, it is possible not only to optimize well-established solutions according to certain quality parameters, but also to create new solutions for a world that increasingly depends on Artificial Intelligence to solve old and new problems in society.

In this book, "Swarm Intelligence: New Trends and Applications", we aim to present the principles and advances of Swarm Intelligence and applications on industry and digital health. The book consists of two parts: the first four chapters are dedicated to the fundamentals of Swarm Intelligence algorithms and theoretical advances; from the fifth chapter to the last one, we present several real-world applications, especially regarding machine learning on digital health.

This book is intended for academics, graduate and postgraduate students in Computer Science, Computer Engineering, Biomedical Engineering, Medicine, Biomedicine and everyone interested in understanding the fundamental basis of Swarm Intelligence, both algorithmic and theoretically, presenting the theoretical bases, new trends, emerging algorithms, examples, and real-world applications. This book is intended to be available to undergraduate and postgraduate students, academics and independent data scientists.

The first chapter, "Swarm Intelligence based algorithm for feature selection in high-dimensional datasets", investigates a temperature variable's inclusion to the existing Ant Colony Optimization algorithm that demonstrates a significant increase in classification performance. The objective of this research is to evaluate the performance of hybrid Ant Colony Optimization, Simulated Annealing algorithm with other algorithms on several benchmark datasets using a Decision Tree classifier.

In Chapter 2 "Swarm Intelligence for Data Mining", the authors review the role of Swarm Intelligence-based algorithms in the data mining tasks including association rule mining and clustering. This chapter begins with an overview of Swarm Intelligence with an emphasis on Particle Swarm Optimization, Ant Colony Optimization and Artificial Bee Colony algorithms. It also provides an introduction on the association rule mining and clustering as the main important tasks in data mining and presents an overview of the Swarm Intelligence-based algorithms for these tasks.

In "Leveraging Center-Based Sampling Theory for Enhancing Particle Swarm Classification of Textual Data", in Chapter 3, the authors present the Center-Based sampling theory and how it is employed to develop a variant of Particle Swarm Optimization, CBS-PSO, able to deal with the curse of dimensionality problem in data classification. The center-based sampling theory implies that the center region of a search space is promising for population-based algorithms due to the presence of points with higher probability to be closer to the optimal solution; this probability increases directly with the dimensionality of the search space. Therefore, the authors give PSO two mechanisms to attract the search process toward the center region of the search space. The first mechanism uses Rocchio Algorithm (RA) to estimate the coordinates of the center point in the search space, while the second mechanism uses the RA-based estimation to generate informed particles, located at the center region, and incorporate them in the swarm to gradually attract the search for the optimal classifiers toward this promising region. The performance of the developed proposed CBS-PSO algorithm was evaluated on the classification of three textual datasets from UC Irvine Machine Learning Repository. To position the proposed CBS-PSO within machine learning classifiers, its performance is compared with the performance of three machine learning approaches, and experimented on the same classification tasks. The results demonstrate that the CBS-PSO can constitute a very competitive and promising classifier with much space for improvement, specifically for high dimensional data classification.

In Chapter 4, "Reinforcement Learning for Out-of-the-box Parameter Control for Evolutionary and Swarm-based Algorithm", the author discusses the application of Reinforcement Learning in out-of-the-box parameter control for evolutionary and swarm-based algorithms. According to reviews of the state-of-the-art performed by the author, despite the well succeeded applications of evolutionary and swarm-based algorithms in several areas, it is well known that these algorithms are quite sensitive to their parameters: the majority of the studies published so far on parameter control for evolutionary and swarm-based algorithms propose the methods tailored to specific scenarios. Only a few studies on out-of-the-box methods can be found. The authors justify their investigation by the fact that Reinforcement Learning is the paradigm that was most used to design out-of-the-box parameter control methods for such algorithms.

In Chapter 5, "Recognition of Emotions in the Elderly Through Audio Signal Analysis", the authors propose a machine learning approach for the recognition of emotions in elderly people through speech. To validate their proposal, the authors adopted the audio speech dataset RAVDESS. The intention is to build human-machine interfaces to support therapists and physicians to get emotional biofeedback. Initially, a CNN architecture with extraction of the log-mel spectrogram attribute was used. Although the experimental results found did not exceed 61%, they served as a starting experiment for the next models. In the second experiment, the authors applied the wavelet transform, converting sound signals into images through pseudocolors. From these images, 2048 features were extracted by a pre-trained ResNet network. The authors used the Particle Swarm Optimization algorithm (PSO) to select the statistically most significant 410 features. To investigate the effects of PSO on the architecture, the authors generated sub-bases with 2048 and with 410 features. They investigated the following learning machines: Bayesian Network, Naive Bayes classifier, decision tree J48, Random Tree, Random Forests, and Support Vector Machines (SVM). The RBF-kernel SVM with $\gamma = 0.5$ showed great potential. The pre-processing with transfer learning reached an accuracy of 81.1%, being the best model. The authors highlighted the relevance of attribute selection for the simplification of the problem.

In Chapter 6, "Recognition of Emotions in the Elderly through Facial Expressions: A Machine Learning-Based Approach", presents different machine learning approaches to Emotion Recognition in elderly through Facial Expressions. The authors performed two experiments using the FER2013 database. In Experiment 1, they implemented a Convolutional Neural Network to classify emotions and use the Haar Cascade Frontal Face to detect faces. In experiment 2, using Transfer Learning, they applied a pre-trained LeNet network with the MNIST dataset for attribute extraction. The Synthetic Minority

Oversampling Technique method was used to balance the classes and the Particle Swarm Optimization method for feature selection. A Random Forest algorithm was used with several tree configurations to perform the classifications. The results obtained in Experiment 1 demonstrate that the model obtained an accuracy of 0.6375, classifying 52.63% of the images of the elderly correctly and 47.37% incorrectly. In Experiment 2, the Random Forest with 400 trees stood out both in the set with all attributes, with an accuracy of 75.86%, and in the set with the selection of attributes, with 73.87%. The experimental results indicate the possibility of developing intelligent systems that support the recognition of emotions in the elderly population.

In Chapter 7, "Identification of Emotion Parameters in Music to Modulate Human Affective States", proposes the automatic identification of emotions induced by music compositions of different genres based on the prediction of their valence and arousal parameters. To achieve this goal, the authors extracted explicit numerical features from the songs and used this set of features to train regression models based on Linear Regression, Support Vector Machines, Extreme Learning Machines, Random Forests, and Multi-Layer Perceptrons. Random Forest model outperformed the others with better correlation coefficients and lower errors for predicting both arousal and valence values from the music signals. Arousal prediction with Random Forest resulted in a Pearson's correlation coefficient of 0.85 ± 0.01. While valence was predicted with a correlation of up to 0.76 ± 0.02. A Particle Swarm Optimization (PSO) feature selection study was conducted in an attempt to better assess the correlation between the extracted features and the emotional parameters associated with the songs. The use of PSO significantly reduced the dimensionality of the vectors used to represent both valence and arousal information.

In Chapter 8, "Clinical decision support in the care of symptomatic patients with COVID-19: An approach based on machine learning and swarm intelligence", aims to evaluate the performance of intelligent classifiers, to be used to support decision making regarding the type of care that the patient should receive. Patient data corresponded to hematological and biochemical tests. Four families of smart classifiers were investigated. The most relevant hematological parameters for decision making were also analyzed using the particle swarm optimization algorithm. The results demonstrated the possibility to build intelligent decision support systems aimed at attending Covid-19 with good results (accuracies above 80%) based on the most relevant hematological parameters.

In Chapter 9, "The Sound of the Mind: Detection of Common Mental Disorders Using Vocal Acoustic Analysis and Machine Learning", the authors developed a machine learning-based tool to support the diagnosis of mental disorders in an emergency context from the analysis of audio signals. The authors built a model to recognize the following illnesses: major depressive disorder, schizophrenia, bipolar disorder, and generalized anxiety. Evolutionary search, particle swarm optimization and ant colony search are used to build a ranking of the 33 audio attributes used, in order to select those that are statistically more relevant for the correct classification.

We hope that the work presented in this collection will show the theoretical foundations and advancements in Swarm Intelligence, as well as state-of-the-art applications, especially in digital health and real-world health-related problems.

Enjoy your reading!

March 1st, 2022   Prof. Wellington Pinheiro dos Santos, DSc MSc BSc EE
Recife, Brazil   Mrs. Juliana Carneiro Gomes, MSc BSc BME
                Prof. Valter Augusto de Freitas Barbosa, DSc ME, MSc BSc BME

Contents

Contents

Section 1

Fundamentals and Advancements on Swarm Intelligence

Chapter 1

Swarm Intelligence Based Algorithm for Feature Selection in High-Dimensional Datasets

Nandini Nayar,[1] Sachin Ahuja[2] and Shaily Jain[1],*

1 Introduction

The true value of data depends on its ability to extract vital information which is adequate for decision support and exploration. In the case of datasets with a lesser number of features, superior prediction results can be obtained.

However, when the number of features is increased, traditional methods tend to be less-efficient because all the features may not be relevant. Thus there is a need to extract a "feature subset" using feature selection methods that can enhance accuracy. Datasets comprising of "n" features can have "2^n" viable feature subsets, however it is an impractical task to analyze all possible feature subsets for high-dimensional datasets. Building reliable models for classification requires a lesser number of features containing as much vital information as possible. However, due to a lack of prior knowledge of datasets, it becomes tedious to determine the pertinent features. It leads to the inclusion of redundant and irrelevant features that

[1] Chitkara University School of Engineering and Technology, Chitkara University Himachal Pradesh, India.
[2] Chitkara University Institute of Engineering and Technology, Chitkara University, Punjab, India.
  Emails: nandini.nayar@chitkarauniversity.edu.in; sachin.ahuja@chitkara.edu.in
* Corresponding author: shaily.jain@chitkarauniversity.edu.in

reduce training efficacy and negatively impact the model's performance (Nayar et al., 2019a). However, when the number of features is increased, the traditional methods tend to be less efficient because all features may not be relevant. Thus there is a need to extract a "feature subset" using feature selection methods to enhance accuracy. A dataset comprising of "n" features can have "2^n" viable feature subsets, but it is an impractical task to analyse all possible feature subsets for high-dimensional datasets.

The critical factor that influences the performance of the algorithm is the "feature space". Selecting relevant features enhances the quality of feature space and improves the classification rate. Feature selection models aim to develop clean and understandable data, thereby improving the data mining performance.

Feature selection methods efficiently lead to optimal solutions with high computational efficacy. As the traditional methods become inefficient because all features may not be relevant, thus necessitating extracting a "subset of features" using feature selection methods that can elevate accuracy. The traditional approaches were inefficient to solve the feature selection problem in the domain of high-dimensional datasets, which encouraged researchers to develop more efficient approaches using Swarm Intelligence (Too and Mirjalili, 2021).

1.1   Feature Selection

High-dimensional datasets pose numerous challenges, including problems related to the storage and retrieval of data, strenuous interpretation, and reduced accuracy which subsequently decelerates the process of mining, consequently leading to the curse of dimensionality. This has motivated researchers to develop more scalable and efficient feature selection techniques for selecting prominent feature subsets.

Feature Selection can certainly help to reduce the number of features. However, it is a complex task, especially when number of features is exceptionally high. Since the irrelevant and redundant features may have a negative impact on the performance of models. Thus, it becomes imperative to select vital features that are valuable for enhancing the performance of models, thereby enhancing the speed and performance of the prediction system (Abualigah and Dulaimi, 2021).

Generally, the features are categorized as:

➢ Relevant features: These features have a noteworthy influence on output, and their role cannot be assumed by the rest of features.

➢ Irrelevant features: These features don't have any noteworthy influence on the output.

➢ Redundant features: These features can take the role of other features.

Selecting the relevant features from a dataset is challenging, especially when we have to select a valuable subset from hundreds or thousands of features. This research aims to choose a subset of valuable features to determine which of the classifiers performs the best.

The objective of feature selection is to choose a minimal feature subset, *i.e.*, the best feature subset comprising of k-features yielding the least generalization errors. It is expected that feature selection techniques are utilized either as a pre-processing step or in combination with the learning model for the task of classification. Usually, the performance of the model is estimated in terms of the "classification rate" that is obtained on a testing set. The set of all original features are given as an input to feature selection methods, which will subsequently generate "feature subsets". Then, the subset which is selected is evaluated by the learning algorithm or through consideration of data characteristics.

1.2 Swarm Intelligence (SI)

The term "Swarm" is used for a group of birds/animals/insects that evince collaborative behaviour by interacting with each other and with their environment, and eventually solve numerous complex problems. These agents follow local rules that govern their actions, and thereby these swarms achieve their goal.

Swarm Intelligence is an essential topic of interest for researchers that plays a significant role in providing efficient optimization solutions. In SI approaches, "agents" are the key elements determining how solutions will be generated and affect the capability of search procedure. A fascinating property of the Swarm-based system is the capability to behave in self-organized manner without any explicit controlling individual.

Owing to the multi-fold benefits of SI approaches, researchers have widely adopted this concept to tackle the problem of feature selection. SI approaches incorporate enormous benefits that are summarized in Fig. 1. SI algorithms are successfully used to optimize the feature selection process by determining the subset that yields the best predictive performance with the machine learning algorithm. One of the most apparent advantages of Swarm Intelligence is "Autonomy". Although swarms don't have any outside administration, still each swarm agent is able to control its behaviour independently.

The "agent" represents the probable solution of the problem, leading to the second advantage of "self-organization". The intelligence is not focussed on a single agent, but it is exhibited in the swarm itself. Even if the agents (solutions) are unknown in advance, still they change themselves during the running of the program. Moreover, self-organization plays a key role in "adaptability" that is, do the agents react favourably to the desired changes, and adjust their behaviour autonomously.

Even if there is no central control, the swarm possesses the property of "robustness", as there is no existence of a single point of failure. Additionally, the concept of "scalability" implies that swarm can comprise agents that can range up to thousands in number and, in any case, the control architecture would remain same. Also, because of the fact that there is no single essential agent for swarm, the SI advantage of flexibility is wholly fulfilled.

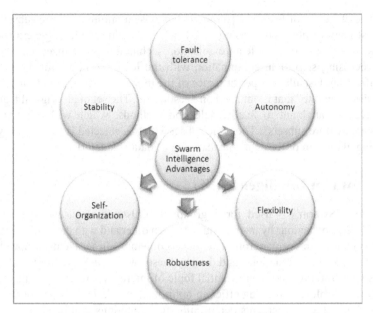

Figure 1: Advantages of Swarm Intelligence.

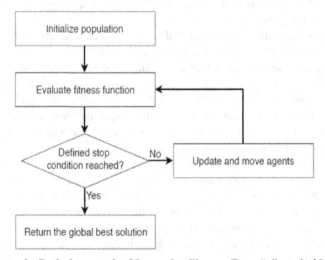

Figure 2: Basic framework of Swarm Intelligence (Brezočnik et al., 2018).

Swarm-based algorithms tend to follow some elementary phases as shown in Fig. 2 that include initializing the population, setting a stop condition, evaluation of the fitness function, moving and updating the agents, and subsequently returning the best solution.

1.3 Ant Colony Optimization (ACO)

The behaviour of ants has inspired many techniques. Ant Colony Optimization (ACO) is one of the most outstanding optimization techniques that is based on the food-finding behaviour of ants, in which ants drop a chemical known as a "pheromone" on their path, which is then perceived by other ants. The subsequent ants tend to follow the path where the pheromone intensity is remarkably high, thereby enabling the subsequent ants to follow the same path and converge more ants towards that path (Dorigo et al., 2006).

It is worth mentioning that in ACO, "probabilistic" decisions are made in terms of local heuristic information and "artificial" pheromone trails. Due to this fact, ACO has capability to explore a larger number of solutions as compared to greedy heuristics. Another interesting trait of ACO is that the evaporation of pheromone trail which reduces its intensity over time, is also that which helps avoid a speedy convergence towards sub-optimal region. Numerous advantages of Ant Colony Optimization have been summarized in Fig. 3.

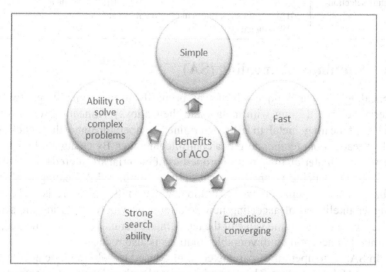

Figure 3: Benefits of Ant Colony Optimization.

Owing to numerous advantages of Ant Colony Optimization, the Ant-based algorithms are being extensively used in various application areas. Some common applications are listed in Table 1.

Table 1: Applications of Ant-based algorithms.

Application area	Authors
Protein folding	Llanes et al. (2016); Kaushik and Sahi (2017)
Multiple sequence alignment	Moss and Johnson (2003); Lee et al. (2008); Liang et al. (2005); Chen et al. (2006)
DNA sequencing	Blum and Yábar Vallès (2006); Kurniawan et al. (2009)
Scheduling	Merkle et al. (2002); Colorni et al. (1994); Forsyth et al. (1997)
Timetabling	Socha and Sampels (2002); Socha et al. (2003); Nothegger et al. (2012); Mayer et al. (2008); Khair et al. (2018); Kenekayoro and Zipamone (2016); Ugat et al. (2018)
Telecommunication networking	Schoonderwoerd et al. (1996); Di Caro and Dorigo (1998)
Cluster analysis	Chiu and Lin (2009); Chiu and Lin (2007); Dai et al. (2009); Korürek and Nizam (2008, 2010)
Feature selection	Aghdam and Kabiri (2016); Dwivedi et al. (2019); Sabeena and Sarojini (2015); Alaoui and Elberrichi (2020); Ghosh et al. (2019); Paniri et al. (2019); Ahmad et al. (2019)

1.4   Simulated Annealing (SA)

"Annealing" is a technique which was primarily used in metallurgy (part of material science dealing with metals and their alloys). Annealing refers to the process of heating metal to a predetermined temperature and then cooling it back to reach room temperature in a controlled manner. By changing the internal structure of a material, the physical properties of material are altered too. To avoid the problem of being trapped in local optima, Simulated Annealing exploits a probability that accepts the worst solution. When the temperature is high, there is higher likelihood of accepting new solutions by widely exploring the search space. However, when the value of the temperature parameter is decremented, the likelihood of accepting unfavourable solutions is also reduced.

In SA, a "temperature" parameter is introduced to help to guide and control iterations of the algorithm. The process is initiated with a high value of temperature and the temperature is decreased until a stage of equilibrium is attained. The cooling schedule must be well-designed so that the final state can be termed as a near-optimal solution.

Section 2 represents a study of the new domain of feature selections and various SI approaches used for this task.

Section 3 outlines the methodology, emphasising Ant Colony Optimization and Simulated Annealing.

Section 4 presents the comprehensive result analysis.

Section 5 comprises a brief conclusion and future scope.

2 Related Work

The various advantages of the ACO algorithm, summarised in Fig. 3, have motivated many researchers to use ACO for optimisation problems (Aghdam and Kabiri, 2016; Jalalinejad et al., 2007). Extensive research on "bio-inspired" algorithms deals with a wide range of optimisation problems, and these algorithms provide a tremendous success rate in computer science (Binitha and Sathya, 2012). The medical knowledge-driven process of feature selection is highlighted for diagnosing heart diseases (Nahar et al., 2013).

The ACO-based feature selection model used various ant groups; the candidate features were selected from each group depending on different criteria. It yielded a 97.95% accuracy for the breast cancer dataset and 96.77% accuracy for heart disease data (El Houby et al., 2017). The correlation-based feature selection method can yield testing accuracy up to 87.71% and is achieved using an average of 100 simulations (Mitra and Samanta, 2013). An approach comprising of Particle Swarm Optimization (PSO) is proposed (Dheeba et al., 2014) which is used for detecting any abnormalities in digital mammograms. The Genetic-SVM system could select a subset of features automatically for optimisation of the SVM classifier.

An "improved" F-score and sequential forward selection method is used for feature selection, that uses KNN and SVM for classification (Niazi et al., 2015). The feature selection process was carried out in two phases: filter part and wrapper part. The wrapper part used SFS and the filter part used improved F-score criteria and achieved an accuracy of 73.8% with KNN classifier.

A Fuzzy inference system (based on adaptive network) provided an accuracy of 94.73% for colon tumour (Zainuddin et al., 2019). It was based on several factors (number of gene attributes, number of ants, and method of data partition). The Fuzzy entropy-based heuristic with ACO was used for finding a global-best smallest set for intrusion detection for identifying top-13 features for detection of real-time intrusion that provided a simple and fast way for exposing real-time intrusion attacks on computer networks (Varma et al., 2016).

Researchers included a penalty function to Binary Firefly algorithm for detection of various types of cancer (Breast/Cervical/Liver), which enhanced classification accuracy and drastically reduced the feature set by using Random Forest classifier (Sawhney et al., 2018).

The BPNN (Back Propagation Neural Network) was trained with a mutation-based Artificial Bee Colony yielding superior local solutions (with 97.32% accuracy) for "PIMA" dataset (Rashid and Abdullah, 2018).

Numerous Swarm Intelligence algorithms are successfully applied in the area of "image segmentation" or "thresholding" (Li et al., 2015; Sornam and Prabhakarn, 2017; Sathya and Rayalvizhi, 2011; Mishra et al., 2015; Mandal et al., 2017). Researchers proposed a Particle Swarm Optimization-based model, with Association rules for prognosis of erythemato-squamous disease using SVM, and achieved 98.91% accuracy (Abdi and Giveki, 2013).

For prognosis of Arrhythmia cordis, PSO-SVM model is proposed (Fei, 2010) that yields superior diagnostic accuracy as compared to artificial neural network.

Numerous SI techniques used for the prognosis of various diseases were surveyed, and it was concluded that SI approaches are the most prevalent for healthcare datasets (Nayar et al., 2019b). For prognosis of hepatitis disease, PSO and case based reasoning is used that is able to diagnose the disease (in the clearest state) with an accuracy of 94.58% (Neshat et al., 2012). Prediction of earthquake time-series data was performed to predict an earthquake's magnitude using the ABC-MLP approach (Shah et al., 2011). Using proper "weights", the initialisation can accelerate training Neural Networks' and enhance it predictive accuracy.

A successfully trained Artificial Bee Colony algorithm was used for training software defect data for the purpose of prediction using Multilayer Perceptron (Farshidpour and Keynia, 2012).

Domains intersected by applying Swarm Intelligence tackles the task of classification in Educational Data Mining by using Particle Swarm Classification (PSC) for classifying the classroom questions of teachers into various categories as identified in "Bloom's taxonomy" (Yaha et al., 2014).

For diagnosis of somatisation disorder, a novel framework adopted an "improved" Bacterial Foraging optimisation algorithm. This algorithm was applied by introducing opposition-based learning strategies that enhanced the bacterial species' diversification by uniformly distributing the initial population. It also enhanced the convergence rate, which could efficiently distinguish severe and mild somatisation, thereby assisting doctors with a more efficient clinical diagnosis (Lv et al., 2018).

In this section, we have analyzed some SI algorithms that are used for feature selection. In recent years, SI algorithms are gaining researchers' attention for feature selection. For improving the efficacy, researchers have combined some specific algorithms to explore optimum solutions. Some researchers have performed specific modifications in the algorithm and some hybrid versions of basic SI algorithms have also been introduced in the recent years that yield superior results. Table 2 summarizes the accuracy value achieved by Swarm Intelligence based algorithms or their hybrid approaches.

Table 2: Comparison of accuracy achieved by SI approaches.

Dataset	Approach	Accuracy achieved (%)
Heart disease	ACO-based feature selection model (El Houby, 2017)	96.77
Breast cancer	ACO-based feature selection model (El Houby, 2017)	97.75
Breast cancer	Particle Swarm Optimized Wavelet-Neural Network (PSOWNN) (Dheeba et al., 2014)	93.67
Colon tumor	ANFIS with ACO (Zainuddin et al., 2019)	94.73
Cervical cancer	BFA + Penalty + RF (Sawhney et al., 2018)	97.36
PIMA	ANN-based ABC with weight-mutation (Rashid and Abdullah, 2018)	97.32
Erythemato-squamous disease	PSO-SVM based on Association rules (Abdi and Giveki, 2013)	98.91
Arrhythmia cordis	PSO-SVM (Fei, 2010)	95.65
Hepatitis	CBR-PSO (Shah et al., 2011)	94.58
Somatization disorder	Improved Bacterial-Foraging Optimization (IBFO) based kernel extreme learning machine (KELM) (Lv et al., 2018)	96.97

3 Methodology

3.1 Hybrid ACO-SA algorithm

An algorithm based on Ant Colony Optimization (ACO) and Simulated Annealing (SA) inspired by the numerous benefits possessed by ACO and SA was proposed by Nayar et al., 2020. ACO is considered a captivating approach for feature selection, as it perpetually leads to the selection of a minimal-optimal subset of features. Moreover, SA has proved to find optimum solutions by carrying out a gradual cooling process. The algorithm runs at different temperature ranges by decrementing the temperature variable to enable gradual cooling (Nayar et al., 2020).

Set $\alpha = 0.0001$, $\beta = 0.1$, $\mu = 0.2$. The algorithm uses different values of a "temperature" variable as 100, 80, 60, 40 and 20. Fixed number of iterations are carried out at each temperature value, which leads to the selection of the best three feature sets at that temperature value. Thereafter, temperature value is again decremented and best three feature subsets are obtained. This process continues till the temperature value is greater than zero. Eventually, the algorithm yields three best feature subsets across all iterations.

Step 1: Initialize all the parameters.

Step 2: Define maximum temperature (T_{max}).

Step 3: Random search by all ants with unique paths to get an initial solution.

Step 4: Repeat steps 5 to 7 for $T = T_{max}$; $T > 0$; $T = T$-20.

Step 5: For choosing the subsequent feature, temperature-weighted ACO probability $P_{ij}^k(T)$ is calculated using Equation 1:

$$P_{ij}^k(T) = \frac{\tau_{ij}^{\alpha T} * \eta_{ij}^{\beta}(T)}{\Sigma_e \tau_{ij}^{\alpha T} * \eta_{ij}^{\beta}(T)} \tag{1}$$

Step 6: Features are ranked based on their length and accuracy using Equation 2:

$$\mu * accuracy + \left[(1-\mu) * \frac{Total\ Length}{L_k} \right] \tag{2}$$

Step 7: Pheromone evaporation rate is influenced by temperature T. Pheromone trail update occurs and is derived using Equation 3:

$$\tau_{ij}^{t+1} = (1-\rho^T) * \tau_{ij}^T + \frac{Q_N}{L_k} \tag{3}$$

where ρ^T represents the rate of evaporation at temperature T, which is updated using Equation 4:

$$\rho^T = \frac{1}{1 + e^{-QT}} \tag{4}$$

where Q is a constant, τ_{ij}^T represents the intensity of pheromone at the edge (i,j) at temperature T.

τ_{ij}^{t+1} represents the extent of pheromone on edge (i,j) for next iteration. L_k is the length of the selected subset by k^{th} ant-τ_{ij} indicates the "pheromone intensity" at edge i,j. η_{ij} is the "heuristic information" for choosing feature j after feature i. α and β are parameters belonging to range 0–1 that determine the significance of pheromone trail and heuristic information respectively. "μ" symbolizes a constant for adjustment of classification error-rate importance and number of selected features.

"L_k" represents the length of subset chosen by k^{th} ant (Nayar et al., 2020).

The ACO-SA algorithm (Nayar et al., 2020) was applied for classification of Arrhythmia that achieved an accuracy of 94.07%. As a part of this research, we have done further validation of results by applying the hybrid ACO-SA algorithm on various benchmark datasets to explore its capabilities for other problem areas. Also, as a measure of the classification performance, Precision, Recall, AUROC, F1 score are also considered.

We have taken publicly available datasets from LIBSVM/KDD/UCI repositories. Experiments were conducted on 6 datasets. The coil_2000 dataset contains details of an Insurance company's clients' details, comprising of 85 features. The Ozone_level dataset has 72 features and 2,536 instances. The libras_move dataset has 15 classes for referencing the hand-movement type using Brazilian signal language. The Spectrometer dataset comprising 531 instances from the IRAS-LRS database is also used, this dataset has 93 features. The scene dataset has 294 features based on real-world images. Lastly, we have used the Optical digits dataset which has 64 features for extraction of normalized bitmaps of the handwritten digits using pre-processing programs by NIST.

The information of each dataset is summarized in Table 3. Data is divided into "balanced" subsets and in order to control overfitting, we used the "Extremely randomized trees (extra-trees) classifier" on the data sub-samples. The algorithm was implemented in Python language which has a vast set of libraries including Scikit-learn, TensorFlow, Keras, SciPy, Numpy, etc., suitable for machine learning, computing and analysis.

Table 3: Summary of datasets.

Dataset	Repository	No. of instances	No. of features
Coil_2000	KDD	9,822	85
Ozone_level	UCI	2,536	72
Libras_move	UCI	360	90
Spectrometer	UCI	531	93
Scene	LIBSVM	2,407	294
Optical_digits	UCI	5,620	64

4   Result and Discussion

The approach proposed by Nayar et al. (2020) is tested on various high-dimensional datasets which are fetched from UCI and LIBSVM repositories. Table 4 represents the accuracy rate, AUROC, Recall, Precision, F1-Score and the number of features selected for each dataset.

Table 4: Comparison of Accuracy, AUROC, Recall, Precision and F1 score.

Dataset	Actual number of features	Number of selected features	Accuracy	AUROC	Recall	Precision	F1 score
Coil_2000	85	17	92.97	98.03	90.42	95.38	92.40
Ozone_level	72	18	93.55	96.16	93.31	93.31	88.98
Libras_move	90	23	77.77	85.36	66.36	84.28	75.32
Spectrometer	93	22	97.48	98.76	97.41	96.45	95.74
Scene	294	22	85.45	72.38	75.96	73.48	73.28
Optical_digits	64	21	94.42	97.91	96.32	97.24	97.52

We performed feature selection on different datasets, and considerably reduced the number of features, and ultimately reached the optimum solution, thereby escalating the accuracy value as shown in Table 5. We have also compared the results with prominent "RUSBoost" and "HUSBoost" methods (Popel et al., 2018), in which feature selection for high-dimensional datasets is not done. Figure 4 demonstrates the accuracy achieved after applying ACO-SA algorithm, HUSBoost and RUSBoost methods on six different datasets. We compared the ACO-SA approach with the HUSBoost and RUSBoost methods because both the methods were already applied for imbalanced datasets without performing the task of feature selection (Popel et al., 2013). According to the results, ACO-SA

Table 5: Comparison of accuracy with other approaches.

Dataset	Approach	Accuracy (%)
Coil_2000	ACO-SA	**92.97**
	RUSBoost (Popel et al., 2018)	67.24
	HUSBoost (Popel et al., 2018)	65.94
	GMDH-SSFS(Xiao et al., 2017)	73.02
Ozone_level	ACO-SA	**93.55**
	RUSBoost (Popel et al., 2018)	72.18
	HUSBoost (Popel et al., 2018)	77.65
	FSNTDJE with Naive Bayes (Sun et al., 2019)	78.08
Libras_move	ACO-SA	77.77
	RUSBoost (Popel et al., 2018)	76.57
	HUSBoost (Popel et al., 2018)	**84.96**
	MIGM (Salem et al., 2020)	78.3
Spectrometer	ACO-SA	**97.48**
	RUSBoost (Popel et al., 2018)	95.89
	HUSBoost (Popel et al., 2018)	92.65
Scene	ACO-SA	**85.45**
	RUSBoost (Popel et al., 2018)	60.86
	HUSBoost (Popel et al., 2018)	67.96
	FSVD-MLRBF(Aggarwal et al., 2018)	71.4
Optical_digits	ACO-SA	**94.42**
	RUSBoost (Popel et al., 2018)	93.58
	HUSBoost (Popel et al., 2018)	91.05
	CC-LF with SVM De Stefano et al., 2014)	90.43

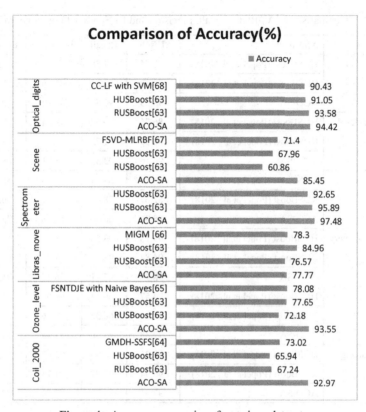

Figure 4: Accuracy comparison for various datasets.

achieved highest accuracy of 97.48 in case of "Spectrometer" dataset whereas in case of "Libras_move" dataset, ACO-SA approach achieved slightly lesser accuracy as compared to the HUSBoost method.

Moreover, comparing the results for selected datasets using the ACO-SA approach with similar studies for Precision, Recall, F1 Score and AUROC (as shown in Table 6) concluded that the ACO-SA technique provides superior results in most of the cases.

5 Conclusion and Future Work

On the basis of enormous advantages of ACO, SA and decision trees, these approaches are outstandingly implemented in the domain of feature selection. For verifying the effectiveness of ACO-SA algorithm, it was applied on various datasets. The experimental results showed that this approach yields promising results, by constructively searching the feature-space. It is revealed that ACO-SA

Table 6: Comparison of AUROC, Recall, Precision and F1 Score with other approaches.

Dataset	Approach	AUROC	Recall	Precision	F1 score
Coil_2000	HUSBoost (Popel et al., 2018)	72.75	67.55	64.91	65.90
	RUSBoost (Popel et al., 2018)	73.32	62.61	66.30	66.62
	ACO-SA	98.03	90.42	95.38	92.40
Ozone_level	HUSBoost (Popel et al., 2018)	86.75	79.56	79.24	78.44
	RUSBoost (Popel et al., 2018)	80.39	71.72	73.44	73.25
	ACO-SA	96.16	93.31	93.31	88.98
Libras_move	HUSBoost (Popel et al., 2018)	93.70	84.53	83.63	85.34
	RUSBoost (Popel et al., 2018)	82.67	78.97	82.67	60.42
	ACO-SA	85.36	66.36	84.28	75.32
Spectrometer	HUSBoost (Popel et al., 2018)	99.18	93.50	95.70	94.15
	RUSBoost (Popel et al., 2018)	94.84	92.87	94.75	95.05
	ACO-SA	98.76	97.41	96.45	95.74
Scene	HUSBoost (Popel et al., 2018)	74.57	66.44	66.03	64.93
	RUSBoost (Popel et al., 2018)	59.19	66.32	61.06	59.70
	ACO-SA	72.38	75.96	73.48	73.28
Optical_digits	HUSBoost (Popel et al., 2018)	98.25	93.85	94.57	93.30
	RUSBoost (Popel et al., 2018)	96.94	93.77	94.75	94.28
	ACO-SA	97.91	96.32	97.24	97.52

method provides superior result in terms of Accuracy, Precision, Recall, AUROC, F1 Score and number of selected features as compared to the approaches that use whole set of features. Overall, the algorithm yields a stable performance in most of the cases. Thus, it is concluded that feature selection plays an integral role in enhancing models' performance, particularly in high-dimensional datasets.

In future, we will extend our work by scrutinising datasets comprising of thousands to millions of features.

References

Abdi, M.J. and D. Giveki. Automatic detection of erythemato-squamous diseases using PSO–SVM based on association rules. Engineering Applications of Artificial Intelligence, 26(1): 603–608, 2013.

Abualigah, L. and A.J. Dulaimi. A novel feature selection method for data mining tasks using hybrid sine cosine algorithm and genetic algorithm. Cluster Computing, pp.1–16, 2021.

Aghdam, M.H. and P. Kabiri. Feature selection for intrusion detection system using ant colony optimization. IJ Network Security, 18(3): 420–432, 2016.

Agrawal, S., J. Agrawal, S. Kaur and S. Sharma. A comparative study of fuzzy PSO and fuzzy SVD-based RBF neural network for multi-label classification. Neural Computing and Applications, 2018 Jan 1; 29(1): 245–56, 2018.

Ahmad, S.R., A.A. Bakar and M.R. Yaakub. Ant colony optimization for text feature selection in sentiment analysis. Intelligent Data Analysis, 23(1): 133–158, 2019.

Alaoui, A. and Z. Elberrichi. Enhanced ant colony algorithm for best features selection for a decision tree classification of medical data. In Critical Approaches to Information Retrieval Research, pp. 278–293. IGI Global, 2020.

Binitha, S. and S.S. Sathya. A survey of bio inspired optimization algorithms. International Journal of Soft Computing and Engineering, 2(2): 137–151, 2012.

Blum, C. and M. Yábar Vallès. Multi-level ant colony optimization for DNA sequencing by hybridization. pp. 94–109. In: Almeida, F., M. Blesa, C. Blum, J.M. Moreno, M. Pérez, A. Roli and M. Sampels (eds.). Proceedings of HM 2006—3rd International Workshop on Hybrid Metaheuristics, Volume 4030 of Lecture Notes in Computer Science. Springer-Verlag, Berlin, Germany, 2006.

Brezočnik, L., I. Fister and V. Podgorelec. Swarm intelligence algorithms for feature selection: A review. Applied Sciences 8(9): 1521, 2018.

Chen, Y., Y. Pan, J. Chen, W. Liu and L. Chen. Multiple sequence alignment by ant colony optimization and divide-and-conquer. In International Conference on Computational Science, pp. 646–653. Springer, Berlin, Heidelberg, 2006, May.

Chiu, C.Y. and C.H. Lin. Cluster analysis based on artificial immune system and ant algorithm. In: Third International Conference on Natural Computation (ICNC 2007), Vol 3, pp 647–650. IEEE, 2007.

Chiu, C.Y., I.T. Kuo and C.H. Lin. Applying artificial immune system and ant algorithm in air-conditioner market segmentation. Expert Syst. Appl., 36(3): 4437–4442, 2009.

Colorni, A., M. Dorigo, V. Maniezzo M. Trubian. Ant system for job shop scheduling. J. Oper. Res. Stat. Comput. Sci., 34(1): 39–53, 1994.

Dai, W., S. Liu and S. Liang. An improved ant colony optimization cluster algorithm based on swarm intelligence. JSW, 4(4): 299–306, 2009.

De Stefano, C., F. Fontanella, C. Marrocco and A.S. Di Freca. A GA-based feature selection approach with an application to handwritten character recognition. Pattern Recognition Letters, 2014 Jan 1; 35: 130–41, 2014.

Dheeba, J., N.A. Singh and S.T. Selvi. Computer-aided detection of breast cancer on mammograms: A swarm intelligence optimized wavelet neural network approach. Journal of Biomedical Informatics, 49: 45–52, 2014.

Di Caro, G. and M. Dorigo. Antnet: distributed stigmergetic control for communications networks. J. Artif. Intell. Res., 9: 317–365, 1998.

Dorigo, M., M. Birattari and T. Stutzle. Ant colony optimization. IEEE Computational Intelligence Magazine, 1(4): 28–39, 2006.

Dwivedi, R., R. Kumar, E. Jangam and V. Kumar. An ant colony optimization based feature selection for data classification. International Journal of Recent Technology and Engineering, pp. 35–40, 2019.

El Houby, E.M., N.I. Yassin and S. Omran. A hybrid approach from ant Colony optimization and k-nearest neighbor for classifying datasets using selected features. Informatica, 41(4), 2017.

Farshidpour, S. and F. Keynia. Using artificial bee colony algorithm for MLP training on software defect prediction. Oriental Journal of Computer Science & Technology, 5(2), 2012.

Fei, S.W. Diagnostic study on arrhythmia cordis based on particle swarm optimization-based support vector machine. Expert Systems with Applications, 37(10): 6748–6752, 2010.

Forsyth, P. and A. Wren. An ant system for bus driver scheduling. Research Report 97.25, University of Leeds School of Computer Studies, 1997.

Ghosh, M., R. Guha, R. Sarkar and A. Abraham. A wrapper-filter feature selection technique based on ant colony optimization. Neural Computing and Applications, pp. 1–19, 2019.

Jalalinejad, F., F. Jalali-Farahani, N. Mostoufi and R. Sotudeh-Gharebagh. Ant colony optimization: A leading algorithm in future optimization of chemical process. In 17th European Symposium on Computer Aided Process Engineering, pp. 1–6. Elsevier, 2007.

Kaushik, A.C. and S. Sahi. Biological complexity: Ant colony meta-heuristic optimization algorithm for protein folding. Neural Computing and Applications, 28(11): 3385–3391, 2017.

Khair, A.F., M. Makhtar, M. Mazlan, M.A. Mohamed and M.N. Abdul Rahman. Solving examination timetabling problem in UniSZA using ant colony optimization. International Journal of Engineering & Technology, 7(2.15): 132–135, 2018.

Korürek, M. and A. Nizam. A new arrhythmia clustering technique based on Ant Colony Optimization. Journal of Biomedical Informatics, 41(6): 874–881, 2008.

Korürek, M. and A. Nizam. Clustering MIT-BIH arrhythmias with Ant Colony Optimization using time domain and PCA compressed wavelet coefficients. Digital Signal Processing, 20(4): 1050–1060, 2010.

Kurniawan, T.B., N.K. Khalid, Z. Ibrahim, M.S.Z. Abidin and M. Khalid. Sequence design for direct-proportional length-based DNA computing using population-based ant colony optimization. In 2009 ICCAS-SICE, pp. 1486–1491. IEEE, 2009, August.

Lee, Z.J., S.F. Su, C.C. Chuang and K.H. Liu. Genetic algorithm with ant colony optimization (GA-ACO) for multiple sequence alignment. Applied Soft Computing, 8(1): 55–78, 2008.

Li, Y., L. Jiao, R. Shang and R. Stolkin. Dynamic-context cooperative quantum-behaved particle swarm optimization based on multilevel thresholding applied to medical image segmentation. Information Sciences, 294: 408–422, 2015.

Liang, D. and H.W. Huo. An adaptive ant colony optimization algorithm and its application to sequence alignment. Computer Simulation, 22(1): 100–106, 2005.

Llanes, A., C. Velez, A.M. Sanchez, H. Perez-Sanchez and J.M. Cecilia. Parallel ant colony optimization for the hp protein folding problem. In International Conference on Bioinformatics and Biomedical Engineering, pp. 615–626. Springer, Cham, 2016, April.

Lv, X., H. Chen, Q. Zhang, X. Li, H. Huang and G. Wang. An improved bacterial-foraging optimization-based machine learning framework for predicting the severity of somatization disorder. Algorithms, 11(2): 17, 2018.

Mandal, D., A. Chatterjee and M. Maitra. Particle swarm optimization based fast Chan-Vese algorithm for medical image segmentation. In Metaheuristics for Medicine and Biology, pp. 49–74. Springer, Berlin, Heidelberg, 2017.

Mayer, A., C. Nothegger, A. Chwatal and G. Raidl. Solving the post enrolment course timetabling problem by ant colony optimization. In Proceedings of the 7th International Conference on the Practice and Theory of Automated Timetabling (PATAT 2008), Montreal, CA. Université de Montréal, 2008.

Merkle, M., M. Middendorf and H. Schmeck. Ant colony optimization for resource-constrained project scheduling. IEEE Transactions on Evolutionary Computation, 6(4): 333–346, 2002.

Mishra, D., I. Bose, U.C. De and M. Das. Medical image thresholding using particle swarm optimization. In Intelligent Computing, Communication and Devices, pp. 379–383. Springer, New Delhi, 2015.

Mitra, M. and R.K. Samanta. Cardiac arrhythmia classification using neural networks with selected features. Procedia Technology, 10: 76–84, 2013.

Moss, J.D. and C.G. Johnson. An ant colony algorithm for multiple sequence alignment in bioinformatics. pp. 182–186. In: Pearson, D.W., N.C. Steele and R.F. Albrecht (eds.). Artificial Neural Networks and Genetic Algorithms. Springer, Berlin, Germany, 2003.

Nahar, J., T. Imam, K.S. Tickle and Y.-P.P. Chen. Computational intelligence for heart disease diagnosis: A medical knowledge driven approach. Expert Syst. Appl., 40(1): 96–104, 2013.

Nayar, N., S. Ahuja and S. Jain. Swarm intelligence and data mining: A review of literature and applications in healthcare. In Proceedings of the Third International Conference on Advanced Informatics for Computing Research, pp. 1–7, 2019a, June.

Nayar, N., S. Ahuja and S. Jain. Swarm intelligence for feature selection: A review of literature and reflection on future challenges. Advances in Data and Information Sciences, pp. 211–221, 2019b.

Nayar, N., S. Ahuja and S. Jain. Meta-heuristic Swarm Intelligence based algorithm for feature selection and prediction of Arrhythmia. International Journal of Advanced Science and Technology, 29(02): 61–71, 2020.

Neshat, M., M. Sargolzaei, A. Nadjaran Toosi and A. Masoumi. Hepatitis disease diagnosis using hybrid case based reasoning and particle swarm optimization. ISRN Artificial Intelligence, 2012.

Niazi, K.A.K., S.A. Khan, A. Shaukat and M. Akhtar. Identifying best feature subset for cardiac arrhythmia classification. In 2015 Science and Information Conference (SAI), pp. 494–499. IEEE, 2015, July.

Nothegger, C., A. Mayer, A. Chwatal and G.R. Raidl. Solving the post enrolment course timetabling problem by ant colony optimization. Annals of Operations Research, 194(1): 325–339, 2012.

Paniri, M., M.B. Dowlatshahi and H. Nezamabadi-Pour. MLACO: A multi-label feature selection algorithm based on ant colony optimization. Knowledge-Based Systems, p. 105285, 2019.

Patrick, K. and Z. Godswill. Greedy ants colony optimization strategy for solving the curriculum based university course timetabling problem. Journal of Advances in Mathematics and Computer Science, pp. 1–10, 2016.

Popel, M.H., K. Md. Hasib, S.A. Habib and F.M. Shah. A hybrid under-sampling method (HUSBoost) to classify imbalanced data. In 2018 21st International Conference of Computer and Information Technology (ICCIT), pp. 1–7. IEEE, 2018.

Rashid, T.A. and S.M. Abdullah. A hybrid of artificial bee colony, genetic algorithm, and neural network for diabetic mellitus diagnosing. ARO-The Scientific Journal of Koya University, 6(1): 55–64, 2018.

Sabeena, S. and B. Sarojini. Optimal feature subset selection using ant colony optimization. Indian Journal of Science and Technology, 8(35): 1–5, 2015.

Salem, O.A., F. Liu, Y.P. Chen and X. Chen. Ensemble fuzzy feature selection based on relevancy, redundancy, and dependency criteria. Entropy, 2020 July; 22(7): 757, 2020.

Sathya, P.D. and R. Kayalvizhi. Modified bacterial foraging algorithm based multilevel thresholding for image segmentation. Engineering Applications of Artificial Intelligence, 24(4): 595–615, 2011.

Sawhney, R., P. Mathur and R. Shankar. A firefly algorithm based wrapper-penalty feature selection method for cancer diagnosis. In International Conference on Computational Science and Its Applications, pp. 438–449. Springer, Cham, 2018, May.

Schoonderwoerd, R., O.E. Holland, J.L. Bruten and L.J.M. Rothkrantz. Ant-based load balancing in telecommunications networks. Adapt. Behav., 2: 169–207, 1996.

Shah, H., R. Ghazali and N.M. Nawi. Using artificial bee colony algorithm for MLP training on earthquake time series data prediction. arXiv preprint arXiv:1112.4628, 2011.

Socha, K. and J. Knowles and M. Sampels. AMAX-MINant system for the university timetabling problem. pp. 1–13. *In*: Dorigo, M., G. Di Caro and M. Sampels (eds.). Proceedings of ANTS2002—Third International Workshop on Ant Algorithms. Lecture Notes in Computer Science, Vol 2463. Springer, Berlin, Germany, 2002.

Socha, K., M. Sampels and M. Manfrin. Ant algorithms for the university course timetabling problem with regard to the state-of-the-art. pp. 334–345. *In*: Cagnoni, S., J.J. Romero Cardalda, D.W. Corne, J. Gottlieb, A. Guillot, E. Hart, C.G. Johnson, E. Marchiori, J.-A. Meyer, M. Middendorf and G.R. Raidl (eds.). Applications of Evolutionary Computing, Proceedings of EvoWorkshops 2003, volume 2611 of Lecture Notes in Computer Science. Springer, Berlin, Germany, 2003.

Sornam, M. and M. Prabhakaran. A new linear adaptive swarm intelligence approach using back propagation neural network for dental caries classification. In 2017 IEEE International Conference on Power, Control, Signals and Instrumentation Engineering (ICPCSI), 2698–2703, 2017.

Sun, L., L. Wang, Y. Qian, J. Xu and S. Zhang. Feature selection using Lebesgue and entropy measures for incomplete neighborhood decision systems. Knowledge-Based Systems, 2019 Dec 15; 186: 104942, 2019.

Too, J. and S. Mirjalili. A hyper learning binary dragonfly algorithm for feature selection: A COVID-19 case study. Knowledge-Based Systems, 212: 106553, 2021.

Ugat, E.B., J.J.M. Montemayor, M.A.N. Manlimos and D.D. Dinawanao. Parallel Ant Colony Optimization on the University Course-Faculty Timetabling Problem in MSU-IIT. GSTF J. Comput., 2018.

Varma, P.R.K., V.V. Kumari and S.S. Kumar. Feature selection using relative fuzzy entropy and ant colony optimization applied to real-time intrusion detection system. Procedia Computer Science, 85: 503–510, 2016.

Xiao, J., H. Cao, X. Jiang, X. Gu and L. Xie. GMDH-based semi-supervised feature selection for customer classification. Knowledge-Based Systems, 2017 Sep 15; 132: 236–48, 2017.

Yahya, A.A., A. Osman and A. Taleb. Swarm intelligence in educational data mining. In Proceedings of the Machine Learning and Data Analytics Symposium MLDAS', 2014.

Zainuddin, S., F. Nhita and U.N. Wisesty. Classification of gene expressions of lung cancer and colon tumor using Adaptive-Network-Based Fuzzy Inference System (ANFIS) with Ant Colony Optimization (ACO) as the feature selection. In Journal of Physics: Conference Series, 1192(1): 012019. IOP Publishing, 2019, March.

Chapter 2

Swarm Intelligence for Data Mining

Razieh Sheikhpour

1 Swarm Intelligence

Swarm Intelligence (SI) is a subset of artificial intelligence inspired by the collective behavior of social swarms in nature, such as bird flocks, ant colonies, honey bees and bacteria. Swarm intelligence-based algorithms are placed in the category of population-based algorithms which are able to generate low cost, fast, and robust solutions to solve optimization problems (Mishra et al., 2021; Yang et al., 2020).

The principles of SI have been applied in a wide-range of domains such as function optimization problems, scheduling, finding optimal routes, structural optimization, and data analysis. Computational modeling of swarms has been widely used in various domains such as data mining, machine learning, bioinformatics, medical informatics, finance and business (Ahmed et al., 2012).

SI-based algorithms have some benefits compared to traditional methods or other evolutionary algorithms. Some of these advantages are (Figueiredo et al., 2019):

(1) The implementation of SI-based algorithms is relativity simple.

(2) Few parameters are required to be set for SI-based algorithms.

Department of Computer Engineering, Faculty of Engineering, Ardakan University, P.O. Box 184, Ardakan, Iran.
Email: rsheikhpour@ardakan.ac.ir

(3) The convergence rate of SI-based algorithms is high.

(4) The exploitation capability of SI-based algorithms is excellent.

A number of SI-based algorithms have been proposed in the last two decades. Particle Swarm Optimization (PSO), Ant Colony Optimization (ACO) and Artificial Bee Colony (ABC) are the most well-known SI-based algorithms widely used to solve optimization problems.

There are some libraries and toolkits for swarm intelligence available. PySwarms (Miranda, 2018) is a research toolkit in python developed for particle swarm optimization. SwarmOpt (Cronin, 2018) is a library of swarm optimization algorithms implemented in python to optimize continuous single-objective functions. SwarmPackagePy (SwarmPackagePy, 2017) is another library of swarm optimization algorithms which contains 14 swarm optimization algorithms. DeepSwarm (Byla et al., 2020) is an open-source library which applies ACO to tackle the neural architecture search problem.

1.1   Particle Swarm Optimization

Particle swarm optimization is a SI-based algorithm introduced by Kennedy and Eberhart (Kennedy et al., 1995), and inspired from the social behavior of bird flocks and fish schools. It is an optimization algorithm used to solve nonlinear, nonconvex or combinatorial optimization problems that exist in many science and engineering applications (Bernal Baró et al., 2020; Su et al., 2019).

In PSO, a number of potential solutions known as the swarm are generated in the search space. Each individual solution is called a particle characterized by a position and velocity and allowed to move around in the search space and determine its movement through the search space by combining its best position with the best one obtained by other particles. A fitness function is usually applied to evaluate the quality of the particles (Kuo et al., 2011; Sheikhpour et al., 2016).

Each particle consists of two D-dimensional vectors, where D is the dimensionality of the search space. The velocity of ith particle at the time step is represented by $v_i^t = \{v_{i1}^t, vx_{i2}^t, ..., v_{iD}^t\}$ and the position of this particle is represented by $x_i^t = \{x_{i1}^t, x_{i2}^t, ..., x_{iD}^t\}$. The velocity and position of the ith particle at iteration t+1 are updated using Equation 1 and Equation 2, respectively.

$$v_{id}^{t+1} = v_{id}^t + c_1 r_1 (p_{id} - x_{id}^t) + c_2 r_2 (p_{gd} - x_{id}^t) \qquad (1)$$

$$x_{id}^{t+1} = x_{id}^t + v_{id}^{t+1} \qquad (2)$$

where $d = \{1, 2, ..., D\}$ represents the dimension, and c_1 and c_2 denote the personal and social learning parameters, respectively. r_1 and r_2 represent uniform random numbers within the range [0, 1]. p_{id} and p_{gd} denote the *pbest* and *gbest* in the dth dimension. The flowchart and procedure of PSO algorithm is provided in Fig. 1 and Algorithm 1, respectively.

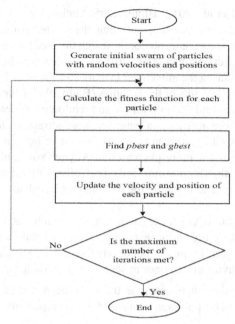

Figure 1: Flowchart of PSO algorithm.

Algorithm 1   Basic procedure of PSO algorithm.

---

1. Initialize a swarm of particles with random velocities and positions on D dimensions in the search space

Repeat

    2. Calculate the desired optimization fitness function for each particle

    3. Find *pbest*. If the fitness value for each particle i is better than its best fitness value found so far, then the current fitness value is set as the new *pbest* of particle i

    4. Find the *gbest*. If any *pbest* is better than the *gbest*, *gbest* is set to the current value of *pbest*

    5. Update the velocity and position of each particle according to Equation 1 and Equation 2, respectively

until the stopping criteria are met (usually if the maximum number of iterations is met)

1.2   Ant Colony Optimization

Ant colony optimization is a SI-based algorithm introduced by Dorigo et al. (1991, 1996) to solve combinatorial optimization problems such as the Traveling Salesman Problem (TSP), DNA sequencing, scheduling, 2D-HP protein folding, and so on (Ahmed et al., 2012; Blum, 2005; Shelokar et al., 2004). ACO was inspired by the behavior of real ants in finding the shortest paths between the food sources and their nest. Real ants randomly search the area around their nest to find a food source (Chandra Mohan et al., 2012). They leave a chemical pheromone trail on the ground during the movement to mark some favorable paths that should be followed by the other ants of the colonies (Blum 2005; Chandra Mohan et al., 2012). Other ants that find the trail, follow and reinforce it by leaving pheromones on the path. The more ants trace a path, the more attractive this path becomes, and it is thus followed by other ants. This cooperative behavior leads to finding the shortest path that has more pheromones (Michelakos et al., 2011; Shelokar et al., 2004). ACO algorithm mimics this mechanisms by selecting the solutions based on pheromones and updating the pheromones based on the solution quality (Runkler, 2005).

The main idea in ACO is to create a weighted graph, called the construction graph, and model the problem for searching the optimal path in the graph (Ahmed et al., 2012). ACO uses simple agents or artificial ants to search for quality paths and mimic the behavior of real ones in several ways (Ahmed et al., 2012):

(1) Artificial ants deposit pheromone trails on the nodes of quality paths for reinforcement of the most appropriate solution components of the construction graph.

(2) Artificial ants move through the construction graph to generate the solutions and select their path according to probabilities that depend on the pheromone trail previously deposited.

(3) Pheromone trails decrease at each iteration as the pheromone evaporation observed in real ants.

The basic components of an ACO algorithm is as follows (Michelakos et al., 2011):

- A *representation*, that allows the artificial ants to generate a solution by means of a probabilistic transition rule
- A *local heuristic*, that helps an ant select the next node for the path it is building
- A *transition rule*, that determines which node an ant will visit next
- A *constraint satisfaction*, that forces it to construct the feasible rules
- A *fitness function*, that evaluates the quality of the solution generated by an ant
- A *pheromone update rule*, that determines how the pheromone is modified

The flowchat and procedure of the ACO algorithm is provided in Fig. 2 and Algorithm 2, respectively.

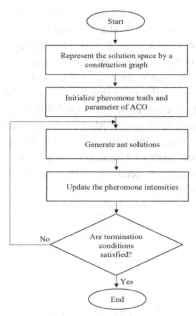

Figure 2: Flowchart of ACO algorithm.

Algorithm 2 Basic procedure of ACO algorithm.

---

1. The solution space is represented by a construction graph

2. Parameters of ACO is set, and pheromone trails are initialized

Repeat

    3. Ant solutions are generated from the movement of each ant on the construction graph mediated by pheromone trails

    4. The pheromone intensities are updated

until termination conditions are satisfied

1.3 Artificial Bee Colony

Artificial bee colony algorithm is a SI-based algorithm, developed by Karaboga (Karaboga, 2005) for optimization problems, which mimics the intelligent behavior of honey bees searching for food sources around their hives (Alshamiri et al., 2016). The colony members share the information about the quality of food sources using the dance language (Kumar et al., 2017). A possible solution to the optimization problem is represented by a food source evaluated by the amount of nectar in the food source (Karaboga et al., 2008; Zhang et al., 2010). Artificial bee colony consists of three types of bees: employed bees, onlookers and scouts. The first half of the colony contains employed bees and the second one consists of the onlookers. There is only one employed bee for every food source. Therefore, the number of employed bees is equal to the number of food sources (solutions) (Alshamiri et al., 2016; Zhang et al., 2010). The employed bees search for food sources and collect information about them such as location, quality and quantity of nectar, and share this information with the onlooker bees within the hive. Onlooker bees select one of the food sources based on the information obtained by the employed bees to exploit with a probability proportional to its quality. The employed bee whose food source has been abandoned becomes a scout and randomly searches for a new food source. A scout bee turns into an employed bee when it finds a food source (Alshamiri et al., 2016; Karaboga et al., 2008). The flowchart and a simple procedure of ABC algorithm is given in Fig. 3 and Algorithm 3, respectively.

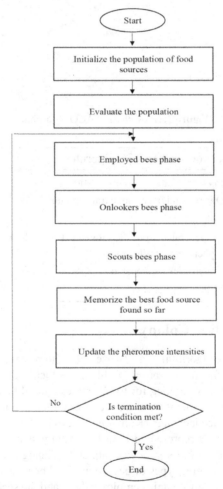

Figure 3: Flowchart of ABC algorithm.

Algorithm 3 The procedure of ABC algorithm.

---

1. Initialize the population of food sources (solutions)

2. Evaluate the population

Repeat

    3. Employed bees phase

    4. Onlookers bees phase

    5. Scouts bees phase

    6. Memorize the best food source found so far

    7. The pheromone intensities are updated

until termination condition is met

Employed bees phase

Each employed bee determines a new food source in the vicinity of its old food source and evaluates the amount of its nectar (fitness). The employed bee replaces the old food source with the new one when the fitness value of the new food source is better than that of the old one. In other words, a greedy selection procedure is used as the selection operation between the old and new food sources (Alshamiri et al., 2016).

Onlooker bees phase

When the process of determining a new food source is completed by all employed bees, the information is shared with the onlooker bees. The fitness information obtained from all employed bees is evaluated by each onlooker bee to select a food source for exploiting according to its fitness. Each onlooker bee finds a new food source in the neighborhood of the selected food source. Similar to an employed bee, the onlooker bee replaces the old food source with the new one when the quality of the new food source is better than that of the old one (Alshamiri et al., 2016).

Scout bees phase

If the quality of a food source does not improve up to a predetermined limit, the food source is abandoned and the corresponding employed bee becomes a scout bee. This scout becomes an employed bee when it generates a new food source (Alshamiri et al., 2016).

These three phases are repeated until the stopping condition is satisfied.

2 Data Mining

Knowledge discovery from data (KDD) is the process of extracting useful and implicit information in data, which is useful for different applications (Figueiredo et al., 2019).

The KDD process consists of the following steps (Han et al., 2011):

(1) Data cleaning (for removing noise and inconsistent data).

(2) Data integration (for combining multiple data sources).

(3) Data selection (for retrieving relevant data to the analysis task from the database).

(4) Data transformation (for transforming and consolidating data into appropriate forms for mining).

(5) Data mining (a basic process in which intelligent methods are applied to discover data patterns).

(6) Pattern evaluation (for identification of the interesting patterns representing knowledge).

(7) Knowledge presentation (for presenting the mined knowledge to users using the visualization and knowledge representation methods).

Data mining as an essential step in KDD process, is the process of discovering interesting patterns and information from large amounts of data. The data can come from different sources such as relational databases, data warehouses, semi-structured documents, or the Web (Alam et al., 2014; Han et al., 2011). Association rule mining (ARM) and clustering are the main tasks in data mining. ARM aims in identifying interesting relations between items in a transactional or relational database (Kou, 2019; Sarath et al., 2013; Sheikhan et al., 2013). Clustering is a process which divides data into different groups based on the similarities and dissimilarities between data objects (Alam et al., 2014).

Optimization-based pattern discovery is recognized as an important field in data mining and is utilized to increase the efficiency of association rule mining and clustering. The increasing complexity and a large amount of data in the database has made the association rule mining and data clustering a popular focus for the use of optimization-based algorithms. SI-based algorithms have been successfully used for different domains of association rule mining and data clustering (Alam et al., 2014).

2.1   Association Rule Mining

Association rule mining derives interesting relations among various items in the large transactional or relational data sets (Kou, 2019; Sarath et al., 2013; Sheikhan et al., 2013). Due to the huge amount of data collected and stored in many industries, the interest in extracting the relations among their data and mining frequent itemsets is growing which can then be used for the decision-making processes such as cross-marketing, catalog design, business intelligence and customer shopping behavior analysis (Han et al., 2011; Indira et al., 2015; Sarath et al., 2013).

An association rule is an implication of the form $A{\rightarrow}B$, where A and B are the subsets of the itemset, $A \neq \emptyset$, $B \neq \emptyset$ $A \cap B \neq \emptyset$. Let $I = \{I_1, I_2, \ldots, I_m\}$ be an itemset and $D = \{T_1, T_2, \ldots, T_k\}$ a transaction database, where each transaction is a nonempty itemset.

Association rule mining is a two-step process:

1. Find frequent patterns or itemsets

Frequent itemsets should occur at least as frequently as a predetermined minimum support. The support is calculated as Equation 3.

$$\text{Support}(A \rightarrow B) = P(A \cup B) = \frac{\text{\# of transactions which contain A \& B}}{\text{\# of transactions in the database}} \quad (3)$$

2. Generate strong association rules from the frequent itemsets

The strong rules should satisfy minimum support and minimum confidence. The confidence of an association rule is computed as Equation 4.

$$\text{Confidence}(A \rightarrow B) = P(B|A) = \frac{\text{\# of transactions which contain A \& B}}{\text{\# of transactions in A}}$$
$$= \frac{\text{suppor}(A \cup B)}{\text{suport}(A)} \quad (4)$$

Many algorithms have been presented to mine frequent itemsets in the database of which Apriori (Agrawal et al., 1993) is the most well-known algorithm for determining the frequent itemsets. Apriori uses an iterative approach to generate candidate itemsets and utilizes minimum support and minimum confidence for filtering the candidate itemsets to find frequent itemsets. Apriori is a level-wise approach which explores k-itemsets utilizing (k-1)-itemsets. In the first step of this algorithm, the database is scanned and the support of each item is calculated to find the frequent 1-itemsets that satisfy minimum support. The resulting set is shown by L_1. Then, the set of frequent 2-itemsets (L_2) is found using L_1. The procedure continues until no more frequent k-itemsets can be found.

2.2   Clustering

Clustering is a process where the data objects are grouped into several clusters where the data within a cluster are similar to one another according to a similarity measure, and dissimilar to the data in other clusters (Alam et al., 2014; Cura, 2012; Han et al., 2011). Clustering can be used in a wide range of applications such as pattern recognition, machine learning, image analysis and other applications of science and engineering such as biology, bioinformatics, security, information retrieval, web mining and business intelligence (Esmin et al., 2015; Tsai et al., 2015).

The clustering methods are basically classified into hierarchical and partitional methods. In the hierarchical clustering, data objects are organized into a hierarchical structure based on the proximity matrix. The hierarchical methods are split into the agglomerative and divisive methods. In the agglomerative method, one-point (singleton) clusters are initially generated, and recursively two or more most suitable clusters are merged based on the distance between the clusters (Alam et al., 2014; Jarboui et al., 2007). In the divisive method, a large cluster containing all the data objects is initially formed. The cluster is then split into smaller clusters based on the proximity matrix until the termination criteria are met. The termination criteria can be the number of data objects in each cluster or the number of clusters (Alam et al., 2014).

Partitional clustering splits the data into a set of disjointed clusters based on the similarities and dissimilarities among the data objects. The most common similarity measures are distance-based, density-based and pattern-based similarity measures. The distance-based clustering uses a distance function to calculate the position of a data object relative to the cluster center called centroid. The position of the centroid is changed in different iterations to enhance the quality of the clusters according to the intra-cluster and inter-cluster distances. The quality of a cluster is determined based on the objective function that can be maximization of inter-cluster distance, minimization of intra-cluster distance, maximization of similarities and minimization of dissimilarities among the data objects (Armano et al., 2016).

One of the most well-known partitional methods is K-means clustering which utilizes a distance function for splitting data into K clusters. In K-means clustering, K initial cluster centroids are chosen, and the distance of every data object to each of the K cluster centroids is calculated to find the minimum distance and place the object into nearest cluster centroid. After the clusters are generated, the mean value of all data objects in each cluster is computed and considered as a new value of the cluster centroid. The process of calculating the distance of every data object to new cluster centroids and classifying the data objects into clusters continues until the cluster members change (Han et al., 2011).

3   Overview of SI-based Algorithms for Association Rule Mining

Apriori is the most popular algorithm for finding frequent item sets that needs a full scan of the database to find each L_k. This process requires plenty of time and increases the input/output overhead of the system (Han et al., 2011). Many efforts have been done to improve the computational efficiency of the Apriori and many algorithms have been presented to extract association rules. In many association rule mining algorithms, a large number of rules are generated such that the extraction of useful knowledge from these rules is difficult, so pruning and summarizing are required to filter the important rules (Indira et al., 2015; Kuo et al., 2007).

The values of minimum support and minimum confidence play an important role in the association rule mining and affect the quality of the rules. These values are set by the user in traditional algorithms and are largely influenced by the user subjectivity. If the values of these parameters are too small, more rules will be generated. Moreover, if the values are too high, less rules will be generated (Nandhini et al., 2012; Sarath et al., 2013; Su et al., 2019; Tyagi et al., 2013). Some researchers have addressed the issue of setting the optimal values for minimum support and minimum confidence to obtain more effective association rules.

Association rule mining is a challenging task due to the nature of high-dimensional space such that traditional algorithms cannot provide sophisticated solutions to solve it (Telikani et al., 2020). In the last two decades, swarm intelligence has been widely used to mine association rules due to its simplicity, effective search mechanism and natural representation.

3.1   Overview of PSO Algorithm for Association Rule Mining

Particle swarm optimization is the most well-known SI-based algorithm used to mine association rules. As stated in the earlier subsection, setting the optimal values for minimum support and minimum confidence is an important issue in association rule mining which is determined by the user in traditional algorithms. Some studies have presented a PSO-based algorithm that can automatically provide the suitable values for minimum support and confidence.

Kuo et al. (2011) proposed an algorithm based on PSO for generating association rules that improves the computational efficiency of the Apriori algorithm and determines the values of minimum support and confidence automatically and objectively. This algorithm contains preprocessing and mining stages. In the first stage of this algorithm, the data transformation into the binary format is done, and the search range of the particle swarm is set using the IR (itemset range) value. In the second stage, the PSO algorithm is used to extract association rules which contains encoding, calculating the fitness value of each particle, generating the population, searching for the best particle and termination condition. Eventually, after finding the best particle, its support and confidence values are determined as the minimum support and minimum confidence. The determined values are employed to derive association rules.

One of the important issues that affects the quality of association rules is the number of rules extracted. An algorithm was proposed by Nandhini et al. (Nandhini et al., 2012) to decrease the quantity of the redundant rules and enhance the computational efficiency of rule mining. This algorithm contains two mining and post-mining phases so that in the mining phase, the PSO algorithm is utilized to calculate the optimal values for minimum support and confidence and generate association rules. Then, domain ontology is used in the post-mining phase to decrease the number of rules and discover the most interesting rules. In this algorithm, binary transformation of data and encoding should be carried out as the steps of preprocessing for applying PSO. In the mining phase using PSO, calculation of the fitness value, generation of the population, evaluation of the best particle and termination condition are done to consider the support and confidence of the best particle as the optimal values for minimum support and minimum confidence.

Su et al. (2019) proposed a PSO-based association rule mining algorithm for the big data environment. They utilized particle swarm optimization to obtain the optimal value of minimum support. Then, the FP-growth algorithm was employed to mine association rules based on the minimum support found by PSO algorithm. This association rule mining algorithm applies information entropy as the degree of interest to measure the effectiveness of association rules and extracts the rules that satisfies the degree. This algorithm can decrease memory consumption, enhance the effectiveness of association rules and improve user experience.

An association rule mining algorithm based on binary particle swarm optimization was proposed by Sarath and Ravi (Sarath et al., 2013). This algorithm includes preprocessing and mining phases by which the fitness values of the particle swarm are calculated and the data are transformed into a binary format in the first phase. In the second phase, the PSO algorithm is utilized for association rule mining which contains particle swarm encoding, population generation of the particle swarm based on the calculated fitness value and stopping condition. Eventually, the top association rule is considered as the output of that run of the algorithm. For generating M association rules, the algorithm should be run M times to obtain the top M rules. In this algorithm, there is no need to predetermine the values of minimum support and minimum confidence, and no redundant rules are generated. This algorithm generates the association rules with variable itemset length unlike Apriori algorithm that generate the rules with the same frequent itemset length. Moreover, in this algorithm, the CPU time consumed to generate association rules is less than that of Apriori algorithm.

Some studies have considered association rule mining as a multi-objective problem and solved the problem using PSO-based multi-objective algorithms.

Kuo et al. (2019) proposed an adaptive archive grid multi-objective PSO based on pareto optimal strategy to mine association rules from numerical database. The aim of this algorithm was to optimize three objectives namely confidence, comprehensibility and interestingness for association rule mining. This algorithm does not require any preprocessing to discretize numerical data. Moreover, this algorithm does not need to predetermine the values of minimum support and confidence. This algorithm includes three phases: initialization, adaptive archive grid and particle swarm optimization searching. Similar to this algorithm, Piri and Dey (Piri et al., 2014) also considered confidence, comprehensibility and interestingness as three objective for extracting association rules and used a pareto based particle swarm optimization for numerical association rule mining.

Tyagi and Bharadwaj (Tyagi et al., 2013) used a multi-objective particle swarm optimization algorithm for association rule mining in the framework of collaborative filtering recommendation systems, which does not require the determination of the minimum support and minimum confidence values in advance. This algorithm simultaneously considers support and confidence as two objectives for multi-objective PSO association rule mining algorithm which leads to derive only useful and interesting rules. Moreover, this algorithm was designed for the framework of recommender system, and therefore it extracts the rules only for a given user that improves the computational efficiency.

One the important issues in SI-based algorithms is setting the suitable values for the control parameters. Indira and Kanmani (Indira et al., 2015) presented an adaptive approach for the control parameters in PSO to extract association rules. They focused on the quality of the extracted rules and considered the association rule mining problem as a multi-objective problem and evaluated the rules quantitatively and qualitatively based on confidence, Laplace, conviction, leverage and lift.

3.2   Overview of ACO Algorithm for Association Rule Mining

ACO algorithm can be useful in solving the problems that need finding paths to destinations. Artificial ants determine the optimal solutions by moving in a parameter space to find superior paths through the graphs.

Al-Dharhani et al. (2014) proposed a graph-based ant colony optimization algorithm for association rule mining (ACO-ARM) that consists of two main phases. In the first phase, the data are represented in the form of a boolean matrix using a boolean transactional data representation scheme. Then, the Apriori algorithm is used to generate n-frequent itemsets from the represented data. In the second phase, a completely connected, weighted graph is created using the 2-frequent itemsets in the first phase which is used by the ACO algorithm to generate the final frequent itemsets. The result of the experiments done by Al-Dharhani et al., showed that the graph-based ACO-ARM improves the execution time in comparison with Apriori algorithm.

Ameta and Vibhakar (Ameta et al., 2013) proposed an algorithm for optimization of association rule mining using the distance weight and ant colony optimization. In this algorithm, the second odder quadratic equation and nearest neighbor classification method are used to choose the candidate set of superiority of key for rule generation. Moreover, a heuristic search method is used to search for the best support value for the generation of optimized association rules. ACO algorithms are used in the whole process of optimizing the rule set. The results of the experiments done by Ameta and Vibhakar revealed that when the distance weight is modified, a large number of new rules are created. This shows that when the weight is only determined based on support and confidence, interesting rules may be ignored.

Some studies (Dong et al., 2019; Patel et al., 2011; Sadh et al., 2013) uses ant colony optimization to propose an algorithm for optimizing the association rules generated by Apriori algorithm. The aim of these algorithms is to prune the association rules and minimize the number of association rules.

3.3   Overview of Artificial Bee Colony and Bee Swarm Optimization Algorithms for Association Rule Mining

Qureshi et al. (2019) proposed a walk back artificial bee colony algorithm namely Walk-BackABC to optimize association rule mining. The Walk-BackABC includes four phases: primary phase, employed bees phase, the onlooker bees phase and the scout bees phase. In all phases of this algorithm, the random walk back process are performed by the onlooker bees to carry out the local optimization process and search of the food process in the neighborhood. In Walk-BackABC, the termination condition is initially set, then the Walk-BackABC algorithm is applied on the rules generated by Apriori or FP growth algorithm to optimize the association rules. The fitness values of the generated rules are calculated, and the rules that satisfy the required condition are added to the output set.

An algorithm based on an improved bee swarm optimization was proposed by Djenouri et al. (2014) for association rule mining. They also proposed an encoding solution and three different strategies for determining the search area. This algorithm consists of four steps: computing the neighborhood search, determining the search area, computing the fitness and dancing step. In this algorithm, the best solution found in each pass is saved in the best list to keep the memory of the best solution. At the end of the algorithm, the rules are generated from the best list.

Sharma et al. (2015) utilized ABC algorithm with mutation operator for the generation of high quality association rules which has six phases: Initialization phase, fitness value calculation phase, employed bees phase, onlooker bees phase, scout bees phase and mutation phase. The mutation operator is utilized after the scout bees phase. Using the mutation operator, there may be a possibility to change the local best position and the algorithm may not be trapped into local optima. Sharma et al., used Apriori algorithm to generate association rules and set the termination condition for artificial bee colony with mutation algorithm. Then, ABC with the mutation algorithm are applied on the rules generated by Apriori algorithm, and the fitness value of each rule is evaluated to add the rules that meet the desired criteria in the output set.

An association rules mining algorithm based on bees swarm optimization metaheuristic named Modified Bees Swarm Optimization for Association Rules Mining (MBSO-ARM) was proposed by Mohammed et al. (2017). This algorithm contains rule representation, initialization, search area determination strategy, neighborhood space calculation and fitness function evaluation phases. The search area determination strategy phase explores the search area regions and selects K bees with the highest fitness values from the search area. At this phase, the region of each bee is explored via neighborhood search operation. Then, the bees communicate with each other to select the best neighborhood (solutions) using a table called the dance table. The best solutions in each pass are kept in the best list. The operations are repeated until the termination criteria are met. After completing this algorithm, the rules are generated from the best list.

4 Overview of SI-based Algorithms for Data Clustering

Quality of the partitional clustering depends on the position of initial cluster centroids and the number of clusters that should be specified in advance (Alam et al., 2014). In hierarchical clustering, a data object cannot be assigned to different clusters in successive passes. While in partitional clustering a data object can be assigned into different clusters in successive passes. The execution time and computational complexity of partitional clustering is lower than those of hierarchical clustering (Esmin et al., 2015).

Hierarchical and partitional clustering have some advantages and disadvantages in terms of creating clusters with different shapes, boundaries of clusters and creating cluster numbers.

The selection of initial cluster centroids, the exact number of natural groups in the data objects, sensitivity to outliers and computational complexity are the problems that affect on the performance of clustering methods. To overcome these problems, optimization-based methods have been used in data clustering to optimize an objective function that can be minimizing the intra-cluster distance or maximizing the inter-cluster distance. The optimization methods can be used as data clustering algorithms or optimize existing data clustering methods (Alam et al., 2014). Optimization based on swarm intelligence has been widely used for data clustering.

4.1 Overview of PSO Algorithm for Data Clustering

The PSO-based clustering methods are divided into two general categories. The first category contains the methods which utilize PSO with other clustering methods such as K-means, K-Harmonic mean, self-organizing maps, and neural networks. In these methods, PSO is used for parameter optimization, parameter selection, and centroid selection or updating. The second category includes the methods where PSO is independently used for clustering of data. In these methods, issues such as parameter selection and initialization, number of particles and evaluation of particles by a fitness function can be discussed (Alam et al., 2014).

Particle swarm optimization was first utilized by Van der Merwe and Engelbecht (Van Der Merwe et al., 2003) for data clustering. They used a fixed number of particles so that each particle denotes a different clustering solution. The centroids of all the clusters are assigned to a single particle. In each iteration of this algorithm, a set of candidate solutions is created and the best solution is chosen. This process continues until the final best solution is achieved. In K-means clustering, one solution is created and it is tried to optimize the solution in successive iterations. The fitness function of this algorithm evaluates each candidate solution based on the positions of the cluster's centroids. They also presented a hybrid PSO algorithm which uses K-means clustering to seed the initial swarm, and then utilizes PSO to refine the clusters created by K-mean.

Chen and Ye (Chen et al., 2012) proposed a PSO-clustering algorithm in which a particle is considered for representing the centroids of all clusters. The initial swarm of particles are randomly produced so that each particle represents the vector of different cluster centroids. The positions and velocity of all particles are randomly initialized. The fitness value is calculated for each particle and compared with the local and global best values to update them. The velocity and position of each particle is updated based on Equation 1 and Equation 2, respectively. The steps of calculating fitness values to update the velocity and position are repeated until a stopping condition is satisfied.

A hierarchical PSO clustering was proposed by Alam et al. (2010) which combines the agglomerative hierarchical and partitional clustering methods and adds PSO to the process for data clustering. In this algorithm, each cluster centroid is modeled by a single particle and the solution of clustering problem is represented by complete swarm. This algorithm generates a large number of particles and combines them until only a final particle remains based on the agglomerative hierarchical clustering methods. The positions of the first generation particles are adjusted in successive iterations. In the transition of swarm from one generation to another one, two selected particles are merged and the swarm is transformed into a smaller swarm.

An integration of PSO with K-means clustering algorithm was presented by Kuo et al. (2011). The first phase of this algorithm is initializing the swarm of particles randomly with initial positions and velocities so that each particle is a vector containing K cluster centroids. The number of clusters should be determined in advance, so that the ART2 neural network is used to provide the desired information. The second phase is calculating the fitness value for each particle. Then, the local and global best are updated and the velocity and position of each particle are calculated based on the best position of the local and global best. In the next phase, the Euclidean distance of every piece of data to all cluster centroids for each particle is calculated. Then, for each particle, each piece of data is assigned to the cluster with the closest cluster centroid. The cluster centroid vector for each particle is calculated again. The algorithm terminates if the maximum number of iterations is met, otherwise it returns to the second phase.

Omran et al. (2006) proposed a hybrid clustering algorithm based on PSO and K-means where binary PSO is used for the clustering of data and K-means is utilized for the refinement of the clusters. This algorithm also finds the number of optimal clusters. The first phase of this algorithm is initializing the swarm parameters such as initial partition of the dataset, number of particles and velocity. Then, calculating the fitness of particles and updating velocity and position are performed. The process is iteratively carried out until the termination condition is satisfied.

4.2   Overview of ACO Algorithm for Data Clustering

Ant-based clustering methods are classified into two main groups: the first group directly mimics the clustering behavior observed in real ant colonies. In the algorithms of this group, clustering objective is implicitly defined, meaning that the overall objective of the clustering and the types of clusters sought are not explicitly defined. The second group reformulates the clustering as an optimization problem, with clustering quality as the objective, and utilizes the general-purpose ant-based optimization to find good or near optimal clusters. One of the advantages of the algorithms in this group is the explicit objective function, which leads to a better understanding and predicting the performance of the clustering algorithm on particular types of data. The explicit objective function also customizes the clustering objective for specific types of data and particular tasks. A number of ant-based clustering algorithms fall between these two groups: They are derived from ant-based general purpose optimization algorithms, but have been modified so that an explicit global objective does not exist anymore (Handl et al., 2007).

Shelokar et al. (2004) presented an ant colony optimization methodology for optimally clustering data objects into several clusters. In this algorithm, a population of agents or ants are generated to build the solutions. An agent is a string in which each element corresponds to one of the test samples. The value of an element of the solution indicates the cluster number assigned to the test sample. To construct a solution, the agent uses the information of the pheromone trail matrix to assign each element of the string to a suitable cluster. At the start of the algorithm, the pheromone matrix is initialized to some small values and evolved in the successive iterations. After generating a population of the solutions, fitness values are calculated for the solution defined as the sum of squared Euclidean distances between each data object and the cluster centroid. Then, a local search is applied on the generated solutions to further enhance the fitness of the solutions. The pheromone trial matrix is then updated depending on the quality of solutions generated by the agents.

In summary, in each iteration of this algorithm, three steps are performed.

(1) New solutions are generated by the artificial ants based on the modified pheromone matrix available from previous iteration.

(2) The local search procedure is performed on the newly generated solutions.

(3) Pheromone trail matrix is updated.

The algorithm repeatedly performs these three steps for a certain number of iterations, and the solution with the lowest fitness value represents the optimal partitioning of data objects into several clusters.

Inkaya et al. (2015) proposed an ACO based algorithm in a multi-objective framework for the spatial clustering that does not require prior information on the number of clusters and the neighborhoods. They also proposed two multiple-objective functions to evaluate the quality of a clustering solution with the arbitrary shaped clusters and different densities. Adjusted compactness and relative separation are considered as the main idea in designing the objective functions. The goal is to maximize the minimum relative separation and minimize the maximum adjusted compactness. This algorithm has two pre-processing steps: neighborhood construction and data set reduction. The former is used for extracting the local characteristics of data objects applied in the solution evaluation, and the latter for ensuring the scalability of the approach. In this algorithm, artificial ants are the search agents that construct tours by inserting the edges between pairs of data objects. Connected data objects in a tour form a cluster. This algorithm consists of six steps: initialization of parameters, solution construction that consists of point selection and edge insertion, solution evaluation, local search applied to each constructed clustering solution, pheromone update carried out for each solution component (edge), and non-dominated set update. Steps 2–6 are repeated until the maximum number of iterations is reached.

Menéndez et al. (2016) proposed two medoid-based clustering algorithms that use ACO to choose an optimal medoid set for determining the clusters. The first algorithm, called METACOC, selects the best medoids based on distance information which the number of clusters is defined in advance. The METACOC algorithm has the following steps:

(1) The pheromone matrix is initialized.

(2) Each ant is initialized: the number of clusters and the visited data objects are set.

(3) For each ant, it is checked that all data objects have been visited or all medoids have been selected.

(4) Each data object is assigned to the closest medoid and the objective function is calculated for each ant.

(5) The best solution is selected which consists of a set of medoids.

(6) The pheromone trails (global updating rule) are updated.

(7) Termination condition is checked, if the maximum number of iterations is not met, go to step 2, otherwise the best solution is provided.

The second algorithm, called METACOC-K, is an extension of the METACOC where the number of clusters is automatically adjusted. The difference between two algorithms is in the selection of the number of clusters and the solution evaluation.

4.3 Overview of ABC Algorithm for Data Clustering

Zhang et al. (2010) proposed an artificial bee colony clustering algorithm for partitioning data objects into different clusters which uses Deb's rules to direct the search direction of each candidate. A population of solutions is initialized, and the first half is considered as the employed bees and the second one as the onlookers. Each bee includes an encoding of a candidate solution (food source) and a fitness that indicates its quality. The floating-point arrays are used to encode cluster centers. Then, the first half of the colony is ordered, and the bees with the worst solution quality are considered as scouts. This algorithm creates new solutions for each employed bee and evaluates it. Then the selection process is done by using the Deb's method. Moreover, this algorithm sends each scout into the search area to find a new food source, evaluates it and applies the selection process using the Deb's method. The probability value is calculated for each employed bee and the new solutions are generated for the onlookers and evaluated. Then, the selection process using the Deb's method is used. The best position achieved so far is memorized, and the termination condition is checked.

A two-step artificial bee colony algorithm was proposed by Kumar and Sahoo (Kumar et al. 2017) for data clustering. This algorithm contains four phases: initialization phase, employed bees phase, onlooker bees phase, abandoned food source and scout bees phase. In this algorithm, the K-means algorithm is used to determine the initial food source positions in a random search space. On the other hand, the positions of the cluster centers generated by the K-means algorithm act as the initial positions of food sources in the employed bees phase of ABC algorithm. In the employed bees phase, the new food sources positions close to the old ones are exploited. The quality of food sources is determined in the onlooker bees phase by a random function. If the quality of the food source is good enough, the source is selected; otherwise, the new food source position is searched by the onlooker bees. Moreover, in the onlooker bees phase of ABC algorithm, an improved solution search equation based on the social behavior of PSO is used to discover the promising search areas. In the scout bee or abandoned food source phase, the position of the abandoned food source is found using Hooke and Jeeves-based classical search method. The output of the two-step ABC algorithm is the optimal cluster centers.

Alshamiri et al. (2016) proposed an algorithm that uses the extreme learning machine (ELM) to project the input data into a high-dimensional feature space and performs the data clustering in this feature space using ABC algorithm. The K-means and heuristic clustering algorithms which use the distance criteria as the measure of the similarity between data objects, are appropriate for data with an ellipsoidal or hyper-spherical distribution. If the separation boundaries between clusters are nonlinear, then the distance based algorithms will fail. One approaches to solve this problem is nonlinear transformation of data into a high-dimensional feature space using kernel functions or ELM, and then, carry out the clustering within the new feature space. For the clustering of data in the high-dimensional feature space using ABC algorithm, initial solutions are generated and their fitness are evaluated. In the employed bees phase, each employed bee creates a new solution and evaluates the fitness value of the solution. If the fitness value of the new solution is better than that of the old one, the old one is replaced by the new one. The fitness information of the solutions related to the employed bees is shared with the onlooker bees. Based on this information, each onlooker bee chooses a solution with a probability related to its fitness value in the onlooker phase. Then, every onlooker bee creates a new solution, evaluates the fitness value of the solution and uses a greedy selection on the new and old solutions. If the fitness value of a solution is not improved after performing a predetermined number of trials, the solution will be abandoned, and the associated employed bee becomes a scout and creates a new solution. The search processes of the employed, onlooker and scout bees are repeated until the stopping condition is satisfied.

A combined algorithm based on the ABC algorithm and k-means method was presented by Armano and Farmani (2014) for solving the clustering problem. In this algorithm, the positions of food sources (each food source represents a set of centroids) are randomly initialized. Then, new food sources are searched, and the places of food sources are updated by the employed bees. Afterward, k-means algorithm and a greedy selection are used to evaluate the new fitness values. In the onlooker bees phase, the food source values are computed, and their place is updated based on to the probability values by the onlooker bees. The k-means algorithm and the greedy selection are applied again to finish the clustering task, the new fitness values are evaluated and compared with the original fitness values to update them. In the scout bees phase, a new food source is created in the search space that exceeds the value of the "limit" parameter. The steps of employed bees phase, onlooker bees phase and scout bees phase are repeated until the stopping condition is met.

Kumar et al. (2018) proposed a hybrid algorithm based on a modified artificial bee colony and K-means algorithm for data clustering. This algorithm initializes the food sources using the chaotic sequences which generates better initial solutions compared to the random sequence, and evaluates the fitness of food sources. For each employed bee, a new food source is found in the neighborhood of old food source and evaluated. Then, the greedy selection on the original food source and the new one is applied. After the employed bees phase, the probability values is calculated for each food source. In the onlooker bees phase, the tournament selection mechanism is used instead of roulette wheel selection to provide better exploration and exploitation of solution space. The tournament size is selected based on the population size and the cycle number. Then, the food source with the maximum probability value is found and the new solution is generated for the selected food source. The fitness value of the new food source is evaluated and the greedy selection is applied on the original food source and the new one. In the second step of the onlooker bees phase, the worst fitness food source is replaced by a randomly generated better food source. If the food source is not upgraded up to the limit, a scout bee will be sent to the solution of food source in the scout bees phase. Then, the best solution obtained so far is memorized. The best solution obtained by the modified ABC is taken as the initial solution for the K-means clustering algorithm. The K-means algorithm is applied to obtain and evaluate the better solutions until the termination condition is satisfied.

5   Conclusion

In today's world, there is a large amount of data in various applications that contain valuable information for decision making. Data mining involves all methods that use data analysis techniques to discover hidden patterns in the data. Association rule mining and clustering are the important techniques in data mining that have been considered by many data mining researchers and have led to the presentation of a number of algorithms to address various aspects of ARM and clustering. ARM is extracting important correlation among the set of items in data and discovering association rules. The large number of rules generated by many association rule mining algorithms makes it difficult to extract knowledge from the rules. Moreover, threshold values of support and confidence parameters affect the quality of association rule mining such that many researchers have addressed to setting the optimal values for these parameters to extract efficient rules. Clustering is grouping similar data objects into one cluster which may be encountered with the problems such as computational complexity, selection of initial cluster centroids, converging to a local optimum and sensitivity to outliers. These problems have a great impact on the quality of clusters formed. SI-based algorithms have been widely used as the solutions to deal with the problems of association rule mining and clustering in the last two decades. In this chapter, the role of SI-based algorithms in the data mining tasks such as association rule mining and clustering was investigated, and a review on the well-known SI-based algorithms for these tasks was carried out.

A survey of the relevant literature showed that the SI-based algorithms for association rule mining and clustering are divided into two groups. In the first group, SI-based algorithms are utilized to optimize other association rule mining and clustering algorithms while in the second one, SI-based algorithms are independently used to solve the association rule mining and clustering problems. The survey also revealed that the efficiency of the SI-based algorithms for association rule mining and clustering depend on the issues such as parameter setting and initialization, number of swarms, the fitness function used for evaluation of the solution and stopping condition.

References

Agrawal, R., T. Imieliński and A. Swami. Mining association rules between sets of items in large databases. Proceedings of the 1993 ACM SIGMOD International Conference on Management of Data—SIGMOD, 93: 207–216, 1993. doi: 10.1145/170035.170072.

Ahmed, H. and J. Glasgow. 2012. Swarm intelligence: Concepts, models and applications. Technical Report, 585(February): 1–50, 2012.

Al-Dharhani, G.S., Z.A. Othman and A.A. Bakar. A graph-based ant colony optimization for association rule mining. Arabian Journal for Science and Engineering, 39(6): 4651–4665, 2014. doi: 10.1007/s13369-014-1096-5.

Alam, S., G. Dobbie, P. Riddle and M.A. Naeem. Particle swarm optimization based Hierarchical Agglomerative clustering. 2010 IEEE/WIC/ACM International Conference on Intelligent Agent Technology, IAT, 2010, 2: 64–68, 2010. doi: 10.1109/WI-IAT.2010.75.

Alam, S., G. Dobbie, Y.S. Koh, P. Riddle and S. Ur Rehman. Research on particle swarm optimization based clustering: A systematic review of literature and techniques. Swarm and Evolutionary Computation, 17: 1–13, 2014. doi: 10.1016/j.swevo.2014.02.001.

Alshamiri, A.K., A. Singh and B.R. Surampudi. Artificial bee colony algorithm for clustering: An extreme learning approach. Soft Computing, 20(8): 3163–3176, 2016. doi: 10.1007/s00500-015-1686-5.

Ameta, G.K. and V. Pathak. An improved association rule mining approach using distance weight and ant colony algorithm. International Journal of Innovative Research in Technology & Science, 1(4): 27–32, 2013.

Armano, G. and M.R. Farmani. Clustering analysis with combination of artificial bee colony algorithm and k-means technique. International Journal of Computer Theory and Engineering, 6(2): 141–145, 2014. doi: 10.7763/ijcte.2014.v6.852.

Armano, G. and M.R. Farmani. Multiobjective clustering analysis using particle swarm optimization. Expert Systems with Applications, 55: 184–193, 2016. doi: 10.1016/j.eswa.2016.02.009.

Bernal Baró, G., J.F. Martínez-Trinidad, R.M. Valdovinos Rosas, J.A. Carrasco Ochoa, A.Y. Rodríguez González and M.S. Lazo Cortés. A PSO-based algorithm for mining association rules using a guided exploration strategy. Pattern Recognition Letters, 138: 8–15, 2020. doi: 10.1016/j.patrec.2020.05.006.

Blum, C. Ant colony optimization: Introduction and recent trends. Physics of Life Reviews, 2(4): 353–373, 2005. doi: 10.1016/j.plrev.2005.10.001.

Byla, E. and W. Pang. DeepSwarm: Optimising convolutional neural networks using swarm intelligence. In UK Workshop on Computational Intelligence UKCI 2019: Advances in Computational Intelligence Systems, pp. 119–130, 2020. doi: 10.1007/978-3-030-29933-0_10.

Chakraborty, A. and A.K. Kar. Swarm intelligence: A review of algorithms. Modeling and Optimization in Science and Technologies, 10: 475–494, 2017. doi: 10.1007/978-3-319-50920-4_19.

Chandra Mohan, B. and R. Baskaran. A survey: Ant Colony Optimization based recent research and implementation on several engineering domain. Expert Systems with Applications, 39(4): 4618–4627, 2012. doi: 10.1016/j.eswa.2011.09.076.

Chen, C.-Y. and F. Ye. Particle swarm optimization algorithm and its application to clustering analysis. 2012 Proceedings of 17th Conference on Electrical Power Distribution. IEEE, 789–794, 2012. Retrieved from https://ieeexplore.ieee.org/abstract/document/6254579.

Cronin, S.K. SwarmOpt. GitHub Repository, 2018. Retrieved from https://github.com/SioKCronin/SwarmOpt.

Cura, T. A particle swarm optimization approach to clustering. Expert Systems with Applications, 39(1): 1582–1588, 2012. doi: 10.1016/j.eswa.2011.07.123.

Djenouri, Y., H. Drias and Z. Habbas. Bees swarm optimisation using multiple strategies for association rule mining. International Journal of Bio-Inspired Computation, 6(4): 239–249, 2014. doi: 10.1504/IJBIC.2014.064990.

Dong, D., Z. Ye, Y. Cao, S. Xie, F. Wang and W. Ming. An improved association rule mining algorithm based on ant lion optimizer algorithm and fp-growth. Proceedings of the 2019 10th IEEE International Conference on Intelligent Data Acquisition and Advanced Computing Systems: Technology and Applications, IDAACS, 1(07): 458–463, 2019. doi: 10.1109/IDAACS.2019.8924290.

Dorigo, M., V. Maniezzo and A. Colorni. Positive feedback as a search strategy. Tech. Report 91-016, Dipartimento Di Elettronica, Politecnico Di Milano, Italy, 1991.

Dorigo, M., V. Maniezzo and A. Colorni. Ant system: Optimization by a colony of cooperating agents. IEEE Transactions on Systems, Man, and Cybernetics, Part B: Cybernetics, 26(1): 29–41, 1996. doi: 10.1109/3477.484436.

Esmin, A.A.A., R.A. Coelho and S. Matwin. A review on particle swarm optimization algorithm and its variants to clustering high-dimensional data. Artificial Intelligence Review, 44(1): 23–45, 2015. doi: 10.1007/s10462-013-9400-4.

Figueiredo, E., M. Macedo, H.V. Siqueira, C.J. Santana, A. Gokhale and C.J.A. Bastos-Filho. Swarm intelligence for clustering—A systematic review with new perspectives on data mining. Engineering Applications of Artificial Intelligence, 82(August 2018): 313–329, 2019. doi: 10.1016/j.engappai.2019.04.007.

Han, J., J. Pei and M. Kamber. Data Mining: Concepts and Techniques. Elsevier, 2011.

Handl, J. and B. Meyer. Ant-based and swarm-based clustering. Swarm Intelligence, 1(2): 95–113, 2007. doi: 10.1007/s11721-007-0008-7.

Indira, K. and S. Kanmani. Association rule mining through adaptive parameter control in particle swarm optimization. Computational Statistics, 30(1): 251–277, 2015. doi: 10.1007/s00180-014-0533-y.

Inkaya, T., S. Kayaligil and N.E. Özdemirel. Ant Colony Optimization based clustering methodology. Applied Soft Computing, 28: 301–311, 2015. doi: 10.1016/j.asoc.2014.11.060.

Jarboui, B., M. Cheikh, P. Siarry and A. Rebai. Combinatorial particle swarm optimization (CPSO) for partitional clustering problem. Applied Mathematics and Computation, 192(2): 337–345, 2007. doi: 10.1016/j.amc.2007.03.010.

Karaboga, D. An idea based on honey bee swarm for numerical optimization. Technical Report-Tr06, Erciyes University, Engineering Faculty, Computer Engineering Department, 2005.

Karaboga, D. and B. Basturk. On the performance of artificial bee colony (ABC) algorithm. Applied Soft Computing Journal, 8(1): 687–697, 2008. doi: 10.1016/j.asoc.2007.05.007.

Kennedy, J. and R. Eberhart. Particle swarm optimization. Proceedings of ICNN'95—International Conference on Neural Networks, 4: 1942–1948, 1995. doi: 10.1109/ICNN.1995.488968.

Kou, Z. Association rule mining using chaotic gravitational search algorithm for discovering relations between manufacturing system capabilities and product features. Concurrent Engineering Research and Applications, 27(3): 213–232, 2019. doi: 10.1177/1063293X19832949.

Kumar, A., D. Kumar and S.K. Jarial. A review on artificial bee colony algorithms and their applications to data clustering. Cybernetics and Information Technologies, 17(3): 3–28, 2017. doi: 10.1515/cait-2017-0027.

Kumar, A., D. Kumar and S.K. Jarial. A novel hybrid K-means and artificial bee colony algorithm approach for data clustering. Decision Science Letters, 7(1): 65–76, 2018. doi: 10.5267/j. dsl.2017.4.003.

Kumar, Y. and G. Sahoo. A two-step artificial bee colony algorithm for clustering. Neural Computing and Applications, 28(3): 537–551, 2017. doi: 10.1007/s00521-015-2095-5.

Kuo, R.J. and C.W. Shih. Association rule mining through the ant colony system for National Health Insurance Research Database in Taiwan. Computers and Mathematics with Applications, 54(11-12): 1303–1318, 2007. doi: 10.1016/j.camwa.2006.03.043.

Kuo, R.J., C.M. Chao and Y.T. Chiu. Application of particle swarm optimization to association rule mining. Applied Soft Computing Journal, 11(1): 326–336, 2011. doi: 10.1016/j.asoc.2009.11.023.

Kuo, R.J., M. Gosumolo and F.E. Zulvia. Multi-objective particle swarm optimization algorithm using adaptive archive grid for numerical association rule mining. Neural Computing and Applications, 31(8): 3559–3572, 2019. doi: 10.1007/s00521-017-3278-z.

Kuo, R.J., M.J. Wang and T.W. Huang. An application of particle swarm optimization algorithm to clustering analysis. Soft Computing, 15(3): 533–542, 2011. doi: 10.1007/s00500-009-0539-5.

Menéndez, H.D., F.E.B. Otero and D. Camacho. Medoid-based clustering using ant colony optimization. Swarm Intelligence, 10(2): 123–145, 2016. doi: 10.1007/s11721-016-0122-5.

Michelakos, I., N. Mallios, E. Papageorgiou and M. Vassilakopoulos. Ant Colony Optimization and data mining. In Next Generation Data Technologies for Collective Computational Intelligence, Springer, Berlin, Heidelberg, pp. 31–60, 2011. doi: 10.1007/978-3-642-20344-2_2.

Miranda, J.V.L. PySwarms: A research toolkit for particle Swarm Optimization in Python. The Journal of Open Source Software, 3(21): 433, 2018. doi: 10.21105/joss.00433.

Mishra, S., R. Sagban, A. Yakoob and N. Gandhi. Swarm intelligence in anomaly detection systems: An overview. International Journal of Computers and Applications, 43(2): 109–118, 2021. doi: 10.1080/1206212X.2018.1521895.

Mohammed, R.A., M.G. Duaimi and A.T. Sadiq. Modified bees swarm optimization algorithm for association rules mining modified bees swarm optimization algorithm for association rules mining. Iraqi Journal of Science, 58(1B): 364–376, 2017.

Nandhini, M., M. Janani and S.N. Sivanandham. Association rule mining using swarm intelligence and domain ontology. International Conference on Recent Trends in Information Technology, ICRTIT, 2012: 537–541, 2012. doi: 10.1109/ICRTIT.2012.6206763.

Omran, M.G., A. Salman and A.P. Engelbrecht. Dynamic clustering using particle swarm optimization with application in image segmentation. Pattern Analysis and Applications, 8(4): 332–344, 2006.

Patel, B.P., N. Gupta, R.K. Karn and Y. Rana. Optimization of association rule mining Apriori algorithm using ACO. International Journal on Emerging Technologies, 2(1): 87–92, 2011.

Piri, J. and R. Dey. Quantitative association rule mining using multi-objective particle swarm optimization. International Journal of Scientific & Engineering Research, 5(10): 155–161, 2014.

Qureshi, I., B. Mohammad and M.A. Habeeb. Optimizing association rule mining using Walk Back Artificial Bee Colony (WalkBackABC) Algorithm. In Innovations in Computer Science and Engineering. Lecture Notes in Networks and Systems, vol 74. Springer, Singapore (Vol. 74, pp. 39–48). Springer Singapore, 2019. doi: 10.1007/978-981-13-7082-3_6.

Runkler, T.A. Ant colony optimization of clustering models. International Journal of Intelligent Systems, 20(12): 1233–1251, 2005. doi: 10.1002/int.20111.

Sadh, A.S. and N. Shukla. Apriori and ant colony optimization of association rules. International Journal of Advanced Computer Research, 3(10): 35–42, 2013.

Sarath, K.N.V.D. and V. Ravi. Association rule mining using binary particle swarm optimization. Engineering Applications of Artificial Intelligence, 26(8): 1832–1840, 2013. doi: 10.1016/j. engappai.2013.06.003.

Sharma, P., S. Tiwari and M. Gupta. Optimize association rules using artificial bee colony algorithm with mutation. Proceedings—1st International Conference on Computing, Communication, Control and Automation, ICCUBEA, 2015, 116(13): 370–373, 2015. doi: 10.1109/ICCUBEA.2015.77.

Sheikhan, M. and M. Sharifi Rad. Gravitational search algorithm-optimized neural misuse detector with selected features by fuzzy grids-based association rules mining. Neural Computing and Applications, 23(7-8): 2451–2463, 2013. doi: 10.1007/s00521-012-1204-y.

Sheikhpour, R., M.A. Sarram and R. Sheikhpour. Particle swarm optimization for bandwidth determination and feature selection of kernel density estimation based classifiers in diagnosis of breast cancer. Applied Soft Computing Journal, 40, 2016. doi: 10.1016/j.asoc.2015.10.005.

Shelokar, P.S., V.K. Jayaraman and B.D. Kulkarni. An ant colony approach for clustering. Analytica Chimica Acta, 509(2): 187–195, 2004. doi: 10.1016/j.aca.2003.12.032.

Su, T., H. Xu and X. Zhou. Particle swarm optimization-based association rule mining in big data environment. IEEE Access, 7: 161008–161016, 2019. doi: 10.1109/ACCESS.2019.2951195.

SwarmPackagePy. 2017. GitHub Repository. Retrieved from https://github.com/SISDevelop/SwarmPackagePy.

Telikani, A., A.H. Gandomi and A. Shahbahrami. A survey of evolutionary computation for association rule mining. Information Sciences, 524: 318–352, 2020. doi: 10.1016/j.ins.2020.02.073.

Tsai, C.W., K.W. Huang, C.S. Yang and M.C. Chiang. A fast particle swarm optimization for clustering. Soft Computing, 19(2): 321–338, 2015. doi: 10.1007/s00500-014-1255-3.

Tyagi, S. and K.K. Bharadwaj. Enhancing collaborative filtering recommendations by utilizing multi-objective particle swarm optimization embedded association rule mining. Swarm and Evolutionary Computation, 13: 1–12, 2013. doi: 10.1016/j.swevo.2013.07.001.

Van Der Merwe, D.W. and A.P. Engelbrecht. Data clustering using particle swarm optimization. 2003 Congress on Evolutionary Computation, CEC 2003—Proceedings, 1: 215–220, 2003. doi: 10.1109/CEC.2003.1299577.

Yang, J., L. Qu, Y. Shen, Y. Shi, S. Cheng, J. Zhao and X. Shen. Swarm Intelligence in Data Science: Applications, Opportunities and Challenges. In International Conference on Swarm Intelligence. Springer, Cham, 3–14, 2020. doi: 10.1007/978-3-030-53956-6_1.

Zhang, C., D. Ouyang and J. Ning. An artificial bee colony approach for clustering. Expert Systems with Applications, 37(7): 4761–4767, 2010. doi: 10.1016/j.eswa.2009.11.003.

Chapter 3

Leveraging Center-Based Sampling Theory for Enhancing Particle Swarm Classification of Textual Data

Anwar Ali Yahya[1,2]

1 Introduction

In swarm intelligence field, Particle Swarm Optimization (PSO) is a population-based algorithm proposed by Kennedy and Eberhart (1995), who took its inspiration from the cooperation and communication behavior of birds swarm. It maintains a population of particles (swarm), where each particle, represents a potential solution to the optimization problem at hand, and is defined by its location in a multidimensional search space. Iteratively, the particles adjust their own positions toward better ones in the space by combining some aspects of the history of its own current and best position with those of one or more members of the swarm, with some random perturbations. Over a number of iterations, the swarm as a whole, like a flock of birds collectively foraging for food, moves more close to an optimum position (Martens et al., 2011; Englebreht, 2006). Thanks to its simplicity, fast convergence, and the fewer parameters it demands, PSO has

---

[1] Najran University, Najran, Saudi Arabia.
[2] Thamar University, Thamar, Yemen.
  Email: aaesmail@nu.edu.sa

been successfully applied to solve optimization problems in various domains (del Valle et al., 2008). A recent domain of applications where PSO has been found efficient is data mining (Abraham et al., 2006b), where PSO has been applied to tackle many problems such as clustering (Figueiredo et al., 2019), classification (Nouaouria et al., 2013), feature selection (Nayar et al., 2019).

As for data classification, the first PSO application dates back to 2004 (Sousa et al., 2004), and since that time PSO has been widely applied (Nouaouria and Boukadoum, 2010; Nouaouria et al., 2013), where it was found suitable and competitive in many demanding domains, especially when accurate, yet comprehensible classifiers, fit for dynamic distributed environments, are required (Abraham et al., 2006b). Recently a major concern has been raised regarding PSO performance when applied to classify data in high dimensional domains (Nouaouria et al., 2013). In such domains, the PSO performance deteriorates drastically, because the particles become highly sparse and achieving a uniform coverage of the search space is almost meaningless. This concern was initially addressed in (de Falco et al., 2006), where PSO is applied to classify nine UCI datasets, and the conclusion is that PSO performance tends to decrease with increasing values of classes, and also with increasing values of the product of data set size and dimension. In (Nouaouria and Boukadoum, 2010) (these conclusions are questioned by investigating PSO on a more complex dataset and positive results are obtained, when using a confinement mechanism. A more through investigation is carried out in (Nouaouria and Boukadoum, 2010) with more datasets and the conclusion is that a PSO with wind dispersion and confinement mechanisms has a good potential as a classification tool even for high dimensioned problems with a large number of instances and multiple classes.

In continuation of the forgoing research efforts, this paper proposes a center-based sampling theory method to enhance PSO performance in data classification. This results in a PSO variant, dubbed CBS-PSO, capable of dealing with the curse of dimensionality problem, an inherent problem in data classification. The center-based sampling theory (Rahnamayan and Wang, 2009; Esmailzadeh and Rahnamayan, 2011), states that in the search space of a given problem, the center region contains points with a higher chance to be closer to the solution and this chance increases directly with the dimensionality of the search space. On this basis, it is hypothesized that if the PSO evolution is attracted toward the center region of the search space, the probability that the PSO evolution converges to the global optimum becomes higher. Nonetheless, utilizing the center-based sampling theory for the PSO model of text classification, requires overcoming two inevitable obstacles: identifying the center of the search space and attracting the PSO evolution toward this promising region. In overcoming these obstacles, the CBS-PSO method applies the Rocchio Algorithm (RA) to estimate the center of the search space for the data classification problem, and to develop a systematic mechanism to generate and incorporate informed particles in the PSO swarm, so that the PSO evolution is attracted to the center region of the search space. While the use of RA to estimate the center point of a search space is motivated by its outstanding performance as a centroid-based classifier for data classification (Sebastiani, 2002; Vinciarelli, 2005), the systematic mechanism of attracting the swarm towards the center region is based on the social learning behavior of the swarm, where all the particles are attracted by the global best particle and move toward it (Liu et al., 2007). As will be elaborated later, in the CBS-PSO, the RA is applied first to estimate the coordinate of the center point in the search space, then iteratively this estimation is used to generate informed particles, one in every PSO iteration. Since these particles are located at the center region of the search space; when they are incorporated in the swarm, they attract other particles toward the center region. Obviously, by constantly incorporating informed particles from the center region of the search space in the swarm, there is an increasing probability of designating some as global best particles and consequently attracting the swarm to converge closer to the optimal solution.

The remaining sections of this paper describe the research background, introduce the center-based sampling theory and its role to improve population-based algorithms, present the proposed CBS-PSO, demonstrate how the proposed CBS-PSO can be applied for text classification, and present the results of validation experiments, and lastly to conclude this work.

2   Background

PSO is a simple yet powerful swarm intelligence algorithm that mimics the behavior of bird flocking and fish schooling (Englebreht, 2006; Abraham et al., 2006b). Formally it is described as a swarm of M particles, so that each particle is composed of three N-dimensional vectors: the current position (p_i), the previous best position (b_i), and the velocity (v_i), where N is the dimensionality of the search space. The current position (p_i) is considered as a set of coordinates representing a candidate solution. In the standard PSO algorithm, shown below, each particle iteratively moves with an adaptable velocity within the search space and retains in memory the best position it ever reached. The objective is to keep finding a better position and updating p_i and b_i by adding v_i coordinates to p_i and adjusting v_i from one iteration to the next as follows: for a particle i its velocity $v_i(t+1)$ at time $t+1$ is the linear combination of its velocity $v_i(t)$ at time t, the difference, $b_i(t)-p_i(t)$, between the position of the best particle found by the particle up to time t and its current position, and the difference, $b_g(t)-p_i(t)$, between the best position ever found by the total swarm and the particle's current position.

$$v_i(t+1) = w.v_i(t) + c_1.U(0,1) \otimes (b_i(t) - p_i(t))$$
$$+ c_2.U(0,1) \otimes (b_g(t) - p_i(t)) \tag{1}$$

where $\otimes$ denotes point-wise vector multiplication, $U(0,1)$ is a function that returns a vector whose positions are randomly generated by a uniform distribution in the range [0,1], c_1 is the cognitive parameter, c_2 is the social parameter, and w is the inertia factor whose range is [0, 1]. The velocity values must be within a range defined by two parameters v_{min} and v_{max}. The position of each particle i at the next step is then computed by summing up its current position and its velocity:

$$p_i(t+1) = p_i(t) + v_i(t+1) \qquad (2)$$

These operations are repeated for T_{max} iterations or until some other stopping criterion is met. A typical stopping criterion is the achievement of some desired minimal error with respect to the optimal solution.

Standard PSO Algorithm

begin
  for each particle i
    randomly initialize particle's position p_i and velocity v_i
  while (t < T_{max})
    for each particle i
      determine particle fitness value f_i
      if f_i is better than f_{bi} // f_{bi} is the fitness of the current local best position
        then $b_i = p_i$ // b_i is current local best position
          $f_{bi} = f_i$
      if f_i is better than f_g // f_g is the fitness of the current global best position
        then $p_g = p_i$ // p_g is current global best position
          $f_g = f_i$
    end for
    for each particle i
      calculate particle velocity v_i // Equation 1
      update particle position p_i // Equation 2
    end for
  end while
end

Due to its ease implementation and fast convergence to acceptable solutions, PSO has been successfully applied to various problems such as function optimization, fuzzy control, Scheduling, clustering, and classification (Abraham et al., 2006b) to name a few. As for data classification, it may seems at first glance that PSO and classification do not have much in common, however, by transforming the data classification problem into a form of optimization problem, *PSO* can be applied to explore the space of all classifiers and find the optimal one according to some pre-specified measures. In this regards, it is worth mentioning that there are two methods of using PSO for data classification: rule-based method and nearest neighbor-based method (Martens et al., 2011). While in the rule-based PSO, the classifiers are a set of rules usually represented in a form of IF-THEN rules, in the nearest neighbor-based PSO method the classifiers are a set of prototype vectors representing the centroids of data set classes. For the nearest neighbor-based PSO method, PSO works as a centroid discovery algorithm to find the optimal centroids representing data classes. As depicted in Fig. 1, the dataset is divided into a training set and testing set, which are processed, through different steps of feature extraction and selection, and transformed into a vector space representation suitable for PSO. Afterward, the PSO is applied as a centroid discovery algorithm as follows: given a data set of C classes and N dimensions data instances, the PSO finds optimal real-valued coordinates in N-dimensional space representing a centroid for each class. The process starts with a swarm of M particles whose coordinates are different tentative centroids for the given class, hence each particle has $2 \cdot N$ components, encoding for the N-dimensional centroid location and velocity. In the training stage, the PSO iteratively refines the positions to find the best position representing the centroid of the class. During a subsequent validation stage, the discovered centroid is evaluated with respect to class instances in a testing set to evaluate performance (the percentage of classification errors). After finding centroids for all classes, a new data instance can be classified by assigning it to a class with a centroid that is nearest (Nouaouria et al., 2013).

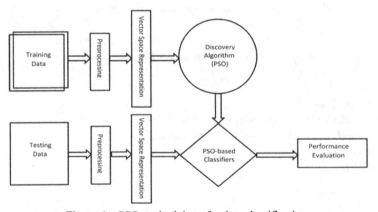

Figure 1: *PSO* methodology for data classification.

As the interest in applying PSO for data classification grows, its effectiveness for classifying high dimensional data becomes questionable. This concern was initially addressed in (de Falco et al., 2006; Falco et al., 2007), where the PSO was applied to nine UCI datasets (Card, Diabetes, Glass, Heart, Horse, Iris, Wdbc, Wdbc-I, and Wine). The obtained results are compared with the results provided by nine classical classification algorithms. More specifically, in these works, the effects of the number of classes and data size and dimensionality are investigated (the number of classes ranges from 2 to 6, the dimensions range from 4 to 58, and the sizes range from 150 to 768. It was concluded that the PSO classification accuracy tends to decrease with increasing values of classes in the dataset and with the value of the product of dataset size by dimensionality. The researchers in Nouraouria and Boukadoum, 2009 questioned the conclusions of de Falco et al., 2006 and Falco et al., 2007 by investigating performance of the PSO on a more complex dataset (Fluorescence measurements on substance datasets with 19 classes, 2,103 data instances, and 64 space dimensions). The results show the positive performance of PSO when using a mechanism of confinement of the data values. Further investigation is implemented in order to evaluate the extent to which the generalization of the previous conclusions holds for three additional datasets with sizes of 2,103, 16,000, and 3,823; dimensions of 64, 16, and 64; and class numbers of 19, 26, and 10. The results bring to surface the fact that PSO has good potential as a classification tool, even for high dimensioned problem spaces with a large number of instances and multiple classes.

It is obvious from the above that the high dimensionality of the high dimensional data presents a serious challenge to the PSO applications in data classification. Therefore, equipping PSO with coping mechanisms to improve its performance for high dimensional data classification becomes crucially important. For this sake, a Center Based Sampling theory method is proposed as will be elaborated in the following Sections.

3   Center-Based Sampling Theory

The center-based sampling theory states that the center region of the search space is very useful for population-based algorithms, because the points located in the center region have a higher chance to be closer to the solution of a given problem. It was introduced by Rahnamayan and Wang (2009), who measured the closeness of points in a search space from an unknown solution using the Euclidean distances. They observed that as the points got closer to the center of the search space, the probability of closeness to the unknown solution rose drastically. They also investigated the validity of the center-based sampling theory for high-dimensional problems; and interestingly found that with the increase of the problem dimensionality, the probability of the closeness to the solution increases on the center of the search space, as well. More specifically, having assumed that the search space is bounded by the interval [0, 1] in all dimensions, there is a specific range, [0.2, 0.8], where the probability of closeness to the solution starts to rapidly increase, as shown in Fig. 2(a) (Rahnamayan and Wang, 2009), and as the dimensionality increases, this probability becomes closer to one. They also measured the average distance of a point from the solution and observed that with the increases of the dimensionality, as the points move closer to the center their average distance from the solution decreases to very low values as shown in Fig. 2(b). Obviously, the center point has the minimum average distance from the unknown solution and thus the maximum chance to be closer to it. In other words, as shown in Fig. 2(c), the probability of the closeness of the center point (p_c) to the solution, compared to a second random point increases sharply with the dimension and interestingly for the higher dimensions ($D > 30$), it is very close (converges) to one.

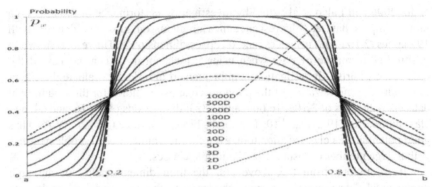

Figure 2(a): Probability of closeness of candidate-solution to an unknown solution, for different interval points and dimensions (Rahnamayan and Wang, 2009).

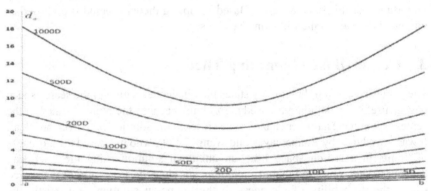

Figure 2(b): The average distance of candidate-solution to an unknown solution, for different high dimensions (Rahnamayan and Wang, 2009).

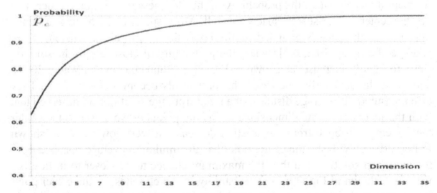

Figure 2(c): Probability of closeness of candidates generated randomly in the center-based region, compared to random candidate generated in the entire range, for dimensions of 1 to 100 (Rahnamayan and Wang, 2009).

It follows from the center-based sampling theory that the center region of the search space is a valuable point for the population-based algorithms searching for an optimal solution in high dimensional spaces. It can serve as a landmark of the center region in the search space, which can be exploited by the population-based algorithms to focus the search on this promising region, thus accelerating the convergence, and yielding better results. Nonetheless, utilizing the center-based sampling in this way requires us to identify the center of the search space of the given problem and to develop a mechanism to guide the search toward this region. The survey of the related literature reveals two manners of exploiting the center-based sampling theory in population-based algorithms. In the first manner, the center-based sampling theory inspires the development of initialization mechanisms so as to start the search from the center region of the search space (Rahnamayan and Wang, 2009). More to this point, the center-based sampling theory is the inspiration source behind the development of initialization mechanisms for the Cooperative Co-evolutionary Algorithm (Mahdavi et al., 2016), differential evolution algorithm (Esmailzadeh and Rahnamayan, 2011), and PSO (Yahya et al., 2018). In the second manner, the concepts of the center-based sampling theory is utilized to guide the evolution of the population-based algorithms toward the center region of the search space. A prominent example is Center Particle Swarm Optimization algorithm (CPSO) (Liu et al., 2007), in which the center of the search space is estimated by the mean values of all particles positions in the current swarm. These values are then used as the position of an informed particle, called center particle. The center particle has no explicit velocity, and is set to the center of the swarm at every iteration, however, other aspects of the center particle are the same as that of the ordinary particle, such as fitness evaluation and competition for the best particle of the swarm. As the center particle generally gets good fitness value, it is often selected as the best particle of swarm, and consequently attracts other particles of the swarm toward the region where it is located. In the following sections, the idea of utilizing the center-based theory to improve the performance of PSO for data classification is described in more details.

4   CBS-PSO for Data Classification

CBS-PSO is a PSO variant developed specifically to tackle data classification tasks. It is inspired by center-based sampling theory, which emphasizes the usefulness of the center region of the search space for population-based algorithms, particularly when applied to high dimensional spaces (Rahnamayan and Wong, 2009; Esmailzadeh and Rahnamayan, 2011). According to this theory, as a point they move closer to the/center of the search space, its average distance to the optimal solution becomes lower, and for higher dimensions this distance decreases even sharply. In light of this, the CBS-PSO hypothesizes that attracting the search toward the center region of the search space provides a higher chance of convergence to the optimal solution. To realize this hypothesis, it is required to develop mechanisms to identify the center point of the search space and guide the search toward the center region of the search space. In doing so, the CBS-PSO uses Rocchio algorithm (Rocchio, 1971), an efficient information retrieval algorithm, as an estimation method of the center point of the search for the data classification problem. RA is used as a centroid-based classifier to generate for each class c a prototype vector, which is the average vector overall training set vectors that belong to the class c and uses it to classify a new data instance by calculating the similarity between the vector of the new data instance and each of prototype vectors and assigns it to the class with maximum similarity. The main advantage of the RA method is its simplicity and efficiency in terms of computation time, which is linear in the dataset size and the number of classes (Aggarwal and Zhai, 2012). Moreover, the CBS-PSO uses the generated RA estimation of the center point to generate informed particles and incorporate them in the swarm to attract the PSO evolution toward the center region of the search space. The rationale behind this lies in the searching behavior of the swarm, in which the velocities of particles are determined by their previous velocities, cognitive learning, and social learning. While the social learning drives all particles to be attracted by the global best particle and move toward it, the other two parts, previous velocities and cognitive learning, are corresponded to the autonomy property, which makes particles keep their own information. Therefore, during the search all particles move in the region where the global best is located, but their positions are usually different and approximately around the global best (Liu et al., 2007). Following this, the incorporation of the RA-based informed particle in the CBS-PSO swarm, considering that its high chance to be selected as the global best, it will definitely attracts all particles toward the center region of the search space where it is located, and ultimately enables the swarm to converge around this promising region.

Formally speaking, for a given class c whose data instances, represented as vector space models $<x_1, ..., x_j, ..., x_N>$, in the dataset is denoted D_c, the CBS-PSO first applies RA to estimate the center of the search space of the class c by computing the vector average or center of mass of its members in the data set as follows:

$$\vec{\mu}^c = \frac{1}{|D_c|} \sum_{x \in D_c} \vec{x}$$ (3)

Then the RA-based estimation of the center point is used to generate informed particles located at the center region of the search space as follows:

$$\vec{p}_i^c = \vec{\mu}^c + \vec{\alpha}_i$$ (4)

where $\vec{\mu}^c$ is a vector of mean values $<\mu_1, ..., \mu_j, ..., \mu_N>$, such that μ_j is the mean value of dimension j over all data instances x_j of in D_c and $\vec{\alpha}_i$ is a random vector $<\alpha_1, ..., \alpha_j, ..., \alpha_N>$, such that α_j is a small random value generated independently for dimension j in the interval $[-R, R]$, such that the dimension j of the generated particle $\vec{p}_i^c$ falls in the range $[\mu_j - R, \mu_j + R]$ centered at μ_j. After generation of the informed particles, they are incorporated in the swarm gradually, such that one informed particle replaced a randomly selected particle at every PSO iteration. During the PSO evolution, it is highly probable that the incorporated informed particle is selected as the global best particle, which attract other particles toward the center region of the search space.

As described in the CBS-PSO algorithm below, it starts with random initialization of the swarm and finding the RA estimation of the center of the search space, Equation 3, afterward the PSO iteratively generate an informed particle, Equation 4, and select a random position in the swarm where the generated particle is incorporated. Following that, the PSO evolution pursues as described in the standard PSO.

CBS-PSO Algorithm

begin
for each particle i
   randomly initialize particle's position p_i and velocity v_i
compute RA estimation of the center of the search space // Equation 3
  while (t < T_{max})
     generate an informed particle in the center region P_{cent} // Equation 4
     select a random particle P_{rand}
     replace P_{cent} with P_{rand} ;
     for each particle i
       determine particle fitness value f_i
       if f_{bi} is better than f_{bi} // f_{bi} is the fitness of the current local best position
          then $b_i = p_i$ // bi is current local best position
             $f_{bi} = f_i$
       if f_i is better than f_g // f_g is the fitness of the current global best position
          then $p_g = p_i$ // p_g is current global best position
             $f_g = f_i$
     end for
     for each particle i
       calculate particle velocity v_i // Equation 1
       update particle position p_i // Equation 2
     end for
  end while
end

---

5   CBS-PSO for Text Classification

In this section, a detailed description of how the proposed CBS-PSO is applied to a text classification task is presented, however prior to this, the text classification problem is briefly introduced. Text classification is the automated assignment of natural language texts to predefined categories based on their content (Sebastiani, 2002; Kowsari et al., 2019). It is a supporting technology in several information processing tasks, including controlled vocabulary indexing, routing and packaging of news and other text streams, content filtering, information security, help desk automation, and others. Research interest in text categorization has been growing in machine learning, information retrieval, computational linguistics, and other fields. Formally text classification is defined as follows. Given a set of documents $D = \{d_1, d_2, ..., d_n\}$ and a predefined set of classes $C = \{c_1, c_2, ..., c_m\}$, text classification is the task of assigning a Boolean value to each pair (d_i, c_j). A value of T assigned to (d_i, c_j) indicates a decision to classify d_i under c_j, while a value of F indicates a decision not to classify d_i under cj. More formally, the task is to approximate the unknown target function $\hat{\Phi} : D \times C \rightarrow \{T, F\}$ (that describes how documents ought to be classified) by means of a function $\Phi : D \times C \rightarrow \{T, F\}$, called the *classifier* (aka *rule*, or *hypothesis*, or *model*) such that $\hat{\Phi}$ and Φ coincide as much as possible (Sebastiani, 2002).

The methodology of applying CBS-PSO to a given text classification task begins with a preprocessing step, followed by classifiers induction, and finally classifiers evaluation.

5.1   Preprocessing

Since the textual data are not suitable for most classifier learning algorithms, a transformation of the documents dataset into a suitable representation (*e.g.*, vector space representation) must be carried out. Typically, this involves the following steps:

- *Tokenization (Term Extraction)*: reducing the document text to lower case characters and generating its terms set.
- *Unuseful Term Removal*: removing the stop words (Salton, 1989), Punctuation marks, Numbers, and less frequent terms.
- *Stemming*: reducing the inflected words to their roots or base forms using a porter stemmer (Porter, 1980).
- *Term Selection*: selecting the most representative terms from the original terms using Term Frequency (TF) metric (Xu and Chen, 2010).
- *Term Weighting*: assigning a non-binary weight in the form of term frequency inverse document frequency (*tfidf*) (Sebastiani, 2002). First, the *tfidf* of each term t_k in a document d_j is computed as follows:

$$tfidf\ (t_k, d_j) = tf(t_k, d_j) \times \log\left[\frac{N(Tr)}{N(d_{t_k}, Tr)}\right] \tag{5}$$

where $tf(t_k, d_j)$ denotes the number of times t_k appears in d_j, $N(Tr)$ represents the number of questions in the training set Tr, and $N(d_{t_k}, Tr)$ expresses the number of questions in Tr where the term, t_k, is encountered. Then term weight is then computed as follows

$$w(t_k, d_j) = \frac{tfidf\ (t_k, d_j)}{\sqrt{\sum_{k=1}^{T}\left(tfidf\ (t_k, d_j)\right)^2}} \tag{6}$$

where T is the number of unique terms in Tr.

- *Vector Space Representation:* each document d_j is represented as a vector of term weights $<w_{1j}, ..., w_{Tj}>$, where $0 \le w_{kj} \le 1$ represents the weight of term t_k in d_j.

After the preprocessing steps, the processed data is divided into training set which is used in classifiers induction stage and testing set which is used in classifiers evaluation.

5.2 Classifiers Induction

In this phase, *CBS-PSO* is applied to induce a classifier for each class from the training set. Given a training set of a given *class C* divided into instances labeled with that C (D_C) and instances labeled with non-C ($D_{\bar{C}}$) represented in N-dimensional vector space, the *CBS-PSO* searches for the optimal centroids of the C and $\bar{C}$ as described in Section 4. More specifically, it starts with a swarm of random particles, where each particle represents potential centroids of the C and $\bar{C}$, then iteratively generates RA-based informed particle, incorporates it in the swarm, and updates the velocity and position of all particles until the maximum number of iteration is reached. The ith particle in the swarm is encoded as a concatenation of four vectors as follows:

$$\{p_i^C, p_i^{\bar{C}}, v_i^C, v_i^{\bar{C}}\} \tag{7}$$

In this representation, $\vec{p}_i^C$ and $\vec{p}_i^{\bar{C}}$ of particle i represents the candidate centroid of the given C and $\bar{C}$ as follows:

$$\vec{p}_i^C = \{p_{i1}^C, ..., p_{iN}^C\} \tag{8}$$

$$\vec{p}_i^{\bar{C}} = \{p_{i1}^{\bar{C}}, ..., p_{iN}^{\bar{C}}\} \tag{9}$$

Similarly, $\vec{v}_i^C, \vec{v}_i^{\bar{C}}$ of particle i express the velocity components of the particle as follows:

$$\vec{v}_i^C = \{v_{i1}^C, ..., v_{iN}^C\} \tag{10}$$

$$\vec{v}_i^{\bar{C}} = \{v_{i1}^{\bar{C}}, ..., v_{iN}^{\bar{C}}\} \tag{11}$$

During the search, each particle i is evaluated in order to assess its suitability by a fitness function f computed over all training set instances, D_C and $D_{\bar{C}}$, as the sum of two components: the summation of the Euclidean distance between a data instance $\vec{x}_j$ and $\vec{p}_i^C$ divided by the number of data instances in D_C, and the summation of the Euclidean distance between $\vec{x}_j$ and $\vec{p}_i^{\bar{C}}$ divided by the number of data instances in $D_{\bar{C}}$ as follows:

$$f(i) = \frac{1}{D_C}\sum_{j=1}^{D_C} d(\vec{x}_j, \vec{p}_i^C) + \frac{1}{D_{\bar{C}}}\sum_{j=1}^{D_{\bar{C}}} d(\vec{x}_j, \vec{p}_i^{\bar{C}}) \qquad (12)$$

As such, the problem is transformed into a typical minimization problem to which *CBS-PSO* can be applied. At the end of this process, the best particles found is used as the centroid representing the C and $\bar{C}$ classes in the subsequent evaluation phase.

5.3   Classifiers Evaluation

The performance of the *CBS-PSO* classifiers depends essentially on computing a contingency table obtained from the classification of a sub-set of questions referred to as the testing set. For a given C classifier, the contingency table consists of the following

- True Positive (*TP*): number of questions a classifier correctly assigns to the given C.
- False Positive (*FP*): number of questions a classifier incorrectly assigns to a given C.
- False Negative (*FN*): number of questions belonging to a given C which the classifier incorrectly assigns to none-C.
- True Negative (*TN*): number of questions a classifier correctly assign to none-C.

The following are the common measures used to evaluate the performance of a given C classifier:

- Precision (*P*): probability that if a random question is classified under C, then this classification is correct, that is,

$$P = \frac{TP}{TP + FP} \qquad (13)$$

- Recall (*R*): probability that if a random question ought to be classified under a given C, then this classification is done, that is

$$R = \frac{TP}{TP + FN} \qquad (14)$$

Normally, the P and R measures are combined into a single F_β measure (harmonic mean), which is defined for $\beta = 1.0$, as follows:

$$F_{1.0} = \frac{2\ RP}{R + P} \qquad (15)$$

Using the above measures, the performance across a set of Cs classifiers can be measured by Macro-Average (unweighted mean of performance across all classes) and/or Micro-Average (performance computed from the sum of per-class contingency tables). In this work, the Macro-Average of F_1 is used.

6 Validation Experiments

In order to evaluate the performance of the proposed CBS-PSO on the text classification, the proposed *CBS-PSO* and the three ML approaches are experimented on three UCI datasets, which are characterized as high dimensional datasets. The selected ML approaches are k-Nearest Neighbor (kNN), Naïve Bayes (NB), Support Vector Machine (SVM), are amongst the most successful ML approaches used for text classification. Table 1 shows the specification of the three UCI datasets.

Table 1: Specifications of the three UCI datasets.

Dataset name	Language	No. of classes	No. of instances	No. of attributes
DBWorld e-mails	English	2	64	4702
Opinion Corpus for Lebanese Arabic Reviews (OCLAR)	Arabic	2	3916	7095
Benchmark dataset for Turkish text categorization	Turkish	6	3600	4814

The first dataset, DBWorld e-mails, have been collected manually and represented by a term-document matrix using bag of words. Every document (e-mail) in the dataset is represented as a vector containing n binary values (n is the size of the vocabulary from the entire corpus). In this representation, the binary value is 1 if the corresponding word belongs to the document, 0 otherwise. The dataset is processed by removing stop words which results in 4702 features. Moreover, each document in the dataset contains also a binary feature that indicates its class: 1 if the document is an announcement of conference, 0 otherwise (Filannio, 2011). The second dataset, Opinion Corpus for Lebanese Arabic Reviews (OCLAR), is collected using Google map and Zomato. The collected reviews are 3,916 reviews, 3,500 reviews from Google and 416 reviews from Zomato. The reviews are about public services, including hotels, restaurants, shops, and others, collected over a period from October 23rd , 2018 to November 22nd , 2018. Each document is processed and represented as TFIDF representation as described in (Al Omari et al., 2020). The third dataset, Benchmark dataset for Turkish text categorization, consists of a total of 3,600 documents including 600 news/texts from six categories in economy, culture-arts, health, politics, sports and technology, obtained from six well-known news portals and agencies (Hurriyet,

Posta, Iha, HaberTurk, Radikal and Zaman). The documents of the dataset were collected between May and July 2015 via Rich Site Summary (RSS) feeds from six categories of the respective portals. All java scripts, HTML tags ($<$ img $>$, $<$ a $>$, $<$ p $>$, $<$ strong$>$, etc.), operators, punctuations, non-printable characters and irrelevant data such as advertising are removed (Kilinic et al., 2015).

The parameters of the three ML approaches are set with the default values of Weka (Hall et al., 2009), while the *CBS-PSO* are set as described as follows. This section presents the results obtained from experiments conducted to evaluate the effectiveness of the *CBS-PSO* for text classification. The performance of *CBS-PSO* is compared with three machine learning approaches. The comparison between these approaches is based on the best macro-average of F_1 obtained using any number of terms. Moreover, in all experiments the dataset is divided into a training set and testing set, and the PSO variant is repetitively applied in 50 experimental cases, where each case uses different number of terms, k, to represent documents ($k = 10, 20,\ldots,500$). In addition, in all experiments, the PSO variant is applied with the parameters settings used in (Nouaouria et al., 2013; Nouaouria and Boukadoum, 2010). That's to say, the PSO parameters are set as follows: $T_{max} = 1000$, $v_{max} = 0.5$, $v_{min} = -0.5$, $c1 = 2.0$, $c2 = 2.0$, $v_{op} = -1$, $v_{su} = 1$, and $M = 80$ particles. Moreover, the value of the particular parameter of the proposed *CBS-PSO*, R, is set to 0.1. In these experiments, no attribute selection methods are used, which means all attributes are used in the representation of each instance.

The obtained results are summarized in Table 2 and Table 3 in terms of the best macro-average F_1 obtained for each experimental case. The comparison between the performance of the standard PSO and the CBS-PSO, as shown in Table 2, demonstrates evidently the superiority of the CBS-PSO over the standard PSO. This is as empirical evidence on the role of the center-based sampling theory for improving the performance of PSO when it is applied to high dimensional spaces. In such spaces, as the dimensionality rises linearly, the uniformity of the swarm

Table 2: *CBS-PSO* vs. *Standard PSO* performance (Macro-average F_1).

Dataset	Standard PSO	CBS-PSO
DBWorld e-mails	0.377	0.857
Arabic Reviews (OCLAR) Data Set	0.398	0.839
Benchmark dataset for Turkish text categorization	0.424	0.851

Table 3: *BS-PSO* vs. *ML Approaches* (Macro-average F_1).

Dataset	kNN	NB	SVM	CBS-PSO
DBWorld e-mails	0.533	0.833	0.840	0.857
Arabic Reviews (OCLAR) Data Set	0.777	0804	0.846	0.839
Benchmark dataset for Turkish text categorization	0.471	0.756	0.844	0.851

drops exponentially and as a result the particles' coverage and diversity becomes low, and ultimately the quality of the solution degrade dramatically. Therefore, guiding the search toward promising regions such as the center of the search spaces is a vital technique to avoid the adverse effect of curse of dimensionality.

On the other hands, the results of the three ML approaches and the CBS-PSO are shown in Table 3. Among ML approaches the ability of kNN is the lowest, NB is better than kNN, however the performance of SVM is the best. The comparison between *CBS-PSO* and the best ML performer, SVM, shows the competitive performance of the CBS-PSO.

In summary, the comparison between *CBS-PSO* and ML approaches provides empirical evidence on the effectiveness of the PSO variants for the classification of high-dimensional data when a proper estimation mechanism of the center region of the search space is used. As discussed in (Kazimipour and Qin, 2014), the low uniformity of the search space affects the performance of the PSO significantly, however with the help of center-based sampling theory, the PSO performance is competitive to the best ML approaches. It could be argued that the high learning time needed by the *CBS-PSO* makes it uncompetitive to the ML approaches, particularly SVM, however, bearing in mind the fact that the *CBS-PSO* still have much room for improvement through fin-tuning its control parameters and the triviality of the learning time factor for most of the real applications, it can be concluded that the *CBS-PSO* is still considered a promising approach for high dimensional data classification.

7   Conclusions

This paper proposes a center-based sampling theory method to improve the performance of PSO applied to text. This results in a new variant of PSO, dubbed CDS-PS, that applies the Rocchio Algorithm to estimate the center of the search space and then to generate informed particles, located at that region, which are incorporated gradually in the swarm to attract PSO evolution to direct the convergence at this promising region. The obtained results confirm the role of the center-based sampling theory for improving the performance of the PSO for the data classification, particularly in high dimensional domains. The results also confirms that a proper estimation mechanism of the center of the search space is crucial for effective classification of text classification. Furthermore, the comparison with three conventional ML approaches on the questions data set and three additional high dimensional datasets from UCI ML repository confirms that the CBS-PSO is very competitive classifier with much space for improvement, particularly for text classification and high dimensional data classification at large.

References

Abraham, A., C. Grosan and V. Ramos. Swarm intelligence in data mining. Studies in Computational Intelligence, 2006a.

Abraham, A., H. Guo and H. Liu. Swarm intelligence: Foundations, perspectives and applications. Swarm Intelligent Systems, Studies in Computational Intelligence, pp. 3–25, 2006b.

Aggarwal, C.C. and C. Zhai. A survey of text classification algorithms. Mining Text Data, pp. 163–222, 2012.

Al Omari, M., M. Al-Hajj, N. Hammami and A. Sabra. Sentiment classifier: Logistic regression for arabic services' reviews in lebanon. In 2019 International Conference on Computer and Information Sciences (ICCIS), Skaka, Alouf, Saudi Arabia, 2020.

del Valle, Y., G.K. Venayagamoorthy, S. Mohagheghi, J.C. Hernandez and R.G. Harley. Particle swarm optimization: Basic concepts, variants and applications in power systems. IEEE Transactions on Evolutionary Computation, 12(2): 171–195, 2008.

Engelbreht, A.P. Fundamentals of Computational Swarm Intelligence, John Wiley & Sons, 2006.

Esmailzadeh, A. and S. Rahnamayan. Enhanced differential evolution using center-based sampling. In IEEE Congress on Evolutionary Computation, 2011.

Falco, I.D., A. Della Cioppa and E. Tarantino. Evaluation of particle swarm optimization effectiveness in classification. Lecture Notes in Computer Science, 3849: 164–171, 2006.

Falco, I.D., A.D. Cioppa and E. Tarantino. Facing classification problems with particle swarm optimization. Applied Soft Computing, 7(3): 652–658, 2007.

Figueiredo, E., M. Macedo, H.V. Siqueira, C.J. Santana, A. Gokhale and C.J. Bastos-Filho. Swarm intelligence for clustering—A systematic review with new perspectives on data mining. Engineering Applications of Artificial Intelligence, 82: 313–329, 2019.

Filannino, M. DBWorld E-Mail Classification Using a Very Small Corpus. University of Manchester, 2011.

Hall, M., E. Frank, G. Holmes and B.R. Pfahringer. The WEKA data mining software: An update. ACM SIGKDD Explorations Newsletter, 19(2): 10–18, 2009.

Kazimipour, B. and A.K. Qin. Why advanced population initialization techniques perform poorly in high dimension? Simulated Evolution and Learning. SEAL 2014. Lecture Notes in Computer Science, Vol. 8886, 2014.

Kennedy, J. and R. Eberhart. Particle swarm optimization. In IEEE International Conference on Neural Networks, 1995.

Kılınc, D., A. Ozçift, F. Bozyigit and P. Ylldlrl. TTC-3600: A new benchmark dataset for Turkish text categorization. Journal of Information Science, pp. 174–185, 2015.

Kowsari, K., K.J. Meimandi, M. Heidarysafa, S. Mendu, L. Barnes and D. Brown. Text classification algorithms: A survey. Information, 10: 1–68, 2019.

Liu, Y., Z. Qin, Z.W. Shi and J. Lu. Center particle swarm optimization. Neurocomputing, 70(4-6): 672–679, 2007.

Mahdavi, S., S. Rahnamayan and K. Deb. Center-based initialization of cooperative co-evolutionary algorithm for large-scale optimization. In IEEE Congress on Evolutionary Computation (CEC), Vancouver, Canada, July 25–29, 2016.

Martens, D., B. Baesens and T. Fawcett. Editorial survey: Swarm intelligence for data mining. Machine Learning, 82(1): 1–42, 2011.

Nayar, N., S. Ahuja and S. Jain. Swarm intelligence for feature selection: A review of literature and reflection on future challenges. In Advances in Data and Information Sciences, Lecture Notes in Networks and Systems, vol. 39, Springer, 2019.

Nouaouria, N. and M. Boukadoum. A particle swarm optimization approach for substance identification. In GECCO'2009, 2009.

Nouaouria, N. and M. Boukadoum. Particle swarm classification for high dimensional data sets. In 22th International IEEE Conference on Tools with Artificial Intelligence, 2010.

Nouaouria, N., M. Boukadoum and R. Proulx. Particle swarm classification: a survey and positioning. Pattern Recogn., 46(7): 2028–2044, 2013.

Porter, M.F. An algorithm for suffix stripping. Program, 14(3): 130–137, 1980.

Chapter 4

Reinforcement Learning for Out-of-the-box Parameter Control for Evolutionary and Swarm-based Algorithm

Marcelo Gomes Pereira de Lacerda

1 Introduction

Despite the well succeeded applications of evolutionary (EA) and swarm-based algorithms (SI) in several areas (Aleti and Moser, 2016), it is well known that these algorithms are quite sensitive to their parameters (Eiben and Smit, 2011). The parameters of a metaheuristic can be classified either as numerical or categorical. Such groups are defined below:

- Numerical parameters: Parameters that assume only integer or real values.

- Categorical parameters: Parameters that assume categorical values, *i.e.*, unordered values taken from a finite set of discrete values. Usually these parameters determine the logic that will be used in the operators of the metaheuristic.

According to the No Free Lunch Theorem (NFL), there is no parameter adjustment for a certain algorithm that works optimally for every problem (Wolpert and Macready, 1997). Thus, different scenarios require different parameter settings.

Escola Politécnica de Pernambuco, Universidade de Pernambuco, Recife, Brazil.
Email: mgpl@ecomp.poli.br

However, manual parameter adjustment for EA and SI algorithms can be very hard to develop and costly, which means that the automation of this task has been one of the greatest and most important challenges in the field (Eiben et al., 1999).

The automatic adjustment methods can be divided into two groups (Karafotias et al., 2015b):

- Tuning algorithms: The parameters are adjusted before the optimization problem is solved, usually via previous runs on a set of training problems. The chosen values are kept constant during the entire execution of the optimization process.

- Control algorithms: The parameters are adjusted on-the-fly, *i.e.*, while the target problem is solved. The parameter controller, therefore, tries to maximize the performance of the optimization algorithm by making the best choice for each moment of the optimization process.

From now on, whenever the word "parameter" is used in this chapter, the class of numerical parameters is referred. The adjustment of categorical parameters is often called *Adaptive Operator Selection*, and the algorithms that present such a feature are usually classified as *hyperheuristics* (Consoli et al., 2016; DaCosta et al., 2008; Consoli et al., 2014; Drake et al., 2020). Therefore, there is a well-established field already existent that is out of the scope of this chapter.

Control methods can be divided into two groups (Karafotias et al., 2015b):

- Methods tailored to a specific application: In this group, the techniques are conceived to work with specific scenarios.

- Out-of-the-box control methods: These methods are general enough to be used in multiple scenarios.

According to the literature on the field, the vast majority of the studies published so far on parameter control for EA and SI algorithms propose using the methods tailored to specific scenarios. Therefore, only a few studies on out-of-the-box methods can be found. Surveys on the topic of parameter adjustment have been published by Eiben et al., in 1999 (Eiben et al., 1999), Zhang et al., in 2012 (Zhang et al., 2012), Karafotias et al., in 2015 (Karafotias et al., 2015b), Aleti et al., in 2016 (Aleti and Moser, 2016), Guan et al., in 2017 (Guan et al., 2017) and Parpinelli et al., in 2019 (Parpinelli et al., 2019).

In 2021, a systematic literature review on out-of-the-box parameter control for EA and SI algorithms was published (de Lacerda et al., 2021). In this study, it was found that Reinforcement Learning-based algorithms (RL) were used to create out-of-the-box parameter control techniques in most of the studies (Eiben et al., 2007; Karafotias et al., 2012, 2014a,b, 2015a; Rost et al., 2016).

RL algorithms are machine learning techniques where an agent interacts with its surrounding environment by taking actions and receiving rewards, improving its performance by trial and error (Sutton and Barto, 2018). They are useful in sequential decision problems, especially when the training data is not independent and identically distributed (i.i.d.). This is the case of parameter control for EA and

SI algorithms, since a decision context at a given time t can be highly correlated with a scenario at $t + 1$, which explains the success of RL-based methods in such problems. Therefore, this chapter is intended to present and discuss the RL-based approaches proposed so far in the literature for out-of-the-box parameter control for EA and SI algorithms.

2 A Brief Introduction to Reinforcement Learning

This section introduces the concepts of Reinforcement Learning necessary to understand the studies discussed in this chapter.

Reinforcement Learning (RL) is a machine learning paradigm where an agent interacts with its surrounding environment by taking actions and receiving rewards, improving its performance regarding the solution of a certain problem by trial-and-error. This chapter provides the basics of RL and discusses how algorithms of this kind can be applied to address the parameter control problem for EA and SI algorithms.

In RL methods, an agent makes a sequence of decisions according to what is perceived from an *environment*. Such decisions are *actions* taken by the agent in the environment according to its current observed *state*. When an action is taken, the environment modifies its state and returns a *reward* to the agent, which represents the quality of the action that has been just taken. A positive reward reinforces the taken action for the observed state when the given action was taken (Sutton and Barto, 2018). This reward is generated by a function that must "guide" the agent towards its goal, which is to solve a certain problem represented by the agent's surrounding environment. The set of "rules" that defines the action to be taken for each state of the environment is called *policy*.

As already mentioned, in an RL problem the learning agent interacts with the environment over and over through a trial-and-error process. In this iterative process, it is expected that the agent learns optimum actions for different scenarios (*i.e.*, states of the environment). Figure 1 shows this mechanism, where the agent takes and action A_t at time t, and the environment "reacts" to the action, returning a new state S_{t+1} alongside a reward R_{t+1}. The sequence of states, actions, and rewards $S_0, A_0, R_1, S_1, A_1, R_2, S_2, A_2, R_3...$ is called *trajectory* (Sutton and Barto, 2018).

An RL problem can be formulated as a Markov Decision Problem (MDP), which is a classical formulation of sequential decision making processes. Equation 1 shows the probability of reaching a state s' at time t and receive a reward r after taking an action a at time t, when the environment was in a previous state S_{t-1} at time $t - 1$. In such a formulation, R_t and S_t depends only on the preceding state and action. Such a definition defines the dynamics of the MDP (Sutton and Barto, 2018).

$$p(s', r|s, a) = P_r\{S_t = s', R_t = r|S_{t-1} = s, A_{t-1} = a\}. \tag{1}$$

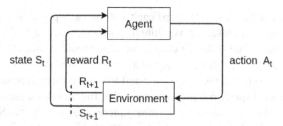

Figure 1: The agent-environment interaction in a Markov decision process (based on (Sutton and Barto, 2018)).

The objective of an RL agent is to maximize the cumulative reward received along the trajectory. Thus, the reward can be thought of as a scalar signal of which accumulation over time must be maximized. The accumulated reward is also known as *expected return* (Puterman, 1990).

A full trajectory from an initial state to a terminal state is called *episode*. A terminal state is a state in which the agent stops learning when it is reached. Learning tasks with terminal states are called *episodic tasks*, of which the expected return can be calculated according to Equation 2. However, in many situations (especially in robotics), there is no such a state, which means that the agent must learn indefinitely. These tasks are called *continuing tasks*. In both cases, the agent tries to maximize G_t for each time t (Puterman, 1990; Sutton and Barto, 2018).

$$G_t = R_{t+1} + R_{t+2} + R_{t+3} + ... + R_T. \tag{2}$$

In continuing tasks, the expected return is usually infinite. In order to overcome this issue, the agent must consider a decreasing discounting factor for each of the future reward, as described in Equation 3. In this equation, $\gamma \in [0, 1]$ and is called *discounting factor* (Kaelbling et al., 1996; Sutton and Barto, 2018), which reduces the influence of future rewards. The further the reward into the future, the greater the discounting factor. It is important to note that the closer to zero, the more myopic the agent. On the other hand, the closer to one, more importance is given to distant rewards. G_t can also be calculated recursively, as defined in Equation 4.

$$G_t = R_{t+1} + \gamma R_{t+2} + \gamma^2 R_{t+3} + ... = \sum_{k=0}^{\infty} \gamma^k R_{t+k+1}. \tag{3}$$

$$G_t = R_{t+1} + \gamma G_{t+1}. \tag{4}$$

In order to unify the representation of both episodic and continuing tasks, instead of using terminal states, *absorbing states* can be added to the MDP. Absorbing states are states from which transitions take the execution flow back to themselves and the corresponding rewards are zero (Alagoz et al., 2010). Then, the expected return can be defined according to Equation 5, where T can be infinite or not (Sutton and Barto, 2018).

$$G_t = \sum_{k=t+1}^{T} \gamma^{k-t-1} R_k. \tag{5}$$

The probability function that maps each state to each possible action is called *policy*, which can be represented as a function $\pi(a|s)$, where a is the taken action and s is the current state of the environment (Sutton and Barto, 2018). Given an agent with a policy π, the value function of a state s calculates the expected return if the agent starts working in the given state and follows π thereafter, until it reaches an absorbing state. Equation 6 provides the value function for a state s if a policy π is followed, which is called *state-value function for policy π*. Similarly, the *action-value function for policy π*, which is provided in Equation 7, computes the expected return (*i.e.*, quality) of an action a taken in state s. As already mentioned, the value functions v_π and q_π can be learned from experience, when true rewards are received for each state and action taken (Lapan, 2018).

$$v_\pi(s) = \mathbb{E}_\pi[G_t|S_t = s] = \mathbb{E}_\pi\left[\sum_{k=0}^{\infty} \gamma^k R_{t+k+1}|S_t = s\right], \forall s \in S. \tag{6}$$

$$q_\pi(s,a) = \mathbb{E}_\pi[G_t|S_t = s, A_t = a] = \mathbb{E}_\pi\left[\sum_{k=0}^{\infty} \gamma^k R_{t+k+1}|S_t = s, A_t = a\right]. \tag{7}$$

Equation 8 shows the relation between the value function of a state s and the state values of its successor states. This relation is called *Bellman equation*. It computes recursively the expected return by considering all possibilities of states, actions, and rewards from the current state until it reaches an absorbing one. In other words, for each combination of a, s' and r, its probability is calculated as $\pi(a|s)p(s',r|s,a)$. Then, the expected return is calculated by summing over the rewards of all visited states multiplied by their probabilities (Ma and Stachurski, 2019). The *advantage* of an action a given a certain state s can be calculate as the difference between the value of a and the value of the state s, which is the expectation over the qualities of all possible actions, as defined in Equation 9. It means that the advantage value of an action measures how much better this action is to the other possible actions when the environment is in a given state.

$$\begin{aligned}
v_\pi(s) &= \mathbb{E}_\pi[G_t|S_t = s] \\
&= \mathbb{E}_\pi[R_{t+1} + \gamma G_{t+1}|S_t = s] \\
&= \sum_a \pi(a|s) \sum_{s'} \sum_r p(s',r|s,a)\left[r + \gamma \mathbb{E}_\pi[G_{t+1}|S_{t+1} = s']\right] \\
&= \sum_a \pi(a|s) \sum_{s',r} p(s',r|s,a)\left[r + \gamma v_\pi(s')\right], \forall s \in S.
\end{aligned} \tag{8}$$

$$A_\pi(s,a) = q_\pi(s,a) - v_\pi(s). \tag{9}$$

Given the definitions presented so far, the goal of an RL agent can be redefined as the search for a policy that maximizes the expected return for each visited state in its trajectory. A policy π is better or equal than a policy π' if and only if $v_\pi(s) \geq v_{\pi'}(s), \forall s \in S$. There is always a policy that is better than or equal to all other policies. Such a policy is called *optimal policy* and can be denoted as π_*. Optimal policies make optimal decisions, which means that they are taken through an optimal state-action value function (Lapan, 2018). Equation 10 shows the definition of the optimal state-action value function, where $v_*(S_{t+1})$ is the optimal state value function, as defined in Equation 11.

$$q_{\pi_*}(s, a) = \mathbb{E}[R_{t+1} + \gamma v_*(S_{t+1})|S_t = s, A_t = a]. \tag{10}$$

$$v_{\pi_*}(S_{t+1}) = \max_{\pi} v_\pi(s). \tag{11}$$

Since v_* is the value function of a policy, it must satisfy the self-consistency posed by the Bellman equation. Equation 12 shows the Bellman equation for v_*, also known as *Bellman Optimality equation*, where $A(s)$ is the set of available actions for the state s. Such an equation is built upon the idea that optimal actions are always taken with optimal policies, as previously mentioned (Bellman, 1957; Lapan, 2018).

$$
\begin{aligned}
v_*(s) &= \max_{a \in A(s)} q_{\pi_*}(s, a) \\
&= \max_{a} \mathbb{E}_{\pi_*}[G_t|S_t = s, A_t = a] \\
&= \max_{a} \mathbb{E}_{\pi_*}[R_{t+1} + \gamma G_{t+1}|S_t = s, A_t = a] \\
&= \max_{a} \mathbb{E}[R_{t+1} + \gamma v_{\pi_*}(S_{t+1})|S_t = s, A_t = a] \\
&= \max_{a} \sum_{s',r} p(s', r|s, a)[r + \gamma v_{\pi_*}(s')].
\end{aligned}
\tag{12}
$$

The Bellman optimality equation can be used to compute the state-action value function for the optimal policy, as defined in Equation 13.

$$q_{\pi_*}(s, a) = \sum_{s',r} p(s', r|s, a) \left[r + \gamma \max_{a'} q_{\pi_*}(s', a') \right]. \tag{13}$$

The Bellman optimality equation has an exact solution. However, it can only be found under three conditions: the dynamics of the environment is accurately known; there is enough computational resource to compute the exact solution in a reasonable time; the RL problem presents the Markov property. *Dynamic Programming* (DP) is a set of widely known iterative algorithms that guarantee optimal policies in MDPs where their dynamics are perfectly known. They are quite efficient under such conditions when compared to other methods such as linear programming or direct search. Two of the most common DP approaches are Policy Iteration and Value Iteration (Bertsekas, 2000; Lapan, 2018).

In the Policy Iteration method, two iterative processes are interchangeably executed: policy evaluation and policy improvement. The output of the policy evaluation affects the policy improvement and vice-versa. Such a "cooperation" happens until the the optimal policy is reached (Lapan, 2018). The policy evaluation and the policy improvement processes are shown in Equations 14 and 15, respectively, which are computed for each state $s \in S$.

$$v_{k+1}(s) = \sum_{s',r} p(s', r|s, \pi_k(s))[r + \gamma v_k(s')]. \tag{14}$$

$$\pi_{k+1}(s) = \arg\max_a \sum_{s',r} p(s', r|s, \pi_k(s))[r + \gamma v_{k+1}(s')]. \tag{15}$$

It is important to mention that each of these iterative processes are executed until they converge to the optimal policy or other stopping criteria is met. However, defining effective and efficient criteria can be hard. Therefore, the Value Iteration method can be used to overcome such an issue, where a single iteration is performed for both iterative processes. Thus, it can be written as a single iterative process that combines the policy improvement and the policy evaluation steps, as shown in Equation 16.

$$v_{k+1}(s) = \max_a \sum_{s',r} p(s', r|s, \pi_k(s))[r + \gamma v_k(s')]. \tag{16}$$

Although these techniques guarantee the return of the optimal policy, a perfect model of the environment's dynamics is almost unlikely to be obtained in real world possibilities. Therefore, methods that do not guarantee such an optimal solution, but are still capable of finding very good policies are mandatory for such cases. The following subsections present some of the most common algorithms of this group.

2.1   Temporal-Difference Learning

Monte Carlo methods are RL methods that do not rely on the complete knowledge of the environment. Instead, they learn the value functions from a set of *experiences*, *i.e.*, sequence of states, actions, and rewards sampled from the interactions between the agent and the environment. However, in such methods, the approximated value functions are updated only after a full episode is executed. Waiting until the end of an episode may cause the assignment of the contributions of each taken action to be inaccurate. Like DP, Temporal-Difference (TD) methods wait only until the next step, with the advantage that, like Monte Carlo methods, there is no need for the perfect model of the environment's dynamics (Sutton and Barto, 2018).

Sarsa is a TD method that updates a state-action value *Q-function* as described in Equation 17. For each step t of an episode, an action a_t is chosen according to the current state s_t following a given policy. For example, an ϵ-greedy policy chooses the action with the highest state-action value with a probability ϵ. Then, r_{t+1} and s_{t+1} are received from the environment. Finally, a subsequent action a_{t+1} is chosen according to s_{t+1} and $Q_{t+1}(s_t, a_t)$ is computed (Sutton and Barto, 2018).

$$Q_{t+1}(s_t, a_t) = Q_t(a_t, s_t) + \alpha\left[r_{t+1} + \gamma Q(s_{t+1}, a_{t+1}) - Q_t(s_t, a_t)\right]. \tag{17}$$

One of the most important TD methods proposed in the early years of the RL field is known as *Q-learning*. Instead of using the same policy to choose both the action a_t and the subsequent action a_{t+1}, it chooses the action that maximizes the function Q. The update of such a function is provided in Equation 18 (Sutton and Barto, 2018).

$$Q_{t+1}(s_t, a_t) = Q_t(a_t, s_t) + \alpha \left[r_{t+1} + \gamma \max_a Q_t(s_{t+1}, a) - Q_t(s_t, a_t) \right]. \quad (18)$$

In Equation 18, which is called Q-function, the choice of a that maximizes $Q(s_{t+1}, a)$ is made using the same Q-function that is used to evaluate the chosen action. Thus, decisions are made based on an approximate function, which has an estimation error. In other words, if a wrong decision is made using the Q-function, it might be reinforced by the same Q-function. This issue causes the algorithm to exploit bad decisions and, therefore, suboptimal policies, which slows down the convergence to the optimal Q* (Lapan, 2018).

Double Q-Learning is an algorithm that address the aforementioned issue by learning two different Q-functions (*i.e.*, state-action value functions): Q_1 that guides the choice of actions, and Q_2 that evaluates the chosen actions, or vice-versa (van Hasselt et al., 2015). In this approach, for each step t of an episode, an action a_t is chosen using the policy $\epsilon - greedy$ with Q_1, Q_2, or the combination of both functions. After taking the action a_t, the agent receives r_{t+1} and s_{t+1} from the environment. Then, with a probability of 50%, Equation 19 is used to update the Q_1. Otherwise, Equation 20 is used to update Q_2.

$$Q_{1,t+1}(s_t, a_t) = Q_{1,t}(s_t, a_t) + \alpha \left[r_{t+1} + \gamma Q_{2,t}(s_{t+1}, \arg\max_a Q_{1,t}(s_{t+1}, a)) - Q_{1,t}(s_t, a_t) \right]. \quad (19)$$

$$Q_{2,t+1}(s_t, a_t) = Q_{2,t}(s_t, a_t) + \alpha \left[r_{t+1} + \gamma Q_{1,t}(s_{t+1}, \arg\max_a Q_{2,t}(s_{t+1}, a)) - Q_{2,t}(s_t, a_t) \right]. \quad (20)$$

In the Q-Learning-based methods presented above, it is important for the algorithm to visit the majority of all possible combinations between states and actions, so that the Q-function can be accurately approximated. In the real world this is usually impractical, since the set of possible states, and sometimes the set of actions, are usually large. In order to give the Q-Learning the capability of accurately estimating the state-action values for unseen combinations of states and actions, ML algorithms have been used to approximate the Q-functions. In 2013, Mnih et al., proposed an algorithm that uses deep neural networks to approximate the Q-function in Q-Learning, called *Deep Q-Netowrk* (DQN) (Mnih et al., 2013). In this technique, a neural network, called *Q-network*, receives the state of the environment encoded as an input vector of observed variables and outputs the state-action values of the possible actions. For each learning epoch, the Q-network is trained through gradient descent with a batch of experiences, *i.e.*, triplets of observed states, their taken actions, and the target Q values computed as $r_{t+1} + \gamma \max_a Q_t(s_{t+1}, a)$. In order to avoid the previously mentioned bias overestimation effect, in 2015, Mnih et al., proposed the *Double DQN* algorithm, a version of the DQN algorithm with two Q-networks. Like in Double Q-Learning, one of the networks is used to choose actions, while the other one evaluates the chosen actions (Mnih et al., 2015).

From Equation 9, it can be seen that the value of an action a in a state s, *i.e.*, $Q(s, a)$, can be decomposed into the sum of the value of the state s, *i.e.*, $V(s)$, and the advantage of a in s, *i.e.*, $A(s, a)$. In 2016, Wang et al., proposed that both the values of a state s, $V(S)$, and the advantage of all possible actions for the state s, $A(s, a), \forall a \in A$, where A is the set of all possible actions, can be learned separately, *i.e.*, learned in different streams of neurons. Then, the outputs of these streams can be combined in order to calculate the state-action values of all actions in s, $Q(s, a), \forall a \in A$. This architecture is called Dueling DQN (Wang et al., 2016).

Figure 2 illustrates the architecture of the Dueling DQN algorithm. It can be seen that the observables that represent the state s are connected to the scalar $V(s)$ and to the layer $A(s, a)$, which represents the vector of advantages of all actions $a \in A$ in state s, through two separate streams of neurons. Then, $V(s)$ and $A(s, a)$ are combined to calculate $Q(s, a), \forall a \in A$ according to Equation 21, which represents the Q-function for the action a in state s at time t with the parameters θ, α, β. In this equation, α and β are the parameters of the neuron streams that compute $V(s)$ and $A(s, a)$, respectively. It is important to notice that any neural network-based architecture can be appended to the input layer to serve as a preprocessing layer to the raw observed data. In Equation 21, θ is the parameter vector of such a preprocessing layer, and is surely optional (Wang et al., 2016).

$$Q_{\theta,\alpha,\beta}(s_t, a_t) = V_{\theta,\beta}(s_t) + \left(A_{\theta,\alpha}(s_t, a_t) - \frac{1}{|A|} \sum_{a_{t+1}} A_{\theta,\alpha}(s_t, a_{t+1}) \right). \quad (21)$$

In this work, the authors highlighted that this idea can be applied to any variation of DQN, such as Double DQN. The results showed significant improvements to different DQN architectures (Wang et al., 2016).

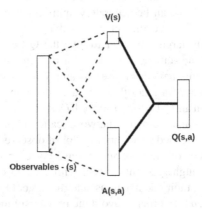

Figure 2: Architecture of the Dueling DQN algorithm (Wang et al., 2016).

2.2 Policy Gradient Methods

Q-Learning-based methods indirectly learn optimal policies by maximizing their state-action value functions, and not by directly evolving the policy itself. *Policy Gradient Methods*, on the other hand, directly learn the optimal policy by dynamically adjusting the parameters of the evolving policy (Lapan, 2018). In such methods, $\pi(a|s, \boldsymbol{\theta}) = Pr\{A_t = a|S_t = s, \boldsymbol{\theta}_t = \boldsymbol{\theta}\}$ is the probability of taking an action a in a state s when the policy's parameter vector is $\boldsymbol{\theta} \in \mathbb{R}^{d'}$, where d' is the number of policy's parameters. These algorithms learn $\boldsymbol{\theta}$ through gradient ascent on the gradient of some scalar performance measure $J(\boldsymbol{\theta})$ (see Equation 22), thus maximizing the agent's performance (Sutton et al., 1999).

$$\boldsymbol{\theta}_{t+1} = \boldsymbol{\theta}_t + \alpha \nabla_\theta J(\boldsymbol{\theta}_t). \tag{22}$$

In order to ensure the exploration in the optimal policy search, the policy is usually required to be stochastic, which are policies that choose actions probabilistically. It means that $\pi(a|s, \boldsymbol{\theta}) \in]0, 1[$ for all a, s and $\boldsymbol{\theta}$. If the action space is discrete, the most common function used to define the probabilities of each action in the action space is the exponential softmax distribution over all possible actions. Such a function is shown in Equation 23, where $h(s, a, \boldsymbol{\theta}) \in \mathbb{R}$ is a parameterized numerical preference. These action preferences can be parameterized by a deep artificial neural network (ANN), where $\boldsymbol{\theta}$ is the weight vector of all connection between neurons. This parameterization is called *softmax in action preferences* (Lapan, 2018). It is important to mention that deterministic policies are special cases of stochastic policies, where, for each state, there is one action with 100% of probability of being chosen.

$$\pi(a|s, \boldsymbol{\theta}) = \frac{e^{h(s, a, \boldsymbol{\theta})}}{\sum_b e^{h(s, b, \boldsymbol{\theta})}}. \tag{23}$$

As shown in Equation 22, in order to maximize the agent's performance by adjusting θ, it is necessary to calculate the gradient $\nabla_\theta J(\boldsymbol{\theta})$. Let τ be a trajectory $s_0, a_0, r_1, s_1, a_1, r_2, s_2, a_2, r_3$.... In a stochastic policy π_θ, the probability of an agent taking the trajectory τ can be calculated as provided in Equation 24. The log-probability of $p(\tau|\pi_\theta)$ is defined as shown in Equation 25, and therefore its gradient in θ can be calculated according to Equation 26. However, the probabilities related to the environment, *i.e.*, $p(s_{t+1}|s_t, a_t)$ and $p(s_0)$, do not change when θ changes. Therefore, their gradients and, therefore, the gradients of their logarithms, are zero, which means that the gradient of the log-probability of a trajectory τ can be reduced to Equation 27 (Sutton et al., 1999).

$$p(\tau|\pi_\theta) = p(s_0) \prod_{t=0}^{T} p(s_{t+1}|s_t, a_t) \pi_\theta(a_t|s_t), \tag{24}$$

$$\log p(\tau|\pi_\theta) = \log p(s_0) + \sum_{t=0}^{T} \left(\log p(s_{t+1}|s_t, a_t) + \log \pi_\theta(a_t|s_t) \right), \tag{25}$$

$$\nabla_\theta \log p(\tau|\pi_\theta) = \nabla_\theta \log p(s_0) + \sum_{t=0}^{T} \left(\nabla_\theta \log p(s_{t+1}|s_t, a_t) + \nabla_\theta \log \pi_\theta(a_t|s_t) \right),$$

$$(26)$$

$$\nabla_\theta \log p(\tau|\pi_\theta) = \sum_{t=0}^{T} \nabla_\theta \log \pi_\theta(a_t|s_t). \tag{27}$$

$J(\theta_t)$ can be defined as the expected performance of π_θ, i.e., $E_{\tau \sim \pi_\theta}[\phi(\tau)]$, where $\phi(\tau)$ is the performance of the π_θ if the trajectory τ is taken. If we define the performance of a policy π_θ in a single step t as the advantage $A(s_t, a_t)$, defined in Equation 9, of the action a_t taken in the state s_t, its expected performance related to all possible trajectories can be calculated as defined in Equation 28. Since the expected value of a random variable can be calculated as its mean, the expected performance of a policy π_θ can be calculated as the average performance in several trajectories, i.e., in a batch of episodes D previously collected with an agent following π_θ, as defined in Equation 29. Therefore, following the same rationale as in the derivation of Equation 27, the gradient of the logarithm of the expected performance of π_θ can be calculated as provided in Equation 30, and it can be used as the gradient in the gradient ascent algorithm defined in Equation 22 (Sutton et al., 1999).

$$\mathop{E}_{\tau \sim \pi_\theta} [\phi(\tau)] = \mathop{E}_{\tau \sim \pi_\theta} \left[\sum_{t=0}^{T} \pi_\theta(a_t|s_t) A(s_t, a_t) \right], \tag{28}$$

$$\mathop{E}_{\tau \sim \pi_\theta} [\phi(\tau)] = \frac{1}{|D|} \sum_{\tau \sim D} \sum_{t=0}^{T} \pi_\theta(a_t|s_t) A(s_t, a_t). \tag{29}$$

$$\nabla_\theta J(\theta_t) = \frac{1}{|D|} \sum_{\tau \sim D} \sum_{t=0}^{T} \nabla_\theta \log \pi_\theta(a_t|s_t) A(s_t, a_t). \tag{30}$$

In current Vanilla Policy Gradient (VPG) implementations, just like DQN, the policy π_θ has been represented with a neural network that receives the observables from the environment as input, and outputs the distribution of probabilities for the possible actions. In this neural network, the weights are the parameters θ of the policy π, and must be adjusted through gradient ascent or any other modern gradient ascent-like algorithm, where the gradient is computed according to Equation 30. It is important to notice that the calculation of the advantage $A(s_t, a_t)$ needs to compute the estimated value $V(s_t)$ of the state s_t. In VPG, this function is also parameterized with parameters ϕ, and in modern implementations a second neural network is used, where the inputs are the observables and the output is the estimated value of the state inferred from these observables. This neural network is trained usually by fitting its parameters by regression using the mean-squared error defined in Equation 31 as loss function and some gradient descent-like algorithm (Duan et al., 2016). Algorithm 1 provides the pseudocode for VPG.

$$\phi_{k+1} = \arg\min_\phi \frac{1}{|D_k|T} \sum_{\tau \in D_k} \sum_{t=0}^{T} \left(V_\phi(s_t) - \sum_{t'=t}^{T} r_t \right). \tag{31}$$

Algorithm 1 Pseudocode of the Vanilla Policy Gradient algorithm.

Initialize θ and ϕ with $\theta_{\nvdash}$ and $\phi_{\nvdash}$, respectively.
$k \leftarrow 0$;
while stopping condition is not met **do**
    Collect a batch of trajectories D_k using the policy π_{θ_k};
    Compute advantages of all actions taken for all trajectories in D_k using ϕ_k to estimate state values;
    Calculate policy gradient using Equation 27;
    Update policy π_{θ_k} with Equation 22 or using any other gradient ascent-like algorithm;
    Update parameters ϕ through Equation 31 and some gradient descent-like algorithm;
    $k \leftarrow k + 1$;
end while

One of the most widely known modern policy gradient algorithm in the literature is the Proximal Policy Optimization (PPO), proposed by Schulman et al., in 2017 (Schulman et al., 2017). The motivation of the authors of this work was to insert a regularization mechanism in VPG, which prevents new policies to be created too far from the previous one. It follows the same sequence of steps of VPG, but uses a different equation to calculate the loss to update the policy parameters θ. Equation 32 shows the function used in PPO for such an update, where ϵ is a hyperparameter the limits the distance between the new and the old policies, and $g(\epsilon, A(s_t, a_t))$ returns $(1 + \epsilon)A(s_t, a_t)$ if $A(s_t, a_t) \geq 0$, and $(1 - \epsilon)A(s_t, a_t)$ otherwise.

$$\theta_{k+1} = \arg\max_{\theta} \frac{1}{|D_k|T} \sum_{\tau \in D_k} \sum_{t=0}^{T} \min\left(\frac{\pi_{\theta_{k-1}}(a_t|s_t)}{\pi_{\theta_k}(a_t|s_t)} A(s_t, a_t), g(\epsilon, A(s_t, a_t)) \right).$$

$$(32)$$

3 Applying Reinforcement Learning to Out-of-the-box Parameter Control for EA and SI Algorithms

As previously mentioned, RL has been used to control parameters of EA and SI algorithms. In such approaches, the environment represents the optimization algorithm solving an optimization problem, while the agent dynamically sets the parameters of the algorithm through actions. For each taken action, *i.e.*, parameter setting defined by the agent, the underlying optimization algorithm runs for a certain number of iterations and returns a reward based on how well its solution has been improved on the optimization problem during this execution. The parameter control policy for EA and SI algorithms must be learned through a training process. This policy is usually trained with a set of trained optimization problems solved by a certain metaheuristic. It is important to note that, since each EA or SI algorithm has specific parameters, a policy must be trained for a single algorithm. Therefore if a policy was trained with a set of training problems for a given metaheuristic A, it cannot be used with a given metaheuristic B. Therefore, after a policy is trained, it can be used only with the same metaheuristic it was trained for solving a certain target problem, which is different from the problems in the training set. Figure 3 shows the basic general of RL-based parameter controllers for EA and SI algorithms as proposed in (Eiben et al., 2007).

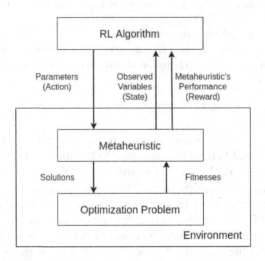

Figure 3: General scheme of RL-based parameter controllers for EA and SI algorithms.

According to (de Lacerda et al., 2021), the majority of the out-of-the-box approaches proposed for parameter control for EA and SI algorithms use RL techniques to create control policies. From the 16 studies that have proposed out-of-the-box parameter control techniques for EA and SI algorithms since 2007, 7 have used RL, of which 5 used Temporal-Difference-based algorithms.

3.1 Temporal-Difference on Out-of-the-box Parameter Control for EA and SI Algorithms

The first RL-based out-of-the-box control method for EA and SI algorithms was proposed in 2007 by Eiben et al. (Eiben et al., 2007), despite other studies on RL applied to non-out-of-the-box parameter control have been published before, *e.g.* (Muller et al., 2002). In their approach, the RL layer is composed by three components: a State-Action Evaluator, an Action Optimizer, and a General Manager. The State-Action Evaluator is intended to learn the quality of each action for each state, *i.e.*, the *state-action value function*, while the Action Optimizer chooses the action that maximizes the future cumulative reward among all possible actions for the current state. This choice is made through the execution of a Genetic Algorithm (GA) (Goldberg, 1989). Finally, the General Manager is responsible for managing the interface between the environment and the RL layer. The State-Action Evaluator is learned through a REPTree regression algorithm (Witten et al., 2011).

Algorithm 2 provides the pseudocode of the proposed approach, which is a combination of Sarsa and Q-Learning (Sutton and Barto, 2018). In this algorithm, a^*_{t+1} can be an action chosen with a GA that approximately maximizes Q, which represents the current policy, or a random action close to the optimal found by the GA. The algorithm randomly switches between these modes with a predefined frequency.

Algorithm 2 Pseudocode of the algorithm proposed by Eiben et al. (2011).

Initialize State-Action value function of the State-Action Evaluator;
Initialize an *experience batch.*
Define ϵ as the probability of choosing a random action;
$episode \leftarrow 0$;
while $episode <$ maximum number of episodes **do**
    Get the first state s_0 of the environment;
    With probability ϵ, choose a random action a_0. Otherwise, choose a_0 that approximately maximizes $Q(s_0, a_0)$ through a GA.
    $t \leftarrow 0$;
    while $t <$ maximum number of steps **do**
        Do the chosen action a_t and get the associated reward r_t and new state s_{t+1};
        Add the tuple $< s, a, r + \gamma Q(s_{t+1}, a^*_{t+1}) - Q(s_t, a_t)$ to the experience batch;
        if Batch size reaches a predefined size **then**
            Update the State-Action value function;
        end if
        $t \leftarrow t + 1$;
    end while
    $episode \leftarrow episode + 1$
end while

The following variables were used to describe the state of the environment (*i.e.,* metaheuristic solving an optimization problem): Best fitness among the solutions of the optimization algorithm, mean fitness, standard deviation over the fitnesses, breeding success number, average distance to the best individual, number of objective function calls made so far, fitness growth, and the vector of the previous action. The reward was defined as the improvement of the best fitness. In this work, the crossover rate, mutation rate, tournament size, and population size of a Genetic Algorithm with binary encoding were controlled. It is important to mention that the policy for parameter control is evolved while the underlying GA solves the optimization. The hyperparameters of the RL algorithm were tuned through a previously performed tuning process.

In 2014, Karafotias et al., proposed an out-of-the-box parameter controller based on Sarsa with eligibility traces (Karafotias et al., 2014a,b). Eligibility traces is a way to assign positive or negative credits to actions according to their influence in future steps. In this paper, the reward for a state-action pair (s_t, a_t) is calculated according to Equation 33, where f^t_b and f^{t+1}_b are the best fitnesses among the population at times t and $t + 1$ (*i.e.,* before and after the action taken by the agent), and

$Evals_t$ and $Evals_{t+1}$ are the numbers of fitness evaluations performed at times t and $t + 1$ (*i.e.*, before and after the action taken by the agent).

$$r(s_t, a_t) = C \cdot \frac{\frac{f_b^{t+1}}{f_b^t} - 1}{Evals_{t+1} - Evals_t}. \tag{33}$$

The set of actions is composed by all possible combinations of all possible values of the controlled parameters. For discrete parameters, the number of possible values is already finite. However, continuous parameters have infinite possible values. In order to turn the action set finite, the authors decided to split the parameter ranges into equally-sized intervals. Thus, for such parameters, each one of these intervals represent one possible action. When one of them is selected, the final parameter value can chosen through interpolation or probabilistic sampling.

In this approach, the genotypic and phenotypic diversities, fitness standard deviation, fitness improvement and a stagnation counter were used as observed variables. The state of the metaheuristic is inferred from such variables through a binary decision tree that is built throughout the execution of the algorithm. It means that the states are discovered as the training process goes on. In this technique, each node of the tree represents an observed variable and a cutting point, while each leaf represents one of the discrete states of the environment (*i.e.*, metaheuristic). The tree starts with a single leaf that represents the only state known by the algorithm in the beginning of the learning process. During the training process, new observed variables and rewards are computed and passed through the tree. The path along the branches is defined according to the values of the observed variables and the sequence of encountered nodes. When this tree walk reaches one of the leaves, a state is assigned to the given set of observed variables. Then, the observables vector is "stored" in the given leaf. Whenever a leaf presents a set of observed variables that can be segmented into two clearly disjoint groups, the leaf will be turned into a decision node and two new child leaves are created. Thus, the state space is gradually segmented over time. Two groups of vectors of observables are said to be disjoint if they present a significant difference their v-values, where a v-value of an observables vector is the sum between the reward received when an action was taken when such a vector was observed and the value of the state observed after the chosen action was taken. The variable that present the largest difference between these groups is chosen as the splitting variable of the new decision node. Hypothesis tests such as the Rank-sum Wilcoxon test can be used to decide whether a leaf can be turned into a decision node. The mean value of a splitting variable is used as its splitting point.

Each state-action pair has an estimated state-action value $Q(s_i, a_i)$ value and an eligibility trace $e(s_i, a_i) \in [0, 1]$. After an action a_t is taken in a state s_t, the eligibility trace is calculated for each known state-action pair. It means that the influence of each state-action pair on the current reward is calculated. The more recent a state-action pair was chosen, the greater its eligibility trace. Algorithm 3 provides the pseudocode of the proposed algorithm.

Algorithm 3 Pseudocode of the algorithm proposed by Karafotias et al. (2014a).

Initialize state inference decision tree with one leaf node (single state);
Initialize hyperparameters;
$episode \leftarrow 0$;
while $episode <$ maximum number of episodes **do**
    Get the first observables vector of the environment;
    Infer the first state s_0 from the previously fetched observables vector;
    With probability ϵ, choose a random action a_0. Otherwise, choose a_0 that approximately maximizes $Q(s_0, a_0)$.
    $t \leftarrow 0$;
    while $t <$ maximum number of steps **do**
        Do the chosen action a_t and get the associated reward r_t and new observables vector;
        Infer the new state s_{t+1} from the observables vector;
        Set the eligibility trace of the previous state action pair (s_{t-1}, a_{t-1}) to 1.
        Calculate δ as shown in Equation 35.
        Calculate the eligibility traces for all state-action pairs through Equation 34;
        Update the state-action values functions $Q(s_i, a_i)$ of all state-action pairs as provided in Equation 35;
        $t \leftarrow t + 1$;
    end while
    $episode \leftarrow episode + 1$
end while

In Equations 34, 35, 36, α, γ, and λ are hyperparameters that need to be previously defined. It is important to mention that the eligibility traces must be greater than a minimum value, which is defined as a hyperparameter. The value of a state s_t is calculated as its maximum Q-value among the Q-values of all possible actions. In this work, just like in (Eiben et al., 2007), the policy for parameter control is evolved while the underlying GA solves the optimization. The hyperparameters of the RL algorithm were tuned through a previously performed tuning process.

$$e(s_i, a_i) = e(s_i, a_i) \cdot \gamma \cdot \lambda. \tag{34}$$

$$\delta = r(s_t, a_t) + \gamma Q(s_t, a_t) - Q(s_{t+1}, a_{t+1}), \tag{35}$$

$$Q(s_i, a_i) = Q(s_i, a_i) + \alpha \cdot \delta \cdot e(s_i, a_i), \tag{36}$$

In 2015, Karafotias et al., tried four different reward functions in their previously published technique (Karafotias et al., 2015a):

1. Improvement of the best fitness over the needed amount of time, as originally proposed in (Karafotias et al., 2014a)(Karafotias et al., 2014b), which is defined in Equation 33;

2. A binary function, which returns 1 when there is an improvement on the best fitness, and returns 0 otherwise;

3. The difference between the reward calculated with Equation 33 and the average return across the N last non-zero values, where N becomes a hyperparameter of the method;

4. The raw value of the fittest candidate solution.

The experimental results showed that the binary function is the most effective approach. It is important to notice that, since this reward does not use the fitness values of the candidate solutions, the reward values are not affected by the order of magnitude of the objective function. In optimization problems where the solutions present high fitness values and high fitness variation along the search space, rewards with excessively high values may be returned to the agent, what may lead the iterative learning process to numerical issues, such as the overestimation of bad decisions.

As already mentioned, in he technique proposed by Karafotias et al., in (Karafotias et al., 2014a), (Karafotias et al., 2014b), and (Karafotias et al., 2015a), the range of values of numerical parameters of the underlying metaheuristic must be split into a certain number of sub-intervals. This poses a challenging choice: since the lower the number of sub-intervals, the smaller the number of possible actions, what eases the learning problem, but the wider their length. Given that the final parameter value must be calculated through interpolation or random value sampling within the chosen interval, wide ranges lead to inaccurate actions. However, even though smaller sub-intervals increase the accuracy of the chosen actions, it leads to a higher number of possible actions, which increases the size of the action set and, therefore, makes the learning problem harder to solve. Unfortunately, a balanced solution can be very hard to find.

In 2016, Rost et al., proposed two improvements to the aforementioned approach (Rost et al., 2016):

1. Application of an entropy-based adaptive range parameter control (EARPC) proposed by Aleti and Moser (Aleti and Moser, 2013), so that the number of intervals should not be defined by the user, which means that the user would not have to be concerned about the granularity of the action space);

2. Training one agent for each parameter, where the action space is segmented following the ideas of state space segmentation used in (Karafotias et al., 2014a), (Karafotias et al., 2014b), and (Karafotias et al., 2015a).

In order to understand the entire approach proposed by Rost et al., 2016 it is necessary to first understand the EARPC algorithm. EARPC was designed as an out-of-the-box parameter controller method for EA. In this method, the parameter ranges are split into two sub-intervals. The choice of the splitting points is made independently for each parameter. After a splitting point is defined, one of the two sub-intervals is randomly chosen, where the probability of choice of an sub-interval is proportional to the average quality of the entries placed within the given sub-interval. An entry is a pair of parameter vector and its quality, which, at some point of the optimization process, was stored in an experience database. The quality of a parameter vector is the performance of the underlying EA when it was executed with the given setup.

The choice of the splitting point is made as follows. Let $\gtrsim$ be a parameter vector chosen by the EARPC algorithm. To choose the splitting point for the parameter v_i, the values of v_i stored in the experience database must be sorted in ascending order, where the mid-point between each pair of neighbor values of v_i is a splitting point candidate. Then parameter vectors that had been stored so far in the experience database are divided into two clusters c_1 and c_2, which can be done through K-means (Jin and Han, 2010). For each $k - th$ splitting point s_k, let $p_{1,k}$ and $p_{2,k}$ be the set of entries where $v_i \leq s_k$ and $v_i > s_k$, respectively. Also, denote $c_1(p_{1,k})$ and $c_1(p_{2,k})$ as the set of entries that is part of c_1 and $p_{1,k}$, and c_1 and $p_{2,k}$, respectively, and $c_2(p_{1,k})$ and $c_2(p_{2,k})$ as the set of entries that is part of c_2 and $p_{1,k}$, and c_2 and $p_{2,k}$, respectively. The entropy H_k of the splitting point s_k is calculated as provided in Equation 37. Then, the splitting point s_k that minimizes the entropy H_k is chosen.

$$H_k = \frac{|p_{1,k}|}{c_1} e_{p_{1,k}} + \frac{|p_{2,k}|}{c_2} e_{p_{2,k}}, \qquad (37)$$

$$e_{p_{1,k}} = -\frac{|c_1(p_{1,k})|}{|p_{1,k}|} ln\left(\frac{|c_1(p_{1,k})|}{|p_{1,k}|}\right) - \frac{|c_2(p_{1,k})|}{|p_{1,k}|} ln\left(\frac{|c_2(p_{1,k})|}{|p_{1,k}|}\right), \qquad (38)$$

$$e_{p_{2,k}} = -\frac{|c_1(p_{2,k})|}{|p_{2,k}|} ln\left(\frac{|c_1(p_{2,k})|}{|p_{2,k}|}\right) - \frac{|c_2(p_{2,k})|}{|p_{2,k}|} ln\left(\frac{|c_2(p_{2,k})|}{|p_{2,k}|}\right). \qquad (39)$$

In their work, Rost et al., use EARPC to improve the technique proposed in (Karafotias et al., 2014a), (Karafotias et al., 2014b), and (Karafotias et al., 2015a). The EARPC algorithm is used to choose the action at each learning iteration. It means that when a vector of observables is observed, the current state s_t of the underlying metaheuristic is inferred through the previously mentioned tree-based method, and then an action a_t is chosen through EARPC. After that, a reward r_t is received and a new state s_{t+1} is inferred from the new observables vector. Then transition vector $(s_t, a_t, r_t, s_{t+1}$ is stored in the experience database. The reward of a transition vector is used as the quality of the parameter vector chosen by the EARPC algorithm, which is needed to define the splitting points. The value of the state s_{t+1}, which is used in the leaf node splitting process in the tree-based state inference method defined in (Karafotias et al., 2014a), is calculated as $\sum_{i=1}^{2} \frac{Q_i^2}{Q_1+Q_2}$, where Q_1 and Q_2 are the average rewards on intervals 1 and 2 defined through EARPC, respectively.

The experiments showed that as the number of states explodes, the algorithm could not significantly improve the performance of the metaheuristic used in the experiments. Therefore, in order to simplify the learning process by reducing the number of possible states and the number of possible actions, the authors proposed a second method where one separate agent was used for each parameter to be controlled.

In this second approach, for each parameter v_i, the action spaces of each agent i are dynamically segmented, similarly to the state space segmentation method proposed in (Karafotias et al., 2014a) and also used in this approach. Initially, the action is chosen from the range $[min_i, max_i]$, which are the minimum and the maximum values of the $i - th$ parameter. The reward is then stored alongside the chosen parameter. After a certain amount of action-reward pairs are stored in an experience database, a splitting point is tried to be defined using the same procedure as in the state-space segmentation technique. If a splitting point is defined, two new sub-intervals are created, which means that the action corresponding to the previous range is removed from the action state, while two new actions are added. Such a procedure is executed after each action is taken throughout the learning process.

The results showed that the approach number 2 is more sample-efficient. The drawback of this approach is that using a single isolated agent for each parameter may not capture any dependency between these parameters.

As previously mentioned, neural networks-based RL methods are able to accurately approximate state-action value functions without the need for visiting the vast majority of the combinations between states and actions. In 2019, Lacerda et al., used the Dueling Double DQN algorithm to train out-of-the-box parameter controls policies for EA and SI (de Lacerda et al., 2019). In this approach, the agent sets the parameters of the underlying metaheuristic, and the metaheuristic runs until the fitness of its best individual stops improving. When this happens, the agent receives a reward, which is the difference between the fitness of the best solution found before and after the latest execution of the underlying metaheuristic. The training episode runs until a budget for the running metaheuristic is over, which is predefined in number of fitness evaluations.

In this work, the observables are numerical variables between 0 and 1. They were defined as follows:

- $\frac{f_{bsf} - \overline{F}}{f_{bsf} - f_{wsf}}$, where f_{bsf} is the best fitness so far, $\overline{F}$ is the average fitness among the individuals of the metaheuristic and f_{wsf} is the worst fitness so far. Length: 1 variable.

- $\frac{std(F)}{str(\{f_{bsf}, f_{wsf}\})}$, where $std(F)$ is the standard deviation of the fitnesses of the individuals of the metaheuristic, and $str(\{f_{bsf}, f_{wsf}\})$ is the standard deviation between the best and the worst fitness so far (*i.e.*, maximum standard deviation among the individuals). Length: 1 variable.

- $\frac{b}{B}$, where b is the current budget left and B is the initial available budget. Budgets can be defined in terms of number of agent's iteration, metaheuristic's iteration, fitness calls for the metaheuristic's population, or execution time in seconds. Length: 1 variable.

- $\frac{b_e}{B}$, where b_e is the elapsed budget (*i.e.*, time unit) since the last improvement of the best fitness so far. Length: 1 variable.

- $\frac{\|p_{a_i} - p_{b_i}\|}{\|max - min\|}$, $\forall i \in \{0, 1, 2, 3, 4\}$, where p_{a_i} is an individual with index a_i, p_{b_i} is an individual with index b_i, both picked from the metaheuristic, a_i and b_i are random indexes, and max and min are the vectors with all their values set to the maximum and minimum values for each dimension of the metaheuristic's search space, respectively. Length: 5 variables.

- $\frac{\|p_{bf} - p_{a_i}\|}{\|max - min\|}$, $\forall i \in \{0, 1, 2, 3, 4\}$, where p_b is the individual of the metaheuristic with the best fitness. Length: 5 variables.

- $\frac{|f_{a_i} - f_{b_i}|}{f_{bsf} - f_{wsf}}$, $\forall i \in \{0, 1, 2, 3, 4\}$, where f_{a_i} is the fitness of an individual with index a_i, f_{b_i} is the fitness of an individual with index b_i, both picked from the metaheuristic. Length: 5 variables.

- $\frac{|f_{a_i} - f_{bf}|}{f_{bsf} - f_{wsf}}$, $\forall i \in \{0, 1, 2, 3, 4\}$, where f_{bf} is the best fitness among all individuals of the metaheuristic. Length: 5 variables.

- $\frac{\|p_{bsf} - p_{a_i}\|}{\|max - min\|}$, $\forall i \in \{0, 1, 2, 3, 4\}$, where p_{bsf} is the position of the solution with the best fitness so far. Length: 5 variables.

- $\frac{I_{t-k}}{N_{t-k}}$, $\forall k \in \{0, 1, 2, 3, 4, 5, 6, 7, 8, 9\}$, where I_{t-k} is the number of individuals that improved its fitness during the $(t - k)^{th}$ agent's iteration (*i.e.*, $k = 0$ is the current t^{th} iteration), and N_{t-k} is the number of individuals in the metaheuristic in the $(t - k)^{th}$ agent's iteration. Length: 10 variables.

- $I_{bsf_{t-k}}$, $\forall k \in \{0, 1, 2, 3, 4, 5, 6, 7, 8, 9\}$, where $I_{bsf_{t-k}}$ is a boolean variable that is set if the best fitness so far was improved during the $(t - k)^{th}$ agent's iteration, and reset otherwise. Length: 10 variables.

Such as (Karafotias et al., 2014a) and (Karafotias et al., 2014b), the action set is composed by all possible combinations of parameter values, and the final value chosen for the continuous parameters, taken from equally-sized sub-intervals, were picked randomly with a uniform probability distribution. However, any of the previously published studies on RL applied to out-of-the-box parameter control for EA and SI has presented a solution for the adjustment of the population size in SI algorithms. In EA algorithms, changing the population size is quite straightforward, since it can be adjusted through any selection operator. However, a mechanism of addition or removal of individuals had be designed for SI algorithms.

    Considering only minimization problems, in the removal process, an individual is randomly chosen with probability equals to the ratio between its current fitness and the sum of the current fitnesses of all remaining individuals in the population.

It means that the lower its fitness, the higher its probability of being chosen. This process is executed until the new population size meets the new value of the parameter. Regarding the addition process, an individual is randomly chosen with probability equals to the complement to 1 of the aforementioned ratio. Then, it serves as a generator for a new individual, which is created by adding a vector randomly generated with a normal distribution with zero mean and variance v to a copy of the chosen individual. In this work, v is defined separately for each dimension d of the objective space as $\sigma \delta B_d \frac{\sqrt{D}}{6D}$, where B_d is the distance between the upper and the lower bounds of the dimension d, D is the number of dimensions, and σ is a parameter controlled by the RL agent, *i.e.*, added to the set of parameters to be controlled.

It is important to mention that, in this approach, the agent must be trained in a set of training functions before it is applied to unseen problems. In the training process, each episode is performed with one function. When an episode ends, another function is randomly chosen for the next episode.

3.2 Other Approaches

Only 2 of the 7 studies presented in this chapter applied other techniques than Temporal-Difference-based methods for out-of-the-box parameter control for EA and SI algorithms. In 2012, Karafotias et al., proposed the use of a neural network-based RL technique for out-of-the-box parameter control for EA and SI algorithms (Karafotias et al., 2012). In this approach, a fully-connected neural network with no hidden layers is used to "encode" the control policy, where the input (*i.e.*, observables) and the output variables (*i.e.*, the variables that "encode" the chosen actions) must be between 0 and 1, and the weights (*i.e.*, the parameters that represent the policy) must be always between -1 and 1. The latest chosen action, the Population Diversity Index (PDI) (Smit et al., 2011b), the current normalized best fitness, and the latest history of the variation of the best fitness are calculated from the set of solutions of the underlying metaheuristic and are used to describe its state.

Instead of using a traditional training method for neural networks (*e.g.* Adam (Kingma and Ba, 2017) and RMSprop (Ruder, 2017)) over a batch of experiences as in DQN, a tuning algorithm called BONESA (Smit et al., 2011a) was used beforehand in order to tune the weights of the neural network. It means that before using the proposed technique to solve a certain target problem, the parameter control policy must be trained on a set of training problems. In the training process, for each policy generated by BONESA, the candidate solution must be used to control the underlying metaheuristic while it solves a training problem for a given number of iterations. Its performance is used as reward to guide the policy search.

In 2019, Schuchardt et al., proposed a PPO-based approach for out-of-the-box parameter control for EA and SI algorithms (Schuchardt et al., 2019). Figure 5 provides the architecture of the neural network used to choose actions (Actor) and compute the values of the states visited by the agent throughout the optimization

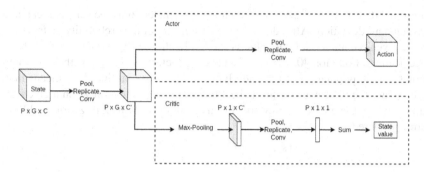

Figure 4: Diagram of the neural network architecture used in (Schuchardt et al., 2019).

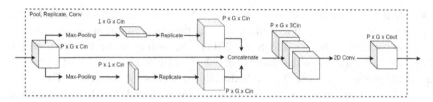

Figure 5: Diagram of the *Pool, Replicate, Conv* block (based on (Schuchardt et al., 2019)).

process (Critic). In this architecture, the input of the neural network is the a P x G x C matrix, where P is the population size of the underlying metaheuristic, G is the number of genes of each individual, and C is the number of channels. Each channel represents one source of information. For example, if the underlying metaheuristic is the PSO algorithm (Kennedy and Eberhart, 1995), the first channel can be the current positions of the individuals in the search space, the second channel can be their current velocities, and the third channel can represent their fitnesses. In the case of scalar variables such as fitness or remaining fitness calls, such a value can be replicated along the gene dimension for each individual. From this input matrix, a sequence of max-pooling, replication and convolution operations extracts the relevant features from the environment, instead of relying on manual definition of features to be extracted and used as observables for the decision process. It is important to notice that the first layers of the neural network followed by the Actor part represents the policy to be learned, and the first layers plus the Critic part encodes the state value function used to calculate the advantage in the PPO algorithm, as described in Algorithm 1.

It is important to mention that PPO supports continuous actions. The output of the Actor network are the parameters of the probability distribution that stochastically determines the final parameter values. In this work, a beta distribution with parameters α and β is used to determine the final values of the bounded parameters of the underlying metaheuristic. Therefore, if the mutation and crossover probabilities of a GA needs to be set, the neural network needs to output 4 numerical variables, *i.e.*, α and β values for each parameter. For the unbounded parameters, a normal distribution is used, for which two parameters must be set: its mean and its standard deviation. After defining the parameters of the probability distribution for a given parameter, a final value is randomly chosen. The reward is calculated according to Equation 40, where C is a scaling factor and $f_{max}s_t$ is the maximum fitness in the population of the underlying metaheuristic at time t. It means that, the greater the improvement of the best fitness in the population when a given action is taken, the greater the reward. In this formula, only maximization problems are considered.

$$r(s_t, a_t) = C \cdot \log_{10} \frac{f_{max}s_t}{f_{max}s_{t-1}}. \tag{40}$$

4   Conclusion

Despite the well succeeded applications of EA and SI algorithms in several areas (Aleti and Moser, 2016), it is well known that these algorithms are quite sensitive to their parameters (Eiben and Smit, 2011). According to the literature on the field, the vast majority of the studies published so far on parameter control for EA and SI algorithms propose the methods tailored to specific scenarios. Therefore, only a few studies on out-of-the-box methods can be found. In 2021, a systematic literature review on out-of-the-box parameter control for EA and SI algorithms was published (de Lacerda et al., 2021). In this study, it was found that Reinforcement Learning is the paradigm that was most used to design out-of-the-box parameter control for EA and SI algorithms: 7 out of 16 studies.

Even though the results achieved in the studies discussed in this chapter are quite promising, there is still a lot to improve. A few important open challenges are, but not limited to:

- RL algorithms can be quite expensive to be trained, especially when the interaction between the agent and the environment triggers a computationally expensive process. In these algorithms, the generation of a trajectory requires the full execution of a metaheuristic over a given optimization problem, which is quite expensive, especially when several trajectories must be generated per training iteration. Therefore, parallel/distributed implementations of such algorithms should be proposed in order to speed-up this expensive training process.

- RL algorithms usually require the adjustment of a considerable amount of hyperparameters. Besides, these algorithms are quite sensitive to their hyperparameters. Therefore, the use of such algorithms usually increases the number of parameters to be adjusted instead of reducing it. Despite the capacity of generating parameter control policies better than humans, these techniques are even harder to use than the original metaheuristics. Thus, the proposal of a parameter-free approaches for out-of-the-box parameter control methods or algorithms that are not too sensitive to their hyperparameters is still an open challenge.

- Some of the proposed algorithms use a set of training problems to train a parameter control policy before using it in unseen problems. The experimental results have been shown that these algorithms are able to learn general enough rules so that they can be applied in problems that are different from the problems it was trained for. It is straightforward to see that the more similar the unseen problem to the training ones, the better the policy performs. Therefore, given a target unsolved problem, it is important to choose a training set with functions that share at least some characteristics with it. However, the extraction of features from optimization problems in order to compare them with each other is a big challenge.

- Even though the authors of the reviewed studies argue that they propose out-of-the-box methods, very limited benchmarks have been used to assess such a generality, what reduces the scope and generality of these methods. Therefore, more extensive benchmarks should be used to truly assess the generality of the proposed methods.

References

Alagoz, O., H. Hsu, A.J. Schaefer and M.S. Roberts. Markov decision processes: A tool for sequential decision making under uncertainty. Medical Decision Making, 30(4): 474–483, 2010.

Aleti, A. and I. Moser. Entropy-based adaptive range parameter control for evolutionary algorithms. In Proceedings of the 15th Annual Conference on Genetic and Evolutionary Computation, GECCO'13, pp. 1501–1508. New York, NY, USA: ACM, 2013.

Aleti, A. and I. Moser. A systematic literature review of adaptive parameter control methods for evolutionary algorithms. ACM Comput. Surv., 49(3): 56:1–56:35, 2016.

Bellman, R. Dynamic Programming. Dover Publications, 1957.

Bertsekas, D.P. Dynamic Programming and Optimal Control (2nd ed.). Athena Scientific, 2000.

Consoli, P.A., L.L. Minku and X. Yao. Dynamic selection of evolutionary algorithm operators based on online learning and fitness landscape metrics. pp. 359–370. In: Dick, G., W.N. Browne, P. Whigham, M. Zhang, L.T. Bui, H. Ishibuchi, Y. Jin, X. Li, Y. Shi, P. Singh, K.C. Tan and K. Tang (eds.). Simulated Evolution and Learning. Cham: Springer International Publishing, 2014.

Consoli, P.A., Y. Mei, L.L. Minku and X. Yao. Dynamic selection of evolutionary operators based on online learning and fitness landscape analysis. Soft Comput., 20(10): 3889–3914, 2016.

DaCosta, L., A. Fialho, M. Schoenauer and M. Sebag. Adaptive operator selection with dynamic multi-armed bandits. In Proceedings of the 10th Annual Conference on Genetic and Evolutionary Computation, GECCO'08, pp. 913–920. New York, NY, USA: Association for Computing Machinery, 2008.

de Lacerda, M.G.P., F.B. de Lima Neto, H. de Andrade Amorim Neto, H. Kuchen and T.B. Ludermir. On the learning properties of dueling ddqn in parameter control for evolutionary and swarm-based algorithms. In 2019 IEEE Latin American Conference on Computational Intelligence (LA-CCI), pp. 1–6, 2019.

de Lacerda, M.G.P., L.F. de Araujo Pessoa, F.B. de Lima Neto, T.B. Ludermir and H. Kuchen. A systematic literature review on general parameter control for evolutionary and swarm-based algorithms. Swarm and Evolutionary Computation, 60: 100777, 2021.

Drake, J.H., A. Kheiri, E. Özcan and E.K. Burke. Recent advances in selection hyper-heuristics. European Journal of Operational Research, 285(2): 405–428, 2020.

Duan, Y., X. Chen, R. Houthooft, J. Schulman and P. Abbeel. Benchmarking deep reinforcement learning for continuous control, 2016.

Eiben, A.E., R. Hinterding and Z. Michalewicz. Parameter control in evolutionary algorithms. IEEE Transactions on Evolutionary Computation, 3(2): 124–141, 1999.

Eiben, A.E., M. Horvath, W. Kowalczyk and M.C. Schut. Reinforcement learning for online control of evolutionary algorithms. In Proceedings of the 4th International Conference on Engineering Self-organising Systems, ESOA'06, pp. 151–160. Berlin, Heidelberg: Springer-Verlag, 2007.

Eiben, A.E. and S.K. Smit. Evolutionary algorithm parameters and methods to tune them. In: Hamadi, Y., E. Monfroy and F. Saubion (eds.). Autonomous Search. Berlin, Heidelberg: Springer, 2011.

Goldberg, D.E. Genetic Algorithms in Search, Optimization and Machine Learning (1st ed.). USA: Addison-Wesley Longman Publishing Co., Inc, 1989.

Guan, Y., L. Yang and W. Sheng. Population control in evolutionary algorithms: Review and comparison. In Bio-inspired computing: Theories and Applications, pp. 161–174, 2017.

Jin, X. and J. Han. K-means clustering. pp. 563–564. In: Sammut C. and G. I. Webb (eds.). Encyclopedia of Machine Learning. Boston, MA: Springer US, 2010.

Kaelbling, L.P., M.L. Littman and A.W. Moore. Reinforcement learning: A survey. J. Artif. Int. Res., 4(1): 237–285, 1996.

Karafotias, G., A.E. Eiben and M. Hoogendoorn. Generic parameter control with reinforcement learning. In Proceedings of the 2014 Annual Conference on Genetic and Evolutionary Computation, GECCO'14, pp. 1319–1326, 2014a.

Karafotias, G., M. Hoogendoorn and B. Weel. Comparing generic parameter controllers for eas. In Proceedings of the 2014 IEEE Symposium Series on Computational Intelligence, SSCI'14, pp. 16–53, 2014b.

Karafotias, G., M. Hoogendoorn and A.E. Eiben. Evaluating reward definitions for parameter control. In Proceedings of the 2015 European Conference on the Applications of Evolutionary Computation, EvoApplications'15 pp. 667–680, 2015a.

Karafotias, G., M. Hoogendoorn and A.E. Eiben. Parameter control in evolutionary algorithms: Trends and challenges. IEEE Transactions on Evolutionary Computation, 19(2): 167–187, 2015b.

Karafotias, G., S.K. Smit and A.E. Eiben. A generic approach to parameter control. In Proceedings of the 2012 European Conference on the Applications of Evolutionary Computation, EvoApplications'12, 2012.

Kennedy, J. and R. Eberhart. Particle swarm optimization. In Proceedings of ICNN'95—International Conference on Neural Networks, 4: 1942–1948, 1995.

Kingma, D.P. and J. Ba. Adam: A method for stochastic optimization, 2017.

Lapan, M. Deep Reinforcement Learning Hands-On: Apply Modern RL Methods, with Deep Q-Networks, Value Iteration, Policy Gradients, Trpo, Alphago Zero and More. Packt Publishing, 2018.

Ma, Q. and J. Stachurski. Dynamic programming deconstructed: Transformations of the bellman equation and computational efficiency, 2019.

Mnih, V., K. Kavukcuoglu, D. Silver, A. Graves, I. Antonoglou, D. Wierstra and M. Riedmiller. Playing atari with deep reinforcement learning, 2013.

Mnih, V., K. Kavukcuoglu, D. Silver, A.A. Rusu, J. Veness, M.G. Bellemare and D. Hassabis. Human-level control through deep reinforcement learning. Nature, 518(7540): 529–533, 2015.

Muller, S., N. Schraudolph and P. Koumoutsakos. Step size adaptation in evolution strategies using reinforcement learning. In Proceedings of the 2002 Congress on Evolutionary Computation. cec'02 (cat. no.02th8600) Vol. 1, pp. 151–156, 2002.

Parpinelli, R.S., G.F. Plichoski and R.S. da Silva. A review of techniques for on-line control of parameters in swarm intelligence and evolutionary computation algorithms. International Journal of Bio-inspired Computation, 13(1): 1–17, 2019.

Puterman, M.L. Chapter 8 Markov Decision Processes. In Stochastic Models, volume 2 of Handbooks in Operations Research and Management Science, pp. 331–434. Elsevier, 1990.

Rost, A., I. Petrova and A. Buzdalova. Adaptive parameter selection in evolutionary algorithms by reinforcement learning with dynamic discretization of parameter range. In Proceedings of the 2016 on Genetic and Evolutionary Computation, GECCO'16, 2016.

Ruder, S. An overview of gradient descent optimization algorithms, 2017.

Schuchardt, J., V. Golkov and D. Cremers. Learning to evolve, 2019.

Schulman, J., F. Wolski, P. Dhariwal, A. Radford and O. Klimov. Proximal policy optimization algorithms, 2017.

Smit, S.K., A.E. Eiben, J.-K. Hao, P. Legrand, P. Collet, N. Monmarché and M. Schoenauer. Multi-problem parameter tuning using bonesa, 2011a.

Smit, S.K., Z. Szláavik and A.E. Eiben. Population diversity index: A new measure for population diversity. In Proceedings of the 13th Annual Conference Companion on Genetic and Evolutionary

Computation GECCO'11, pp. 269–270, New York, NY, USA. Association for Computing Machinery, 2011b.

Sutton, R.S. and A.G. Barto. Reinforcement Learning: An Introduction. Cambridge, MA, USA: A Bradford Book. Cambridge, MA, USA, 2018.

Sutton, R.S., D. McAllester, S. Singh and Y. Mansour. Policy gradient methods for reinforcement learning with function approximation. In Proceedings of the 12th International Conference on Neural Information Processing Systems, NIPS'99, pp. 1057–1063. Cambridge, MA, USA: MIT Press, 1999.

van Hasselt, H., A. Guez and D. Silver. Deep reinforcement learning with double q-learning, 2015.

Wang, Z., T. Schaul, M. Hessel, H. van Hasselt, M. Lanctot and N. de Freitas. Dueling network architectures for deep reinforcement learning, 2016.

Witten, I.H., E. Frank and M.A. Hall. Data Mining: Practical Machine Learning Tools and Techniques. Morgan Kaufmann Series in Data Management Systems. Morgan Kaufmann, Amsterdam, 3 edition, 2011.

Wolpert, D.H. and W.G. Macready. No free lunch theorems for optimization. IEEE Transactions on Evolutionary Computation, 1(1): 67–82, 1997.

Zhang, J., W.-N. Chen, Z.-H. Zhan, W.-J. Yu, Y.-L. Li, N. Chen and Q. Zhou. A survey on algorithm adaptation in evolutionary computation. Frontiers of Electrical and Electronic Engineering, 7(1): 16–31, 2012.

Section 2

Applications

Chapter 5

Recognition of Emotions in the Elderly Through Audio Signal Analysis

Flávio S. Fonseca,[1] Arianne S. Torcate,[1] Maíra A. Santana,[1] Juliana C. Gomes,[1] Nicole Charron,[2] José Daniel S. do Carmo,[2] Giselle M.M. Moreno[3] and *Wellington P. dos Santos[1,2],**

1 Introduction

Population aging is an expanding phenomenon at a global level (Oliveira, 2019). In opposition to this growth, we have the decline in the quality of life of these individuals (Dantcheva et al., 2017). In addition to the various motor and health problems intrinsic to advancing age, the ability to communicate vocally, and especially emotionally, generally becomes much more subtle (Lagacé et al., 2012). This difficulty becomes even more evident when we talk about dementia.

In this context, according to the work of (de Souza et al., 2017; Torcate et al., 2020), there is a growing need for therapies that support the quality of life of these patients. Also reducing pressure on health professionals and family members involved. For this age group, aging well is essential. But, satisfaction measurements, often understood merely as happiness or sadness, are difficult factors to quantify.

[1] Polytechnic School of the University of Pernambuco, Recife, Brazil.
[2] Department of Biomedical Engineering, Federal University of Pernambuco, Recife, Brazil.
[3] Institute of Astronomy, Geophysics and Atmospheric Sciences, University of São Paulo, São Paulo, Brazil.
* Corresponding author: wellington.santos@ufpe.br

Even more when these feelings occur, almost always, in rare moments of distraction.

Given this reality, it is important to think about ways to stimulate this rehabilitation process. The use of games, alternative therapies or other digital resources are good examples. For this, technology must emerge as an ally to promote the well-being and comfort of these people (Dornelles and Corrêa, 2020). We are also aware of the barriers naturally imposed when we talk about new technologies. Elderly people often find it difficult to keep up with this rapid evolution. However, new devices and software have helped to break this paradigm, and approaching the older audience (Zilidis and Zilidou, 2018).

Essentially, we have an increase in life expectancy. Therefore, the demand for resources and trained health professionals increases, at ever greater intervals. Thus, when we talk about policies for a population that is constantly growing, these resources become insufficient. In this environment, assistive technologies and studies that support possible solutions in health are the only way out, as stated by Iancu and Iancu (2017). Furthermore, to help the development of intelligent solutions for the patient and healthcare professional, technology must integrate the elderly in a society that, for the most part, excludes them digitally.

From both human and technological perspective, Affective Computing (AC) emerges. This field of science combines Psychology, Cognitive Sciences and Computer Science (Torcate et al., 2020), integrating humans and machines through, mainly, the recognition of emotions Han et al. (2019) and the creation of devices that deal with the human factor. It is precisely from the perspective of AC that we guide the work developed in this chapter.

Moreover, there is a lack of research focused on the elderly in this field of computing (Ma et al., 2019). Thus, our work aims to contribute to the improvement of computational techniques aimed at recognizing emotions in the elderly through speech analysis. The idea is that our final application will support therapists, doctors and caregivers. Also narrowing the interpersonal relationships with the patient.

To perform the recognition of emotions through voice, two methodologies were applied. Initially, we used the Google Colab development environment, in Python programming language with libraries such as TensorFlow, NumPy and Scikit-learn. In this first experiment, we developed a Convolutional Neural Network (CNN) to extract the Log-Mel spectrogram feature of each audio file from the RAVDESS database (Livingstone et al., 2012) and, later, perform the classification. Then, in a second experiment, we applied the Wavelet transform on the same database. The results obtained were plotted in the form of an image using pseudocolors, creating then a new database. By using transfer learning approach (Yang et al., 2020) and Weka software (Witten and Frank, 2002), we applied a pretrained ResNet network (Residual-Net) (Targ et al., 2016) to extract features from the generated images.

The extraction of these features through the deep network ended up overestimating the problem. Then the idea of using swarm methods to simplify the architecture came up. The particle swarm optimization (PSO) was then applied and the results from this step were also compared with models without PSO. These bases with different features served as input to several intelligent classifiers, which were trained and exhaustively tested.

This chapter has been divided into 6 sections. In addition to the Introduction, Section 2 presents some works related to voice recognition of emotions. Then, in Section 3, together with its respective subsections, we perform a contextualization of aging and its consequences on the speech, interpretation and emotional expression of these elderly people. In Section 4 we present the methodological path, together with the diagram with the two proposals, each of its stages and configurations. We discuss and analyze the results found in each approach in Section 5. Finally, in Section 6 we conclude the chapter and present our perspectives for future work.

2   Related Works

In the recent work of Mustaqeem and Kwon (2020), they developed a new CNN architecture using different strategies to extract data from speech signals and reduce the sampling of feature maps. In this case, they chose to work with convolutional layers and special strides, using 2 datasets: IEMOCAP and RAVDESS. In this context, the changes found were greater in the pre-processing steps, CNN model and computational complexity. In the first one, the authors developed a new technique to remove noise and silent parts in the data. As for the CNN and the computational complexity, few layers were used in the architecture, making it possible to improve model accuracy while maintaining reduced complexity. At the end, an accuracy of 81.75% for the IEMOCAP and 79.5% for the RAVDESS was obtained, a higher value when compared to other models of CNNs.

In the article of Issa et al. (2020), to obtain a better accuracy and improve the classification model, the researchers, in addition to making certain modifications to the baseline, also extracted 5 different features from the audio files and turned them into an array, which served as input for the one-dimensional CNN that was used. In total, 4 models of simple architecture were developed and they were more accurate than almost all the models compared. Finally, they concluded that the combination of these features generated a much better representation of the database and helped in the emotion recognition process, reaching an accuracy of 71.6% with the RAVDESS database. However, the authors emphasized that in order to have greater accuracy in the models, they need an auxiliary neural network and improved techniques to increase the amount of data in the testing set.

Özseven (2018) proposed a method to investigate the effects of texture analysis and spectrogram images on speech emotion recognition. Four texture analysis methods were applied to extract features from the spectrogram images of speech. Then the author subjected these feature sets to emotion classification using SVM. This approach achieved 74.9% of accuracy using EMO-DB database, 57.2% using Enterface'05, and 59.8% of success when applied to the data in SAVEE database. These results were reasonable and showed that texture analysis methods may be promising for speech emotion recognition. Further in the study the author compared the success of the texture analysis with acoustic analysis methods. Texture methods performed slightly worse than the acoustic analysis, with a 0.4% reduction in accuracy. However, the author also found that this performance may be increased when combining both analyses, specially the GLCM, wavelet and acoustic features. An important finding was that method performance is highly dependent on the data used since performances vary according to the database. These changes are probably due to the voice acquisition protocol in each dataset, these differences are usually not well described in the spectrogram images. Some limitations of the study are associated to the conversion of the images to grayscale, which may provide a small data loss. The lack of other preprocessing methods and the unbalanced databases may also have negatively influenced the outcome (Özseven, 2018).

In the study from Wei and Zhao (2019) the authors came up with a novel speech recognition algorithm to overcome the common decrease in the performance of the existing methods applied in real-life speech emotion recognition. Their approach is a kernel sparse deep model based on auto-encoder, denoising autoencoder, and sparse auto-encoder. These auto-encoder methods are used to extract and select features from the data. Then, they applied a wavelet-kernel SVM as classifier. This algorithm is applied to a Chinese speech dataset that has spontaneous emotion data. Their method achieved a maximum recognition rate of 80.95%, outperforming other previously tested approaches. However, further studies should be conducted to assess model performance for other language databases (Wei and Zhao, 2019).

The work of Hamsa et al. (2020) introduces an artificial emotional intelligence system able to identify in real-time the emotions of the speaker. They conducted experiments with speech data from RAVDESS, SUSAS, and ESD databases, comprising two different languages: English and Arabic. Their approach uses wavelet packet transform (WPT) to assess emotions based on energy, time and spectral parameters. As classifier they used a random forest model, which overcame the performances of other algorithms in literature, achieving recognition rates between 86.38% and 89.60% for the different datasets. One of the main advantages of this method is the ability to recognize emotions in the presence of noise and interference. On the other hand, its main limitation is that all speech signals used to build and evaluate the system are from non-spontaneous speech due to the lack of natural emotional speech datasets (Hamsa et al., 2020).

Table 1 below brings a summary of the works cited with the respective results achieved.

Table 1: Summary of related works: Authors; Applied methods; Result of the achieved accuracy.

Author	Method	Result(%)
Mustaqeem and Kwon (2020)	CNN	81,75
Issa et al. (2020)	CNN	71.6
Özseven (2018)	SVM	74.9
Wei and Zhao (2019)	SVM	80.9
Hamsa et al. (2020)	Random Forest	86.3
Our approach	SVM	81.1

3   Background

To support this chapter, we deal in Subsection 3.1 with the difficulties related to aging and their relationship with the interpretation and recognition of emotions. We highlight these adversities mainly in the artificial scope and human-machine interfaces. In Subsection 3.2, we detail the most common models in the literature to classify an emotion.

3.1   Aging and Speech Difficulty

As we get older, we tend to have several changes in our body, personality and cognitive functions of our organism (Kremer and den Uijl, 2016). These changes affect the way we express ourselves. Interacting and recognizing emotions, both between humans and, mainly, between man and machine becomes a very difficult task

Speech is one of the skills that can suffer from these changes. Vocal communication depends on numerous muscle structures that, with age, lose mass and strength. Vocal cords, larynx, tongue and lips are just some of the most affected parts. In view of these changes, it is common for older people to present hoarseness, breathiness and decreased speech rate (Vipperla, 2011). Furthermore, the elderly express themselves less fluently, with more errors, using more words and repetitions compared to younger people (Mortensen et al., 2006). Due to such differences in vocalization and acoustics, adjustments are often necessary for models that perform voice recognition in the elderly, so that they have a satisfactory performance (Vipperla, 2011).

Something similar also happens with regard to facial recognition. It is known that the elderly, when sketching emotions with the face, present more wrinkles and are less expressive than the young. This is something that can negatively interfere with the results of a (Lopes et al., 2018) classifier. We still had many difficulties regarding the lack of research in this context. It is indisputable the small amount of databases that are exclusive or involve the elderly, expressing emotions through speech, face or physiological signs.

3.2   The Interpretation of Emotions

To recognize an emotion, we need, first of all, to understand what they are and how to differentiate them. At first, they are sensations that compose an important function in the empirical and social construction of the human being. They guide our actions, tastes, desires and memories, thus shaping the being itself. In the scientific literature, we do not find a consensus on the definition of what emotion is. Although the representation of these feelings may seem very subjective. Some theories have already managed to model, analyze and interpret this natural human affective behavior (Pereira, 2018).

Emotion operates in each individual in a distinct and complex way. Thus, we do not understand each feeling in isolation, but integrated into a whole. This feature is straight related to the cognitive aspects (Izard, 1977). In this context, emotion recognition is one of the most complex fields of study in modern science. According to Le and Provost (2013), this complexity in emotional expression occurs because it is a dynamic process, involving several areas of knowledge.

Based on this, work on the classification of emotions by two fundamental models, the categorical and the dimensional (de Santana et al., 2020).

The categorical models used in Ekman and Friesen's (1971)' research are quite simple compared to the complexity in identifying emotions. However, they are still promising as they bring up cultural issues related to this representation. The authors identified 7 emotions namely "universal": neutral, anger, disgust, fear, happiness, sadness, and surprise. These emotional states could be recognized regardless of culture or geographic location. After their work, several other models such as Plutchik (2001) Wheel of Emotions were published, detailing or even expanding the number of primary and secondary emotions.

Considering that it is possible to identify and relate emotions in different ways, subjectivity becomes one of the main problems incategorical models. Another way to represent emotions is to identify and assign values to components in which emotions are made. The works of Russell (1980) propose to describe emotional experience in 2 dimensions. The valence measures how positive or negative an experience can be felt, and arousal measures how active the experience was.

4   Materials and Methods

This work is part of a larger and more complex project, which involves the acquisition of several types of signals, the production of its own database, the creation of an efficient hybrid model and the development of the application for the end user. In this document, however, 2 approaches regarding the recognition of emotions exclusively with audio signals will be presented. Data acquisition, pre-processing, extraction and features selection and classification are some steps present in this chapter. Each approach and its respective phases are illustrated in the diagram in Fig. 3 and Fig. 4, and will be explained in sequence.

In approach A, we represent the signals by Log-Mel Coefficients and use a convolutional network for classification. In approach B, the voice signals were converted to images, from which features were extracted using deep transfer learning methods. The base was balanced, and then we used the swarm particle optimization method to features selection. Finally, we implement classical algorithms for classifying emotions and analyzing the results.

4.1   Database Description

The RAVDESS (Ryerson Audio-Visual Database of Emotional Speech and Song) database originally contains 7356 files, totaling about 25 GB. It is divided into 3 different audiovisual modes: audio only, video only and audio-video.

For data collection, the researchers hired 24 professional actors from Toronto, Canada, aged between 21 and 33 years, there were 12 male and 12 female actors. Most of the actors were self-declared Caucasians and all had to have English as their first language. That was because for data collection a neutral North American accent was needed.

In this context, each actor performed twice by speaking the following expressions in English: ("Kids are talking by the door", "Dogs are sitting by the door"), followed by singing tests, accompanied by a piano, with predefined settings. For oral expression, eight feelings were chosen to be shown by the actors, such as: neutral, calm, joy, sadness, anger, fear, surprise and disgust, whereas for the melodies there were only six: neutral, calm, joy, sadness, anger and fear. It is noteworthy that the expressions were created in an induced way, aiming to get as close as possible to the desired emotion, so each actor used different techniques to achieve the result and, in the end, the expressions were recorded at 2 different levels of emotional intensity, normal and strong , with additional neutral expressions.

Still in the recording phase, the actors spent an average of 4 hours and were paid for that time. They all wore black shirts, had very little makeup, no jewelry, beards or accessories. In addition, all video recordings were made with a resolution 1920x1080 pixels with the camera facing the actor, without the arms or hands appearing in the recordings, while for voice recordings a microphone was used that was placed 20 cm in front of the actor.

For this work, we selected only the portion of audio files containing the 24 actors' speeches, each with 60 tracks, totaling 1440 .WAV files, with 48kHz and 16 bit.

Each of the files used were named according to 7 identifiers in the following order: Modality, Channel, Emotion, Intensity, Statement, Repetition and Actor, causing the file names to be formed with 7 2-digit numbers (ex. 02- 01-06-01-02-01-12.mp4 or .wav), the numbers corresponding to each identifier, described in Table 2 below.

Table 2: Description of RAVDESS filenames. The 7 identifier and respective codes.

Identifier	Coding description of factor levels
Modality	01 = Audio-video, 02 = Video-only, 03 = Audio-only
Channel	01 = Speech, 02 = Song
Emotion	01 = Neutral, 02 = Calm, 03 = Happy, 04 = Sad, 05 = Angry, 06 = Fear, 07 = Disgust, 08 = Surprised
Intensity	01 = Normal, 02 = Strong
Statement	01 = "Kids are talking by the door", 02 = "Dogs are sitting by the door"
Repetition	01 = First repetition, 02 = Second repetition
Actor	01 = First actor, ..., 24 = Twenty-fourth actor

As for the distribution of files among the 8 emotions, the database is unbalanced. Neutral emotion has half the audio files of other classes, as shown in Fig. 1 (Livingstone and Russo, 2018).

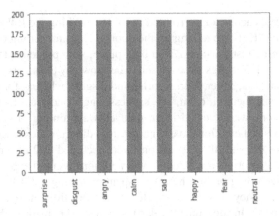

Figure 1: Distribution of classes in the RAVDESS Emotional Speech Audio base.

4.2   Approach A

In the first experiment, called Approach A, we used a classical method in the literature for recognizing emotions in audio signals. The diagram in Fig. 2 illustrates each of the steps in this experiment.

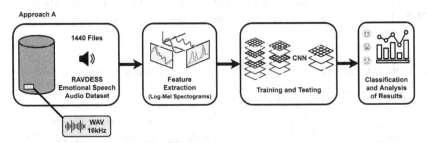

Figure 2: Diagram A: The RAVDESS Emotional Speech Audio Dataset was the input for approach A (Extracting the Log-Mel spectogram attribute of each audio signal; training and testing the CNN architecture; Classification and analysis of results).

Initially, we prepared the RAVDESS database extracting the Log-Mel spectrogram feature from each audio file. These data served as input to train and test a Convolution Neural Network (CNN). We chose this attribute and architecture for its popularity in well-recognized speech emotion classification models. Another purpose was to get initial parameters for comparison with future experiments.

In the Pre-processing step, we structure the data in their respective classes. Then we created a function to extract emotion labels from each file. Attribute extraction is important in modeling because it converts audio files into a format that can be understood by algorithms, generating a new database. After examining the wave graph of some audio signals, we extract the cepstral Mel Coefficients from each file.

4.2.1 Mel-Frequecy Coefficients

According to Han and Chan (2006), Mel's spectrogram is a parametric representation of the frequency spectrum of the audio signal. This attribute is one of the most common in applications that work on voice emotion recognition (Espinola et al., 2021a,b; Meghanani et al., 2021; Suhas et al., 2020). The spectrum of the signal is obtained through a Fourier transform of the signal in the time domain (Kui et al., 2021). The use of the Mel scale is very close to the human auditory system. Mainly because it is a scale with a non-linear behavior in the frequency domain.

4.2.2 CNN-Training and Testing

Regarding classification, the data generated from the feature extraction served as input for the training and testing of a Convolution Neural Network (CNN) (Barbosa et al., 2020; da Silva et al., 2020; dos Santos et al., 2019; Silva et al., 2019). We chose this architecture because it is a common and easy-to-implement model, according to the emotion classification literature.

The architecture used has 3 convolutional layers and an output layer. The input data was divided into the proportion of 75% for training and 25% for model testing. We performed this experiment in the Google Colab environment in Python language. We use libraries such as TensorFlow, NumPy and Scikit-learn, on an Intel i5 desktop with 8GB of RAM memory.

Regarding a convolutional neural network, we are talking about a specific type of deep architecture widely used in the classification of digital images (Mustaqeem and Kwon, 2020). CNNs are inspired by the biological and neural patterns of animals. Generally, compared to other image classification algorithms, CNNs require less pre-processing capacity. The lack of prior knowledge and independence of human support in the development of its basic functions are the biggest advantage for its application (Barbosa et al., 2020; da Silva et al., 2020; dos Santos et al., 2019; Haikel, 2021; Silva et al., 2019).

4.3 Approach B

In this approach, we used the Wavelet transform to describe the audio signals and a hybrid architecture to perform emotions recognition.

Different from the previous procedure, here we use the ResNet deep network to extract image features. The new generated base was then balanced and expanded with the SMOTE method. Then the experiment proceeded along 2 paths. Each one

with 1 ARFF file that served as the basis for the various classification models. The
first of these files was from the balancing step. The other went through an attribute
selection step by particle swarm optimization.

Figure 3 illustrates all the steps in this approach, which will be detailed below.

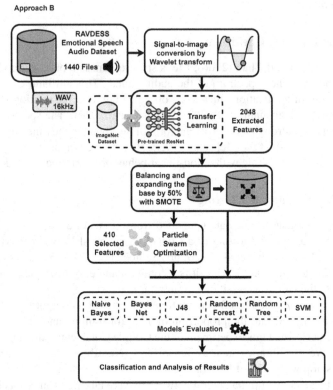

Figure 3: The RAVDESS database served as input to approach B using transfer learning:
Application of the wavelet transform; features extraction through the ResNet pre-trained
network; feature selection by PSO; models' valuation in different configurations; classification and analysis of results.

4.3.1 Signal to Image

Wavelet Transform is an effective tool for representing multi-resolution signals
since it provides both temporal and frequency information (Mallat, 1999). The result of this transformation was plotted as an image using pseudocolors in GNU/Octave
6.2.0 software (Eaton et al., 2015).

Figure 4 brings examples of the images created in this step for all 8 classes.

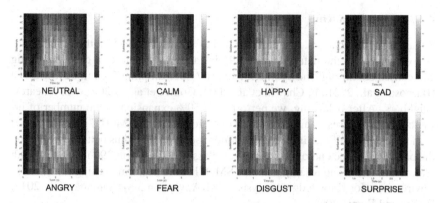

Figure 4: Examples of images created after Wavelet transform. Image of emotions Neutral, Calm, Happy, Sad, Angry, Fear, Disgust and Surprise.

4.3.2   Feature Extraction and Transfer Learning

Transfer Learning (TL) is a technique that allows you to transfer knowledge acquired in a given approach to solving problems in another context (Zhuang et al., 2020).

According to Liu et al. (2021), TL allows the absorption of knowledge in a vast data field (source domain) to be used in another field with insufficient data (destination domain). According to Pan and Yang (2009), TL is inspired by the fact that humans often intelligently reuse acquired knowledge. For us, previous solutions often serve as inspiration for solving new problems, faster and more creatively.

If we look from the perspective of educational psychology, transferring learning would be the result of the ability to generalize the experience (Ying et al., 2018; Zhuang et al., 2020). For this theory, it is necessary first of all to have some similarity between both activities. Otherwise, TL becomes unfeasible.

In short, traditional machine learning models and algorithms, in principle, start each task without any prior knowledge. Transfer learning techniques, on the other hand, transfer the knowledge acquired in known tasks to a target task in order to improve the performance of the models (Pan and Yang, 2009).

Knowing these benefits, for feature extraction we used tre Residual Networks (ResNet) pre-trained with ImageNet database (Deng et al., 2009; Targ et al., 2016). ResNet is a deep-learning network first proposed in 2015 by He et al. (2016) in an attempt to overcome optimization issues due to a vanishing gradient problem. Thus, this network used shortcut connections aiming to reduce the difficulty of training and test errors. In our approach we used the pre-trained ResNet configuration with 50 weighted layers, ReLu as the activation function and an average pooling. This pre-trained model may be used to learn patterns in other problems through transfer learning. Finally, the ResNet already trained for image classification was applied to the emotion recognition in voice signals represented by the generated images. This network extracted 2048 features for each instance of the 8 classes.

4.3.3   Class Balancing

Regarding to the classes, "Neutral" class has 96 instances while the others emotion categories in the database have 192 instances. Therefore, a class balancing was carried out through the Synthetic Minority Oversampling Technique (SMOTE) (Barbosa et al., 2021a,b; Chawla et al., 2002; Gomes et al., 2020a) with 3 nearest neighbors. After balancing, we performed a 50% expansion in the number of instances of all classes. This step was also performed with SMOTE and was added with the intention of making the dataset more populous and thus better representing the problem. At the end of this step, each class ended up with 290 instances. Both feature extraction and resampling with SMOTE were performed using the Waikato Environment for Knowledge Analysis (WEKA, version 3.8) (Santana et al., 2018; Witten and Frank, 2005).

4.3.4   Attribute Selection

In the context of machine learning and data mining, one of the biggest challenges is analyzing high-dimensional data (Zebari et al., 2020). In order to reduce this dimensionality, researchers usually select relevant and potentially useful features in databases (Gomes et al., 2021a).

Features selection is a simple but effective way to eliminate redundant and irrelevant data (El-Hasnony et al., 2020). By removing this data, we can improve learning accuracy, reduce training time and model complexity. These simplifications also facilitate the interpretation and understanding of the learning algorithm and/or data (Raj et al., 2020).

Knowing this, we use the Particle Swarm Optimization method (PSO) (Kennedy and Eberhart, 1995; Poli et al., 2007; Wang et al., 2007). PSO is a heuristic algorithm, that is, it finds an approximate solution when classical methods do not find an exact solution. This method was initially proposed in 1995 by Kennedy and Eberhart (1995). It is based on patterns in nature, where each particle would represent an individual in a population of birds. In this analogy, populations are modeled as dynamic systems with a global leader. In a hierarchical dynamic, the birds with the best performance are promoted to local leaders. Of these, the global leader leads the swarm and its local leaders with the aim of optimizing a certain behavior, guiding the general dynamics of the group.

In PSO, each individual is modeled using pairs of velocity and spatial position vectors. These vectors are constantly changing according to Equation 1 for velocity and Equation 2 for position. The system evolves in such a way that, along the process, local leaders can become simple members or a global leader.

$$v_{k+1} = wv_k + c_1 r_1 (p_{best_k} - x_k) + c_2 r_2 (g_{best} - x_k) \qquad (1)$$

$$x_{k+1} = x_k + v_k \qquad (2)$$

In the equations, for a swarm with K particles, w is the coefficient of inertia; p_{best_k} is the best known position of the k particle; g_{best} is the best position among all the particles; c_1 and c_2 are acceleration constants; r_1 and r_2 are random numbers between 0 and 1.

It is noteworthy that in the PSO, each individual represents a possible candidate for solving the problem of maximizing or minimizing an objective function. However, as the algorithm uses a population of randomly generated particles, there is no guarantee that an ideal solution will be found (Bratton and Kennedy, 2007; Kennedy and Eberhart, 1995).

This optimization and search algorithm has few parameters to be defined, which justifies its choice. In this experiment, we used 50 individuals and 50 interactions. In addition, we adopted the following settings: individual weight of 0.34, inertia weight of 0.33, mutation probability of 0.01, reporting frequency of 20, and social weight of 0.33.

Thus, the database generated during pre-processing had its number of features reduced from 2048 to 410 potentially more relevant features. This experimental step was performed using Weka software, version 3.8.

4.3.5   Model's Evaluation

In the next steps, we test six classification models with different configurations. We chose to work with Bayes Net, Naive Bayes, J48 Decision Tree, Random Tree, Random Forest and Support Vector Machines. More information about its parameters will be described below. At this stage, all these models were tested 30 times. Also, to avoid overfitting, we ran all tests with 10-time cross-validation and k-fold method.

Among the supervised methods, the support vector machine (SVM) is a probabilistic model used for both classification and regression. Created by Cortes and Vapnik (1995), this algorithm is used to identify patterns and solve complex problems with many variables. SVM works by identifying hyperplanes capable of separating different groups or classes in some database (Pal, 2005; Pham et al., 2019; Skariah et al., 2021). With changes to the kernel functions, we can find the ideal hyperplanes for each situation. Of these functions, the most common and also used in this chapter were the Linear Kernel, Polynomial ($d = 2$ and $d = 3$) and Radial Basis Function ($\gamma = 0.01$, 0.25 and 0.5). In Table 3 we visualize the respective functions and its formulas.

Random Forest (RF) and Random Tree are joint learning algorithms, also supervised, structured by hierarchically organized decision trees (Jackins et al., 2021; Pal, 2005). These trees are uncorrelated and trained for greater statistical validation. They then make predictions based on the most common generated results in

Table 3: Kernel functions used on SVM models.

Kernel type	Kernel function
Linear	$K(\mathbf{x}, \mathbf{y}) = \mathbf{x} \bullet \mathbf{y}$
Polynomial	$K(\mathbf{x}, \mathbf{y}) = (1 + \mathbf{x} \bullet \mathbf{y})^d$
Radial Basis Function (RBF)	$K(\mathbf{x}, \mathbf{y}) = \exp(-\gamma\,(\mathbf{x} - \mathbf{y}) \bullet (\mathbf{x} - \mathbf{y}))$

case of a classification problem. In case of regression or, the values found by the model are averaged.

Another important point of RF is its low computational cost in relation to its performance. Compared to deep learning methods with similar performance, RF is much simpler and easier to implement (Pavani et al., 2021). In this chapter we use RF with configurations of 10, 20, 30, 40, 50, 60, 70, 80, 90 and 100 trees.

Naive Bayes is one of the best known machine learning models. This probabilistic model is very fast, simple and efficient, even in predictions with multiple classes. It uses the Bayes theorem, created by Thomas Bayes, as a foundation and it does not consider correlations between features, but it can still have good results in databases that have their dependent features (Zhang, 2004).

BayesNet is also a probabilistic classification model, made up of numerous features. It is represented by graphs and it is possible to identify the influence of one feature on the occurrence of the others. This dependency is represented by probabilities, called conditional probability, which also uses Bayes theorem for the calculation. Furthermore, it is a supervised classifier and capable of making predictions with multiple classes (Ben-Gal, 2008).

The J48 classifier seeks to subset a chosen attribute until it repeats itself (a divided subset has a similar class). It labels each attribute with different classes, until it finds instances belonging to a common class, thus labeling the node. Depending on the chosen selection parameter, the best attribute will be obtained based on the calculated data (Saravana and Gayathri, 2018).

Table 4, below, summarizes all the classifiers used in this approach.

Table 4: Configuration of classifiers used in approach B.

Classifier	Parameters
Support Vector Machine	Linear Kernel Polynomial Kernel (P=2 and P=3) RBF Kernel ($\gamma = 0.01, 0.25$ and 0.5)
Random Forest	Trees: 10, 20, 30, 40, 50, 60, 70, 80 90, 100
Bayes Net	- -
Naive Bayes	- -
Random Tree	- -
J48	- -

4.3.6   Analysis of Results

In the metrics for analyzing the results with each classifier, we used the Accuracy, Area Under the ROC Curve, the Sensitivity and the Specificity. We represent each formula respectively in Table 5.

Accuracy is common in any neural network training, where you want to calculate the frequency of equal predictions (Espinola et al., 2021a,b; Gomes et al., 2020b).

Table 5: Mathematical Expressions for the Metrics used to evaluate the method. TP, TN, FP and FN are the quantity of True Positives, True Negatives, False Positives and False Negatives, respectively. TPR and FPR are the True Positive Rate and False Positive Rate, respectively.

Metric	Mathematical expression
Accuracy	$\frac{TP+TN}{TP+TN+FP+FN}$
Sensitivity	$\frac{TP}{TP+FN}$
Specificity	$\frac{TN}{TN+FP}$
Kappa	$\frac{(\rho_o-\rho_e)}{(1-\rho_e)}$
Area Under the ROC Curve	$AUC = \int TPR d(FPR)$

The Area Under the ROC Curve (Receiver operating characteristic), unlike the previous metric, evaluates all operating points of a model, through a Riemann sum for the area. It uses the height of values by the false positive rate. It is also widely used to assess the predictive performance of models (de Oliveira et al., 2020; Gomes et al., 2021b).

Sensitivity and Specificity take 4 variables (True/False and positives/negatives). Sensitivity measures the proportion of real positives. Specifity measures the proportion of real negatives (Gomes et al., 2021b).

In Table 5, ρ_o is the observed agreement rate, also called accuracy. The expected agreement rate is defined by ρ_e, in Equation 3

$$\rho_e = \frac{(TP+FP)(TP+FN)+(FN+TN)(FP+TN)}{(TP+FP+FN+TN)^2}. \qquad (3)$$

5   Results and Discussion

In this section we present the results found in Approach A and Approach B.

5.0.1   Results of Approach A

In the initial tests, we extracted the log-mel spectrogram of each emotion as an example for comparing this attribute. In Fig. 5 we see an example of a log-mel spectrogram extracted from a female audio of "Neutral" emotion, female of "Fear" and male of "Anger" emotion.

The initial model of CNN trained and validated in the proportion 75/25 with 40 epochs showed maximum accuracy of 61.3% in the training stage and 53.6% during validation. In Fig. 6 we see the evolution of accuracy over the epochs for the CNN training and testing stages.

Analyzing the graph in Fig. 6, we observe that from epochs 25 the model improves its performance during training, while showing a certain stability in the test accuracy. This means that the model is a better fit for the training set but is losing its ability to predict new data. In other words, it's a strong indication of overfitting.

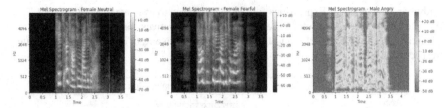

Figure 5: Example of images created by extracting the Log-Mel-Spectrogram attribute from emotions (A) Neutral-Female, (B) Fear-Female and (C) Anger-Male.

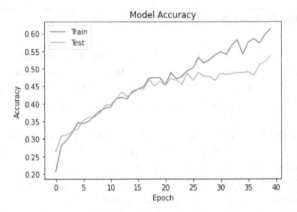

Figure 6: Evolution of Accuracy. CNN architecture training and testing steps in 40 epochs.

In Table 6 we present the Sensitivity, Specificity and Area accuracies under the ROC Curve of all emotions. The emotion anger (71%), calm (58%) and fear (57%) showed the best results. The happy emotion (44%) had the worst result of the 8, while for the others the model reached very similar values.

Table 6: Accuracy, sensitivity, specificity and area under the ROC curve for the eight emotions.

	Accuracy (%)	Sensitivity	Specificity	AUC
Angry	71.2 ± 2.4	0.62 ± 0.02	0.91 ± 0.03	0.74 ± 0.08
Calm	58.6 ± 3.6	0.69 ± 0.08	0.94 ± 0.07	0.77 ± 0.13
Disgust	52.0 ± 1.5	0.69 ± 0.06	0.89 ± 0.03	0.78 ± 0.07
Fear	$57.5 \pm 3, 1$	0.25 ± 0.14	0.98 ± 0.01	0.71 ± 0.11
Happy	44.5 ± 4.5	0.29 ± 0.22	0.94 ± 0.04	0.65 ± 0.09
Neutral	56.4 ± 0.8	0.83 ± 0.06	0.93 ± 0.06	0.84 ± 0.10
Sad	51.3 ± 3.0	0.42 ± 0.07	0.92 ± 0.05	0.59 ± 0.04
Surprise	45.4 ± 1.2	0.65 ± 0.21	0.92 ± 0.02	0.69 ± 0.11

Figure 7 shows the confusion matrix with the current and predicted values for the 8 classes. It confirms the values presented above and shows us how for some emotions the model is still quite inefficient.

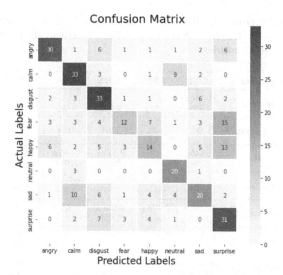

Figure 7: Results presented through the Confusion Matrix. The X (horizontal) axis of the matrix represents predicted emotions and the Y (vertical) axis represents the correct classification of actual emotions.

5.0.2   Results of Approach B

We observe all the results of approach B in Table 8 to the original base with all features, and in Table 9 the results for selected features with PSO. We measured the performance of each classifier using the Accuracy (ACC), Kappa Index (KPP), Sensitivity (SENS), Specificity (ESP) and Area Under the ROC Curve (AUC-ROC) metrics, with their respective means and standard deviations.

We also noticed some inconsistencies regarding the results of the Naive Bayes model. A possible cause would be the fact that the data are not so close to a Gaussian distribution. Data with this format tends to disfavor Baysean models.

From a thorough analysis of the average values found by all metrics, we distinguished between the best and worst models. Among these, we positively highlight the 0.5 gamma SVM RBF classifier. At the opposite extreme, the Bayes Net model presented the worst performance, with results about 60% lower than those obtained by the SVM classifier. Table 7 presents the detailed results between the best and worst classifiers.

Table 7: Results of models that performed better and worse.

	SVM RBF	Bayes Net
Accuracy (%)	81.184 ± 2.383	31.094 ± 2.716
Kappa Index	0.784 ± 0.027	0.212 ± 0.014
Sensitivity	0.926 ± 0.045	0.616 ± 0.090
Specificity	0.998 ± 0.004	0.831 ± 0.025
Area under the ROC Curve	0.972 ± 0.020	0.815 ± 0.037

Table 8: Results of Approach B, without PSO. Classifiers and results obtained for the Accuracy (ACC %), Kappa Index (KPP), Sensitivity (SENS), Specificity (ECP) and Area under the ROC Curve (A_ROC) metrics.

Classifier	ACC %	KPP	SENS	ESP	A_ROC
Bayes Net	31.094 ± 2.716	0.212 ± 0.013	0.616 ± 0.090	0.832 ± 0.023	0.815 ± 0.037
Naive Bayes	0	1	NaN	NaN	0.5
J 48	45.845 ± 3.184	0.381 ± 0.036	0.699 ± 0.091	0.945 ± 0.016	0.837 ± 0.043
Rdm Tree	40.423 ± 3.053	0.319 ± 0.348	0.626 ± 0.101	0.938 ± 0.017	0.782 ± 0.050
Rdm Forest_10	56.207 ± 3.129	0.499 ± 0.035	0.898 ± 0.056	0.922 ± 0.019	0.970 ± 0.016
Rdm Forest_20	64.149 ± 2.957	0.590 ± 0.033	0.933 ± 0.048	0.942 ± 0.017	0.985 ± 0.010
Rdm Forest_30	68.286 ± 2.964	0.637 ± 0.338	0.948 ± 0.040	0.950 ± 0.016	0.990 ± 0.007
Rdm Forest_40	70.436 ± 2.917	0.662 ± 0.033	0.954 ± 0.037	0.955 ± 0.015	0.991 ± 0.006
Rdm Forest_50	72.022 ± 2.894	0.680 ± 0.033	0.961 ± 0.036	0.957 ± 0.014	0.993 ± 0.006
Rdm Forest_60	72.910 ± 2.824	0.690 ± 0.032	0.962 ± 0.035	0.958 ± 0.013	0.993 ± 0.005
Rdm Forest_70	73.534 ± 2.877	0.697 ± 0.032	0.964 ± 0.034	0.959 ± 0.013	0.994 ± 0.005
Rdm Forest_80	74.163 ± 2.737	0.704 ± 0.031	0.966 ± 0.034	0.960 ± 0.014	0.994 ± 0.005
Rdm Forest_90	74.533 ± 2.726	0.708 ± 0.031	0.966 ± 0.032	0.960 ± 0.014	0.994 ± 0.004
Rdm Forest_100	74.912 ± 2.613	0.713 ± 0.029	0.968 ± 0.032	0.961 ± 0.013	0.995 ± 0.004
SVM POLY 1	75.040 ± 2.603	0.714 ± 0.029	0.952 ± 0.040	0.957 ± 0.013	0.981 ± 0.007
SVM POLY 2	76.948 ± 2.579	0.736 ± 0.029	0.952 ± 0.038	0.936 ± 0.012	0.985 ± 0.006
SVM POLY 3	78.737 ± 2.588	0.756 ± 0.029	0.957 ± 0.036	0.966 ± 0.012	0.986 ± 0.006
SVM RBF 0.01	50.994 ± 2.876	0.439 ± 0.032	0.849 ± 0.069	0.861 ± 0.021	0.907 ± 0.018
SVM RBF0.25	80.428 ± 2.460	0.776 ± 0.028	0.956 ± 0.037	0.986 ± 0.007	0.988 ± 0.009
SVM RBF 0.5	81.184 ± 2.383	0.784 ± 0.027	0.926 ± 0.045	0.997 ± 0.002	0.972 ± 0.020

Relatively faster models than the SVM, the Random Forest, more specifically the configuration with 100 trees, reached accuracies of $74.9 \pm 2.4\%$. About 6% less than the best models, however 40% higher than the worst classifiers. This result makes this Random Forest a still viable alternative if training time is a critical

Table 9: Results of Approach B, with features selection (PSO). Classifiers and results obtained for the Accuracy (ACC%), Kappa Index (KPP), Sensitivity (SENS), Specificity (ECP) and Area under the ROC Curve (A_ROC) metrics.

Classifier	ACC %	KPP	SENS	ESP	A_ROC
Bayes Net	30.57 ± 2.80	0.21 ± 0.03	0.60 ± 0.09	0.83 ± 0.02	0.81 ± 0.04
Naive Bayes	0	1	NaN	NaN	0.5
J 48	47.73 ± 3.33	0.36 ± 0.04	0.69 ± 0.09	0.94 ± 0.02	0.83 ± 0.05
Rdm Tree	40.91 ± 3.28	0.32 ± 0.04	0.63 ± 0.1	0.94 ± 0.02	0.78 ± 0.05
Rdm Forest_10	56.82 ± 3.04	0.51 ± 0.03	0.90 ± 0.06	0.92 ± 0.02	0.97 ± 0.02
Rdm Forest_20	64.44 ± 3.29	0.59 ± 0.04	0.93 ± 0.04	0.94 ± 0.02	0.98 ± 0.01
Rdm Forest_30	67.98 ± 3.02	0.63 ± 0.03	0.95 ± 0.04	0.95 ± 0.02	0.99 ± 0.01
Rdm Forest_40	70.12 ± 2.88	0.66 ± 0.03	0.95 ± 0.04	0.95 ± 0.01	0.99 ± 0.01
Rdm Forest_50	71.33 ± 2.92	0.67 ± 0.03	0.96 ± 0.04	0.95 ± 0.01	0.99 ± 0.01
Rdm Forest_60	72.22 ± 3.05	0.68 ± 0.03	0.96 ± 0.03	0.96 ± 0.01	0.99 ± 0.01
Rdm Forest_70	73.02 ± 2.91	0.69 ± 0.03	0.96 ± 0.04	0.96 ± 0.01	0.99 ± 0.01
Rdm Forest_80	73.59 ± 2.86	0.70 ± 0.03	0.96 ± 0.03	0.96 ± 0.01	0.99 ± 0.01
Rdm Forest_90	74.02 ± 2.82	0.70 ± 0.03	0.97 ± 0.03	0.96 ± 0.01	0.99 ± 0.01
Rdm Forest_100	74.36 ± 2.84	0.71 ± 0.03	0.97 ± 0.03	0.96 ± 0.01	0.99 ± 0.01
SVM POLY 1	67.39 ± 2.77	0.63 ± 0.03	0.92 ± 0.05	0.94 ± 0.02	0.97 ± 0.01
SVM POLY 2	72.12 ± 2.74	0.68 ± 0.03	0.93 ± 0.05	0.96 ± 0.01	0.98 ± 0.01
SVM POLY 3	74.96 ± 2.64	0.71 ± 0.03	0.94 ± 0.05	0.96 ± 0.01	0.98 ± 0.01
SVM RBF 0.01	40.08 ± 2.88	0.32 ± 0.03	0.77 ± 0.08	0.80 ± 0.03	0.85 ± 0.03
SVM RBF0.25	72.27 ± 2.73	0.68 ± 0.03	0.95 ± 0.04	0.95 ± 0.01	0.97 ± 0.01
SVM RBF 0.5	77.60 ± 2.56	0.74 ± 0.03	0.96 ± 0.04	0.97 ± 0.01	0.98 ± 0.01

factor in the process. We note, so, that if the goal is precision and processing speed, we must be cautious when considering only deep architectures. In view of the good performance achieved here by the simpler classifiers.

Regarding the features selection by Particle Swarm Optimization, it is possible to observe that the results were very similar to the approach without selection. This will raise promising discussions about using this method with deep networks.

Among the simplest models, we see that the J48 decision tree still had a small improvement in accuracy, when applied only to the best features. Bayes Net, Random Tree and Random Forests showed variations in the second or third decimal place. This reinforces the optimization obtained in these models, with the reduction from 2048 to 410 relevant features in the input data.

On the other hand on support vector machines we see a slight drop in metrics. This could be seen in all SVM configurations. The most pronounced difference reached 10% in the accuracy, in the configuration with kernel RBF of degree 0.01. This distinction between SVM with and without features selection had an impact on the best model found. The rbf 0.5 kernel SVM after PSO achieved 77.6% accuracy (a 4% drop over the same model without PSO).

6   Conclusion

This work proposes the development of deep and hybrid architecture models for emotion recognition in elderly people through speech analysis. Given the importance of the problem, the demand for solutions that help therapists and support the quality of life of the elderly is increasingly urgent. Thus, we hope that the models proposed here will bring the necessary benefits to the development of a simple and efficient human-machine interface.

The results so far are promising, mainly because it is a complex problem. The analysis of voice signals with the initial approach reached an average accuracy of 61.3% during the training phase and 53.6% during the tests. The neural network showed little generalization capacity, being unable to predict new data. We believe that this is mainly due to the scarcity of data by class in the database used. As observed in related works, similar models trained with more data variability, obtained much better results.

This problem, however, was worked around in the second approach. Even knowing that the ideal would be the collection of voice signals in elderly patients, the use of public databases together with Learning through Transfer created good prospects for the validation of the project. Wavelet pre-processing, followed by ResNet pre-training with a larger image bank, gave strength to the final classifiers. Even so, we cannot discard the hypothesis that better-tuned algorithms could achieve results higher than the 81% accuracy achieved by the SVM RBF Kernel 0.5.

The implementation of Particle Swarm Optimization brought good prospects for the development of an optimal model. The algorithm reduced the original base with 2048 features to a sub base with 410 most influential features. In addition to demonstrating the hyper-dimensionality created by some models of deep networks, the PSO appears as an alternative to simplifying the architecture. If, on the one hand, adding the PSO adds another step to the process, on the other hand, we greatly reduced its dimensionality. By improving the interpretation of both the data and the model, the selection of features also showed that for 16 of the 20 models tested, the classification performance remained practically the same.

In the future, it is intended to join other deep networks to the tests, combining them with larger and different databases. Finally, we suggest that this proposal be linked to a hybrid model, with analysis of voice, physiological and facial image signals. With this, we hope to achieve the goal of an architecture that is robust, lightweight and practical enough to be deployed in a human-machine interface that helps patients and therapists.

Acknowledgements

This study was financed in part by the Coordenação de Aperfeiçoamento de Pessoal de Nível Superior - Brazil (CAPES) - Finance Code 001, and by the Fundação de Amparo à Ciência e Tecnologia do Estado de Pernambuco (FACEPE), Brazil, under the code IBPG-0013-1.03/20.

Disclosure Statement

No potential conflict of interest was reported by the authors.

References

Barbosa, V.A.d.F., J.C. Gomes, M.A. de Santana, C.L. de Lima, R.B. Calado, C.R. Bertoldo Júnior, J.E.d.A. Albuquerque, R.G. de Souza, R.J.E. de Araújo, L.A.R. Mattos Júnior, R.E. de Souza and W.P. dos Santos. Covid-19 rapid test by combining a random forest-based web system and blood tests. Journal of Biomolecular Structure and Dynamics, pp. 1–20, 2021a.

Barbosa, V.A.d.F., J.C. Gomes, M.A. de Santana, E.d.A. Jeniffer, R.G. de Souza, R.E. de Souza and W.P. dos Santos. Heg.IA: An intelligent system to support diagnosis of Covid-19 based on blood tests. Research on Biomedical Engineering, pp. 1–18, 2021b.

Barbosa, V.A.F., M.A. Santana, M.K.S. Andrade, R.C.F. Lima and W.P. Santos. Deep-wavelet neural networks for breast cancer early diagnosis using mammary termographies. In: Das, H., C. Pradhan and N. Dey (eds.). Deep Learning for Data Analytics: Foundations, Biomedical Applications, and Challenges. Elsevier, London, 1st edition, 2020.

Ben-Gal, I. Bayesian networks. Encyclopedia of Statistics in Quality and Reliability, 1, 2008.

Bratton, D. and J. Kennedy. Defining a standard for particle swarm optimization. In 2007 IEEE Swarm Intelligence Symposium, pp. 120–127. IEEE, 2007.

Chawla, N.V., K.W. Bowyer, L.O. Hall and W.P. Kegelmeyer. Smote: Synthetic minority oversampling technique. Journal of Artificial Intelligence Research, 16: 321–357, 2002.

Cortes, C. and V. Vapnik. Support-vector networks. Machine Learning, 20(3): 273–297, 1995.

da Silva, I.R.R., G.d.S.L. e Silva, R.G. de Souza, M.A. de Santana, W.W.A. da Silva, M.E. de Lima, R.E. de Souza, R. Fagundes and W.P. dos Santos. Deep learning for early diagnosis of Alzheimers disease: A contribution and a brief review. pp. 63–78. In: Das, H., C. Pradhan and N. Dey (eds.). Deep Learning for Data Analytics: Foundations, Biomedical Applications, and Challenges. Elsevier, 2020.

Dantcheva, A., P. Bilinski, H.T. Nguyen, J.-C. Broutart and F. Bremond. Expression recognition for severely demented patients in music reminiscence-therapy. In 2017 25th European Signal Processing Conference (EUSIPCO), pp. 783–787, 2017.

de Oliveira, A.P.S., M.A. de Santana, M.K.S. Andrade, J.C. Gomes, M.C. Rodrigues and W.P. dos Santos. Early diagnosis of Parkinsons disease using EEG, machine learning and partial directed coherence. Research on Biomedical Engineering, 36(3): 311–331, 2020.

de Santana, M.A., J.C. Gomes, G.M. de Souza, A. Suarez, A.S. Torcate, F.S. Fonseca, G.M.M. Moreno and W.P. dos Santos. Reconhecimento automático de emoçoes a partir de sinais multimodais e inteligência artificial. Anais do IV Simpósio de Inovação em Engenharia Biomédica-SABIO, pp. 43, 2020.

de Souza, M.C., A.B. da Rocha Alves, D.S. de Lima, L.R.F.A. de Oliveira, J.K.B. da Silva, E.C. de Oliveira Ribeiro, M.E.S. Lopes, A.S. Aureliano, G.A. da Silva, I.D. de Oliveira, E.C. de Oliveira, J.J.C. do Nascimento, E.G.S. Araújo, W.A. Miranda, M.B.A. Bezerra, C.F. Siqueira, K.I.T. Lobo, M.F.B.L. Silva, L.M. dos Anjos, V.C. Lima and A.S. da Cunha. The treatment of Alzheimer in the context of musicotherapy. International Archives of Medicine, 10, 2017.

Deng, J., W. Dong, R. Socher, L.-J. Li, K. Li and L. Fei-Fei. Imagenet: A large-scale hierarchical image database. In 2009 IEEE Conference on Computer Vision and Pattern Recognition, pp. 248–255. IEEE, 2009.

Dornelles, V.J. and E.A. Corrêa. Atividade de lazer e novas tecnologias em pessoas com doença de Alzheimer. Revista MotriSaúde, 2(1), 2020.

dos Santos, M.M., A.G. da Silva Filho and W.P. dos Santos. Deep convolutional extreme learning machines: Filters combination and error model validation. Neurocomputing, 329: 359–369, 2019.

Eaton, J.W., D. Bateman, S. Hauberg and R. Wehbring. Gnu octave version 4.0. 0 manual: A high-level interactive language for numerical computations, 2015. URL http://www. gnu.org/software/octave/doc/interpreter, 8:13, 2015.

Ekman, P. and V. Friesen. Constants across cultures in the face and emotion. Journal of Personality and Social Psychology, pp. 124–129, 1971.

El-Hasnony, I.M., S.I. Barakat, M. Elhoseny and R.R. Mostafa. Improved feature selection model for big data analytics. IEEE Access, 8: 66989–67004, 2020.

Espinola, C.W., J.C. Gomes, J.M.S. Pereira and W.P. dos Santos. Detection of major depressive disorder using vocal acoustic analysis and machine learning an exploratory study. Research on Biomedical Engineering, 37(1): 53–64, 2021a.

Espinola, C.W., J.C. Gomes, J.M.S. Pereira and W.P. dos Santos. Vocal acoustic analysis and machine learning for the identification of schizophrenia. Research on Biomedical Engineering, 37(1): 33–46, 2021b.

Gomes, J.C., V.A.d.F. Barbosa, M.A. Santana, J. Bandeira, M.J.S. Valença, R.E. de Souza, A.M. Ismael and W.P. dos Santos. Ikonos: An intelligent tool to support diagnosis of Covid-19 by texture analysis of x-ray images. Research on Biomedical Engineering, 2020: 1–14, 2020a.

Gomes, J.C., L.H.d.S. Silva, J. Ferreira, A.A.F. Junior, A.L.d.S. Rocha, L. Castro, N.R.C. da Silva, B.J.T. Fernandes and W.P. dos Santos. Optimizing the molecular diagnosis of Covid-19 by combining RT-PCR and a pseudo-convolutional machine learning approach to characterize virus DNA sequences. BioRxiv, 2020b.

Gomes, J.C., V.A. de Freitas Barbosa, M.A. de Santana, C.L. de Lima, R.B. Calado, C.R.B. Junior, J.E. de Almeida Albuquerque, R.G. de Souza, R.J.E. de Araujo, G.M.M. Moreno, L.A.L. Soares, L.A.R. Mattos Júnior, R.E. de Souza and W.P. dos Santos. Rapid protocols to support covid-19 clinical diagnosis based on hematological parameters. MedRxiv, 2021a.

Gomes, J.C., A.I. Masood, L.H.d.S. Silva, J.R.B. da Cruz Ferreira, A.A.F. Júnior, A.L. dos Santos Rocha, L.C.P. de Oliveira, N.R.C. da Silva, B.J.T. Fernandes and W.P. Dos Santos. Covid-19 diagnosis by combining rt-pcr and pseudo-convolutional machines to characterize virus sequences. Scientific Reports, 11(1): 1–28, 2021b.

Haikel, A. Cnn ensemble approach to detect covid-19 from computed tomography chest images. Computers, Materials, & Continua, pp. 3581–3599, 2021.

Hamsa, S., I. Shahin, Y. Iraqi and N. Werghi. Emotion recognition from speech using wavelet packet transform cochlear filter bank and random forest classifier. IEEE Access, 8: 96994–97006, 2020.

Han, J., Z. Zhang, N. Cummins and B. Schuller. Adversarial training in affective computing and sentiment analysis: Recent advances and perspectives [review article]. IEEE Computational Intelligence Magazine, 14(2): 68–81, 2019.

Han, W. and C. Chan. An efficient MFCC extraction method in speech recognition. International Symposium on Circuits and Systems, 2006.

He, K., X. Zhang, S. Ren and J. Sun. Deep residual learning for image recognition. In Proceedings of the IEEE Conference on Computer Vision and Pattern Recognition, pp. 770–778, 2016.

Iancu, I. and B. Iancu. Elderly in the digital era theoretical perspectives on assistive technologies. Technologies, 5(3): 60, 2017.

Issa, D., M.F. Demirci and A. Yazici. Speech emotion recognition with deep convolutional neural networks. Biomedical Signal Processing and Control, 59: 101894, 2020.

Izard, C.E. Human Emotions. New York: Springer, 1977.

Jackins, V., S. Vimal, M. Kaliappan and M.Y. Lee. Ai-based smart prediction of clinical disease using random forest classifier and naive bayes. The Journal of Supercomputing, 77(5): 5198–5219, 2021.

Kennedy, J. and R. Eberhart. Particle swarm optimization. In Proceedings of ICNN'95-International Conference on Neural Networks, volume 4, pp. 1942–1948. IEEE, 1995.

Kremer, S. and L. den Uijl. Studying emotions in the elderly. In Emotion measurement, pp. 537–571. Elsevier, 2016.

Kui, H., J. Pan, R. Zong, H. Yang and W. Wang. Heart sound classification based on log mel-frequency spectral coefficients features and convolutional neural networks. Biomedical Signal Processing and Control, 69: 102893, 2021.

Lagacé, M., A. Tanguay, M.-L. Lavallée, J. Laplante and S. Robichaud. The silent impact of ageist communication in long term care facilities: Elders' perspectives on quality of life and coping strategies. Journal of Aging Studies, 26(3): 335–342, 2012.

Le, D. and E.M. Provost. Emotion recognition from spontaneous speech using hidden markov models with deep belief networks. IEEE Workshop on Automatic Speech Recognition and Understanding, pp. 216–221, 2013.

Liu, J., Q. Zhang, X. Li, G. Li, Z. Liu, Y. Xie, K. Li and B. Liu. Transfer learning-based strategies for fault diagnosis in building energy systems. Energy and Buildings, 250: 111256, 2021.

Livingstone, S.R. and F.A. Russo. The ryerson audio-visual database of emotional speech and song (ravdess): A dynamic, multimodal set of facial and vocal expressions in North American english. PloS One, 13(5): e0196391, 2018.

Livingstone, S.R., K. Peck and F.A. Russo. Ravdess: The ryerson audio-visual database of emotional speech and song. In Annual Meeting of the Canadian Society for Brain, Behaviour and Cognitive Science, pp. 205–211, 2012.

Lopes, N., A. Silva, S.R. Khanal, A. Reis, J. Barroso, V. Filipe and J. Sampaio. Facial emotion recognition in the elderly using a svm classifier. In 2018 2nd International Conference on Technology and Innovation in Sports, Health and Wellbeing (TISHW), pp. 1–5. IEEE, 2018.

Ma, K., X. Wang, X. Yang, M. Zhang, J.M. Girard and L.-P. Morency. Elderreact: A multimodal dataset for recognizing emotional response in aging adults. In 2019 International Conference on Multimodal Interaction, pp. 349–357, 2019.

Mallat, S. A Wavelet Tour of Signal Processing. Elsevier, 1999.

Meghanani, A., C. Anoop and A. Ramakrishnan. An exploration of log-mel spectrogram and MFCC features for Alzheimers dementia recognition from spontaneous speech. In 2021 IEEE Spoken Language Technology Workshop (SLT), pp. 670–677. IEEE, 2021.

Mortensen, L., A.S. Meyer and G.W. Humphreys. Age-related effects on speech production: A review. Language and Cognitive Processes, 21(1-3): 238–290, 2006.

Mustaqeem, M. and S. Kwon. A cnn-assisted enhanced audio signal processing for speech emotion recognition. Sensors, 20(1): 183, 2020.

Oliveira, A.S. Transição demográfica, transição epidemiológica e envelhecimento populacional no brasil. Hygeia-Revista Brasileira de Geografia Médica e da Saúde, 15(32): 69–79, 2019.

Özseven, T. Investigation of the effect of spectrogram images and different texture analysis methods on speech emotion recognition. Applied Acoustics, 142: 70–77, 2018.

Pal, M. Random forest classifier for remote sensing classification. International Journal of Remote Sensing, 26(1): 217–222, 2005.

Pan, S.J. and Q. Yang. A survey on transfer learning. IEEE Transactions on Knowledge and Data Engineering, 22(10): 1345–1359, 2009.

Pavani, G., B. Biswal and P. Biswal. Robust classification of neovascularization using random forest classifier via convoluted vascular network. Biomedical Signal Processing and Control, 66: 102420, 2021. ISSN 1746-8094. URL https://www.sciencedirect.com/science/article/pii/S1746809421000173.

Pereira, I.V.d.S.T. Uma representação geral da fala para reconhecimento de emoção com uma rede semi-supervisionada utilizando gan. Master's thesis, University of Pernambuco, 2018.

Pham, B.T., I. Prakash, K. Khosravi, K. Chapi, P.T. Trinh, T.Q. Ngo, S.V. Hosseini and D.T. Bui. A comparison of support vector machines and Bayesian algorithms for landslide susceptibility modelling. Geocarto International, 34(13): 1385–1407, 2019.

Plutchik, R. The nature of emotions: Human emotions have deep evolutionary roots, a fact that may explain their complexity and provide tools for clinical practice. American Scientist, 89(4): 344–350, 2001.

Poli, R., J. Kennedy and T. Blackwell. Particle swarm optimization. Swarm Intelligence, 1(1): 33–57, 2007.

Raj, R.J.S., S.J. Shobana, I.V. Pustokhina, D.A. Pustokhin, D. Gupta and K. Shankar. Optimal feature selection-based medical image classification using deep learning model in internet of medical things. IEEE Access, 8: 58006–58017, 2020.

Russell, J.A. A circumplex model of affect. Journal of Personality and Social Psychology, 39(6): 1161, 1980.

Santana, M.A.d., J.M.S. Pereira, F.L.d. Silva, N.M.d. Lima, F.N.d. Sousa, G.M.S.d. Arruda, R.d.C.F.d. Lima, W.W.A. d. Silva and W.P.d. Santos. Breast cancer diagnosis based on mammary thermography and extreme learning machines. Research on Biomedical Engineering, 34: 45–53, 01 2018. ISSN 2446-4740.

Saravana, N. and D.V. Gayathri. Performance and classification evaluation of j48 algorithm and kendalls based j48 algorithm (knj48). Int. J. Comput. Trends Technol. (IJCTT)–Volume, 59, 2018.

Silva, I.R., G.S. Silva, R.G. de Souza, W.P. dos Santos and A.d.A. Roberta. Model based on deep feature extraction for diagnosis of alzheimers disease. In 2019 International Joint Conference on Neural Networks (IJCNN), pp. 1–7. IEEE, 2019.

Skariah, A., R. Pradeep, R. Rejith and C. Bijudas. Health monitoring of rolling element bearings using improved wavelet cross spectrum technique and support vector machines. Tribology International, 154: 106650, 2021.

Suhas, B., J. Mallela, A. Illa, B. Yamini, N. Atchayaram, R. Yadav, D. Gope and P. K. Ghosh. Speech task based automatic classification of als and parkinsons disease and their severity using log mel spectrograms. In 2020 international conference on signal processing and communications (SPCOM), pp. 1–5. IEEE, 2020.

Targ, S., D. Almeida and K. Lyman. Resnet in resnet: Generalizing residual architectures. arXivpreprint arXiv:1603.08029, 2016.

Torcate, A.S., M.A. de Santana, G.M.M. Moreno, A. Suarez, J.C. Gomes, W.P. dos Santos, F.S. Fonseca and G.M. de Souza. Intervenções e impactos da musicoterapia no contexto da doença de alzheimer: Uma revisão de literatura sob a perspectiva da computação afetiva. Anais do IV Simpósio de Inovação em Engenharia Biomédica-SABIO 2020, pp. 31, 2020.

Vipperla, R. Automatic speech recognition for ageing voices. Master's thesis, The University of Edinburgh, 2011.

Wang, X., J. Yang, X. Teng, W. Xia and R. Jensen. Feature selection based on rough sets and particle swarm optimization. Pattern Recognition Letters, 28(4): 459–471, 2007.

Wei, P. and Y. Zhao. A novel speech emotion recognition algorithm based on wavelet kernel sparse classifier in stacked deep auto-encoder model. Personal and Ubiquitous Computing, 23(3): 521–529, 2019.

Witten, I.H. and E. Frank. Data mining: Practical machine learning tools and techniques with java implementations. Acm Sigmod Record, 31(1): 76–77, 2002.

Witten, I.H. and E. Frank. Data Mining: Pratical Machine Learning Tools and Technique. Morgan Kaufmann Publishers, San Francisco, CA, USA, 2005.

Yang, Q., Y. Zhang, W. Dai and S.J. Pan. Transfer Learning. Cambridge University Press, 2020.

Ying, W., Y. Zhang, J. Huang and Q. Yang. Transfer learning via learning to transfer. In International Conference on Machine Learning, pp. 5085–5094. PMLR, 2018.

Zebari, R., A. Abdulazeez, D. Zeebaree, D. Zebari and J. Saeed. A comprehensive review of dimensionality reduction techniques for feature selection and feature extraction. Journal of Applied Science and Technology Trends, 1(2): 56–70, 2020.

Zhang, H. The optimality of naive bayes. AA, 1(2): 3, 2004.

Zhuang, F., Z. Qi, K. Duan, D. Xi, Y. Zhu, H. Zhu, H. Xiong and Q. He. A comprehensive survey on transfer learning. Proceedings of the IEEE, 109(1): 43–76, 2020.

Zilidis, G. and V. Zilidou. The use of new technologies addressing social exclusion and improving the quality of life of the elderly. Interscientific Health Care, 10(4), 2018.

Chapter 6

Recognition of Emotions in the Elderly through Facial Expressions: A Machine Learning-Based Approach

Arianne Sarmento Torcate,[1] Maíra Araújo Santana,[1] Juliana Carneiro Gomes,[1] Ingrid Bruno Nunes,[1] Flávio Secco Fonseca,[1] Gisele M.M. Moreno[2] and Wellington Pinheiro dos Santos[1,3,]*

1 Introduction

An aging population is a global phenomenon that has been growing steadily in recent years. About half of the current population of elderly people over 75 years old suffers from physical and/or mental disabilities, with dementia being one of the major challenges affecting the quality of life of the elderly and also of their caregivers (Dantcheva et al., 2017). It is important to clarify that along with the aging process, changes in perception and cognition can damage the recognition of facial emotions (Ferreira and Torro-Alves, 2016). Ochi and Midorikawa (2021) emphasize that in the literature the relationship between emotion recognition and cogni-

[1] Polytechnic School of the University of Pernambuco, Recife, Brazil.
[2] Institute of Astronomy, Geophysics and Atmospheric Sciences, University of São Paulo, São Paulo, Brazil.
[3] Department of Biomedical Engineering, Federal University of Pernambuco, Recife, Brazil.
* Corresponding author: wellington.santos@ufpe.br

tive function during aging is still unclear. However, works in the literature (Ferreira and Torro-Alves, 2016; Grondhuis et al., 2021; Ko et al., 2021) highlight at least four possible causes: (i) impairment of brain structures responsible for processing emotions; (ii) issues related to the natural aging process, such as wrinkles and folds that mask the emotion displayed, thus making the process of interpreting emotions difficult; (iii) the socio-emotional selectivity theory, which states that the elderly would have greater preservation in the recognition of positive emotions; and, finally, (iv) atrophy of the facial skeleton, loss of soft tissue and poor muscle positioning.

Basic emotions can be understood as involuntary physiological responses shared by human beings, visually distinguishable and shaped by lifelong experiences (Bomfim et al., 2019). Therefore, the ability to express and recognize emotions through facial expressions is considered a fundamental stage of basic communication (Ko et al., 2021) and an essential skill to get along in society (Bomfim et al., 2019). Not being able to express emotions such as anger, sadness or disgust can result in social isolation (Grondhuis et al., 2021) or negatively affect non-verbal communication. In this sense, by decreasing the ability to express emotions, older people may have difficulty communicating important messages such as discomfort associated with treatments and others complications.

With this problem in mind, technology has become a strong ally to increase the quality of life of the elderly (Dornelles and Corrêa, 2020), whether they have any cognitive impairment or not. Although the technological barrier is still a very present point in older generations, current devices and software have broken paradigms and have been adapted to achieve this audience (Zilidis and Zilidou, 2018). Basically, what we have is a context in which the increase in life expectancy generates more demands for assistance, care and trained professionals, which are required for longer and longer periods of time. These very specific health resources become unfeasible when we talk about large-scale policies. Iancu and Iancu (2017) state that assistive technologies are the only solution for this problem. In addition to supporting possible responses to health, assistive technologies seek to integrate these elderly people in a society that is sometimes distant and in which isolation has become not only social but also digital.

It is in this digitalized world that Affective Computing emerges. Uniting Psychology, Cognitive Sciences and Computer Science. This research area seeks to integrate the human emotional side to machines. Either through the recognition of emotions (Han et al., 2019) or even in the development of devices and studies that deal with the human aspect. It is precisely from the perspective of affective computing that we will conduct this work.

The main objective of this research is to investigate different machine learning approaches for the recognition of emotions in the elderly. In all, two experiments were carried out using the FER2013 database (Goodfellow et al., 2013). Basically, in experiment 1, in an earlier study, we developed a Convolutional Neural Network (CNN or ConvNet) for classification of emotions and applied the Haar-cascade Frontal Face (Viola and Jones, 2001) to detect the face in static images of elderly people. In the second experiment, using Transfer Learning, we applied a LeNet network to extract the attributes. Then, in order to balance the classes, we apply the Synthetic Minority Oversampling Technique (SMOTE) method. After that, we performed a selection of attributes using Particle Swarm Optmization (PSO). Finally, we use the Random Forest algorithm with different tree configurations for the classification step.

This chapter is structured as follows: in addition to the Introduction, Section 2 with its respective subsections present important theoretical references for understanding the present research topic. In Section 3 related works are reported. Section 4 presents the methodological approach adopted to carry out the experiments. Section 5 describes the results obtained in detail. Finally, in Section 6 we highlight the final considerations, as well as the perspectives for future work.

2 Background

This section presents the main theoretical references that support the realization and understanding of this research. Thus, in Subsection 2.1 we briefly talk about aging, cognitive deficits and dementias. In Subsection 2.2 we conceptualize emotions and their importance for any human being. Subsection 2.3 presents the field of study of Affective Computing. In Subsection 2.4 we bring an explanation about the recognition of emotions and make a specific topic for facial expressions in Subsection 2.4.1. Finally, in order to logically limit the theoretical framework to the scope of this study, we end with Subsection 2.5, where we present a discussion on the recognition of emotions in the elderly through facial expressions.

2.1 Aging, Cognitive Deficits and Dementias

According to the WHO (2018), the number of people aged 60 years or more in the population is gradually increasing, where projections for 2030 indicate that there will be 1.4 billion elderly people and in 2050 it will reach 2.1 billion. There are those who see this milestone from two perspectives. The first of them we can understand based on Tavares et al. (2017) explanation, where the authors point out that being able to achieve this longevity is a success for humanity since the elderly can contribute to society through knowledge, skills and experiences. On the other hand, the second perspective exposed by Rudnicka et al. (2020) states that population aging is the most important medical and social demographic problem in the world. The WHO (2021) emphasizes that it is necessary to deconstruct these ideas and attitudes related to age, as it can lead to discrimination and directly affect the way the elderly and society face aging.

According to Hayashi et al. (2021), as a result of the aging process, people have cognitive, biological and psychological changes. Where about half of the current elderly population over 75 years old suffers from physical and/or mental disabilities, with dementia being one of the great challenges that affects the quality of life of the elderly and their caregivers (Dantcheva et al., 2017). Cognitive deficit can be understood as the difficulty the brain has to learn, concentrate and remember, but it does not change the elderly's quality of life (Hayashi et al., 2021). Dementia, on the other hand, is characterized by a gradual impairment of cognitive function that interferes with social and professional activities (de Sousa Silva et al., 2021), causing damage to the quality of life of the elderly and their families.

Alzheimer's Disease (AD) is the most common form of dementia (Dantcheva et al., 2017; Guo et al., 2020; Reale et al., 2020; Torcate et al., 2020), affecting 47 million people worldwide (Cavalli et al., 2020). In addition to AD, Vascular, Parkinson, Senile, frontotemporal and other dementia also stand out. The WHO (2018) clarifies that current trends, such as technology, should be used to devise strategies aimed to promote health and quality of life of the elderly population. For example, games are already being used to motivate elderly people to practice physical exercise, contributing to their motivation and engagement (Crespo et al., 2016). Virtual Reality (VR) applications are already being used to assist in the rehabilitation of stroke survivors (Cameirão et al., 2017) and personalized therapies based on social robotics (Agres et al., 2021) are also being applied. Based on this, several approaches and contributions have emerged in the field of Artificial Intelligence, mainly focusing on the Affective Computing sub-area.

2.2   Emotions

Although it seems simple, defining what emotions are is complex, as this term is often used in everyday life (Paxiuba and Lima, 2020). Bomfim et al. (2019) states that basic emotions can be understood as involuntary physiological responses, which are visually distinguishable and also molded according to our life experiences. The research carried out by Madeira (2011) explains that emotion is not a single variable or entity that can be easily identified, but it is a process that has distinct elements that can be related, such as sensations, facial expressions, body movement, voice, breathing, and heart rate (de Oliveira and Jaques, 2013).

In this context, emotions can be understood as one of the most important and fundamental daily experiences for the regulation of social interaction and interpersonal functioning (Ferreira and Torro-Alves, 2016), in addition to directly guiding our choices, preferences and decision-making (Chaturvedi et al., 2021), being the basis for our motivation and essential for verbal and non-verbal communication (Dorneles et al., 2020; Marosi-Holczberger et al., 2012).

There are at least two ways to classify emotions, which is through (i) Discrete (or categorical) Model and (ii) Two-Dimensional Model (de Santana et al., 2020). In the Discrete Model, emotional states are represented and can be categorized by six basic emotions, which are: Sadness, Joy, Disgust, Anger, Fear and Surprise (Bomfim et al., 2019; de Oliveira and Jaques, 2013; Han et al., 2021; Khateeb et al., 2021). On the other hand, the Two-Dimensional Model is based on two main categories, which are: Valence and Excitement. The valence dimension represents the degree of likeability or dislike of a signal and is usually measured on a continuous scale ranging from positive (nice) to negative (unpleasant) (Bhattacharya et al., 2021). While the Excitement dimension measures the degree of intensity of an emotional state (Han et al., 2021). The Fig. 1 below illustrates the two-dimensional model, considering valence and excitation.

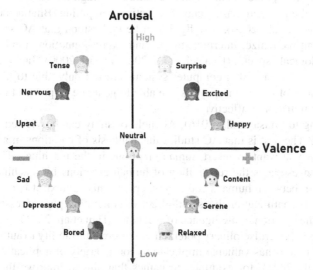

Figure 1: Two-Dimensional Model, also known as Circumplex Model of Affect, proposed by Russell (1980). The representation of the emotions happiness and sadness are located oppositely in two-dimensional space. Neutral emotion represents an intermediate state, that is, the subject does not feel a preominance of valence or manifestation of affective state.

It is important to emphasize that each emotion has a particular definition, characteristic, facial expression and peculiar way of manifesting itself in each individual. Finally, emotions can be understood as brief psychophysiological phenomena, which are adaptive in relation to environmental changes. Therefore, they prepare the organism to act and respond to stimuli (Madeira, 2011). Knowing that emotions are brief, involuntary and with different physiological patterns, there are several methods to recognize the transmitted emotion (Okada, 2018). Moreover, according to Marosi-Holczberger et al. (2012), it is precisely because there are more and more different methods for recognizing emotions that this field of research is constantly growing.

2.3   Affective Computing

It is known that emotions play a vital role in our daily life activities, influencing communication and personal and social development of any individual (Khateeb et al., 2021). The subarea of Artificial Intelligence that studies emotion is called Affective Computing (AC) (Paxiuba and Lima, 2020). Nalepa et al. (2019) explains that the term "Affective Computing" was proposed by Rosalind Picard, in 1997. And, it is an interdisciplinary field of study with other areas of knowledge (such as Biomedical Engineering, Psychology, Computer Science and others) and that it

seeks to develop computational models and emotion recognition methods in order
to improve human-computer interaction (HCI).

For a long time, recognizing human emotions through the computer has been
one of the challenges and main focus of Affective Computing (Bhattacharya et al.,
2021; de Sousa et al., 2020). Briefly, it can be understood that AC studies how
computers can recognize, interpret, model and express emotions (and other human psychological aspects) (Khateeb et al., 2021; Picard, 2000). Tan et al. (2021)
explains that the idea is that computer systems are not only able to identify the
emotional states of users, but may also be able to generate responses that humans
perceive as emotional or affective.

According to Sousa et al. (2016), AC field of study can be viewed from two
perspectives. The first is that AC studies the synthesis of emotions in a machine,
that is, when you want to insert human emotions in the machine. The second
perspective investigates the recognition of human emotions by machines during
the interaction between humans and computers. In this context, it is important to
emphasize that sentiment analysis and affective computing play an essential role
in enabling the emotional intelligence of machines (Han et al., 2021).

Knowing the interdisciplinary potential of this area, the ability to automatically
recognize emotions has valuable implications for a variety of applications (Bhattacharya et al., 2021), for example, in games that aim to improve the user experience (Setiono et al., 2021), on education (Jaques et al., 2012), in analyzing
language-based emotions to measure consumer satisfaction (Ren and Quan, 2012),
stress detection to improve the health of individuals (Greene et al., 2016), and
Emotion analysis of customer telephone complaints (Gong et al., 2015).

2.4   Emotion Recognition

Considering that AC seeks to make the emotion existing in communication between people also present in the interaction between humans and computers, one
of the main objectives is to investigate the recognition of emotions. Therefore,
emotions recognition can be defined as a process of automatic perception of human affection (Han et al., 2021). Abdullah et al. (2021) add that the recognition of
emotions is a dynamic process that aims to identify the emotional state of individuals, where the emotions corresponding to each person's actions are different.

However, for emotion recognition to happen, human data must be collected. It
is worth mentioning that there are several ways for a person to express/communicate
their emotions, which can be either verbal or non-verbal (Abdullah et al., 2021;
de Oliveira and Jaques, 2013). According to González and McMullen (2020),
data can originate from different sources, such as Galvanic Skin Response (GSR),
Facial Expressions, Electroencephalographic (EEG) signals, tone of voice, electro-
cardiograms (ECG), Eye Tracker and others. The authors also clarify that each data
source has specific methodologies and application contexts. For example, the EEG
is most commonly used to provide insights into emotions, while skin conductance
is known to be the most reliable source for assessing stress and arousal.

It is important to highlight that collecting spontaneous data related to emotions is a challenging task due to the duration of emotions, which are usually brief. Knowing this, in research environments it is necessary to place the individual in situations where emotions are aroused/stimulated by using odors (Meska et al., 2020), visual or auditory stimuli, which can be images, videos or music (Vicencio-Martínez et al., 2019) and others. In the literature, it is pointed out that the recognition of emotions can be performed in two ways. The first is unimodal, that is, using only one data source, such as voice (Leão et al., 2012). The second way is multimodal, using combined data sources, such as voice and GSR (de Oliveira and Jaques, 2013; Han et al., 2021).

2.4.1 Facial Expressions

Facial expressions are considered one of the most powerful, immediate and natural ways for human beings to communicate their emotions and intentions (de Sousa et al., 2020). Namba et al. (2021) explain that facial expressions can be understood as affective signals that convey social information about an individual's experience of an emotional event. The ability to recognize and express emotions through the face is a fundamental stage of basic communication (Ko et al., 2021) and an important social skill (Grondhuis et al., 2021).

Tian et al. (2005) reinforce that facial expressions are facial changes in response to a internal emotional states or social communications. Moreover, Ferreira et al. (2013) highlights seven universally recognized facial expressions of emotions, which can be identified as: Disgust, Surprise, Fear, Anger, Happy, Sadness and Contempt (Fig. 2).

Disgusted Surprise   Fear   Anger   Happy   Sadness   Contempt

Figure 2: Images from the FER2013 (Goodfellow et al., 2013) database to illustrate the seven universally recognized facial expressions of emotions.

In the research carried out by Ferreira et al. (2013), two important scales are presented to understand the intensity of emotions in facial expressions. The first is the Intensity Scale, which basically defines the muscular contraction of an expression that starts in the neutral state until the peak emotion, that is, maximum expression of the emotion. The authors present an example adopted by Ekman et al. (2002), which divides the scale into five categories, as shown in Fig. 3, where A means the degree of intensity of the traits, B is the minimum, C means marked/pronounced, D is severe/extreme and E means the maximum.

The second scale presented by Ferreira et al. (2013) it called the energy scale, created by Trnka and Stuchlíková (2011). Such as may be seen in Fig. 4, the

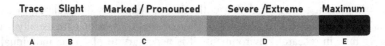

A   B   C   D   E

Figure 3: The Intensity Scale measures in five categories the intensity of facial features to express emotions, ranging from the lowest degree (A), which is when the emotion starts in the neutral state, to the maximum degree (E), which represents when the face reached the peak of the desired emotion (Ekman et al., 2002; Ferreira et al., 2013).

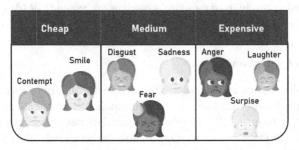

Figure 4: The Energy Scale illustrates and organizes the emotions facials on a scale of Low, Medium and High, highlighting which of them are they emotions most need energy to manifest, as well as those that need it least (Ferreira et al., 2013; Trnka and Stuchlíková, 2011).

authors created three intensities, corresponding to Little, Medium and Very, where emotions are organized in order, from those that need less energy to those that need more energy to manifest.

Finally, it is worth noting that the recognition of emotional facial expressions is directly related to non-verbal social behavior and the adaptation of human beings to different contexts (Nozima et al., 2018). Recognizing emotions through the face consists of identifying patterns of facial features, such as the shape of the mouth, face, distance between eyes and others (de Sousa et al., 2020).

2.5   Recognition of Emotions in the Elderly through Facial Expressions

As already mentioned, recognizing emotional facial expression is an important social skill (Grondhuis et al., 2021). However, the ability to express and recognize emotions through facial expressions changes with age (Ko et al., 2021), especially with old age. Chuang et al. (2021) explain that facial recognition of emotions is one of the essential components of social cognition, being crucial for people to be able to recognize and express emotions (Ochi and Midorikawa, 2021). Ma et al. (2019) clarify that most of the research that covers automatic recognition of emotions is focused on adults and, to a lesser extent, the elderly, even though these are a significant part of the population and that it is constantly growing.

Studies in the literature (Fölster et al., 2014; Grondhuis et al., 2021; Ko et al., 2021) list possible causes of natural changes related to aging that contribute to elderly people having difficulties to express and recognize emotions through the face, such as (i) wrinkles, folds and wear of facial muscles (Fölster et al., 2014; Grondhuis et al., 2021) and (ii) atrophy of the facial skeleton, loss of soft tissue and poor muscle positioning (Ko et al., 2021). These changes contribute for the elderly to have a decline in the recognition/perception of emotions, especially low intensity negative ones (Ferreira and Torro-Alves, 2016), such as Fear, Anger and Sadness (Ko et al., 2021; Micillo et al., 2021).

Elderly people who have Alzheimer's Disease (AD) (Ladislau et al., 2015), Parkinson's (Nozima et al., 2018), Depression (Bomfim et al., 2019) and others diseases also have compromised brain structures that make up the system responsible for processing emotions, which results in damage to the recognition of emotional expressions on the face. In addition, the poor performance in recognizing the emotional facial expression of these elderly people is related to the progression of the disease.

In this scenario, Dantcheva et al. (2017) emphasizes that the recognition of emotions in the elderly through facial expressions is essential, as they have lost their cognitive and verbal communication skills, having difficulties in communicating important messages, such as pain, discomfort associated with treatments and other complications. For example, not being able to signal negative emotions such as anger, sadness and fear can reduce the quality of interpersonal communication (Grondhuis et al., 2021) and even put their own physical integrity at risk, as they are not able to signal risky situations.

As technology has become a strong ally to assist in the treatment of elderly patients with dementia or not, helping them to have a better quality of life (Dornelles and Corrêa, 2020), there is still a need to develop intelligent systems that support the recognition of emotions in this audience. However, it is worth noticing that studies in the literature are fully dedicated to the recognition of emotions in young people and adults, and few studies address the recognition of emotions in the elderly such as stated by Ma et al. (2019). The authors also explain that aging causes many changes in the shape and appearance of the face, so it is important that systems are developed for the automatic recognition of emotions specifically for this audience. However, it is worth mentioning that there are few datasets built to recognize emotions in the elderly. Furthermore, this lack of data is even greater in relation to the recognition of emotions in elderly people with dementias, such as AD.

3   Related Works

In the field of facial expressions, Grondhuis et al. (2021) presents possible answers about why the recognition of emotions in elderly people is more difficult than in young people. Initially, he suggests two hypotheses, relating this difficulty either to (i) excess wrinkles or (ii) atrophy of facial muscles, very common in this age group. For the comparative effect between these two variables (wrinkles/folds vs facial muscles), Generative Adversarial Networks were used in the image treatment. Young individuals have been aged, as well as older people have been artificially rejuvenated. With a database of 28 people, they found that emotions on younger faces when artificially wrinkled are 16% less likely to be identified. However, emotions on the faces of naturally elderly people were 50% less likely to be right. In contrast to this, older faces, artificially rejuvenated, had 74% less chance of getting right compared to young natural ones. The results then suggest that wrinkles and marks on the face of individuals have a much smaller impact than facial musculature on their ability to express emotions.

The research carried out by Micillo et al. (2021) makes an interesting analysis of issues related to the perception and expression of emotions in both elderly and young individuals. The author states that even though the visual recognition of emotions is widely used in the literature, elderly people rarely participate in research. As a way to investigate the interpretation of neutral, happy and angry emotions, 55 elderly people aged between 60 and 85 years and 52 young people aged between 20 and 30 years were tested. At first, the authors did not see a clear relationship for age variations in the perception of correct emotions, contrary to previous studies that said that older adults tend to have greater variability in responses. However, a detail came to light regarding the response time of the 2 groups. Both age groups have a longer response time when subjected to stimuli from emotional faces than to neutral faces. Images of younger people also influenced time and were classified more quickly by the elderly. Images of elderly people did not differ in terms of classification time.

The study carried out by Kuruvayil and Palaniswamy (2021) seeks to investigate the challenges regarding the extraction of facial features. Some of these challenges are partial occlusion, pose and lighting variations. Therefore, the authors propose a modeling of an emotion recognition system based on machine learning and deep learning that aims to generalize well in natural obstructions. The training was carried out using a large volume of data. One challenge was the scarcity of images with the desired characteristics in the basic emotion recognition datasets. The proposed system, ERMOPI (Emotion Recognition using Meta-learning through Occlusion, Pose and Illumination), was trained for 5 basic emotions with facial images having 5 occlusion categories, 7 head poses and 5 lighting levels. The results were 90% accuracy for CMU Multi-PIE images (dataset) and 68% accuracy for AffectNet images (dataset).

The work developed by Zhang et al. (2014) presents a pertinent question, which is: "Does arousal have a greater correlation with a categorized emotion than valence?". From this, the authors propose a framework to evaluate the performance of different texture features merged with geometric distance features to represent facial expressions in a continuous valence-excitation space. Texture features include discriminative subsets of three texture descriptors: local binary patterns—LBP, scale invariant trace transformation—SIFT and Gabor filter outputs that showed state-of-the-art facial expression recognition performance. Correlations between the dimensions of emotion and categorized emotions are investigated from four aspects: spatial distribution, change, similarity (Bhattacharyya distance) and correlation between predicted outcomes and corresponding fundamental truths.

Following an approach similar to the one proposed in this chapter, Mehendale (2020) work uses convolutional neural networks to recognize emotions in faces. Through an architecture divided into 2 parts, the first network removes the background from the images and a second one extracts features from the facial expressions. The background removal step, as well as the division into different steps of the method, helped to deal with various face position and camera distance issues. For training, testing and validation of the model 3 datasets as well as the author's own images were widely used. The Caltech faces, The CMU database and NIST database datasets achieved accuracy of 85%, 78% and 96% respectively. Finally, for the author, the use of larger datasets, such as the CMU with 750.000 images, showed low precision due to overfitting. Very small datasets, likewise, did not perform well, reaching an ideal number of 2000 to 10000 images for the best performance of the model.

4   Methodology

4.1   Database Description

The database used to perform the experiments was the Facial Expression Recognition 2013 (FER-2013), created by Pierre Luc Carrier and Aaron Courville and introduced in the ICML 2013 - Challenges in Representation Learning, by Goodfellow et al. (2013). Briefly, the data in this database was created from searches using the Google Images API. Then, it was searched for faces that matched a set of 184 words related to emotions, such as "Happy", "Raging", "Fear" and others. These words were also combined with gender, age or ethnicity, at the end of this process, 600 strings were obtained to use as a query for facial image research.

The returned images were kept for the processing stage, where OpenCV was used to add bounding boxes around each face in the collected images. After that, the images were resized to 48x48 pixels and converted to scaled in gray. Altogether, the base comprises a total of 35.887 images and comprises seven classes of emotions. In the Fig. 5 it is possible to see the emotion classes included in the dataset, as well as the number of images per class.

It is important to highlight that FER2013 is currently considered the largest facial expression database publicly available for researchers who wish to train machine learning models, mainly Deep Neural Networks (DNNs). In addition to what has already been said, it is worth noting that the winners of the FER2013 challenge obtained 71.2% accuracy in the test set, using Convolutional Neural Networks and Support Vector Machine (SVM).

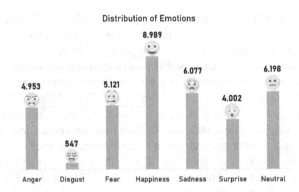

Figure 5: Distribution of Emotions in the FER2013 database.

4.2   Approach A

The approach A adopted in this research is composed of two parts, as shown in Fig. 6. Initially, in part 1, the pre-processing of the FER2013 database was carried out. It is important to highlight that the referred database already has a basic processing, as mentioned in Subsection 4.1, where the authors resized the images to 48x48, so that the face was positioned centrally in the image. Also, all images were already in grayscale. For our work, it was necessary to transform the pixel list into an array, using numpy. After that, the pixels were on a scale from 0 to 255, for better processing by the neural network, we normalized the pixels to a scale from 0 to 1. After pre-processing, we chose Convolutional Neural Networks (CNN) to be the classifier of this research. The choice was due to the fact that this model is the most used in the literature to work with images. To decide which parameters and configurations to use in CNN, five experiments were carried out with different architectures, as presented in Subsection 4.2.1. To train the models, we split the data into 80% for training, 10% for testing, and 10% for validation. It is important to clarify at the end of each epoch the validation of the model in real time was performed. While the test set was used after the model was fully trained. To identify and select the best architecture, we analyzed performance based on evaluative metrics (Subsection 4.2.2) such as Accuracy, Precision, Recall, F1 Score and Zero One Loss.

After selecting the best architecture for us to use, we ran part 2 of the methodology. In this step, we randomly chose 19 images of elderly people by Google Images, from the "Creative Commons License" filter. After obtaining the test images, the Haarcascade Frontal Face (Subsection 4.3) was applied to detect the face and, subsequently, the CNN classifier to attribute emotions to the images. It is important to clarify that the experiments were performed on Google Colab, using Python programming language, along with several libraries, such as Keras and TensorFlow. In addition, the experiments ran on a server with adequate capacity (Intel(R) Xeon(R) Silver 4110 CPU @ 2.10GHz 2.10GHz, RAM: 128GB and 64-bit OS).

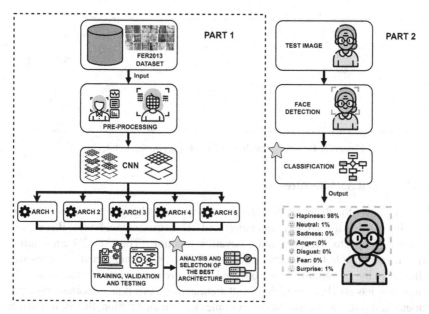

Figure 6: Diagram with the steps of approach A. In Part 1, the pre-processing of the FER2013 base was carried out. Subsequently, we chose the convolutional neural networks to be the classifier and tested five architectures. Tests with the architectures went through training, validation and testing. Based on the metrics analysis, we choose the best architecture to use in the classifier. In Part 2, we chose 19 images of elderly people for testing, we used the frontal face haarcascade to detect the face and the CNN to classify emotions.

4.2.1 Classification

In this approach we tested different CNN architectures to perform classification. Convolutional Neural Networks (Vargas et al., 2016) are deep learning intelligent methods. In this method, the network learns the patterns of a given input from its processing through several layers. The more layers that are inserted, the deeper the network becomes. In the context of image processing, an input image is subjected to successive convolution and pooling processes. At the end of the network there is a data synthesis layer (fully connected), resulting in the output data.

Figure 7 illustrates this network. Each input image is initially subjected to convolution operations. This mathematical operation works like a filtering process, highlighting or fading information of interest. The quantity and orientation of the filters are defined from the neighborhood considered for the convolution. After each convolution layer, the resulting images are subjected to pooling layers. These layers perform the downsampling process which consists of reducing the image size (*e.g.*, four pixels are replaced by just one). This process is essential since it is responsible for reducing memory consumption during the execution of the algorithm. It is particularly helpful in cases where the number of layers in the network is very large.

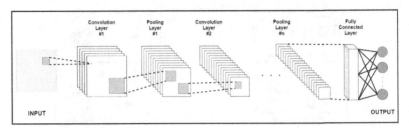

Figure 7: General convolutional neural networks architecture.

4.2.2   Tested Architectures

Table 1 shows the different configurations that were changed in the architecture experiments. Changes refer to the number of 2D Convolutional layers, Batch Size, Number of Epochs, Dropout and Activation function. The Conv2D convolution layer is responsible for extracting the input features, the number of features was different in the five architectures, but the kernel size of 3x3 was applied to all. The Batch Size has also been modified in all architectures, this is an important hyperparameter and refers to the number of examples used in an iteration, that is, it controls the number of training samples to be worked on. Another parameter that differs in architectures is the number of Epochs, which refers to the number of complete passes through the training dataset. In order to avoid overfitting, we tested different values for the Dropout function, which is responsible for turning off some neurons along with their connections randomly during training, however, during the predictions the neurons are kept active. The activation function determines the output of each neuron, in the experiments we tested three types: Relu, Elu and Softmax. Relu and Elu were used in the Conv2D layers, while Softmax was used only in the last dense layer of CNN, in order to return and assign probabilities to the output ratings.

Table 1: Table with the parameters of the convolution layers (Conv2D), Batch Size, Epochs, Dropout and Activation function that were modified and tested in CNN architectures. It is worth clarifying that each model had a typical single execution, where the expected error had a variation around 10%.

Architectures	Tested configurations				
	Conv2D	Batch Size	Epochs	Dropout	Activation Function
Architecture 1	64, 64, 128, 128, 256, 256, 512, 512	64	100	0.5	Relu and Softmax
Architecture 2	32, 32, 64, 64, 128, 128, 256, 256	16	100	0.2	Elu and Softmax
Architecture 3	64, 64, 128, 128, 256, 256, 512, 512	30	50	0.3	Relu and Softmax
Architecture 4	64, 64, 128, 128, 256, 256, 512, 512	32	70	0.6	Elu and Softmax
Architecture 5	20, 30, 40, 50, 60, 70, 80, 90	256	100	0.2	Relu and Softmax

Some configurations were performed on all architectures. As an example, at the end of two 2D convolution layers both Batch Normalization and Pooling were applied using the Max Pooling technique, with a Pool Size of 2x2 and Strides of 2x2. Pooling layer was applied to reduce the size of input data (feature map) and regularize the network, thus contributing to reduce memory cost and improve processing. We also use a Flatten layer to transform the resulting matrix from the other convoluted layers into a linear array, with a single dimension (1D). In addition, all experiments had four dense layers, where the last dense layer with Softmax activation function had 7 outputs corresponding to emotions classes of Anger, Disgust, Fear, Happiness, Sadness, Surprise and Neutral.

4.2.3   Analysis and Selection of the Best Architecture

To evaluate the performance of the tested architectures, we considered five evaluative metrics, they are: Accuracy, Precision, Recall, F1 Score and Zero One Loss. We can understand accuracy as the most used metric to evaluate algorithm performance. This metric indicates the overall performance of the model, in other words, it is the probability of true positives and true negatives among all results (Barbosa et al., 2021a,b; Commowick et al., 2018; de Lima et al., 2014, 2016; de Souza et al., 2021; Gomes et al., 2020, 2021; Macedo et al., 2021; Pereira et al., 2021). Precision, also known as positive predictive value, can be understood as a metric that indicates the ratio of positive predictions that are actually positive (Barbosa et al., 2021a,b; Commowick et al., 2018; de Lima et al., 2014, 2016; de Souza et al., 2021; Gomes et al., 2020, 2021; Macedo et al., 2021; Pereira et al., 2021). Generally, its value varies, approaching 1 when values are positive and 0 when values tend to be false positive (Arpaci et al., 2021). Recall (also known as sensitivity) is the rate of true positives and seeks to assess the ability of the algorithm to successfully detect results classified as positive. F1 Score (or F-Measure) can be understood as a harmonic average between accuracy and Recall/Sensitivity. In other words, it's a metric that allows us to view Precision and Recall together (Chicco and Jurman, 2020; Lipton et al., 2014). Zero One Loss is a common loss function that is widely used in classification tasks. Its operation is simple, basically, this measure attributes a cost (loss) to the failure to guess the correct class. In some situations, different types of misclassification have different costs associated with them (Domingos and Pazzani, 1997). Generally, the value assigned by this zero one loss metric is 0 for a correct classification and 1 for an incorrect classification (Sammut and Webb, 2010). Having knowledge of the metrics used, the Table 2 presents the results obtained.

Table 2: Performance of tested architectures evaluated based on metrics, such as Accuracy, Precision, Recall, F1 Score and Zero One Loss.

Metric	Architectures				
	Architecture 1	Architecture 2	Architecture 3	Architecture 4	Architecture 5
Accuracy	0.6297	0.6375	0.6090	0.2454	0.5784
Precision	0.6301	0.6428	0.6090	0.2454	0.5784
Recall	0.6297	0.6374	0.5078	0.1428	0.5426
F1 Score	0.6234	0.6337	0.5989	0.0967	0.5756
Zero One Loss	0.3702	0.3624	0.3909	0.7545	0.4215

Among the architectures tested, the one that best stood out in terms of accuracy (0.6375), precision (0.6428), Recall (0.6374), F1 Score (0.6337) and Zero One Loss (0.3624) was architecture 2, followed by architecture 1. On the other hand, as it is noticeable, the worst performance was obtained by architecture 4, with outliers regarding accuracy (0.2454), Precision (0.2454), Recall (0.1428), F1 Score (0.0967) and Zero one Loss (0.7545), followed by architecture 5. The architecture 3 presented mediated values, as it is possible to visualize, the accuracy (0.6090), Precision (0.6090), Recall (0.5078), F1 Score (0.5989) and Zero One Loss (0.3909) are concentrated among the best and worst results obtained. Finally, based on the analysis, the architecture selected to carry out the classifications was architecture 2.

4.2.4   Face Detection

For the face detection step, we use the Haarcascade Frontal Face, introduced by Viola and Jones (2001). Haar cascade is a method of detecting objects in images or videos, based on machine learning (Rudinskaya and Paringer, 2020). By proposing this method, Viola and Jones (2001) highlight three main contributions. The first one of these is a new form of image representation, called an "integral image" that allows the detector to quickly calculate the resources used. The second is an AdaBoost based algorithm, which selects a small number of features from a larger data set to produce more efficient classifiers. The third is to combine the classifiers in a cascade fashion to allow background regions of the image to be quickly discarded, while the detector focuses attention on promising regions of the image.

Verma and P Renukadevi (2021) explain that the Haar cascade works on the basis of positive images (covers the class of objects you want to detect) and negative (contains images that the classifier does not recognize). That is, Haar characteristics are weighted according to their success in accepting positive samples and rejecting negative samples (Varley et al., 2021). Khairuddin et al. (2021) states that this method already contains pre-trained classifiers and that they are available in the .xml format file to perform different types of recognition, such as detecting eyebrows, smile, nose, face, mouth and others (Anand, 2021; Verma and P Renukadevi, 2021). Finally, Haar Cascade is one of the most successful cascading techniques in this context (Varley et al., 2021), standing out for being fast and achieving good detection rates (Kasinski and Schmidt, 2010; Viola and Jones, 2001).

4.3   Approach B

As illustrated in the Fig. 8, in the second experiment, also using the FER2013 dataset, we used a transfer learning approach to extract the attributes. For this, a pre-trained LeNet network with the MNIST dataset was used. Since the database we use has a visible unbalance between the classes (Fig. 5), we apply the SMOTE method to balance the data, thus generating a new dataset. After that, using the balanced base, we performed a selection of attributes through the PSO method,

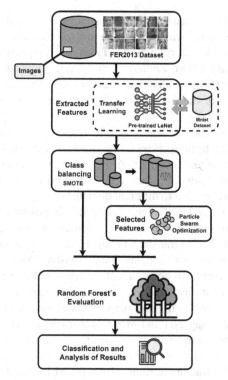

Figure 8: In the second approach of the present work, the extraction of attributes from the FER2013 base was performed through a LeNet network pre-trained with the MNIST dataset. For class balancing, we apply the SMOTE method. In order to perform a selection of attributes, we apply the PSO method. After that we train a Random Forest with several configurations and analyze its performance based on metrics.

generating a second dataset. In order to make a comparison between both generated bases, we train a Random Forest with several tree configurations and analyze its performance based on statistical metrics.

It is important to clarify that the next subsections provide detailed information about each method used, as well as their respective settings. To carry out the experiments of approach B of this work, we used the Weka tool, version 3.8 (Witten et al., 2005). As in approach A, we also have the help of a server with adequate capacity to carry out the experiments in question.

4.3.1 Transfer Learning

Transfer Learning (TL) is a machine learning methodology and aims to transfer knowledge between domains to solve problems (Zhuang et al., 2020). Liu et al. (2021) explain that TL allows the transfer of a rich data field (source domain) to another insufficient data field (destination domain) to occur, in order to achieve better model learning and performance. According to Pan and Yang (2009), we can understand that transference learning is motivated by the fact that human beings can intelligently reuse the knowledge acquired in a previous situation to solve new problems, faster and with better solutions. From the perspective of educational psychology (Ying et al., 2018), Zhuang et al. (2020) point out that learning to transfer is the result of the generalization of experience. That is, according to this theory, the prerequisite of transference is that there is a connection between two learning activities.

Whereas traditional machine learning techniques try to learn each task from scratch, transfer learning techniques try to transfer knowledge from some previous tasks to a target task (Pan and Yang, 2009). According to Sun et al. (2019), what and how to transfer are essential issues to be addressed in transference learning, as different methods are applied to different domains of origin and destination that unite different transference knowledge. For this, it is possible to identify these issues, since once learning to transfer a source domain is considered beneficial to a destination domain (when to transfer), an algorithm (such as transfer) discovers transferable knowledge between domains (the to transfer) (Ying et al., 2018).

The training of deep convolutional neural network models, depending on large datasets, can be a task of days, that is, it has a significant computational cost. One way to ease this process is to reuse the weights of models already pre-trained with data sets (such as ImageNet and MNIST) that are references in the field of computer vision. Some examples of pre-trained models are InceptionNet, ResNet, DenseNet, MobileNet (You et al., 2021) and others. In the case of the present work, for the stage of extracting attributes from the FER2013 database, we use a LeNet architecture, pre-trained with the MNIST dataset (LeCun et al., 1998).

The LeNet architecture was introduced by LeCun et al. (1998) in order to recognize numeric characters in documents. The LeNet is considered the first Convolutional architecture (Krishna and Kalluri, 2019), recognized for being simple, easy to understand and that returns interesting results. The Fig. 9 below shows the LeNet architecture, according to Titos et al. (2019).

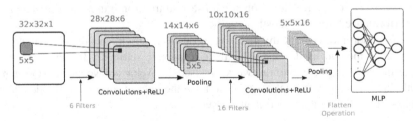

Figure 9: Ilustration of LeNet architecture, according to Titos et al. (2019). Briefly, LeNet architecture consists of two convolutional layers with ReLu activation function and two Pooling layers, followed by a Flatten layer, responsible for flattening the data. After the two layers are fully connected, the softmax activation function is applied.

According to Titos et al. (2019), a LeNet network is a CNN with seven levels of depth trained with the MNIST dataset (divided into 80% for training and 20% for testing) to classify numerical character images. Basically, as exposed in Sreehari et al. (2019), LeNet has three layers, they are: Convolution layer (responsible for extracting resources from the input image along with the Relu activation function), Pooling layer (increases the robustness of resource extraction and decreases the dimensionality of the data) and the fully connected layer (responsible for connecting all neurons to the previous layer followed by the Relu activation function). Finally, at the network exit, to return probabilities for the classifications, the Softmax activation function is used.

It is worth mentioning that with the application of the LeNet network to extract attributes from the FER2013 base, we obtained a set of 500 attributes and 35.887 instances.

4.3.2 Class Balancing

The unbalance of classes can be understood as a scenario where the distribution of data is unequal in a given dataset. Madeira (2011) explain that classifiers are sensitive to imbalance, that is, they tend to value the predominant classes and ignore the underrepresented classes. In an unbalanced dataset, the class with the highest representation is called the majority class or negative class, and the class with a relatively low representation is called the minority class or positive class (Liu, 2021). Knowing this, in order to avoid bias and bias in rankings, techniques are applied in the pre-processing of data in order to reduce imbalance.

A popular approach is the Synthetic Minority Oversampling Technique, proposed by Chawla et al. (2002). SMOTE is an oversampling method that aims to generate synthetic (artificial) data examples to balance minority classes, based on existing samples(Kaur and Gosain, 2021; Madeira, 2011; Özdemir et al., 2021). This is possible because SMOTE randomly selects the smallest class and finds the closest K-neighbors. Selected samples are evaluated using the nearest neighbor for that particular point (Rupapara et al., 2021). To find these neighborhoods, the KNN algorithm is used (Juez-Gil et al., 2021).

Making a specific cut for the experiment we performed and detailed in this section, to balance the classes, we applied the SMOTE with a number of K-Neighbors equal to 3. After balancing, we obtained a dataset with 500 attributes and 62.269 instances.

4.3.3 Feature Selection

The attribute selection process aims to reduce the dimensionality of data that can cause noise in the models. In other words, the selection of attributes aims to remove attributes that are redundant and do not strongly contribute to the model's learning, causing problems such as high computational cost. In order to select potential attributes to use in this experiment, we applied Particle Swarm Optimization (PSO), proposed by Kennedy and Eberhart (1995).

The PSO is a technique in the field of Evolutionary Computing (EC) (Xue et al., 2014) and is based on the collective movement of a group of particles: the particle swarm (Rodrigues et al., 2019). The functioning of the PSO starts with a population of random positions and velocities, where each particle contains a fitness function that must be evaluated and compared with the fitness evaluation of each particle along with its pbest (which means personal experience). If in each iteration the positions and speeds of the particles are better, they should be updated and used to assume the value of pbest. Particle velocities should be updated using the best positions (personal and global) (Barbosa et al., 2021b; Chrouta et al., 2021; Harb and Desuky, 2014; Rodrigues et al., 2019; Zomorodi-moghadam et al., 2021).

In this experiment, we apply PSO to select attributes, where we set the population size equal to 50, as well as 50 iterations. As a result, among the 500 attributes obtained by extracting the LeNet network, the PSO found and selected 148 potentially relevant attributes.

4.3.4 Classification and Analysis

For the classification step, we used the Random Forest (RF) algorithm with 10, 20, 50, 100, 150, 200, 250, 300, 350, 400 and 500 trees. RF is a supervised machine learning algorithm used to solve regression and classification problems. The functioning of Random Forest can be understood as a hierarchical collection of decision trees (Jackins et al., 2021; Pal, 2005) that compose the forests, being these trees responsible for analyzing the input data and assigning values to the outputs of the classes. The Random Forest classifier is widely used for having good performance even with absent data and for being able to reduce the possibility of overfitting in the data set. In addition to its simplicity in formulation, ease of implementation and lower computational cost (Pavani et al., 2021). The performance of the algorithm was evaluated based on metrics such as Accuracy, Kappa Index, Sensitivity, Specificity and ROC Curve Area.

It is worth clarifying that in order to obtain statistical data, each configuration tested against the Random Forest trees was performed with 30 repetitions. We also use the cross-validation method, with 10 folds.

5 Results

In Subsection 5.1 the results referring to approach A are presented. Subsection 5.2 details the results obtained in approach B. Finally, Subsection 5.3 presents a discussion of the results obtained in both experiments.

5.1 Results of Approach A

The Fig. 10 presents the confusion matrix regarding the recognition of emotions in facial expressions using CNN, generated from the prediction of the test dataset (corresponding to 3.589 images). The X (horizontal) axis of the matrix represents predicted emotions and the Y (vertical) axis represents the correct classification of actual emotions.

Confusion Matrix

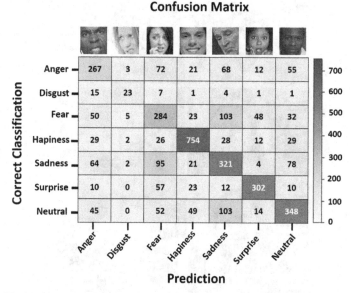

Figure 10: Results presented through the Confusion Matrix. The X (horizontal) axis of the matrix represents predicted emotions and the Y (vertical) axis represents the correct classification of actual emotions.

As can be seen, the model did not perform well in the ratings of Anger, Disgust and Fear emotions. While the emotion Anger is mostly correctly classified (with 267), but still, the model misclassified 231 images, where a significant part was confused with Fear (72), Sad (68) and Neutral (55). With regard to the Disgust emotion, it is important to highlight that it has a low number of representation in the database images, both for training, as well as for validation and testing, this justifies the small number for this class in the matrix of confusion, where out of 52 images, the model was able to correctly classify 23 and confused a significant number of 15 images with rabies. As for the Fear emotion, although the classification was better than the two aforementioned emotions (anger and disgust), out of 545 images, 284 of them were correctly classified, while a considerably high number of 103 was classified as Sad emotion.

On the other hand, the model managed to perform better in the classification of emotions as Happy, Sad, Surprised and Neutral. For Happy class, 754 images were correctly classified and 126 of them were wrongly distributed in the other classes. For sadness, 321 images were correctly classified, however, a high number of 264 images were attributed to other classes of emotions. For the Surprised class, 302 images were correctly classified, but if you look closely, for example, the model tends to classify images of Surprise as Fear (with 57 images). Finally, the Neutral class has 348 correctly classified images and 263 misassigned to other emotion classes.

Figure 11: Result of recognition of emotions in static images of elderly people. In all, of the 19 test images we used, the model was able to detect the face and attribute emotions to 52.63% of them.

This result was possibly influenced by the unbalance of the database, as some classes have much less images than others. As exposed in the confusion matrix (Fig. 10), the classification performance was worse for the disgust, anger and fear classes, exactly the classes that have a smaller amount of images.

In a second moment, in order to verify the effectiveness of the classification model in the researched context, tests were performed to recognize emotions in static images of the elderly. As already mentioned, these images were obtained from Google, using the "Creative Commons Licenses" type of license. It's possible to view the results in the Fig. 11. Along with the classification of emotions, the probability of the emotion belonging to other classes of emotions is also exposed.

Figure 12: Face detection errors and attribution of emotion by the classifier in elderly images. In all, of the 19 images we used for testing, the model had difficulties in detecting the face and correctly attributing emotions to 47.37% of them.

The results obtained by the test image ratings reinforce what is exposed in the confusion matrix. Where, for example, the Neutral emotion also tends to be classified/confused by the model with the sad emotion. While the Happy emotion has chances to belong to the Neutral emotion. These facts can be better observed in the probabilities presented along with each image in Fig. 11.

The images in Fig. 12 evidence an important finding that deserves to be discussed. In some tested images of elderly people two faces were detected and there was difficulty for the classifier to identify emotions. We believe that what may have influenced this failure is that the data used to train the classifier as well as the face detector are not specific to the context of elderly people.

Although good results were achieved, we believe that errors can be even greater when testing the classifier in the real context of the elderly. Thus, considering that this audience has a compromise in brain and facial structures that are important for the emotions processing and expression, it is believed that the classifier may present more difficulties in assertiveness to recognize emotions, as well as the detector to identify the face. Therefore, we emphasize the importance of having another data source (such as voice, electroencephalographic signals, galvanic skin response and others) and also using databases appropriate to the researched context.

5.2   Results of Approach B

It is possible to visualize the results obtained in the experiments of approach B through the Table 3. In the first dataset, with all attributes and classes balanced with the SMOTE, it can be seen that the Random Forest algorithm from 10 to 50 trees presented an accuracy between 55.49% and 67.67%. From the RF of 100 trees, it is clear that the accuracy stabilizes at around 70%. Where, the best performance regarding accuracy (75.86%), Kappa (0.48), Sensitivity (0.46), Specificity (0.86) and AUC (0.74) was obtained by Random Forest with 500 trees. However, the performance difference between the RF of 350, 400 and 500 trees is minimal. Which leads us to understand that both would be appropriate to use as classifiers.

In the dataset with the selection of attributes through the PSO, we can notice that the results obtained are not so discrepant when compared with the results of the dataset with all attributes. It is noticed that the RF with 10 trees showed the worst performance in relation to accuracy (54.83%), Kappa (0.47), Sensitivity (0.46), Specificity (0.86) and AUC (0.75). While the RF from 20 to 100 trees stabilized the performance and presented accuracy between 60.28% to 69.85%. It is visible that from the RF of 150 to 500 trees the difference in performance is minimal. The Random Forest with 500 trees stood out in relation to the other configurations when analyzing the accuracy (73.87%), Kappa (0.70), Sensitivity (0.62), Specificity (0.92) and AUC (0.88).

Table 3: The results obtained in the experiments of approach B are detailed in this Table. In the first part, we have the dataset equivalent to all attributes and balanced classes with SMOTE. In the second set of data, the classification results with the selection of attributes are presented.

Dataset	Classifier	Accuracy	Kappa	Sensitivity	Specificity	AUC
All features	RF 10	55.49% ± 0.63	0.48 ± 0.01	0.46 ± 0.02	0.86 ± 0.00	0.74 ± 0.01
	RF 20	61.18% ± 0.59	0.55 ± 0.01	0.49 ± 0.02	0.88 ± 0.00	0.79 ± 0.01
	RF 50	67.67% ± 0.61	0.62 ± 0.01	0.53 ± 0.02	0.90 ± 0.00	0.84 ± 0.01
	RF 100	71.44% ± 0.54	0.67 ± 0.01	0.57 ± 0.02	0.91 ± 0.00	0.86 ± 0.01
	RF 150	73.07% ± 0.55	0.69 ± 0.01	0.59 ± 0.02	0.92 ± 0.00	0.87 ± 0.00
	RF 200	73.97% ± 0.57	0.70 ± 0.01	0.60 ± 0.02	0.92 ± 0.00	0.88 ± 0.00
	RF 250	74.57% ± 0.54	0.70 ± 0.01	0.60 ± 0.02	0.93 ± 0.00	0.88 ± 0.00
	RF 300	74.98% ± 0.52	0.71 ± 0.01	0.61 ± 0.02	0.92 ± 0.00	0.88 ± 0.00
	RF 350	75.29% ± 0.54	0.71 ± 0.01	0.61 ± 0.02	0.92 ± 0.00	0.89 ± 0.00
	RF 400	75.52% ± 0.52	0.71 ± 0.01	0.62 ± 0.02	0.92 ± 0.00	0.89 ± 0.00
	RF 500	75.86% ± 0.52	0.72 ± 0.01	0.62 ± 0.02	0.92 ± 0.00	0.89 ± 0.00
Selected features	RF 10	54.83% ± 0.58	0.47 ± 0.01	0.46 ± 0.02	0.86 ± 0.00	0.75 ± 0.01
	RF 20	60.28% ± 0.54	0.54 ± 0.01	0.49 ± 0.02	0.88 ± 0.00	0.80 ± 0.01
	RF 50	66.43% ± 0.53	0.61 ± 0.01	0.54 ± 0.02	0.90 ± 0.00	0.84 ± 0.01
	RF 100	69.85% ± 0.53	0.65 ± 0.01	0.57 ± 0.02	0.91 ± 0.00	0.86 ± 0.01
	RF 150	71.35% ± 0.53	0.67 ± 0.01	0.59 ± 0.02	0.91 ± 0.00	0.87 ± 0.01
	RF 200	72.18% ± 0.53	0.68 ± 0.01	0.60 ± 0.02	0.91 ± 0.00	0.87 ± 0.00
	RF 250	72.71% ± 0.52	0.68 ± 0.01	0.60 ± 0.02	0.92 ± 0.00	0.88 ± 0.00
	RF 300	73.08% ± 0.54	0.69 ± 0.01	0.61 ± 0.02	0.92 ± 0.00	0.88 ± 0.00
	RF 350	73.37% ± 0.53	0.69 ± 0.01	0.61 ± 0.02	0.92 ± 0.00	0.88 ± 0.00
	RF 400	73.58% ± 0.53	0.69 ± 0.01	0.61 ± 0.02	0.92 ± 0.00	0.88 ± 0.00
	RF 500	73.87% ± 0.53	0.70 ± 0.01	0.62 ± 0.02	0.92 ± 0.00	0.88 ± 0.00

RF: Random Forest

5.3 Discussion of Results

It is important to emphasize that the experiments carried out in approach A were initial and of great importance to define possibilities for solutions and also to identify difficulties and limitations, such as unbalanced classes and lack of data covering the context of the elderly. These two points directly affected the performance of the model. It was precisely in this scenario and the need to find good configurations and methods that we carried out other experiments and described in approach B.

As mentioned, the balanced base is composed of 500 attributes, after selection with PSO, a new dataset was generated with 150 attributes. That is, attributes have significantly decreased from one dataset to another. A very positive and evident point in the B approach experiments is that Random Forest managed to obtain good and almost equivalent results in both data sets. The difference between metrics, most of the time, did not reach 1%.

This result is quite promising, since the PSO was able to identify potentially useful attributes to represent the data and also reduce the dimensionality and noise in the models, excluding non-informative and irrelevant attributes.

Another curiosity, still in approach B, is that despite using several tree configurations in the Random Forest algorithm, the results were not so different from one to the other. There was even a stabilization of RF performance from a considerably low number of trees. This point leads us to believe that using, for example, the attributes (150) selected by the PSO together with an RF of 200 trees is enough to obtain and achieve good classifications with a minimized computational cost.

6 Conclusion

As mentioned throughout this document and also evidenced by Ma et al. (2019), studies in the literature that address the recognition of emotions in the elderly, with dementia or not, still represent a small portion close to the problem and need for this support. As a result, there is still a scarcity of specific databases for this context, especially those that take into account changes in form, face, changes in non-verbal behavior patterns and others. The scarcity of works also directly impacts the limited variety of publicly available databases. This also affects the quality of available databases, which, in most cases, are heavily unbalanced.

A point that is worth noting is that the results obtained in the initial experiments are considerably good. However, as seen, the classifier had difficulties to attribute emotions and the detector to identify the faces of some of the elderly. It is believed that this problem was caused by the database we used, which is not suitable for the elderly context. For this reason, we believe that these errors can persist and even be greater if applied in real contexts.

However, being aware of these difficulties and limitations reported here, we relate this point to our goals, that is, with what we intend to do from now on, such as searching for public databases in the specific context of elderly people to validate the models. Other studies should also be conducted with the addition of methods for class balancing. The variability of training images can also be improved by inserting new images through the database combination. The acquisition of images of the elderly should also be encouraged, whether they are healthy or affected by pathologies, such as dementia.

Acknowledgement(s)

This study was financed in part by the Coordenação de Aperfeiçoamento de Pessoal de Nível Superior - Brazil (CAPES) - Finance Code 001, and by the Fundação de Amparo à Ciência e Tecnologia do Estado de Pernambuco (FACEPE), Brazil, underthe code IBPG-0013-1.03/20.

Disclosure statement

No potential conflict of interest was reported by the authors.

References

Abdullah, S.M.S.A., S.Y.A. Ameen, M.A. Sadeeq and S. Zeebaree. Multimodal emotion recognition using deep learning. Journal of Applied Science and Technology Trends, 2(02): 52–58, 2021.

Agres, K.R., R.S. Schaefer, A. Volk, S. van Hooren, A. Holzapfel, S. Dalla Bella, M. Müller, M. DeWitte, D. Herremans, R. Ramirez Melendez, M. Neerincx, S. Ruiz, D. Meredith, T. Dimitriadis and W.L. Magee. Music, computing, and health: A roadmap for the current and future roles of music technology for health care and well-being. Music & Science, 4: 2059204321997709, 2021.

Anand, D. Implementation and analysis of sentimental analysis on facial expression using haar cascade methods. Turkish Journal of Computer and Mathematics Education (TURCOMAT), 12(2): 2787–2793, 2021.

Arpaci, I., S. Huang, M. Al-Emran, M.N. Al-Kabi and M. Peng. Predicting the covid-19 infection with fourteen clinical features using machine learning classification algorithms. Multimedia Tools and Applications, 80(8): 11943–11957, 2021.

Barbosa, V.A.d.F., J.C. Gomes, M.A. de Santana, C.L. de Lima, R.B. Calado, C.R. Bertoldo Júnior, J.E.d.A. Albuquerque, R.G. de Souza, R.J.E. de Araújo, L.A.R. Mattos Júnior, R.E. de Souza and W.P. dos Santos. Covid-19 rapid test by combining a random forest-based web system and blood tests. Journal of Biomolecular Structure and Dynamics, 2021: 1–20, 2021a.

Barbosa, V.A.d.F., J.C. Gomes, M.A. de Santana, E.d.A. Jeniffer, R.G. de Souza, R.E. de Souza and W.P. dos Santos. Heg.ia: An intelligent system to support diagnosis of covid-19 based on blood tests. Research on Biomedical Engineering, 2021: 1–18, 2021b.

Bhattacharya, P., R.K. Gupta and Y. Yang. Exploring the contextual factors affecting multimodal emotion recognition in videos. IEEE Transactions on Affective Computing, 2021.

Bomfim, A.J.d.L., R.A.d.S. Ribeiro and M.H.N. Chagas. Recognition of dynamic and static facial expressions of emotion among older adults with major depression. Trends in Psychiatry and Psychotherapy, 41: 159–166, 2019.

Cameirão, M.S., F. Pereira and S.B. i Badia. Virtual reality with customized positive stimuli in a cognitive-motor rehabilitation task. In 2017 International Conference on Virtual Rehabilitation (ICVR), pp. 1–7. IEEE, 2017.

Cavalli, E., G. Battaglia, M.S. Basile, V. Bruno, M.C. Petralia, S.D. Lombardo, M. Pennisi, R. Kalfin, L. Tancheva, P. Fagone, F. Nicoletti and K. Mangano. Exploratory analysis of ipscs-derived neuronal cells as predictors of diagnosis and treatment of Alzheimer disease. Brain Sciences, 10(3): 166, 2020.

Chaturvedi, V., A.B. Kaur, V. Varshney, A. Garg, G.S. Chhabra and M. Kumar. Music mood and human emotion recognition based on physiological signals: A systematic review. Multimedia Systems, pp. 1–24, 2021.

Chawla, N.V., K.W. Bowyer, L.O. Hall and W.P. Kegelmeyer. Smote: Synthetic minority oversampling technique. Journal of Artificial Intelligence Research, 16: 321–357, 2002.

Chicco, D. and G. Jurman. The advantages of the matthews correlation coefficient (MCC) over f1 score and accuracy in binary classification evaluation. BMC Genomics, 21(1): 1–13, 2020.

Chrouta, J., F. Farhani and A. Zaafouri. A modified multi swarm particle swarm optimization algorithm using an adaptive factor selection strategy. Transactions of the Institute of Measurement and Control, pp. 01423312211029509, 2021.

Chuang, Y.-C., M.-J. Chiu, T.-F. Chen, Y.-L. Chang, Y.-M. Lai, T.-W. Cheng and M.-S. Hua. An exploration of the own-age effect on facial emotion recognition in normal elderly people and individuals with the preclinical and demented Alzheimers disease. Journal of Alzheimer's Disease, 2021(Preprint): 1–11, 2021.

Commowick, O., A. Istace, M. Kain, B. Laurent, F. Leray, M. Simon, S.C. Pop, P. Girard, R. Ameli, J.-C. Ferré, A. Kerbrat, T. Tourdias, F. Cervenansky, T. Glatard, J. Beaumont, S. Doyle, F. Forbes, J. Knight, A. Khademi, A. Mahbod, C. Wang, R. McKinley, F. Wagner, J. Muschelli, E. Sweeney, E. Roura, X. Lladó, M.M. Santos, W.P. Santos, A.G. Silva-Filho, X. Tomas-Fernandez, H. Urien, I. Bloch, S. Valverde, M. Cabezas, F.J. Vera-Olmos, N. Malpica, C. Guttmann, S. Vukusic, G. Edan, M. Dojat, M. Styner, S.K. Warfield, F. Cotton and C. Barillot. Objective evaluation of multiple sclerosis lesion segmentation using a data management and processing infrastructure. Scientific Reports, 8(1): 1–17, 2018.

Crespo, A.B., G.G. Idrovo, N. Rodrigues and A. Pereira. A virtual reality UAV simulation with body area networks to promote the elders life quality. In 2016 1st International Conference on Technology and Innovation in Sports, Health and Wellbeing (TISHW), pp. 1–7. IEEE, 2016.

Dantcheva, A., P. Bilinski, H.T. Nguyen, J.-C. Broutart and F. Bremond. Expression recognition for severely demented patients in music reminiscence-therapy. In 2017 25th European Signal Processing Conference (EUSIPCO), pp. 783–787. IEEE, 2017.

de Lima, S.M., A.G. da Silva-Filho and W.P. dos Santos. A methodology for classification of lesions in mammographies using zernike moments, ELM and SVM neural networks in a multikernel approach. In 2014 IEEE International Conference on Systems, Man, and Cybernetics (SMC), pp. 988–991. IEEE, 2014.

de Lima, S.M., A.G. da Silva-Filho and W.P. dos Santos. Detection and classification of masses in mammographic images in a multi-kernel approach. Computer Methods and Programs in Biomedicine, 134: 11–29, 2016.

de Oliveira, E. and P.A. Jaques. Classificação de emoções básicas através de imagens capturadas por webcam. Revista Brasileira de Computação Aplicada, 5(2): 40–54, 2013.

de Santana, M.A., J.C. Gomes, G.M. de Souza, A. Suarez, A.S. Torcate, F.S. Fonseca, G.M.M. Moreno and W.P. dos Santos. Reconhecimento automático de emoçoes a partir de sinais multimodais e inteligência artificial. Anais do IV Simpósio de Inovação em Engenharia Biomédica-SABIO, pp. 43, 2020.

de Sousa, A.L., S.W.S. Costa, Y. Pires and F. Araújo. Fourface: Uma ferramenta de reconhecimento de expressões faciais. Brazilian Journal of Development, 6(10): 81667–81675, 2020.

de Sousa Silva, B., I. dos Santos Zanetti, P.P. de Barros, L.T. de Souza and L.B. Barreto. Diagnósticos diferenciais das deficiências cognitivas em idosos. Revista Eletrônica Acervo Científico, 26: e7565–e7565, 2021.

de Souza, R.G., G. dos Santos Lucas e Silva, W.P. dos Santos and M.E. de Lima. Computer-aided diagnosis of Alzheimers disease by MRI analysis and evolutionary computing. Research on Biomedical Engineering, 37(3): 455–483, 2021.

Domingos, P. and M. Pazzani. On the optimality of the simple Bayesian classifier under zero-one loss. Machine Learning, 29(2): 103–130, 1997.

Dorneles, S.O.D.S.O., D.N.F. Barbosa and J.L.V. Barbosa. Sensibilidade ao contexto na identificação de estados afetivos aplicados à educação: Um mapeamento sistemático. RENOTE, 18(1), 2020.

Dornelles, V.J. and E.A. Corrêa. Atividade de lazer e novas tecnologias em pessoas com doença de Alzheimer. Revista MotriSaúde, 2(1), 2020.

Ekman, P., W.V. Friesen and J.C. Hager. Facial acts coding system: The manual. In Salt Lake. Research Nexus, 2002.

Ferreira, A., P.M. Teixeira and P. Tavares. Estudos de expressões faciais para animação 3d. Edição IPCA ISBN: 978-989-97567-6-2 Design editorial· Cláudio Ferreira, 2013.

Ferreira, C.D. and N. Torro-Alves. Reconhecimento de emoções faciais no envelhecimento: Uma revisão sistemática. Universitas Psychologica, 15(5), 2016.

Fölster, M., U. Hess and K. Werheid. Facial age affects emotional expression decoding. Frontiers in Psychology, 5: 30, 2014.

Gomes, J.C., V.A.d.F. Barbosa, M.A. Santana, J. Bandeira, M.J.S. Valença, R.E. de Souza, A.M. Ismael and W.P. dos Santos. Ikonos: An intelligent tool to support diagnosis of covid-19 by texture analysis of x-ray images. Research on Biomedical Engineering, 2020: 1–14, 2020.

Gomes, J.C., A.I. Masood, L.H.d.S. Silva, J.R.B. da Cruz Ferreira, A.A.F. Júnior, A.L. dos Santos Rocha, L.C.P. de Oliveira, N.R.C. da Silva, B.J.T. Fernandes and W.P. dos Santos. Covid-19 diagnosis by combining rt-pcr and pseudo-convolutional machines to characterize virus sequences. Scientific Reports, 11(1): 1–28, 2021.

Gong, S., Y. Dai, J. Ji, J. Wang and H. Sun. Emotion analysis of telephone complaints from customer based on affective computing. Computational Intelligence and Neuroscience, 2015, 2015.

González, E.J.S. and K. McMullen. The design of an algorithmic modal music platform for eliciting and detecting emotion. In 2020 8th International Winter Conference on Brain-Computer Interface (BCI), pp. 1–3. IEEE, 2020.

Goodfellow, I.J., D. Erhan, P.L. Carrier, A. Courville, M. Mirza, B. Hamner, W. Cukierski, Y. Tang, D. Thaler, D.-H. Lee, Y. Zhou, C. Ramaiah, F. Feng, R. Li, X. Wang, D. Athanasakis, J. Shawe-Taylor, M. Milakov, J. Park, R. Ionescu, M. Popescu, C. Grozea, J. Bergstra, J. Xie, L. Romaszko, B. Xu, Z. Chuang and Y. Bengio. Challenges in representation learning: A report on three machine learning contests. In International Conference on Neural Information Processing, pp. 117–124. Springer, 2013.

Greene, S., H. Thapliyal and A. Caban-Holt. A survey of affective computing for stress detection: Evaluating technologies in stress detection for better health. IEEE Consumer Electronics Magazine, 5(4): 44–56, 2016.

Grondhuis, S.N., A. Jimmy, C. Teague and N.M. Brunet. Having difficulties reading the facial expression of older individuals? Blame it on the facial muscles, not the wrinkles. Frontiers in Psychology, 12, 2021.

Guo, T., D. Zhang, Y. Zeng, T.Y. Huang, H. Xu and Y. Zhao. Molecular and cellular mechanisms underlying the pathogenesis of Alzheimers disease. Molecular Neurodegeneration, 15(1): 1–37, 2020.

Han, J., Z. Zhang, N. Cummins and B. Schuller. Adversarial training in affective computing and sentiment analysis: Recent advances and perspectives [review article]. IEEE Computational Intelligence Magazine, 14(2): 68–81, 2019.

Han, J., Z. Zhang, M. Pantic and B. Schuller. Internet of emotional people: Towards continual affective computing cross cultures via audiovisual signals. Future Generation Computer Systems, 114: 294–306, 2021.

Harb, H.M. and A.S. Desuky. Feature selection on classification of medical datasets based on particle swarm optimization. International Journal of Computer Applications, 104(5), 2014.

Hayashi, C.L., T.H.F. Vasconcellos, D.V. de Oliveira, J.R.A. do Nascimento Júnior, M.F. Franco and J.K.A. Nogueira. Treinamento de dupla tarefa associado a estratégias cognitivas de associação e imagem mental: impacto no equilíbrio, cognição e na saúde mental de idosos. Research, Society and Development, 10(10): e449101018675–e449101018675, 2021.

Iancu, I. and B. Iancu. Elderly in the digital era theoretical perspectives on assistive technologies. Technologies, 5(3): 60, 2017.

Jackins, V., S. Vimal, M. Kaliappan and M.Y. Lee. Ai-based smart prediction of clinical disease using random forest classifier and naive bayes. The Journal of Supercomputing, 77(5): 5198–5219, 2021.

Jaques, P.A., M.A.S. Nunes, S. Isotani and I. Bittencourt. Computaçao afetiva aplicada a educaçao: Dotando sistemas tutores inteligentes de habilidades sociais. In Anais do Workshop de Desafios da Computação Aplicada à Educação, pp. 50–59, 2012.

Juez-Gil, M., Á. Arnaiz-González, J.J. Rodríguez, C. López-Nozal and C. García-Osorio. Approxsmote: Fast smote for big data on apache spark. Neurocomputing, 464: 432–437, 2021.

Kasinski, A. and A. Schmidt. The architecture and performance of the face and eyes detection system based on the haar cascade classifiers. Pattern Analysis and Applications, 13(2): 197–211, 2010.

Kaur, P. and A. Gosain. Gt2fs-smote: An intelligent oversampling approach based upon general type-2 fuzzy sets to detect web spam. Arabian Journal for Science and Engineering, 46(4): 3033–3050, 2021.

Kennedy, J. and R. Eberhart. Particle swarm optimization. In Proceedings of ICNN'95-International Conference on Neural Networks, volume 4, pp. 1942–1948. IEEE, 1995.

Khairuddin, M., S. Shahbudin and M. Kassim. A smart building security system with intelligent face detection and recognition. In IOP Conference Series: Materials Science and Engineering, volume 1176, pp. 012030. IOP Publishing, 2021.

Khateeb, M., S.M. Anwar and M. Alnowami. Multi-domain feature fusion for emotion classification using deap dataset. IEEE Access, 9: 12134–12142, 2021.

Ko, H., K. Kim, M. Bae, M.-G. Seo, G. Nam, S. Park, S. Park, J. Ihm and J.-Y. Lee. Changes in facial recognition and facial expressions with age. Sensors, 2021.

Krishna, S.T. and H.K. Kalluri. Deep learning and transfer learning approaches for image classification. International Journal of Recent Technology and Engineering (IJRTE), 7(5S4): 427–432, 2019.

Kuruvayil, S. and S. Palaniswamy. Emotion recognition from facial images with simultaneous occlusion, pose and illumination variations using meta-learning. Journal of King Saud University-Computer and Information Sciences, 2021.

Ladislau, R., J.G. Guimarães and W.C.d. Souza. Percepção de expressões faciais emocionais em idosos com doença de alzheimer. Psicologia: Reflexão e Crítica, 28: 804–812, 2015.

Leão, L.P., J.S. Bezerra, L.N. Matos and M.A.S.N. Nunes. Detecção de expressões faciais: Uma abordagem baseada em análise do fluxo óptico. REVISTA GEINTEC-GESTAO INOVACAO E TECNOLOGIAS, 2(5): 472–489, 2012.

LeCun, Y., L. Bottou, Y. Bengio and P. Haffner. Gradient-based learning applied to document recognition. Proceedings of the IEEE, 86(11): 2278–2324, 1998.

Lipton, Z.C., C. Elkan and B. Narayanaswamy. Thresholding classifiers to maximize f1 score. ArXiv, pp. 1402–1892, 2014.

Liu, J. Importance-smote: A synthetic minority oversampling method for noisy imbalanced data. Soft Computing, pp. 1–23, 2021.

Liu, J., Q. Zhang, X. Li, G. Li, Z. Liu, Y. Xie, K. Li and B. Liu. Transfer learning-based strategies for fault diagnosis in building energy systems. Energy and Buildings, 250: 111256, 2021.

Ma, K., X. Wang, X. Yang, M. Zhang, J.M. Girard and L.-P. Morency. Elderreact: A multimodal dataset for recognizing emotional response in aging adults. In 2019 International Conference on Multimodal Interaction, pp. 349–357, 2019.

Macedo, M., M. Santana, W.P. dos Santos, R. Menezes and C. Bastos-Filho. Breast cancer diagnosis using thermal image analysis: A data-driven approach based on swarm intelligence and supervised learning for optimized feature selection. Applied Soft Computing, 2021: 107533, 2021.

Madeira, M.A.M. Reconhecimento de emoções faciais na esquizofrenia. PhD thesis, Universidade da Beira Interior, 2011.

Marosi-Holczberger, E., D.M.B. Prieto-Corona, M.G. Yáñez-Téllez, M.A. Rodríguez-Camacho, H. Rodríguez-Camacho and V. Guerrero-Juárez. Quantitative spectral EEG assessments during affective states evoked by the presentation of the international affective pictures. Journal of Behavior, Health & Social Issues (México), 4(2): 23–35, 2012.

Mehendale, N. Facial emotion recognition using convolutional neural networks (ferc). SN Applied Sciences, 2, 2020.

Meska, M.H.G., L.Y. Mano, J.P. Silva, G.A. Pereira and A. Mazzo. Reconocimiento de emociones para ambiente clínico simulado con uso de olores desagradables: estudio cuasiexperimental. Revista Latino-Americana de Enfermagem, 28, 2020.

Micillo, L., F. Stablum and G. Mioni. Do the young and the old perceive emotional intervals differently when shown on a younger or older face? Cognitive Processing, pp. 1–9, 2021.

Nalepa, G.J., K. Kutt and S. Bobek. Mobile platform for affective context-aware systems. Future Generation Computer Systems, 92: 490–503, 2019.

Namba, S., H. Matsui and M. Zloteanu. Distinct temporal features of genuine and deliberate facial expressions of surprise. Scientific Reports, 11(1): 1–10, 2021.

Nozima, A.M.M., B. Demos and W.C.d. Souza. Ausência de prejuízo no reconhecimento de expressões faciais entre indivíduos com parkinson. Psicologia: Teoria e Pesquisa, 34, 2018.

Ochi, R. and A. Midorikawa. Decline in emotional face recognition among elderly people may reflect mild cognitive impairment. Frontiers in Psychology, 12, 2021.

Okada, H.K.R. Detecção automática de fases temporais de emoção em vídeos a partir de características da face. PhD thesis, Universidade Federal do Amazonas, 2018.

Özdemir, A., K. Polat and A. Alhudhaif. Classification of imbalanced hyperspectral images using smote-based deep learning methods. Expert Systems with Applications, 178: 114986, 2021.

Pal, M. Random forest classifier for remote sensing classification. International Journal of Remote Sensing, 26(1): 217–222, 2005.

Pan, S.J. and Q. Yang. A survey on transfer learning. IEEE Transactions on Knowledge and Data Engineering, 22(10): 1345–1359, 2009.

Pavani, P.G., B. Biswal and P.K. Biswal. Robust classification of neovascularization using random forest classifier via convoluted vascular network. Biomedical Signal Processing and Control, 66: 102420, 2021.

Paxiuba, C.M. and C.P. Lima. An experimental methodological approach working emotions and learning using facial expressions recognition. Brazilian Journal of Computers in Education, 28: 92–114, 2020.

Pereira, J., M.A. Santana, J.C. Gomes, V.A. de Freitas Barbosa, M.J.S. Valença, S.M.L. de Lima and W.P. dos Santos. Feature selection based on dialectics to support breast cancer diagnosis using thermographic images. Research on Biomedical Engineering, 37(3): 485–506, 2021.

Picard, R.W. Affective Computing. MIT Press, 2000.

Reale, M., I. Gonzales-Portillo and C.V. Borlongan. Saliva, an easily accessible fluid as diagnostic tool and potent stem cell source for Alzheimers disease: Present and future applications. Brain Research, 1727: 146535, 2020.

Ren, F. and C. Quan. Linguistic-based emotion analysis and recognition for measuring consumer satisfaction: An application of affective computing. Information Technology and Management, 13(4): 321–332, 2012.

Rodrigues, A.L., M.A. de Santana, W.W. Azevedo, R.S. Bezerra, V.A. Barbosa, R.C. de Lima and W.P. dos Santos. Identification of mammary lesions in thermographic images: Feature selection study using genetic algorithms and particle swarm optimization. Research on Biomedical Engineering, 35(3): 213–222, 2019.

Rudinskaya, E. and R. Paringer. Face detection accuracy study based on race and gender factor using haar cascades. Information Technology and Nanotechnology, 2667, 2020.

Rudnicka, E., P. Napierala, A. Podfigurna, B. Meczekalski, R. Smolarczyk and M. Grymowicz. The World Health Organization (WHO) approach to healthy ageing. Maturitas, 139: 6–11, 2020.

Rupapara, V., F. Rustam, H.F. Shahzad, A. Mehmood, I. Ashraf and G.S. Choi. Impact of smote on imbalanced text features for toxic comments classification using RVVC model. IEEE Access, 2021.

Russell, J.A. A circumplex model of affect. Journal of Personality and Social Psychology, 39(6): 1161, 1980.

Sammut, C. and G.I. Webb (eds.). Encyclopedia of Machine Learning. Chapter Zero-One Loss, pp. 1031–1031. Springer US, Boston, MA, 2010.

Setiono, D., D. Saputra, K. Putra, J.V. Moniaga and A. Chowanda. Enhancing player experience in game with affective computing. Procedia Computer Science, 179: 781–788, 2021.

Sousa, A.L.d., S.W.d.S. Costa, Y.P. Pires and F. Araújo. Reconhecimento de expressões faciais e emocionais como método avaliativo de aplicações computacionais. Encontro Regional de Computação e Sistemas de Informação-ENCOSIS, 2016.

Sreehari, R., K. Roopa, P.R. Sarika, J.T. Nevline and K.P.G. Jyothish. Analysis of helmet detection using lenet and transfer learning. International Journal of Innovative Research in Science, Engineering and Technology, 8(5): 5569–5575, 2019.

Sun, Q., Y. Liu, T.-S. Chua and B. Schiele. Meta-transfer learning for few-shot learning. In Proceedings of the IEEE/CVF Conference on Computer Vision and Pattern Recognition, pp. 403–412, 2019.

Tan, C., M. Šarlija and N. Kasabov. Neurosense: Short-term emotion recognition and understanding based on spiking neural network modelling of spatio-temporal eeg patterns. Neurocomputing, 434: 137–148, 2021.

Tavares, R.E., M.C.P.d. Jesus, D.R. Machado, V.A.S. Braga, F.R. Tocantins and M.A.B. Merighi. Healthy aging from the perspective of the elderly: An integrative review. Revista Brasileira de Geriatria e Gerontologia, 20: 878–889, 2017.

Tian, Y.-L., T. Kanade and J.F. Cohn. Facial expression analysis. In Handbook of Face Recognition, pp. 247–275. Springer, 2005.

Titos, M., A. Bueno, L. García, C. Benítez and J.C. Segura. Classification of isolated volcano-seismic events based on inductive transfer learning. IEEE Geoscience and Remote Sensing Letters, 17(5): 869–873, 2019.

Torcate, A.S., M.A. de Santana, G.M.M. Moreno, A. Suarez, J.C. Gomes, W.P. dos Santos, F.S. Fonseca and G.M. de Souza. Intervenções e impactos da musicoterapia no contexto da doença de Alzheimer: Uma revisão de literatura sob a perspectiva da computação afetiva. Anais do IV Simpósio de Inovação em Engenharia Biomédica-SABIO, 2020, pp. 31, 2020.

Trnka, R. and I. Stuchlíková. Anger coping strategies and anger regulation. Re-constructing Emotional Spaces: From Experience to Regulation, pp. 89–103, 2011.

Vargas, A.C.G., A. Paes and C.N. Vasconcelos. Um estudo sobre redes neurais convolucionais e sua aplicação em detecção de pedestres. In Proceedings of the XXIX Conference on Graphics, Patterns and Images, volume 1. sn, 2016.

Varley, P.A., S. Cristina, A. Bonnici and K.P. Camilleri. As plain as the nose on your face? In VISIGRAPP (4: VISAPP), pp. 471–479, 2021.

Verma, P. and H.P. Renukadevi. Face recognition using open cv. Annals of the Romanian Society for Cell Biology, 25(6): 6272–6281, 2021.

Vicencio-Martínez, A.A., B. Tovar-Corona and L.I. Garay-Jiménez. Emotion recognition system based on electroencephalography. In 2019 16th International Conference on Electrical Engineering, Computing Science and Automatic Control (CCE), pp. 1–6. IEEE, 2019.

Viola, P. and M. Jones. Rapid object detection using a boosted cascade of simple features. In Proceedings of the 2001 IEEE Computer Society Conference on Computer Vision and Pattern Recognition. CVPR 2001, volume 1, pp. I–I. IEEE, 2001.

W. H. O. WHO. Ageing. Available in: https://www.who.int/health−topics/ageingtab = tab1, 2018.

W. H. O. WHO. Ageing and health. Available in: https://www.who.int/news − room/fact − sheets/ detail/ageing − and − health, 2021.

Witten, I.H., E. Frank, M.A. Hall, C. Pal and M. Data. Practical machine learning tools and techniques. In Data Mining, Volume 2, pp. 4, 2005.

Xue, B., M. Zhang and W.N. Browne. Particle swarm optimisation for feature selection in classification: Novel initialisation and updating mechanisms. Applied Soft Computing, 18: 261–276, 2014.

Ying, W., Y. Zhang, J. Huang and Q. Yang. Transfer learning via learning to transfer. In International Conference on Machine Learning, pp. 5085–5094. PMLR, 2018.

You, K., Y. Liu, J. Wang and M. Long. Logme: Practical assessment of pre-trained models for transfer learning. In International Conference on Machine Learning, pp. 12133–12143. PMLR, 2021.

Zhang, L., D. Tjondronegoro and V. Chandran. Representation of facial expression categories in continuous arousal–valence space: Feature and correlation. Image and Vision Computing, 32(12): 1067–1079, 2014.

Zhuang, F., Z. Qi, K. Duan, D. Xi, Y. Zhu, H. Zhu, H. Xiong and Q. He. A comprehensive survey on transfer learning. Proceedings of the IEEE, 109(1): 43–76, 2020.

Zilidis, G. and V. Zilidou. The use of new technologies addressing social exclusion and improving the quality of life of the elderly. Interscientific Health Care, 10(4), 2018.

Zomorodi-moghadam, M., M. Abdar, Z. Davarzani, X. Zhou, P. Pławiak and U.R. Acharya. Hybrid particle swarm optimization for rule discovery in the diagnosis of coronary artery disease. Expert Systems, 38(1): e12485, 2021.

Chapter 7

Identification of Emotion Parameters in Music to Modulate Human Affective States

Maíra A. Santana,[1] Ingrid B. Nunes,[1] Andressa L.Q. Ribeiro,[2] Flávio S. Fonseca,[1] Arianne S. Torcate,[1] Amanda Suarez,[2] Vanessa Marques,[2] Nathália Córdula,[3] Juliana C. Gomes,[1] Giselle M.M. Moreno[4] and Wellington P. Santos[1,2,]*

1 Introduction

In recent years, the study of affect has been growing exponentially, especially in the computational field. This is mostly due to the fact that emotions play the role of directing human behaviors and interactions (Suhaimi et al., 2020). Therefore, if emotional states play a central role in our social life, guiding motivations, communication, memory and learning, it is natural and important that there is also progress in the study of affect through artificial intelligence (Suhaimi et al., 2020). In this sense, emotions are understood as subjective, physiological and cognitive reactions to environmental, internal or external events, which define the behavior of an individual when faced with a stimulus (Fonseca, 2016). In general, the lit-

[1] Polytechnic School of the University of Pernambuco, Recife, Brazil.
[2] Federal University of Pernambuco, Recife, Brazil.
[3] Faculdade Pernambucana de Saúde, Recife, Brazil.
[4] IAG, University of São Paulo, São Paulo, Brazil.
* Corresponding author: wellington.santos@ufpe.br

erature considers 6 emotions as basic and universal: joy, sadness, anger, disgust, fear and surprise (Meska et al., 2020). Furthermore, the neutral state is regularly used in the field as an intermediate condition that precedes the other emotional states (Meska et al., 2020).

It is important to highlight that there are several forms of emotional expression, such as changes in the individual's vocal features (rhythm and frequency) (Miguel, 2015). Studies even prove a strong relationship between these features and the musical purpose of communicating these emotional states (Juslin and Laukka, 2003). However, in addition to expressing affectivity, the human ability to recognize these states through bodily, sound, physiological signals, and others is an essential aspect of a healthy social dynamic.

Physiologically, humans are able to demonstrate and recognize emotional behaviors due to some neural structures and connections. These structures make up the brain's limbic system, whose main structures are: the cingulate gyrus, parahippocampal gyrus, hypothalamus, thalamus, hippocampus, amygdala, septum, prefrontal area and cerebellum (Rolls, 2015). The activation of these structures is also part of the brain response to musical stimuli, since music is a way of expressing emotions (Hsieh et al., 2012).

Furthermore, damages to these brain structures is linked to some dysfunctions and diseases, such as Alzheimer's Disease, Parkinson's Disease, Autistic Spectrum Disorder, and depression. In the case of Alzheimer's, Hsieh et al. (2012) shows that with the progression of the disease, the individual usually presents a certain deficiency in the recognition of emotions from facial expressions (Hsieh et al., 2012). A similar behavior was also found in the study by Li et al. (2016), which shows that there are dysfunctions in the connection networks on the limbic system of patients with Alzheimer's, hindering their ability to perceive and express emotions (Li et al., 2016). On the other hand, these pathologies rarely affect brain regions associated with auditory processing. Therefore, auditory stimuli, particularly music, can be used to support perception, control, induction, and expression of emotions in audiences like these.

As one of the oldest ways of human expression and communication, music has the potential to universally and cross-culturally affect human beings (Cowen et al., 2020; Juslin, 2013; Song et al., 2016). The effects of music on the human body are diverse. Such effects start in structures of the Central Nervous System and require complex cognitive functions. Music is capable of activating areas all over the brain, especially those related to the reward system, and to auditory, motor and visual processing (Arjmand et al., 2017; Koelsch, 2018). In addition, musical interaction triggers physiological, hormonal and mood-modulating responses (Arjmand et al., 2017; Schaefer, 2017). Furthermore, during musical composition, melodic parameters are able to incorporate emotional aspects in the music, thus conveying emotions (Juslin, 2013; Song et al., 2016).

The modulation of the affective state by music is a tool that has been explored in the context of music therapy for various cognitive and behavioral disorders. Music therapy is a therapeutic approach in which musical stimuli are used to achieve non-musical goals (de l'Etoile, 2008). In recent years it has been better studied and explored for various applications. Several studies have sought to understand the effects of musical stimuli in the context of therapy for people with Autistic Spectrum Disorder and learning difficulties (Safonicheva and Ovchinnikova, 2021). In these groups, aspects such as attention, socialization and trust are strongly developed. Other studies have identified a number of benefits of these musical stimuli in elderly people with Parkinson's Disease, Alzheimer's Disease and other neurodegenerative disorders (de l'Etoile, 2008). In these groups, music plays an important role in slowing down the progression of the disease. Studies also showed that adequate musical stimuli may have positive effects in reducing depression and anxiety (de l'Etoile, 2008). One of the main musical parameters that allow this modulation of human affective state is the emotions conveyed by the music itself. For example, if music expresses happiness, resonance effects induced by it on brain waves is likely to improve the mood of this individual (Schaefer, 2017). Similar processes may occur for other affective states.

Nevertheless, perceiving, controlling, inducing, and expressing emotions consist in some of the most complex and fundamental aspects of every human being development. These complex abilities also guide our social skills and our interaction with the world elements around us. One of the reasons for this complexity is that an emotion manifests itself differently in each individual. Therefore, studies developed in the last century came up with two main ways to represent affective states: the categorical and the dimensional approaches (Yu et al., 2015). The dimensional approach has particularly drawn attention since it can provide a more fine-grained emotional assessment. In this approach, emotions are represented as continuous numerical values such as valence-arousal two-dimensional space (Russell, 1980). Valence values are related to the degree of positive and negative emotions, while arousal represents the activation degree (excitement and calmness) (Russell, 1980). Based on this emotion representation proposed by Russell (1980), many studies describe emotions as function of these parameters (Cheuk et al., 2020; Grekow, 2018; Vatolkin and Nagathil, 2019; Yu et al., 2015). However, they usually acquire valence and arousal rating from human assessment, which is highly subjective, nonspecific, and subject-dependent. Thus, it is important to work on ways to automatically define valence and arousal ratings. Artificial Intelligence (AI) techniques may be of great help in this context. From this tool, we can train an algorithm to learn how to associate some stimuli to valence-arousal values, thus acquiring emotional information from these stimuli.

Therefore, this chapter proposes an approach to the automatic identification of emotions expressed by music of different genres based on the prediction of valence and arousal parameters. We explore AI regression tools and particle swarm methods in an attempt to find an optimal configuration to associate musical stimuli to valence and arousal values. This method may be of great help to support human emotional perception of music or other kind of content. It may also be useful to improve the affective component of human-computer interaction in several applications, such as recommendation systems. Moreover, it may address some music therapy issues related to creating and recommending personalized content to better achieve patient needs and, consequently, improve the therapeutic intervention.

The chapter is organized as follows: Section 2 will present some related studies that also seek to assess musical content by its emotional effect in human beings. Then, in Section 3, we present the experimental materials and methods proposed in this chapter. This section is followed by the results and discussions, and at the last section we provide some conclusions, highlighting limitations and future perspectives.

2 Related Studies

The research carried out by Sharma et al. (2020) aimed to classify songs in emotions through the prediction of valence and arousal, based on the Russell model. The study was divided into two parts. In the first part, they performed a comparative study between classical algorithms such as SVM, Logistic Regression, KNN, Random Forest, Naive Bayes and decision trees on audio resources. In the second part, a hybrid model based on MLP was developed to increase the accuracy of the forecasts. The database used in their experiments was the PMEmo 2019. Their results demonstrate that, both for prediction of arousal and valence, the SVM algorithm with RBF kernel stood out in terms of accuracy, obtaining, respectively, 68.75% and 61.97%. The proposed model, managed to increase the overall prediction accuracy of some algorithms, such as the Linear SVM, which was equivalent to 50.33%, with the application of the model, the accuracy managed to reach 63%.

In order to classify emotions in music, Chen and Li (2020) proposes a stack-based multifunctional combined network, applying CNN-LSTM (Convolutional neural networks-long term long memory) with a combination of 2D features input and 1D features input through DNN (deep neural networks). The authors used the Last.fm database, composed of one million songs. Following Thayer's emotion model, four emotional tag were extracted. Emotional classes were angry, happy, relaxed and sad, and 500 songs were collected from each emotion category, resulting in 2,000 songs. Their experiments show that the classification of music audios into emotions using the proposed model reached a 68% precision rate. On the other hand, song lyrics rating achieved a precision of 74%. Overall, the average precision obtained by their model was 78%.

The study by Sobeeh et al. (2019) investigates the effect of listening to two pieces of high-excitement music. The snippets have the same square root of the mean amplitude and different valences (positive happy valence and negative anxious valence), in reaction time and Simon effect. The high arousal anxious (AHA) group showed faster reaction time and greater Simon effect than the other groups. Thus, this larger Simon effect was interpreted by poor interference control through an incongruous conflict situation. The high arousal group showed a faster reaction time and greater Simon effect compared to the silent control group. Although the study results are consistent with previous studies of poor interference control with positive mood, it provides a new finding that negative anxious mood tracks faster reaction time, while interference control with positive mood was limited and with greatest Simon effect.

Hizlisoy et al. (2021) proposed an approach to the recognition of musical emotions based on the deep convolutional neural network architecture of long short-term memory. The authors used features extracted by feeding convolutional neural network layers with log-mel filterbank energies and mel-frequency cepstrum coefficients, in addition to standard acoustic resources. The results show that adding new features to the default audio attributes improves classification performance. Improved performance was achieved after selecting features by applying the correlation-based feature selection method.

In the study of Vatolkin and Nagathil (2019) they propose a computational method to associate emotions with music. They tested different linear regression methods to predict arousal and valence values. The features extracted from the audio signals were combinations of energy, harmony, rhythm, and timbre parameters. The greatest contribution of this work was the inclusion of a feature selection step. After extracting the features, they applied a Minimum Redundancy-Maximum Relevance (MRMR) algorithm for feature selection. From this selection they could assess different sets of features to represent audio data. Therefore, the authors found that timbre features are the most relevant in arousal prediction, while valence prediction is mostly associated to rhythm features. In this study RMSE values were close to 1 in most of the tested feature combination. Other sets of audio features and regression algorithms may be included to improve results.

Cheuk et al. (2020) studied a novel approach of Triplet Neural Netwoks (TNNs) in the context of emotion prediction from music. They assess these network's performance in representing musical signals in a regression task by using this representation as input for regression models based on Support Vector Machines and Gradient Boosting Machines. The authors compared the representation provided by TNNs to others feature selection methods such as Principal Component Analysis (PCA) and Autoencoders (AE). Their approach overcame the other methods with higher prediction rates for both valence and arousal, possibly providing new music categorisation and recommendation approaches.

The work from Grekow (2018) also investigates different features combination in an attempt to find an optimal set of features to represent audio signals in order to improve music emotion detection. In their study they applied regression algorithms to estimate valence and arousal values. The authors used 31 features to represent the signals, such as Zero Crossings, Spectral Centroid, Spectral Flux, Spectral Rolloff, Mel-Frequency Cepstral Coefficients (MFCC), chroma, mean, geometric mean, power mean, median, moments up to the 5th order, energy, root mean square (RMS), spectrum, flatness, crest, variance, skewness, kurtosis of probability distribution, and a single Gaussian estimate. They tested different combinations of these features, which were used as input of SMOreg, REPTree, M5P-SMOreg regression algorithms. The authors found that feature selection process improved regression performance in almost 50%. For arousal prediction, their approach achieved Pearson's correlation coefficient of 0.79, and mean absolute error of 0.09. Regarding valence prediction, this best model showed moderate performance, with correlation coefficient 0.58, and 0.10 of error.

The article by Yang and Hirschberg (2018) aimed to perform a study on the continuous tracking of emotions, following Russell's circumplex model of affect, in order to predict arousal and valence. The combination of raw wave form signals inputs and log-mel filterbank features was performed to assess their joint effects. The neural network architecture used contains a set of convolutional neural network layers (CNN) and bidirectional long-term memory layers (BLSTM) to take into account the temporal and spectral variation and the textual content model. In order to evaluate the performance of the model, the SEMAINE database and the RECOLA database were chosen. For all of these experiments, the correlation of agreement coefficient of tension (CCC) was used as the objective function to train the models. The results demonstrate that all models perform significantly better than the baseline model, which indicates that the models can learn important features for the arousal and valence of the data of both databases. Furthermore, the 'W Only' model outperforms the 'S Only' model in predicting arousal, while the 'S Only' model outperforms the 'W Only' model in predicting valence. Finally, by combining the waveform and spectrogram inputs, the 'W + S' model provides further improvement in predicting both arousal (0.680 for SEMAINE database, and 0.692 for RECOLA) and valence (0.506 for SEMAINE and 0.423 for RECOLA data), which show that waveforms and spectrograms contain complementary emotion information. Comparing results, the CCC for predicting valence in SEMAINE is systematically higher than in RECOLA.

In the study of Tan et al. (2019), the objective was to create a system capable of detecting the mood of a song based on the four quadrants of Russell's model. To achieve this, the researchers used two classification algorithms (SVM and Naïve Bayes) to train separate classifier models for valence and arousal using selected audio resources for SVM and lyrical resources for Naïve Bayes. This process returns four trained valence and arousal models for each algorithm. The dataset used for this study consisted of 180 songs that had lyrics annotated while 162 songs had audio annotations. The number of songs that contained both lyrics and audio annotations was of 133 songs. Arousal detection is highly accurate when used with audio features, while valence detection is highly accurate when using letters. The arousal is easily distinguishable when heard, as its range would be from top to bottom. This study focused more on the use of time to detect arousal using audio resources. Valence detection using lyrics with Naïve Bayes resulted in greater accuracy than using audio because it is difficult to distinguish and analyze melody and the positivity or negativity of a word as they cannot be correctly distinguished.

In Table 1 we present the main information from these related studies, such as their main goal, the computation techniques used and their main findings. At the last line of this table is our method, proving that our proposal is well contextualized in the state-of-the-art.

Table 1: Summary of related works.

Work	Main goal	Method	Main results
Sharma et al. (2020)	Emotion classification in musics through the prediction of valence and arousal	Using the PMEmo 2019 database, the authors compared the performance of SVM, Logistic Regression, KNN, Random Forest, Naive Bayes and decision tree architectures.	They found accuracies up to 68.75% to predict arousal, and 61.97% for valence prediction.
Chen and Li (2020)	Classification of music into 4 emotions categories using 2,000 songs from the Last.fm database.	Their classifier was a hybrid approach combining LSTM to features extracted by deep neural networks.	Emotion classification was better when using the song lyrics (precision of 74%) than when using only the melody (68%).
Sobeeh et al. (2019)	Measure the effect of listening two pieces of high-arousal songs, one with positive valence (happy), and the other with negative valence (anxious).	They compared the results in terms of the reaction time and Simon effect.	The main finding of this study was that negative anxious mood tracks faster reaction time than positive happy music stimuli.
Hizlisoy et al. (2021)	Recognition of musical emotions based on arousal and valence parameters.	The authors built their own database composed of 124 Turkish traditional excerpts of 30s. They represented the songs using a combination of CNN and standard acoustic features. It was then used as input to a LSTM classifier	They achieved an overall accuracy of 99.19%. However, the amount of songs in the database is small. This is especially problematic when using deep learning methods and can easily lead to overfitting.
Vatolkin and Nagathil (2019)	Associate emotions with music based on the prediction of arousal and valence values.	The main proposal of this study was the inclusion of a feature selection step using a Minimum Redundancy-Maximum Relevance algorithm. Than, the authors tested different linear regression methods to assess arousal and valence prediction.	They achieved RMSE values close to 1 after adding the feature selection approach, also finding that that timbre features are the most relevant in arousal prediction, while valence prediction is mostly associated to rhythm features.
Cheuk et al. (2020)	Emotion prediction from music in terms of valence and arousal	The authors proposed a novel feature selection approach based on Triplet Neural Networks (TNN). They use 744 music signals from the DEAM database.	Their music representation using TNN overcame other widely used methods such as PCA and autoencoder. The proposed method achieved higher Pearson's correlation coefficient rates for both valence (0.367 ± 0.113) and arousal (0.662 ± 0.065) when compared to these other methods
Grekow (2018)	Improve emotion detection from music by assessing different features combination applied to regression algorithms to estimate valence and arousal values.	The author used different combination of 31 features to represent the signals. As regression algorithms they performed experiments with SMOreg, REPTree, and M5P-SMOreg.	He found that feature selection process improved regression performance in almost 50%. Their approach achieved Pearson's correlation coefficient of 0.79 for arousal and of 0.58 for valence prediction.
Yang and Hirschberg (2018)	Perform a study on the continuous tracking of emotions in terms of arousal and valence.	The authors used convolutional neural network (CNN) and bidirectional long-term memory layers (BLSTM) for feature extraction and classification using two databases: SEMAINE and RECOLA.	Their approach achieved concordance coefficient up to 0.680 for arousal prediction and 0.506 in predicting valence using SEMAINE data. The results were slightly lesse satisfying for RECOLA data for both arousal (0.692) and valence (0.423)
Tan et al. (2019)	Develop a system capable of detecting emotions in songs based on the four quadrants of Russell's model.	The authors used two classification algorithms (SVM and Naïve Bayes) to train separate classifier models for valence and arousal. The dataset consisted of 180 songs with lyrics, 162 songs with only audio annotations, and 133 songs with both audio and lyrics.	They found that SVM was better to predict arousal while Random Forest showed better performance when predicting valence.
Our approach	Emotion prediction in terms of valence and arousal from music signals.	We applied SVM, ELM, MLP, Random Forest, and Linear regression algorithms to predict both arousal and valence parameters	Random Forest outperformed the other models with Pearson's correlation coefficient of 0.76 ± 0.02 for valence prediction, and 0.85 ± 0.01 for predicting arousal values.

3 Materials and Methods

Our proposed method of recognizing emotions in music consists of five main steps (Fig. 1): (1) acquisition and organization of the music database; (2) pre-processing; (3) feature extraction; (4) feature selection; and (5) performing regression experiments to estimate valence and arousal values. Initially, we requested access to the database "Emotions in Music" (Soleymani et al., 2013), it consists of 45-second

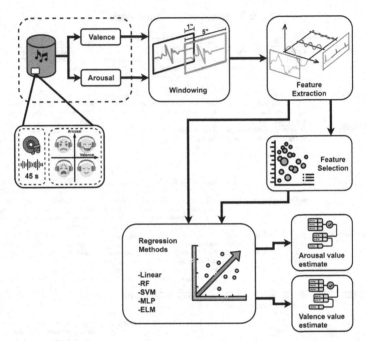

Figure 1: Diagram of the proposed method. First of all we have a database containing 744 music excerpts of 45s with arousal and valence annotations. Then, all songs with their respective valence and arousal data were submitted to a windowing process with windows of 5s and overlapping of 1s. After segmentation, we extracted explicit features from these signals. Then, a feature selection step was conducted. Finally, both arousal and valence knowledge datasets were used as input to assess the performance of different regression models in estimating their values.

excerpts of 744 songs available in the "1 to 1000" package from the Free Music Archive (FMA). All excerpts were pre-processed, then, valence and arousal ratings were assigned to each by the participants.

During the following phases, we performed a 5-second windowing, with a 1-second overlap in the available exertions, in addition to extracting 35 features useful to the regression problem. Subsequently, we performed a feature selection process using the Particle Swarm Optimization (PSO) algorithm. Therefore, we created 4 knowledge bases: 2 with the full set of features, being one with the values of valence and the other for arousal values; and another 2 bases from valence and arousal datasets represented by the selected features. In the fifth step, we assess regression performances from the following algorithms: Random Forest, SVM, MLP, Linear and ELM. All experiments were conducted using k-fold cross-validation with 10 folds and 30 runs in order to generate statistically relevant results and avoid overfitting. Later, to assess the statistical behavior, we plotted the results in boxplot and tables with average and standard deviation values. All these steps are illustrated in Fig. 1.

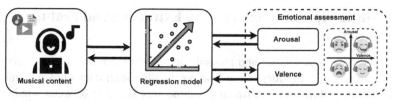

Figure 2: System usability. The optimal trained regression model is able to predict arousal and valence values from musical content, providing emotional information. The system may also recommend musical content from a given emotional state given in terms of valence and arousal.

Our approach of predicting emotional parameters may be applied to situations such as the one represented in Fig. 2, where the trained regression model is able to effectively predict arousal and valence values or recommend musical content from these emotional parameters. Therefore, one may use the system to support human emotional perception of music or other kind of content. It is particularly useful to guide and optimize personalized therapeutic approaches such as music therapy by supporting the perception, control, induction, and expression of emotional states. This way of automatically rate content based on valence and arousal parameters may be also applied to improve human-machine affective interactions, thus refining custom content recommendation systems. The system may also act as the core of assistive solutions so that people with social, learning and communication disabilities would be able to benefit from it.

3.1 Music Database

The database was created by Soleymani et al. (2013) from the music database of the Free Music Archive (FMA) website, which contains several songs of different genres. In all, 1000 songs were selected. For the selection, the 300 songs classified as best are downloaded in MP3 format, and correspond to the genres: Blues, Electronic, Rock, Classical, Folk, Jazz, Country, and Pop. Tracks with more than 10 minutes or less than 1 minute were excluded, resulting in 125 songs of each genre. Due to some redundancies, the dataset has shrunk to 744 songs. After selecting the songs, the authors extracted 45s excerpts from each of them. Snippets are pulled from a random (evenly distributed) starting point for each song. Then, the excerpts were all converted to the same sampling frequency (44100Hz) (Soleymani et al., 2013).

During the assembly of the database, the authors also collected annotations regarding to parameters associated with emotions. For these notes, the participants received the definitions of arousal (emotional intensity) and valence (positive emotion versus negative emotion). They were also asked to provide personal information, including gender, age and nationality. These participants were subjected to two short audio clips of music that contained highly dynamic emotion shifts; they then indicated whether arousal and valence were increasing or decreasing. After annotating songs continuously, the participants were further asked to rate the level of arousal or valence for the entire clip on a 9-point scale.

3.2 Music Segmentation, Feature Extraction and Feature Selection

All instances in both valence and arousal datasets were submitted to a 5-second windowing process. In order to not lose potentially useful data when transitioning between windows, an overlap of 1 second was included between windows. After that, we extracted 35 time-frequency-statistical features from all instances. The list of features can be seen in Fig. 3. It is important to mention that all procedures reported in this subsection were performed in the GNU/Octave mathematical computing environment, version 4.0.3 (Eaton et al., 2015). This step resulted in a dataset with 8184 instances and 35 attributes for both valence and arousal data.

After extracting features we conducted an attribute selection step. Selection was performed using PSO method. Initially proposed by Kennedy and Eberhart

Parameter	Equation	Parameter	Equation
Mean (μ)	$\mu = \frac{1}{N}\sum_{n=1}^{N} x_n$	Waveform length	$WL = \sum_{n=1}^{N-1} |x_{n+1} - x_n|$
Variance	$var = \frac{1}{N-1}\sum_{n=1}^{N}(x_n - \mu)^2$	Zero crossing	$ZC = \sum_{n=1}^{N-1}[sgn(x_n \times x_{n+1}) \cap |x_n - x_{n+1}| \geq threshold]$ $sgn(x) = \begin{cases} 1, if\, x \geq threshold \\ 0, \quad otherwise \end{cases}$
Standard devintion (σ)	$\sigma = \sqrt{\frac{1}{N-1}\sum_{n=1}^{N}|x_n - \mu|^2}$	Slope Sign Changes	$SSC = \sum_{n=1}^{N-1}[f(x_n - x_{n-1}) \times (x_n - x_{n+1})]]$ $f(x) = \begin{cases} 1, if\, x \geq threshold \\ 0, \quad otherwise \end{cases}$
Root mean square	$RMS = \sqrt{\frac{\sum_{n=1}^{N}(x_n)^2}{N}}$	Hjorth parameter activity	$Hjorth_{activity} = \frac{1}{N-1}\sum_{n=1}^{N}(x_n - \mu)^2$
Average Amplitude Changes	$AAC = \frac{1}{N}\left(\sum_{n=1}^{N}\left|\frac{d\,x(t)}{dt}\right|\right)$	Hjorth parameter mobility	$Hjorth_{mobility} = \sqrt{\frac{var\left(\frac{d\,x(t)}{dt}\right)}{var(x(t))}}$
Difference Absolute Deviation	$DASDV = \sqrt{\frac{1}{N}\sum_{n=1}^{N}\left(\frac{d\,x(t)}{dt}\right)^2}$	Hjorth parameter complexity	$Hjorth_{complexity} = \frac{Hjorth_{mobility}\left(\frac{d\,x(t)}{dt}\right)}{Hjorth_{mobility}(x(t))}$
Integrated Absolute Value	$IAV = \sum_{n=1}^{N} x_n$	Mean frequency	$MNF = \frac{\sum_{j=1}^{M} f_j P_j}{\sum_{j=1}^{M} P_j}$ Where f_j, P_j are the frequencies and power of the spectrum, respectively, and M is the length of the frequencies
Logarithm Detector	$LOGD = e^{\left(\frac{1}{N}\sum_{n=1}^{N}\log(|x_n|)\right)}$	Median frequency	$MDF = \frac{1}{2}\sum_{j=1}^{M} P_j$
Simple Square Integral	$SSI = \sum_{n=1}^{N} x_n^2$	Mean power	$MNP = \sum_{j=1}^{M}\frac{P_j}{M}$
Mean Absolute Value	$MAV = \frac{1}{N}\sum_{n=1}^{N}|x_n|$	Peak frequency	$PKF = \max(P_j)$
Mean Logarithm Kernel	$MLOGK = \frac{1}{N}\sum_{n=1}^{N} x_n$	Power Spectrum ratio	$PSR = \frac{PKF}{\sum_{j=1}^{M} P_j}$
Skewness (s)	$s = \frac{\frac{1}{N}\sum_{n=1}^{N}(x_n - \mu)^2}{\sigma^3}$	Total Power	$TP = \sum_{j=1}^{M} P_j$
Kurtosis	$kurt = \frac{\frac{1}{N}\sum_{n=1}^{N}(x_n - \mu)^4}{\sigma^4}$	First Spectral Moment	$SM1 = \sum_{j=1}^{M} f_j P_j$
Maximum Amplitude	$MAX = \max(x_n)$	Second Spectral Moment	$SM2 = \sum_{j=1}^{M} f_j^2 P_j$
Third Moment	$M3 = \left|\frac{1}{N}\sum_{n=1}^{N}(x_n)^3\right|$	Third Spectral Moment	$SM3 = \sum_{j=1}^{M} f_j^3 P_j$
Fourth Moment	$M4 = \left|\frac{1}{N}\sum_{n=1}^{N}(x_n)^4\right|$	Variance of Central Frequency	$VCF = \frac{SM2}{TP} - \left(\frac{SM1}{TP}\right)^2$
Fifth Moment	$M5 = \left|\frac{1}{N}\sum_{n=1}^{N}(x_n)^5\right|$	Shannon's entropy	$E = -\sum_i S_i^2 \log(S_i^2)$, where S is the signal

Figure 3: List of the 35 extracted features with their mathematical representations.

(1995), PSO consists on a bioinspired algorithm that is based on the collective behavior of a group of particles namely swarming. First of all, we initialize a population of particles with random positions and velocities on the dimensions in the problem space. Each particle of the swarm moves through the search space of the problem and have their position and velocity updated during the search for an optimal subset of features. The search procedure proceeds iteratively until the most suitable subset is found or when the algorithm reaches the maximum number of iterations defined by the user. For this study, we set PSO algorithm according to the parameters shown in Table 2. This method has been successively used to select features in a variety of applications (Barbosa et al., 2021; Rodrigues et al., 2019; Zomorodi-moghadam et al., 2021). It can be used as a tool in an attempt to increase the generalization ability; to optimize processing (time and memory consumption); or even to acquire human knowledge from the extracted features. In this chapter, where we extract attributes from the data in an explicit way, it is possible, through the feature selection, to perceive which are the most relevant aspects to represent a given set of data. In particular, it is possible to see which characteristics of time, frequency and statistics may be more relevant for predicting the aspects of valence and arousal induced by certain songs, which can be directly associated with emotions.

Table 2: PSO settings.

Parameter	Setting
Individual weight	0.34
Inertia weight	0.33
Social weight	0.33
Iterations	50
Iterations	50

3.3 Regression Models

To carry out the experiments we used the following algorithms: Random Forest (RF), Support Vector Machine (SVM), Linear Regression, Multilayer Perceptron (MLP) and Extreme Learning Machine (ELM). As shown in Table 3, each of the regressors we used had different settings.

Random Forest is an algorithm that works by combining decision trees. Each of these trees is composed by vectors of clustered samples, randomly obtained. The vectors have a similar distribution for all trees in the forest and select subsets of random samples from the initial data (Biau and Scornet, 2016; Breiman, 2001). This algorithm uses the supervised learning paradigm and are widely applied to solve classification and regression problems. However, for classification problems, the chosen prediction is given by the class most voted by the trees. In regression problems, the prediction is given by the average of the values obtained by each tree (Biau and Scornet, 2016). Due to the operating mode of this algorithm, RF can be applied in databases with large data volumes. In addition, it also adapts well to databases with missing data and does not tend to overfit the model, even

Table 3: Configuration of the regression models.

Regressor	Settings
Random Forest	Trees: 10, 20, 50, 100, 150, 200, 250, 300 and 350
	Batch size: 100
SVM	Kernel functions: linear, polynomial (d = 2, d = 3, and d = 4), and RBF (γ = 0.50)
ELM	Kernel functions: linear, polynomial (d = 2, d = 3, and d = 4), RBF and sigmoid
	Neurons in the hidden layer: 500.
Linear Regression	-
MLP	1 hidden layer: 10, 20, 50, and 100 neurons
	2 hidden layers with 20 neurons each (20, 20)
	2 hidden layers with 100 neurons each (100, 100)

with the increase in the number of trees (Biau and Scornet, 2016; Breiman, 2001; da Silva et al., 2021; de Lima et al., 2020).

The Support Vector Machine is also a supervised machine learning algorithm. SVM algorithm was initially developed by Vapnik and has been applied to classification and regression problems. This algorithm can be used in databases with more than two classes, through the one against all technique (Ahmad et al., 2018; Patle and Chouhan, 2013). SVM works by creating a hyperplane capable of separating the different classes of input data. The optimal hyperplane will be the one that separates the classes in the best way and that is farthest from the support vectors. That is, hyperplanes that have larger margins (Ahmad et al., 2018). These hyperplanes are defined by kernel functions. Kernel functions allow mapping of linearly non-separable data into linearly separable spaces (Patle and Chouhan, 2013). In addition, they help to find the optimal hyperplane by maximizing the hyperplane margins (Ahmad et al., 2018). For the experiments of this research, we tested the SVM with linear kernel, polynomial kernel and Radial Basis Function (RBF) kernel. Such kernel types are mathematically described in Table 4.

Table 4: Kernel functions used in SVM and ELM architectures.

Kernel type	Kernel function
Linear	$K(\mathbf{x}, \mathbf{y}) = \mathbf{x} \bullet \mathbf{y}$
Polynomial	$K(\mathbf{x}, \mathbf{y}) = (1 + \mathbf{x} \bullet \mathbf{y})^d$
Radial Basis Function (RBF)	$K(\mathbf{x}, \mathbf{y}) = \exp(-\gamma (\mathbf{x} - \mathbf{y}) \bullet (\mathbf{x} - \mathbf{y}))$
Sigmoid	$K(\mathbf{x}, \mathbf{y}) = \tanh(b(\mathbf{x}, \mathbf{y}) + c)$

Linear Regression is another machine learning technique used to create a prediction model that already is well studied in the field of statistics. This model is given by the correlation obtained between dependent and independent variables, through a linear adjustment of the data (Kavitha et al., 2016). The model obtained by the Linear Regression seeks to reduce the error associated with the least square of the residuals, given by the original data and the data obtained by the model prediction (Schuld et al., 2016).

Multilayer Perceptron is one of the neural network algorithms that operates following the feedforward model. Therefore, it has input, hidden and output layers. All these layers are made up of several neurons. These neurons can be present in varying amounts in each of the layers. When MLP has more hidden layers in its structure, it is possible to apply it to solve non-linear problems (Desai and Shah, 2020; Driss et al., 2017). In addition, each of these neurons have weights associated with each other, which are adjusted during the training phase usually using a backpropagation procedure. This training phase observed in MLP is of the supervised type. It allows the weights associated with neurons to be adjusted and updated by subtracting the output response (Desai and Shah, 2020; Driss et al., 2017). However, MLP has certain drawbacks in addressing problems. One of them is the fact that it is not possible to have an approximation of the function format when modeling a problem, the commonly called 'black box'. Furthermore, it is important to point out that a greater number of layers and neurons does not guarantee better performance and tend to require more processing time and computational power (Singh and Husain, 2014).

The Extreme Learning Machine, like the MLP, is a type of neural network that operates through the feedforward process. In addition, ELM is also built by input, hidden, and output layers. Unlike MLP, ELM model does not use the back-propagation technique during the training stage. Moreover, the input weights are randomly initialized which leads to a decrease in processing time when compared to MLP (Ahmad et al., 2018). In ELM, the output weights determination is ana-lytically performed. This process does not occur iteratively, which results in faster processing and good applicability to more complex problems (de Moraes Ramos et al., 2021). Furthermore, ELM presents a good performance generalization, due to the tendency to have a lower norm of its weights (Deng et al., 2009; Huang et al., 2006).

All these models were trained using the k-fold cross-validation method with 10 folds to avoid overfitting (Jung and Hu, 2015; Siriyasatien et al., 2018). In addition, we trained the architectures 30 times to assess their statistical behavior and thus measure the reliability of the results. At this stage we used the Waikato Environment for Knowledge Analysis (WEKA), version 3.8, for experiments with Linear Regression, SVM, Random Forest and MLP (Witten and Frank, 2005). For the ELM experiments, we implemented the models in the GNU/Octave program-ming environment (version 4.0.3) (Eaton et al., 2015).

3.4 Metrics

To evaluate the performance obtained by the algorithms, we used seven metrics, which are: Pearson's Correlation Coefficient (PCC), Kendall's Coefficient of Con-cordance (KCC), Spearman's Correlation (SCC), Mean Absolute Error (MAE), Root Mean Squared Error (RMSE), Relative Absolute Error (RAE) and Root Rel-ative Squared Error (RRSE). Table 5 presents each metric along with their respec-tive mathematical expressions.

Table 5: Metrics and their mathematical expressions.

Metric	Mathematical expression
Pearson's Correlation Coefficient	$r_{xy} = \dfrac{\sum (x_i - \overline{x}) \sum (y_i - \overline{y})}{\sqrt{\sum (x_i - \overline{x})^2} \sqrt{\sum (y_i - \overline{y})^2}}$
Kendall's Coefficient of Concordance	$W = \dfrac{12S}{m^2(n^3 - n)}$
Spearman's Correlation	$\rho = 1 - \dfrac{6 \sum d_i^2}{n(n^2 - 1)}$
Mean absolute error	$MAE = \dfrac{1}{n} \sum_{i=1}^{n} |x_i - x|$
Root mean squared error	$RMSE = \sqrt{\dfrac{1}{n} \sum_{i=1}^{n} (S_i - O_i)^2}$
Relative absolute error	$RAE = \dfrac{\sum_{i=1}^{n} |p_i - a_i|}{\sum_{i=1}^{n} |\overline{a} - a_i|}$
Root relative squared error	$RRSE = \sqrt{\dfrac{\sum_{i=1}^{n} (p_i - a_i)^2}{\sum_{i=1}^{n} (a_i \overline{a})^2}}$

According to Zhou et al. (2016), the Pearson Correlation Coefficient is historically the first formal measure of correlation, and it is one of the most used relationship measures in regression problems. PCC is also known as the product-momentum correlation coefficient. The main objective is to measure the strength of the linear association/relation between two variables (Adler and Parmryd, 2010; Sedgwick, 2012). Briefly, Zhou et al. (2016) explains that PCC highlights the strength of the linear relationship between the two random variables x and y. Where, the value of the correlation coefficient is positive if the variables are directly related ($r_{xy} = 1$), and negative if the variables are considered uncorrelated ($r_{xy} = 0$).

Kendall's coefficient of agreement can be understood as a measure of agreement among m judges who rank a set of n entities (Field, 2005). This metric quantitatively assesses the coherence of the collective classification (S) provided by the (Franceschini and Maisano, 2021) models. The main intention is that Kendall's W presents results ranging from 0 (when there is no agreement) to 1 (when there is complete agreement).

Spearman's correlation coefficient is a distribution-free rank statistic, being a measure of the strength of an association between two variables (Hauke and Kossowski, 2011). Xiao et al. (2016) explain that, basically, Spearman's correlation assesses the strength of the relationship between two variables. In other words, it evaluates monotonous relationships, which can be linear or not. Spearman's correlation (ρ) between two variables (d and n) will have a similar (or identical) rank when the correlation is equal to 1, and will have a dissimilar rank when the observations are completely opposite, with correlation value equal to -1.

The mean absolute error is constantly used to evaluate regression models (Chai and Draxler, 2014; Qi et al., 2020) and is derived from a measure of the mean error. In other words, MAE is the mean of all absolute errors. Sammut and Webb (2011) explains that the MAE for a given testing set is the mean of the absolute values of the individual prediction errors over all n instances of that set. That is, each forecast error is the difference between the expected value (x_i) and the predicted value (x) for the instance.

The root mean square error is a widely used statistical metric to measure the performance of models (Chai and Draxler, 2014). The RMSE is the square root of the mean square of all errors. This metric stands out due to its general purpose for numerical predictions (Neill and Hashemi, 2018). In other words, RMSE is a measure that calculates the root mean square of the n errors between real values (S_i) and predictions (O_i). Chai and Draxler (2014) point out that this metric is useful and provides an overview of the error distribution.

Relative Absolute Error is the metric that returns the absolute error between actual and expected values between variables (Dineva and Atanasova, 2019; Mishra et al., 2018). RAE is often used to assess the performance of predictive models, particularly in areas such as machine learning, data mining and Artificial Intelligence (Subasi et al., 2020). The main goal of this metric is to return an error measure regarding the variability of the n results detected ($p_i - a_i$) in relation to the real values ($\bar{a} - a_i$) (Jeyasingh and Veluchamy, 2017).

Subasi et al. (2020) explains that the Root Relative Square Error refers to the result of a simple predictor if it had been used. A simple predictor can be thought as the real values average. Thus, the RRSE takes the total squared error ($(p_i - a_i)^2$) and normalizes it, dividing it by the total squared error of the simple predictor ($(a_i\bar{a})^2$). Later, by taking the square root of the relative squared error, the error is reduced to the same dimensions as the quantity being predicted.

4   Results and Discussion

In this section we first presents the results associated to valence prediction in Table 6 and Fig. 4. Then, Table 9 and Fig. 5 show the regression performance in predicting arousal values from the musics. In Tables 8 and 11 we also present the results regarding the feature selection process, comparing the findings with the entire set of features and the ones with the selected features. Finally, in Tables 7 and 10 we show the selected features for both valence and arousal datasets, discussing their meaning and relevance to the problem.

Table 6: Performance of different models in the prediction of valence values.

Metric	Linear Regression	SVM	ELM	Random Forest	MLP
		poly 4	linear	300 trees	(20, 20) neurons
	-	poly 4	linear	300 trees	(20, 20) neurons
PCC	0.4644 ± 0.0240	0.4603 ± 0.1202	0.2592 ± 0.0091	0.7569 ± 0.0153	0.5293 ± 0.0271
KCC	0.3223 ± 0.0180	0.3761 ± 0.0173	0.1768 ± 0.0053	0.5648 ± 0.0148	0.3709 ± 0.0192
SCC	0.4725 ± 0.0250	0.5398 ± 0.0235	0.2582 ± 0.0070	0.7517 ± 0.0166	0.5352 ± 0.0258
MAE	0.1721 ± 0.0042	0.1738 ± 0.0902	0.3022 ± 0.0033	0.1228 ± 0.0033	0.1836 ± 0.0266
RMSE	0.2138 ± 0.0047	0.2379 ± 0.0832	0.1343 ± 0.0008	0.1614 ± 0.0043	0.2278 ± 0.0291
RAE (%)	86.00 ± 1.38	76.49 ± 5.33	55.58 ± 0.26	61.35 ± 1.37	91.73 ± 13.17
RRSE (%)	88.57 ± 1.27	81.01 ± 3.71	25.04 ± 0.45	66.88 ± 1.46	94.39 ± 11.96

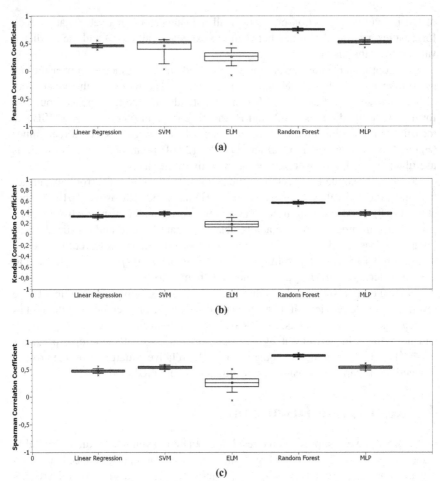

Figure 4: Correlation coefficients from different models to predict valence in songs. Pearson's coefficient is in (a), (b) shows Kendall's coefficient, and Spearman's coefficient is in (c).

4.1 Valence Prediction

Table 6 presents the general performance of the best configurations from the five different families of regression algorithms. These performances are associated to valence prediction. Detailed results are shown in Table A1. For this problem of predicting valence values, SVM with 4th-degree polynomial kernel overcame the other SVM architectures. Performance was also better for ELM of linear kernel, Random Forest with 350 trees, and MLP with 2 layers of 20 neurons.

In this context, Random Forest model fits valence data better than the others, with the highest correlations. This model reached an average Pearson's correlation of 0.7569, Kendall's correlation of 0.5648, and 0.7517 for Spearman's coefficient.

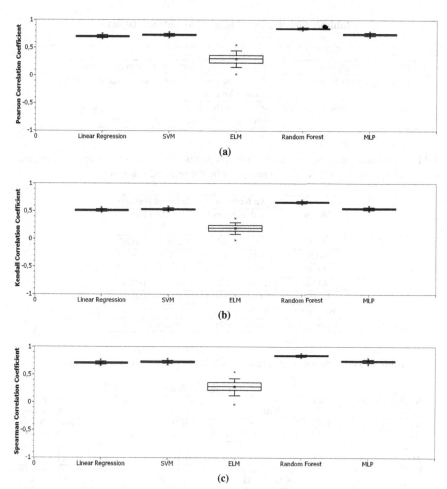

Figure 5: Correlation coefficients from different models to predict arousal in songs. Pearson's coefficient is in (a), (b) shows Kendall's coefficient, and Spearman's coefficient is in (c).

Moreover, data dispersion was minimal for this model, such as may be seen in Fig. 4. Random Forest also achieved the lowest MAE and RMSE, with average values of 0.1228 and 0.1614, respectively. However, the percentage errors associated with this model had high values: 61.35% for relative absolute error, and 66.88% for root relative squared error.

On the opposite side, ELM showed the worse performance regarding to correlation coefficients, with low correlation and more data dispersion. Its MAE and RMSE results were reasonable, relative absolute error was statistically similar to the result of Random Forest, and root relative squared error was the best overall, with average value of 25.04%.

Table 7: List of selected features for valence dataset.

Feature	Meaning
Maximum Amplitude	Represents the volume or strength of the signal.
Power Spectrum Ratio	Shows the power distribution of signals in the frequency domain.
Variance of Central Frequency	It is one of the alternative statistical analysis to extract information from the power spectrum.

Table 8: Comparison of the best results in the prediction of valence values with the complete set of features and with the dataset represented by the selected features.

	All features	Selected features
Metric	Random Forest	Random Forest
	300 trees	300 trees
PCC	0.7569 ± 0.0153	0.5001 ± 0.0267
KCC	0.5648 ± 0.0148	0.3459 ± 0.0199
SCC	0.7517 ± 0.0166	0.4969 ± 0.0269
MAE	0.1228 ± 0.0033	0.1658 ± 0.0043
RMSE	0.1614 ± 0.0043	0.2100 ± 0.0051
RAE (%)	61.35 ± 1.37	82.82 ± 1.82
RRSE (%)	66.88 ± 1.46	87.01 ± 1.80

Table 9: Performance of different models in the prediction of arousal values.

	Regression Model				
Metric	Linear Regression	SVM	ELM	Random Forest	MLP
	-	RBF	linear	300 trees	$(20, 20)$ neurons
PCC	0.7017 ± 0.0159	0.6379 ± 0.1807	0.2988 ± 0.0112	0.8470 ± 0.0107	0.7443 ± 0.0165
KCC	0.5144 ± 0.0143	0.5503 ± 0.0152	0.1928 ± 0.0057	0.6600 ± 0.0124	0.5467 ± 0.0152
SCC	0.7118 ± 0.0166	0.7461 ± 0.0171	0.2838 ± 0.0076	0.8428 ± 0.0116	0.7440 ± 0.0167
MAE	0.1674 ± 0.0042	0.1585 ± 0.0109	0.2626 ± 0.0028	0.1180 ± 0.0031	0.1727 ± 0.0220
RMSE	0.2088 ± 0.0049	0.2810 ± 0.1676	0.1561 ± 0.0012	0.1571 ± 0.0044	0.2152 ± 0.0249
RAE (%)	67.84 ± 1.70	95.74 ± 56.64	51.16 ± 0.20	47.82 ± 1.42	69.98 ± 8.90
RRSE (%)	71.27 ± 1.59	75.23 ± 6.07	25.01 ± 0.34	53.63 ± 1.55	73.48 ± 8.47

In this dataset for the prediction of valence values, the feature selection step resulted in 3 attributes, which are listed in Table 7. This number represents a 91.43% reduction in the amount of features used to describe the dataset. It means that PSO algorithm considers that most features are not strongly relevant to estimate the valence values associated with the songs. In other words, features of time, frequency and statistical domains might not be suitable to describe valence aspects in this kind of data.

After performing feature selection, we assessed prediction performance using all the aforementioned regression models. Table A2 shows these results, where Random Forest performed better than the other algorithms. Such as when using the entire set of features, the model with the best overall performance was Random Forest with 300 trees. Therefore, in Table 8 we present the performance of this model for both sets of features (*i.e.*, with and without feature selection). From

Table 10: List of selected features for arousal dataset.

Feature	Meaning
Shannon's Entropy	Represents the average level of information, surprise or uncertainty associated with a given signal.
Zero crossings	It is a point where the sign of a mathematical function changes. In the context of sound signals, this occurs when there are discontinuities in the wave, which are perceived as clicks or crackles in the sound.
Skewness	It is the measure of the asymmetry of a probability distribution of an ideally symmetric random variable.
Hjorth complexity parameter	It is an indicator of statistical properties that represents the change in frequency.
Difference Absolute Deviation	Is an statistical feature that measures the absolute difference between a specific element, another given point and its median.
Mean Absolute Value	It consists on the distance between a number and zero, without considering the direction.
Root Mean Square	It is the absolute value of the square root of the mean squares, a particular case of the generalized mean with exponent.
Variance	Measures the variability of the data.
Standard Deviation	It is closely related to the variance of the distribution, mathematically it consists of the square root of the variance.
Maximum Amplitude	Represents the volume or strength of the signal.
Power Spectrum Ratio	Shows the power distribution of signals in the frequency domain.
Total Power	It is defined as an aggregate of the power spectrum.
Median Frequency	is a frequency at which the power spectrum is divided into two regions of equal amplitude. In other words, it's half the total power.

Table 11: Comparison of the best results in the prediction of arousal values with the complete set of features and with the dataset represented by the selected features.

Metric	All features Random Forest 300 trees	Selected features Random Forest 300 trees
PCC	0.8470 ± 0.0107	0.8112 ± 0.0127
KCC	0.6600 ± 0.0124	0.6172 ± 0.0136
SCC	0.8428 ± 0.0116	0.8073 ± 0.0135
MAE	0.1180 ± 0.0031	0.1321 ± 0.0035
RMSE	0.1571 ± 0.0044	0.1719 ± 0.0047
RAE (%)	47.82 ± 1.42	53.56 ± 1.59
RRSE (%)	53.63 ± 1.55	58.70 ± 1.65

these results it is possible to see that we experienced a decrease in performance after adding the feature selection process. The correlation coefficients went through a decrease of around 0.25, for example going from a maximum PCC of 0.77 to 0.53. There was also a consequent increase in the errors. This decrease in performance may be due to the small amount of features that remained from the feature selection. It is highly unlikely that a regression model could achieve better results when using only 3 features to describe this complex problem.

4.2   Arousal Prediction

In predicting arousal values, the SVM configuration with the best performance was with the RBF kernel, ELM with the linear kernel, Random Forest with 350 trees and MLP with 2 layers of 20 neurons each. These results are shown in Table 9 (see Table A3 for other architectures). In this context Random Forest also outperformed the other regression models, with the highest correlations coefficients and lowest errors, except for the root relative squared error, which was better for ELM. Linear Regression, SVM, and MLP achieved similar results with low data dispersion, as showed in Fig. 5. Data dispersion for ELM was also low, but greater than the other models.

Using Random Forest architecture with 350 trees our approach achieved an average Pearson's correlation of 0.8470, an average of 0.6600 for Kendall's correlation and 0.8428 for average Spearman's correlation. MAE reached an average value of 0.1180, and RMSE was around 0.1571. The relative absolute error associated with this model was 47.82%, and root relative squared error of 53.63%.

PSO selected 13 features from the arousal dataset, resulting in a reduction of 62.86% in the amount of features. A list of the selected features is in Table 10. Thus, more features were considered relevant than those from valence dataset. After the selection process, we used the reduced set of features to represent the data and we assessed regression performance using the multiple models. These results are shown in Table A4. Again Random Forest with 300 trees achieved the best overall performance. Table 11 shows the best results for both the entire set of features and the dataset with selected features.

Unlike what happened to valence database, the feature selection process applied to arousal database had little effect on the prediction performance. An example of this was the PCC result, which went from around 0.85 using the entire set of features to 0.81 after feature selection. Despite having low data dispersion for all metrics, if you consider the standard deviation these results get even closer together. All metrics follow this same pattern, with high correlations and relatively low errors. This was an interesting finding, since the amount of features was reduced by more than half. Therefore, these findings may indicate that arousal is an aspect that can better be represented by time, frequency and statistical characteristics than valence.

4.3   General Findings

Overall, the models achieved reasonable results for the metrics that perform global assessments, such as Pearson's correlation coefficient, Spearman's coefficient, mean absolute error, and RMSE. However, Kendall's coefficient, RAE, and RRSE usually performed worse, since they are more sensitive to local variations.

Moreover, we observed that there is an agreement between the valence and arousal results. There is even consistency between the best settings on most models. In addition, for both predictions of valence and arousal, the model that best fits the data was Random Forest with 300 trees. Furthermore, we noticed that arousal prediction was better than valence prediction, with higher correlation coefficients and lower errors.

This finding agrees to the ones in Yang and Hirschberg (2018), Grekow (2018) and Cheuk et al. (2020). However, our approach performed better than these other regression models. Random Forest achieved Pearson's correlation up to 0.76 for valence prediction, with Kendall's of 0.56, and 0.75 for Spearman's correlation. In the arousal context, results were even better for the coefficients of Pearson (0.85), Kendall (0.66), and Spearman (0.84). These promising performances demonstrate that the adopted method is suitable for the representation of this kind of data and for the prediction of the parameters of interest. Furthermore, 300-trees Random Forest's good performance confirms the complexity of the emotion recognition problem at hand.

After appling PSO to select features from both datasets we experienced an overall decrease in performance, which was greater for valence than for arousal. At the same time, PSO selected less than half of the original features for both valence and arousal, resulting in 3 features to represent valence data and 13 for arousal's, which is a considerable small set of attributes to describe such a complex data. Although there was a drop in performance in both cases, the arousal prediction remained satisfactory after the feature selection, and were quite close to those with the full set of attributes.

Furthermore, the difference in performance between the valence and arousal datasets after feature selection indicates the difficulty in representing both parameters from the same set of attributes. This is in accordance with what was found by Grekow (2018) and Vatolkin and Nagathil (2019) in their study with different sets of features to estimate valence and arousal values. From Tables 7 and 10 we verified this statement, where the sets of selected features for valence and arousal are almost entirely different. A common point is that parameters associated with signal power were considered relevant for both sets. For arousal, in addition to power information, most of the selected features were related to statistical information and to the identification of signal discontinuities.

5   Conclusion

Emotions are a complex feature of every human being. They mainly affect social skills due to its direct link with the spontaneity and reliability of interpersonal relationships. One of the most popular ways of representing emotions is as a function of valence-arousal values. However, defining degrees of valence and arousal is usually an extremely subjective task since it is highly human-dependent. Thus, in this chapter we proposed an AI-based approach to the automatic identification of emotions in musics of different genres. This identification uses regression algorithms to predict valence and arousal parameters. Therefore, we assessed the performance of different models based on linear regression, SVM, ELM, Random Forest, and MLP.

In this context, Random Forest model with 300 trees performed better for arousal and valence predictions in both scenarios (1) with the full set of extracted features and (2) after feature selection. For the first scenario, this model reached an average Pearson's correlation of 0.7569 for valence, and of 0.8470 for arousal. For the datasets built with the selected features, this regression model achieved average Pearson's correlations of 0.5001 and 0.8112 for valence and arousal, respectively.

In the Random Forest model for regression, each decision tree that builds the forest is responsible for estimating an output value. Thus, the actual output is the average of these estimated values for each tree. The fact that the output is an average makes the Random Forest a smooth models. In other words, a model that tend to present a good global estimation, but tend to fail locally, justifying the high RMSE values found with this model.

The fact that this model was the best one also points to a possible low generalization ability of the problem of predicting valence and arousal values from music. This ability needs to be further investigated in future works. Low generalization may also be associated with the features used for representing the musical signals. From these results we cannot be sure whether valence and arousal are directly functions of these extracted features. They may be functions of other variables and therefore may require more complex representation models.

In this way, other studies with a greater variety of data and models should be conducted. In addition to more in-depth investigations into the relationship of the features with valence and arousal parameters. Even so, the obtained results were already important to trace some relationships between time, frequency and statistical features with valence and arousal parameters. The findings presented here were also promising to enable the prediction of valence and arousal from music. This automatic prediction is certainly useful to provide less subjective assessment of human emotional perception of music. Therefore, this type of prediction can have important contributions in the fields of emotion recognition and personalized content recommendation.

Acknowledgement(s)

This study was financed in part by the Coordenação de Aperfeiçoamento de Pessoal de Nível Superior - Brazil (CAPES) - Finance Code 001, and by the Fundação de Amparo à Ciência e Tecnologia do Estado de Pernambuco (FACEPE), Brazil, under the code IBPG-0013-1.03/20.

Disclosure Statement

No potential conflict of interest was reported by the authors.

References

Adler, J. and I. Parmryd. Quantifying colocalization by correlation: The pearson correlation coefficient is superior to the mander's overlap coefficient. Cytometry Part A, 77(8): 733–742, 2010.

Ahmad, I., M. Basheri, M.J. Iqbal and A. Rahim. Performance comparison of support vector machine, random forest, and extreme learning machine for intrusion detection. IEEE Access, 6: 33789–33795, 2018.

Arjmand, H.-A., J. Hohagen, B. Paton and N.S. Rickard. Emotional responses to music: Shifts in frontal brain asymmetry mark periods of musical change. Frontiers in Psychology, 8: 2044, 2017.

Barbosa, V.A.d.F., J.C. Gomes, M.A. de Santana, E.d.A. Jeniffer, R.G. de Souza, R.E. de Souza and W.P. dos Santos. Heg.ia: An intelligent system to support diagnosis of covid-19 based on blood tests. Research on Biomedical Engineering, 2021: 1–18, 2021.

Biau, G. and E. Scornet. A random forest guided tour. Test, 25(2): 197–227, 2016.

Breiman, L. Random forests. Machine Learning, 45(1): 5–32, 2001.

Chai, T. and R.R. Draxler. Root mean square error (rmse) or mean absolute error (mae)? arguments against avoiding RMSE in the literature. Geoscientific Model Development, 7(3): 1247–1250, 2014.

Chen, C. and Q. Li. A multimodal music emotion classification method based on multifeature combined network classifier. Mathematical Problems in Engineering, 2020, 2020.

Cheuk, K.W., Y.-J. Luo, B. Balamurali, G. Roig and D. Herremans. Regression-based music emotion prediction using triplet neural networks. In 2020 International Joint Conference on Neural Networks (IJCNN), pp. 1–7. IEEE, 2020.

Cowen, A.S., X. Fang, D. Sauter and D. Keltner. What music makes us feel: At least 13 dimensions organize subjective experiences associated with music across different cultures. Proceedings of the National Academy of Sciences, 117(4): 1924–1934, 2020.

da Silva, C.C., C.L. de Lima, A.C.G. da Silva, E.L. Silva, G.S. Marques, L.J.B. de Araújo, L.A.A. Júnior, S.B.J. de Souza, M.A. de Santana, J.C. Gomes, V.A.F. Barbosa, A. Musah, P. Kostkova, W.P. dos Santos and A.G. Silva-Filho. Covid-19 dynamic monitoring and real-time spatio-temporal forecasting. Frontiers in Public Health, 9, 2021.

de l'Etoile, S. Processes of Music Therapy: Clinical and Scientific Rationales and Models. The Oxford Handbook of Music Psychology, 2008.

de Lima, C.L., C.C. da Silva, A.C.G. da Silva, E. Luiz Silva, G.S. Marques, L.J.B. de Araújo, L.A. Albuquerque Júnior, S.B.J. de Souza, M.A. de Santana, J.C. Gomes, V.A.F. Barbosa, A. Musah, P. Kostkova, W.P. dos Santos and A.G. da Silva Filho. Covid-sgis: A smart tool for dynamic monitoring and temporal forecasting of covid-19. Frontiers in Public Health, 8: 761, 2020.

de Moraes Ramos, R.T., M.A.d. Santana, P.A. Sousa, M.R. Assunção Ferreira, W.P. dos Santos and L.A. Lira Soares. Multivariate regression and artificial neural network to predict phenolic content in schinus terebinthifolius stem bark through TLC images. Journal of Liquid Chromatography & Related Technologies, pp. 1–8, 2021.

Deng, W., Q. Zheng and L. Chen. Regularized extreme learning machine. In 2009 IEEE Symposium on Computational Intelligence and Data Mining, pp. 389–395. IEEE, 2009.

Desai, M. and M. Shah. An anatomization on breast cancer detection and diagnosis employing multilayer perceptron neural network (MLP) and convolutional neural network (CNN). Clinical eHealth, 2020.

Dineva, K. and T. Atanasova. Regression analysis on data received from modular IoT system. In Proceedings of the European Simulation and Modelling Conference ESM, 2019.

Driss, S.B., M. Soua, R. Kachouri and M. Akil. A comparison study between MLP and convolutional neural network models for character recognition. In Real-Time Image and Video Processing 2017, volume 10223, pp. 1022306. International Society for Optics and Photonics, 2017.

Eaton, J.W., D. Bateman, S. Hauberg and R. Wehbring. Gnu octave version 4.0. 0 manual: A high-level interactive language for numerical computations, 2015. URL http://www. gnu.org/software/octave/doc/interpreter, 8: 13, 2015.

Field, A. Kendalls coefficient of concordance, encyclopedia of statistics in behavioral science, 2005.

Fonseca,V.d. Importância das emoções na aprendizagem: Uma abordagem neuropsicopedagógica. Revista Psicopedagogia, 33(102): 365–384, 2016.

Franceschini, F. and D. Maisano. Aggregating multiple ordinal rankings in engineering design: The best model according to the kendalls coefficient of concordance. Research in Engineering Design, 32(1): 91–103, 2021.

Grekow, J. Audio features dedicated to the detection and tracking of arousal and valence in musical compositions. Journal of Information and Telecommunication, 2(3): 322–333, 2018.

Hauke, J. and T. Kossowski. Comparison of values of pearsons and spearmans correlation coefficient on the same sets of data. Quaestiones Geographicae, 2011.

Hizlisoy, S., S. Yildirim and Z. Tufekci. Music emotion recognition using convolutional long short term memory deep neural networks. Engineering Science and Technology, an International Journal, 24(3): 760–767, 2021.

Hsieh, S., M. Hornberger, O. Piguet and J. Hodges. Brain correlates of musical and facial emotion recognition: Evidence from the dementias. Neuropsychologia, 50(8): 1814–1822, 2012.

Huang, G.-B., Q.-Y. Zhu and C.-K. Siew. Extreme learning machine: Theory and applications. Neurocomputing, 70(1-3): 489–501, 2006.

Jeyasingh, S. and M. Veluchamy. Modified bat algorithm for feature selection with the wisconsin diagnosis breast cancer (wdbc) dataset. Asian Pacific Journal of Cancer Prevention: APJCP, 18(5): 1257, 2017.

Jung, Y. and J. Hu. A K-fold averaging cross-validation procedure. Journal of Nonparametric Statistics, 27(2): 167–179, 2015. ISSN 10290311.

Juslin, P.N. What does music express? Basic emotions and beyond. Frontiers in Psychology, 4: 596, 2013.

Juslin, P.N. and P. Laukka. Communication of emotions in vocal expression and music performance: Different channels, same code? Psychological Bulletin, 129(5): 770, 2003.

Kavitha, S., S. Varuna and R. Ramya. A comparative analysis on linear regression and support vector regression. In 2016 Online International Conference on Green Engineering and Technologies (ICGET), pp. 1–5, 2016.

Kennedy, J. and R. Eberhart. Particle swarm optimization. In Proceedings of ICNN'95-International Conference on Neural Networks, volume 4, pp. 1942–1948. IEEE, 1995.

Koelsch, S. Investigating the neural encoding of emotion with music. Neuron, 98(6): 1075–1079, 2018.

Li, X., H. Wang, Y. Tian, S. Zhou, X. Li, K. Wang and Y. Yu. Impaired white matter connections of the limbic system networks associated with impaired emotional memory in Alzheimer's disease. Frontiers in Aging Neuroscience, 8: 250, 2016.

Meska, M.H.G., L.Y. Mano, J.P. Silva, G.A. Pereira and A. Mazzo. Emotional recognition for simulated clinical environment using unpleasant odors: quasi-experimental study. Revista latinoamericana de enfermagem, 28, 2020.

Miguel, F.K. Psicologia das emoções: Uma proposta integrativa para compreender a expressão emocional. Psico-usf, 20: 153–162, 2015.

Mishra, S., P. Paygude, S. Chaudhary and S. Idate. Use of data mining in crop yield prediction. In 2018 2nd International Conference on Inventive Systems and Control (ICISC), pp. 796–802. IEEE, 2018.

Neill, S.P. and M.R. Hashemi. Ocean modelling for resource characterization. Fundamentals of Ocean Renewable Energy, pp. 193–235, 2018.

Patle, A. and D.S. Chouhan. Svm kernel functions for classification. In 2013 International Conference on Advances in Technology and Engineering (ICATE), pp. 1–9. IEEE, 2013.

Qi, J., J. Du, S.M. Siniscalchi, X. Ma and C.-H. Lee. On mean absolute error for deep neural network based vector-to-vector regression. IEEE Signal Processing Letters, 27: 1485–1489, 2020.

Rodrigues, A.L., M.A. de Santana, W.W. Azevedo, R.S. Bezerra, V.A. Barbosa, R.C. de Lima and W.P. dos Santos. Identification of mammary lesions in thermographic images: Feature selection study using genetic algorithms and particle swarm optimization. Research on Biomedical Engineering, 35(3): 213–222, 2019.

Rolls, E.T. Limbic systems for emotion and for memory, but no single limbic system. Cortex, 62: 119–157, 2015.

Russell, J.A. A circumplex model of affect. Journal of Personality and Social Psychology, 39(6): 1161, 1980.

Safonicheva, O.G. and M.A. Ovchinnikova. Movements and development art-therapy approach in the complex rehabilitation of children with intellectual disorders, including autism spectrum disorder. In Emerging Programs for Autism Spectrum Disorder, pp. 243–264. Elsevier, 2021.

Sammut, C. and G.I. Webb. Encyclopedia of Machine Learning. Springer Science & Business Media, 2011.

Schaefer, H.-E. Music-evoked emotions current studies. Frontiers in Neuroscience, 11: 600, 2017.

Schuld, M., I. Sinayskiy and F. Petruccione. Prediction by linear regression on a quantum computer. Physical Review A, 94(2): 022342, 2016.

Sedgwick, P. Pearsons correlation coefficient. Bmj, 345, 2012.

Sharma, H., S. Gupta, Y. Sharma and A. Purwar. A new model for emotion prediction in music. In 2020 6th International Conference on Signal Processing and Communication (ICSC), pp. 156–161. IEEE, 2020.

Singh, P.K. and M.S. Husain. Methodological study of opinion mining and sentiment analysis techniques. International Journal on Soft Computing, 5(1): 11, 2014.

Siriyasatien, P., S. Chadsuthi, K. Jampachaisri and K. Kesorn. Dengue epidemics prediction: A survey of the state-of-the-art based on data science processes. IEEE Access, 6: 53757–53795, 2018.

Sobeeh, M., G. Öztürk and M. Hamed. Effect of listening to high arousal music with different valences on reaction time and interference control: Evidence from simon task. IBRO Reports, 6: S441, 2019.

Soleymani, M., M.N. Caro, E.M. Schmidt, C.-Y. Sha and Y.-H. Yang. 1000 songs for emotional analysis of music. In Proceedings of the 2nd ACM International Workshop on Crowd Sourcing for Multimedia, pp. 1–6, 2013.

Song, Y., S. Dixon, M.T. Pearce and A.R. Halpern. Perceived and induced emotion responses to popular music: Categorical and dimensional models. Music Perception: An Interdisciplinary Journal, 33(4): 472–492, 2016.

Subasi, A., M.F. El-Amin, T. Darwich and M. Dossary. Permeability prediction of petroleum reservoirs using stochastic gradient boosting regression. Journal of Ambient Intelligence and Humanized Computing, pp. 1–10, 2020.

Suhaimi, N.S., J. Mountstephens and J. Teo. Eeg-based emotion recognition: A state-of-the-art review of current trends and opportunities. Computational Intelligence and Neuroscience, 2020, 2020.

Tan, K., M. Villarino and C. Maderazo. Automatic music mood recognition using russells two-dimensional valence-arousal space from audio and lyrical data as classified using SVM and naïve bayes. In IOP Conference Series: Materials Science and Engineering, volume 482, pp. 012019. IOP Publishing, 2019.

Vatolkin, I. and A. Nagathil. Evaluation of audio feature groups for the prediction of arousal and valence in music. In Applications in Statistical Computing, pp. 305–326. Springer, 2019.

Witten, I.H. and E. Frank. Data Mining: Pratical Machine Learning Tools and Technique. Morgan Kaufmann Publishers, San Francisco, CA, USA, 2005.

Xiao, C., J. Ye, R.M. Esteves and C. Rong. Using spearman's correlation coefficients for exploratory data analysis on big dataset. Concurrency and Computation: Practice and Experience, 28(14): 3866–3878, 2016.

Yang, Z. and J. Hirschberg. Predicting arousal and valence from waveforms and spectrograms using deep neural networks. In INTERSPEECH, pp. 3092–3096, 2018.

Yu, L.-C., J. Wang, K.R. Lai and X.-j. Zhang. Predicting valence-arousal ratings of words using a weighted graph method. In Proceedings of the 53rd Annual Meeting of the Association for Computational Linguistics and the 7th International Joint Conference on Natural Language Processing (Volume 2: Short Papers), pp. 788–793, 2015.

Zhou, H., Z. Deng, Y. Xia and M. Fu. A new sampling method in particle filter based on pearson correlation coefficient. Neurocomputing, 216: 208–215, 2016.

Zomorodi-moghadam, M., M. Abdar, Z. Davarzani, X. Zhou, P. Pławiak and U.R. Acharya. Hybrid particle swarm optimization for rule discovery in the diagnosis of coronary artery disease. Expert Systems, 38(1): e12485, 2021.

Appendix A: Regression Results for all Tested Configurations

Table A1: Performance for all tested configurations of different models in the prediction of **valence** values.

Regression Model		PCC	KCC	SCC	MAE	RMSE	RAE (%)	RRSE (%)
Linear Regression	-	0.4644 ± 0.0240	0.3223 ± 0.0180	0.4725 ± 0.0250	0.1721 ± 0.0042	0.2138 ± 0.0047	86.00 ± 1.38	88.57 ± 1.27
SVM	linear	0.4512 ± 0.0260	0.3156 ± 0.0189	0.4608 ± 0.0265	0.1721 ± 0.0043	0.2161 ± 0.0051	86.00 ± 1.54	89.55 ± 1.50
	poly 2	0.4889 ± 0.0433	0.3485 ± 0.0185	0.5044 ± 0.0254	0.1665 ± 0.0045	0.2130 ± 0.0237	83.18 ± 1.89	88.26 ± 10.05
	poly 3	0.5079 ± 0.0647	0.3641 ± 0.0186	0.5243 ± 0.0251	0.1642 ± 0.0099	0.2257 ± 0.1631	82.06 ± 5.05	93.61 ± 68.75
	poly 4	0.4603 ± 0.1202	0.3761 ± 0.0173	0.5398 ± 0.0235	0.1738 ± 0.0902	0.2379 ± 0.0832	76.49 ± 5.33	81.01 ± 3.71
	RBF	0.5039 ± 0.0255	0.3519 ± 0.0189	0.5076 ± 0.0260	0.1646 ± 0.0042	0.2088 ± 0.0051	82.23 ± 1.62	86.52 ± 1.60
ELM	linear	0.2592 ± 0.0091	0.1768 ± 0.0053	0.2582 ± 0.0070	0.3022 ± 0.0033	0.1343 ± 0.0008	55.58 ± 0.26	25.04 ± 0.45
	poly 2	0.1614 ± 0.0320	0.1760 ± 0.0223	0.2573 ± 0.0317	0.4107 ± 0.1001	0.9047 ± 0.3076	109.68 ± 18.43	168.93 ± 57.26
	poly 3	0.0419 ± 0.0259	0.0993 ± 0.0301	0.1467 ± 0.0440	1.9223 ± 1.4020	5.1993 ± 4.0065	443.25 ± 252.01	990.93 ± 754.48
	poly 4	0.0162 ± 0.0278	0.0565 ± 0.0332	0.0836 ± 0.0494	1.36E+3 ± 7.43E+3	7.32E+3 ± 39.36E+3	1.55E+5 ± 8.42E+5	1.42E+5 ± 7.67E+5
	RBF	0.1496 ± 0.0178	0.0267 ± 0.0153	0.0288 ± 0.0188	0.9624 ± 0.0032	0.2322 ± 0.0006	96.36 ± 0.24	43.43 ± 0.62
	sigmoid	0.1372 ± 0.0201	0.0931 ± 0.0200	0.1345 ± 0.0280	1.83E+5 ± 8.61E+5	1.45E+6 ± 7.53E+6	1.14E+8 ± 6.00E+8	2.94E+8 ± 1.53E+9
Random Forest	10 trees	0.7003 ± 0.0179	0.5118 ± 0.0164	0.6935 ± 0.0193	0.1304 ± 0.0036	0.1725 ± 0.0045	65.14 ± 1.65	71.47 ± 1.67
	20 trees	0.7283 ± 0.0165	0.5373 ± 0.0157	0.7222 ± 0.0182	0.1265 ± 0.0034	0.1668 ± 0.0043	63.21 ± 1.50	69.10 ± 1.55
	50 trees	0.7459 ± 0.0155	0.5541 ± 0.0148	0.7403 ± 0.0169	0.1242 ± 0.0032	0.1634 ± 0.0042	62.04 ± 1.38	67.71 ± 1.47
	100 trees	0.7523 ± 0.0153	0.5603 ± 0.0147	0.7469 ± 0.0166	0.1234 ± 0.0033	0.1623 ± 0.0043	61.64 ± 1.36	67.23 ± 1.45
	150 trees	0.7545 ± 0.0153	0.5625 ± 0.0147	0.7492 ± 0.0166	0.1231 ± 0.0034	0.1618 ± 0.0043	61.50 ± 1.38	67.06 ± 1.46
	200 trees	0.7555 ± 0.0154	0.5636 ± 0.0148	0.7503 ± 0.0167	0.1229 ± 0.0034	0.1616 ± 0.0043	61.42 ± 1.39	66.97 ± 1.47
	250 trees	0.7561 ± 0.0154	0.5642 ± 0.0149	0.7509 ± 0.0167	0.1229 ± 0.0034	0.1615 ± 0.0043	61.39 ± 1.39	66.93 ± 1.48
	300 trees	0.7566 ± 0.0154	0.5646 ± 0.0149	0.7514 ± 0.0167	0.1228 ± 0.0034	0.1615 ± 0.0043	61.37 ± 1.38	66.90 ± 1.47
	350 trees	0.7569 ± 0.0153	0.5648 ± 0.0148	0.7517 ± 0.0166	0.1228 ± 0.0033	0.1614 ± 0.0043	61.35 ± 1.37	66.88 ± 1.46
MLP	10 neurons	0.4870 ± 0.0355	0.3494 ± 0.0222	0.5064 ± 0.0303	0.1920 ± 0.0292	0.2366 ± 0.0325	95.91 ± 14.40	98.01 ± 13.34
	20 neurons	0.4875 ± 0.0446	0.3506 ± 0.0307	0.5075 ± 0.0434	0.1904 ± 0.0279	0.2359 ± 0.0314	95.1288 ± 13.8311	97.74 ± 12.96
	50 neurons	0.4418 ± 0.1326	0.3230 ± 0.1019	0.4682 ± 0.1477	0.1962 ± 0.0494	0.2474 ± 0.0735	98.0037 ± 24.6803	102.53 ± 30.51
	100 neurons	0.4354 ± 0.1653	0.3066 ± 0.1371	0.4442 ± 0.1997	3.05E+74 ± 5.28E-75	8.72E+75 ± 1.51E+77	1.52E+77 ± 2.63E+78	3.62E+78 ± 6.27E+79
	(20, 20) neurons	0.5293 ± 0.0271	0.3709 ± 0.0192	0.5352 ± 0.0258	0.1836 ± 0.0266	0.2278 ± 0.0291	91.73 ± 13.17	94.39 ± 11.96
	(100, 100) neurons	0.1565 ± 0.2435	0.1334 ± 0.2111	0.1916 ± 0.3055	0.2092 ± 0.0323	0.2569 ± 0.0413	104.48 ± 15.87	106.45 ± 17.02

Table A2: Performance for all tested configurations of different models in the prediction of **valence** values using PSO to select features.

Regression Model		PCC	KCC	SCC	MAE	RMSE	RAE (%)	RRSE (%)
Linear Regression	-	0.4048 ± 0.0281	0.2773 ± 0.0204	0.4060 ± 0.0288	0.1788 ± 0.0043	0.2207 ± 0.0048	89.32 ± 1.29	91.45 ± 1.24
SVM	linear	0.4024 ± 0.0287	0.2782 ± 0.0204	0.4073 ± 0.0288	0.1779 ± 0.0044	0.2219 ± 0.0051	88.90 ± 1.52	91.93 ± 1.50
	poly 2	0.3976 ± 0.0289	0.2800 ± 0.0202	0.4109 ± 0.0286	0.1781 ± 0.0045	0.2221 ± 0.0052	88.97 ± 1.51	92.02 ± 1.46
	poly 3	0.3845 ± 0.0290	0.2776 ± 0.0204	0.4109 ± 0.0286	0.1791 ± 0.0045	0.2232 ± 0.0051	89.50 ± 1.46	92.48 ± 1.39
	poly 4	0.3706 ± 0.0286	0.2787 ± 0.0203	0.4078 ± 0.0290	0.1804 ± 0.0045	0.2245 ± 0.0050	90.15 ± 1.36	93.00 ± 1.27
	RBF	0.4244 ± 0.0277	0.2945 ± 0.0196	0.4094 ± 0.0289	0.1753 ± 0.0044	0.2191 ± 0.0051	87.58 ± 1.50	90.78 ± 1.47
ELM	linear	0.1101 ± 0.0988	0.0739 ± 0.0700	0.1050 ± 0.1015	0.3709 ± 0.0478	0.1450 ± 0.0103	59.73 ± 5.04	27.05 ± 2.37
	poly 2	0.1598 ± 0.1128	0.1278 ± 0.0800	0.1839 ± 0.1150	0.3163 ± 0.0434	0.1353 ± 0.0089	57.28 ± 5.17	25.37 ± 2.12
	poly 3	0.1879 ± 0.1076	0.1425 ± 0.0743	0.2057 ± 0.1075	0.3145 ± 0.0424	0.1348 ± 0.0082	56.97 ± 4.82	25.08 ± 2.04
	poly 4	0.2108 ± 0.1124	0.1570 ± 0.0773	0.2276 ± 0.1121	0.3117 ± 0.0462	0.1342 ± 0.0090	56.78 ± 5.50	25.03 ± 2.15
	RBF	0.2030 ± 0.1051	0.1511 ± 0.0721	0.2189 ± 0.1044	0.3144 ± 0.0440	0.1343 ± 0.0088	56.65 ± 4.78	25.02 ± 2.10
	sigmoid	0.0301 ± 0.1400	0.1747 ± 0.0687	0.2583 ± 0.1003	6.1590 ± 11.2079	11.6962 ± 20.7173	785.31 ± 1288.46	2194.92 ± 3930.87
Random Forest	10 trees	0.4571 ± 0.0289	0.3150 ± 0.0209	0.4545 ± 0.0289	0.1723 ± 0.0047	0.2192 ± 0.0058	86.09 ± 2.09	90.81 ± 2.06
	20 trees	0.4781 ± 0.0277	0.3300 ± 0.0199	0.4751 ± 0.0273	0.1689 ± 0.0044	0.2144 ± 0.0054	84.39 ± 1.92	88.85 ± 1.92
	50 trees	0.4921 ± 0.0272	0.3401 ± 0.0201	0.4888 ± 0.0273	0.1669 ± 0.0044	0.2116 ± 0.0053	83.38 ± 1.88	87.66 ± 1.85
	100 trees	0.4971 ± 0.0268	0.3437 ± 0.0199	0.4937 ± 0.0270	0.1662 ± 0.0043	0.2106 ± 0.0052	83.04 ± 1.84	87.26 ± 1.81
	150 trees	0.4988 ± 0.0268	0.3449 ± 0.0199	0.4953 ± 0.0269	0.1660 ± 0.0043	0.2103 ± 0.0051	82.92 ± 1.84	87.12 ± 1.81
	200 trees	0.4994 ± 0.0267	0.3454 ± 0.0198	0.4960 ± 0.0268	0.1659 ± 0.0043	0.2101 ± 0.0051	82.88 ± 1.83	87.07 ± 1.80
	250 trees	0.4999 ± 0.0267	0.3458 ± 0.0199	0.4965 ± 0.0269	0.1658 ± 0.0043	0.2101 ± 0.0051	82.84 ± 1.83	87.03 ± 1.80
	300 trees	0.5001 ± 0.0267	0.3459 ± 0.0199	0.4967 ± 0.0269	0.1658 ± 0.0043	0.2100 ± 0.0051	82.82 ± 1.82	87.01 ± 1.80
	350 trees	0.5004 ± 0.0267	0.3461 ± 0.0199	0.4969 ± 0.0269	0.1657 ± 0.0042	0.2100 ± 0.0051	82.81 ± 1.82	86.99 ± 1.80
MLP	10 neurons	0.4391 ± 0.0282	0.3039 ± 0.0199	0.4444 ± 0.0278	0.1953 ± 0.0289	0.2409 ± 0.0316	97.53 ± 14.17	99.80 ± 12.89
	20 neurons	0.4424 ± 0.0294	0.3069 ± 0.0201	0.4491 ± 0.0281	0.1950 ± 0.0295	0.2407 ± 0.0321	97.40 ± 14.46	99.72 ± 13.12
	50 neurons	0.4431 ± 0.0288	0.3068 ± 0.0201	0.4497 ± 0.0281	0.1950 ± 0.0295	0.2406 ± 0.0322	97.38 ± 14.46	99.66 ± 13.14
	100 neurons	0.0989 ± 0.2037	0.0383 ± 0.2085	0.0558 ± 0.3047	0.2867 ± 1.2572	1.7444 ± 25.4044	144.55 ± 650.74	739.33 ± 10.81E+3
	(20, 20) neurons	0.4220 ± 0.0272	0.2890 ± 0.0191	0.4246 ± 0.0269	0.1964 ± 0.0287	0.2423 ± 0.0313	98.09 ± 14.04	100.39 ± 12.73
	(100, 100) neurons	0.2176 ± 0.2447	0.1422 ± 0.2120	0.2087 ± 0.3115	0.2069 ± 0.0305	0.2534 ± 0.0347	103.36 ± 14.97	104.98 ± 14.17

Table A3: Performance for all tested configurations of different models in the prediction of **arousal** values.

Regression Model		PCC	KCC	SCC	MAE	RMSE	RAE (%)	RRSE (%)
Linear Regression	-	0.7017 ± 0.0159	0.5144 ± 0.0143	0.7118 ± 0.0166	0.1674 ± 0.0042	0.2088 ± 0.0049	67.84 ± 1.70	71.27 ± 1.59
SVM	linear	0.6976 ± 0.0166	0.5090 ± 0.0148	0.7055 ± 0.0172	0.1669 ± 0.0044	0.2103 ± 0.0052	67.66 ± 1.84	71.79 ± 1.74
	poly 2	0.7199 ± 0.0322	0.5311 ± 0.0142	0.7281 ± 0.0160	0.1597 ± 0.0044	0.2041 ± 0.0144	64.73 ± 1.85	69.69 ± 4.78
	poly 3	0.7190 ± 0.0729	0.5399 ± 0.0144	0.7364 ± 0.0161	0.1588 ± 0.0144	0.2329 ± 0.2734	64.36 ± 5.78	79.42 ± 92.59
	poly 4	0.6379 ± 0.1807	0.5503 ± 0.0152	0.7461 ± 0.0171	0.1585 ± 0.0109	0.2810 ± 0.1676	95.74 ± 56.64	75.23 ± 6.07
	RBF	0.7309 ± 0.0153	0.5338 ± 0.0145	0.7302 ± 0.0163	0.1579 ± 0.0041	0.2001 ± 0.0050	63.99 ± 1.81	68.30 ± 1.71
ELM	linear	0.2988 ± 0.0112	0.1928 ± 0.0057	0.2838 ± 0.0076	0.2626 ± 0.0028	0.1561 ± 0.0012	51.16 ± 0.20	25.01 ± 0.34
	poly 2	0.1886 ± 0.0358	0.1659 ± 0.0234	0.2422 ± 0.0342	0.6160 ± 0.2175	1.1730 ± 0.4356	114.92 ± 23.16	187.81 ± 69.27
	poly 3	0.0402 ± 0.0319	0.0786 ± 0.0198	0.1167 ± 0.0294	2.3917 ± 1.2484	5.7969 ± 2.9025	400.69 ± 131.24	930.57 ± 466.48
	poly 4	0.0195 ± 0.0327	0.0554 ± 0.0244	0.0820 ± 0.0352	6.8994 ± 4.9853	16.4990 ± 11.3780	1004.70 ± 565.66	2640.30 ± 1817.80
	RBF	NaN ± NaN	NaN ± NaN	NaN ± NaN	0.9655 ± 0.0039	0.2856 ± 0.0009	96.59 ± 0.30	45.80 ± 0.49
	sigmoid	0.1282 ± 0.0242	0.0988 ± 0.0159	0.1430 ± 0.0230	1.70E+4 ± 4.59E+4	6.78E+5 ± 1.88E+5	3.28E+6 ± 9.00E+6	1.11E+7 ± 3.05E+7
Random Forest	10 trees	0.8210 ± 0.0124	0.6297 ± 0.0137	0.8160 ± 0.0134	0.1251 ± 0.0035	0.1673 ± 0.0048	50.70 ± 1.64	57.13 ± 1.74
	20 trees	0.8341 ± 0.0117	0.6446 ± 0.0132	0.8295 ± 0.0127	0.1215 ± 0.0032	0.1621 ± 0.0045	49.24 ± 1.53	55.35 ± 1.66
	50 trees	0.8422 ± 0.0111	0.6542 ± 0.0127	0.8379 ± 0.0120	0.1193 ± 0.0031	0.1589 ± 0.0045	48.35 ± 1.46	54.25 ± 1.60
	100 trees	0.8449 ± 0.0108	0.6575 ± 0.0124	0.8407 ± 0.0117	0.1185 ± 0.0031	0.1579 ± 0.0044	48.05 ± 1.44	53.90 ± 1.56
	150 trees	0.8460 ± 0.0107	0.6588 ± 0.0123	0.8417 ± 0.0116	0.1182 ± 0.0031	0.1575 ± 0.0044	47.93 ± 1.42	53.76 ± 1.55
	200 trees	0.8464 ± 0.0107	0.6593 ± 0.0123	0.8422 ± 0.0116	0.1181 ± 0.0031	0.1573 ± 0.0044	47.88 ± 1.41	53.70 ± 1.55
	250 trees	0.8466 ± 0.0107	0.6596 ± 0.0124	0.8424 ± 0.0117	0.1181 ± 0.0031	0.1572 ± 0.0044	47.86 ± 1.42	53.67 ± 1.55
	300 trees	0.8468 ± 0.0107	0.6599 ± 0.0123	0.8427 ± 0.0116	0.1180 ± 0.0031	0.1571 ± 0.0044	47.83 ± 1.41	53.64 ± 1.55
	350 trees	0.8470 ± 0.0107	0.6600 ± 0.0124	0.8428 ± 0.0116	0.1180 ± 0.0031	0.1571 ± 0.0044	47.82 ± 1.42	53.63 ± 1.55
MLP	10 neurons	0.7157 ± 0.0230	0.5303 ± 0.0167	0.7270 ± 0.0184	0.1871 ± 0.0301	0.2320 ± 0.0336	75.8235 ± 12.2587	79.1906 ± 11.4993
	20 neurons	0.6970 ± 0.1017	0.5154 ± 0.0972	0.7066 ± 0.1333	0.1964 ± 0.0884	0.2429 ± 0.0926	79.5956 ± 35.9354	82.9243 ± 31.6468
	50 neurons	0.6823 ± 0.1529	0.5136 ± 0.1019	0.7037 ± 0.1392	6.29E+134 ± 1.09E+136	1.80E+136 ± 3.12E+137	2.53E+137 ± 4.39E+138	6.11E+138 ± 1.06E+140
	100 neurons	0.6790 ± 0.1711	0.4995 ± 0.1486	0.6836 ± 0.2069	9.02E+6 ± 1.56E+8	5.63E+7 ± 9.74E+8	3.67E+9 ± 6.35E+10	1.92E+10 ± 3.34E+11
	(20, 20) neurons	0.7443 ± 0.0165	0.5467 ± 0.0152	0.7440 ± 0.0167	0.1727 ± 0.0220	0.22 ± 0.02	69.98 ± 8.90	73.4750 ± 8.4705
	(100, 100) neurons	0.2162 ± 0.3487	0.1995 ± 0.3523	0.2694 ± 0.4913	0.2389 ± 0.0486	0.2931 ± 0.0663	96.80 ± 19.48	100.01 ± 22.31

"NaN" results correspond to outputs that tend to ±∞, suffering underflow or overflow. In these cases, we used the errors as comparison parameters.

Table A4: Performance for all tested configurations of different models in the prediction of **arousal** values using PSO to select features.

Regression Model		PCC	KCC	SCC	MAE	RMSE	RAE (%)	RRSE (%)
Linear Regression	-	0.6736 ± 0.0197	0.4976 ± 0.0150	0.6928 ± 0.0175	0.1736 ± 0.0042	0.2167 ± 0.0060	70.36 ± 1.6	73.99 ± 1.90
SVM	linear	0.6696 ± 0.0250	0.4996 ± 0.0149	0.6948 ± 0.0175	0.1724 ± 0.0044	0.2189 ± 0.0087	69.88 ± 1.84	74.72 ± 2.92
	poly 2	0.6866 ± 0.0538	0.5091 ± 0.0147	0.7056 ± 0.0169	0.1675 ± 0.0047	0.2157 ± 0.0347	67.91 ± 1.95	73.61 ± 11.66
	poly 3	0.6944 ± 0.0511	0.5110 ± 0.0149	0.7072 ± 0.0172	0.1660 ± 0.0047	0.2131 ± 0.0323	67.28 ± 1.96	72.73 ± 10.87
	poly 4	0.6766 ± 0.0422	0.5100 ± 0.0150	0.7053 ± 0.0174	0.1668 ± 0.0046	0.2182 ± 0.0198	67.60 ± 1.95	74.50 ± 6.66
	RBF	0.7064 ± 0.0157	0.5140 ± 0.0146	0.7113 ± 0.0167	0.1651 ± 0.0042	0.2075 ± 0.0048	66.91 ± 1.82	70.82 ± 1.62
ELM	linear	0.2711 ± 0.0951	0.1721 ± 0.0690	0.2524 ± 0.0999	0.2776 ± 0.0475	0.1559 ± 0.0110	51.56 ± 4.21	25.05 ± 1.74
	poly 2	0.2018 ± 0.1425	0.1336 ± 0.0959	0.1973 ± 0.1409	0.2739 ± 0.1739	0.2279 ± 0.2726	65.78 ± 40.80	36.69 ± 45.56
	poly 3	0.1274 ± 0.1186	0.0953 ± 0.0791	0.1412 ± 0.1162	0.2856 ± 0.1682	0.3679 ± 0.4178	81.12 ± 41.90	59.34 ± 68.84
	poly 4	0.0608 ± 0.1134	0.0652 ± 0.0911	0.0959 ± 0.1333	0.4976 ± 0.6220	0.9510 ± 1.4378	119.08 ± 85.45	153.53 ± 235.13
	RBF	0.1299 ± 0.1094	0.0100 ± 0.0840	0.0084 ± 0.1034	0.9650 ± 0.0194	0.2854 ± 0.0177	96.55 ± 1.54	45.91 ± 3.06
	sigmoid	0.0013 ± 0.0949	0.0807 ± 0.0684	0.1218 ± 0.1020	3.20E6 ± 9.36E6	1.23E7 ± 3.03E7	9.36E8 ± 2.4E9	1.97E9 ± 4.85E9
Random Forest	10 trees	0.8210 ± 0.0124	0.6297 ± 0.0137	0.8160 ± 0.0134	0.1251 ± 0.0035	0.1673 ± 0.0048	50.7053 ± 1.6379	57.1292 ± 1.7365
	20 trees	0.8341 ± 0.0117	0.6446 ± 0.0132	0.8295 ± 0.0127	0.1215 ± 0.0032	0.1621 ± 0.0045	49.24 ± 1.53	55.35 ± 1.66
	50 trees	0.8422 ± 0.0111	0.6542 ± 0.0127	0.8379 ± 0.0120	0.1193 ± 0.0031	0.1589 ± 0.0045	48.35 ± 1.46	54.25 ± 1.60
	100 trees	0.8449 ± 0.0108	0.6575 ± 0.0124	0.8407 ± 0.0117	0.1185 ± 0.0031	0.1579 ± 0.0044	48.05 ± 1.44	53.90 ± 1.56
	150 trees	0.8460 ± 0.0107	0.6588 ± 0.0123	0.8417 ± 0.0116	0.1182 ± 0.0031	0.1575 ± 0.0044	47.93 ± 1.42	53.76 ± 1.55
	200 trees	0.8464 ± 0.0107	0.6593 ± 0.0123	0.8422 ± 0.0116	0.1181 ± 0.0031	0.1573 ± 0.0044	47.88 ± 1.41	53.70 ± 1.55
	250 trees	0.8110 ± 0.0128	0.6169 ± 0.0137	0.8071 ± 0.0136	0.1322 ± 0.0035	0.1720 ± 0.0047	53.58 ± 1.60	58.73 ± 1.66
	300 trees	0.8112 ± 0.0127	0.6172 ± 0.0136	0.8073 ± 0.0135	0.1321 ± 0.0035	0.1719 ± 0.0047	53.56 ± 1.59	58.70 ± 1.65
	350 trees	0.8113 ± 0.0127	0.6173 ± 0.0136	0.8075 ± 0.0135	0.1321 ± 0.0035	0.1719 ± 0.0046	53.55 ± 1.59	58.68 ± 1.65
MLP	10 neurons	0.7092 ± 0.0192	0.5193 ± 0.0158	0.7170 ± 0.0180	0.1872 ± 0.0278	0.2318 ± 0.0311	75.86 ± 11.23	79.11 ± 10.58
	20 neurons	0.7090 ± 0.0289	0.5211 ± 0.0156	0.7190 ± 0.0175	0.1858 ± 0.0266	0.2311 ± 0.0321	75.31 ± 10.74	78.89 ± 10.92
	50 neurons	0.6998 ± 0.0767	0.5160 ± 0.0535	0.7122 ± 0.0726	0.1859 ± 0.0275	0.2339 ± 0.0461	75.36 ± 11.07	79.83 ± 15.58
	100 neurons	0.5923 ± 0.2584	0.4469 ± 0.1954	0.6185 ± 0.2723	0.1948 ± 0.0439	0.2856 ± 0.4234	78.97 ± 17.90	97.48 ± 143.42
	(20, 20) neurons	0.7221 ± 0.0157	0.5253 ± 0.0143	0.7242 ± 0.0161	0.1795 ± 0.0229	0.2229 ± 0.0262	72.74 ± 9.27	76.10 ± 8.88
	(100, 100) neurons	0.3124 ± 0.3697	0.2316 ± 0.3371	0.3188 ± 0.4752	0.2291 ± 0.0493	0.2792 ± 0.0575	92.86 ± 19.87	95.31 ± 19.59

Chapter 8

Clinical Decision Support in the Care of Symptomatic Patients with COVID-19: An Approach Based on Machine Learning and Swarm Intelligence

Ingrid Bruno Nunes,[1] Pedro Vitor Soares Gomes de Lima,[2]
Andressa Laysa Queiroz Ribeiro,[2] Leandro Ferreira Frade Soares,[2]
Maria Eduarda da Silva Santana,[2] Maria Luysa Teles Barcelar,[2]
Juliana Carneiro Gomes,[1] Clarisse Lins de Lima,[1]
Maíra Araújo de Santana,[1] Rodrigo Gomes de Souza,[3]
Valter Augusto de Freitas Barbosa,[4] Ricardo Emmanuel de Souza[2]
and *Wellington Pinheiro dos Santos[1,2,]**

1 Introduction

In December 2019, China, more specifically Wuhan, located in Hubei province, became the scene of an outbreak of pneumonia without a defined cause or etiologic agent. Such an outbreak attracted the attention not only of the Chinese government,

[1] Polytechnic School of the University of Pernambuco, Recife, Brazil.
[2] Department of Biomedical Engineering, Federal University of Pernambuco, Recife, Brazil.
[3] Center for Informatics, Federal University of Pernambuco, Recife, Brazil.
[4] Department of Mechanical Engineering, Federal University of Pernambuco, Recife, Brazil.
* Corresponding author: wellington.santos@ufpe.br

but also of the World Health Organization (WHO). The country's authorities began an immediate investigation to identify and control the disease. Contaminated patients or suspected of contamination were isolated, in addition to monitoring the contact with these patients, accompanied by a clinical epidemiological survey. As of January 7, 2020, Chinese scientists had isolated a new coronavirus (CoV) from patients in Wuhan, the virus was reported as "new Coronavirus 1" on January 9 by the Chinese Center for Disease Control (CCD) Chinese). A few days later, WHO declared that the "new Coronavirus of 2019" (SARSCoV-2) had been responsible for the outbreak in Wuhan city (Chakraborty et al., 2020; Wang et al., 2020a).

The sequencing of the new Coronavirus was quickly obtained thanks to the database of the Global Initiative on Sharing All Influenza Data (GISAID) platform. The availability of the SARS-CoV-2 genetic sequence allowed the development of a specific diagnostic test, using the Reverse Transcription Polymerase Chain Reaction (RT-qPCR) technique (Jin et al., 2020). In addition to the RT-qPCR technique (Gralinski and Menachery, 2020; Su et al., 2016), other diagnostic methods usually applied together are being used, such as: clinical evaluation - observation of symptoms associated with several cases of patients affected by SARS-CoV-2, such as nasal congestion, rhinorrhea and other symptoms associated with the respiratory tract superior (Boncristiani et al., 2009; de Freitas Barbosa et al., 2021; Klopfenstein et al., 2020; Mizrahi et al., 2020; Torcate et al., 2022; Wang et al., 2020a); physical assessment – patients with severe conditions may have respiratory failure, weakened breath sounds, etc.; Computed tomography (CT) images – although the images vary according to the stage of the disease, drug intervention, age and immunity status of the patient, CT shows images of lesions with different distributions, quantities, densities and formats (de Santana et al., 2022; Gomes et al., 2020; Jin et al., 2020); and hematological tests – thrombocytopenia, increased levels of D-dimer and problems with coagulation mechanisms, are associated with a poor prognosis of COVID-19 (Barbosa et al., 2021; Thachil et al., 2020; Xiang-Hua et al., 2010), in addition to an increase in pro-inflammatory cytokines (Levi et al., 2008).

With all the chaotic context of overcrowded hospitals and lack of beds to accommodate patients around the world, it is of great importance that healthcare professionals make correct decisions regarding the treatment and care of patients. The ease of virus contamination and the number of patients who have died so far, which now exceed 5.2 million (Johns Hopkins University, 2021), opens up possibilities for studies and research to help fight the virus, prevent new cases and aid in diagnosis, for example.

This work aims to develop a decision support system capable of assisting the clinical decision of admission to an intensive care unit, semi-intensive care unit or regular care based on the analysis of the most clinically relevant hematological parameters of the complete blood count and biochemical tests. For this, the performance of four smart classifiers was evaluated. It is justified by the need to develop systems that reduce the cost and time of patient care, providing the quality necessary for an effective intervention, even facilitating the reorganization of issues such as bed occupancy rates, medical interventions and the risk of the patient's life. Section 2 brings the theoretical foundation, which brings concepts related to COVID-19, hospitalizations, the criteria for hospitalization of patients and some of the intelligent classifiers that were used in this study. Section 3 brings some related works, studies that are somehow related to the proposal. Section 4 explains the methodology used to develop this work, explaining the database used, defining some parameters for patient examinations, how the pre-processing was carried out, the classification and the metrics used. The fourth and penultimate section brings the results of the experiments, and is divided into intensive, regular, semi-intensive and attribute extraction. Finally, the last section brings the conclusion of this work.

2   Theoretical Foundation

2.1   COVID-19

In 2020 the World Health Organization (WHO) announced the worldwide pandemic caused by the coronavirus, SARS-CoV-2. The transmission of SARS-CoV-2 occurs predominantly through contaminated droplets of oropharyngeal secretions from an infected person to a person free from the infection, along with the role of transmission by aerosols, through contact with surfaces and contaminated objects, where the virus can remain viable for up to 72 hours (Aquino et al., 2020). Many cases have arisen in Asian countries, such as Thailand, Japan, South Korea and Singapore, Europe and other nations. The Covid-19 disease, so named by the WHO, causes dry cough, headache, hypoxia, fever and dyspnea, the acute symptoms such as fever, cough, headache, sore throat, fatigue and shortness of breath, appear after the incubation period, between 5.2 days and the symptoms of severe cases involve sepsis and acute respiratory distress syndrome, which can be fatal in patients with debility and chronic diseases, pulmonary patients, chronic kidney diseases, patients with diabetes, hypertension, heart disease, users of steroids or immunosuppressive drugs, smokers and the elderly, these cases require intensive care, usually deaths occur due to a gradual respiratory failure caused by lung damage (Lins de Lima et al., 2021; Moreira, 2020).

Due to its high contamination capacity, Covid-19 has proven to be one of the greatest sanitary challenges on a global scale of this century. By mid-April, a few months after the epidemic began in Wuhan, China, at the end of 2019, there had already been more than 2 million cases and 120,000 deaths worldwide from Covid-19. In Brazil, until then, there had been around 21 thousand confirmed cases and 1,200 deaths by the Covid-19 (Werneck and Carvalho, 2020). Despite advances in terms of vaccination, the number of infected and dead people is still extremely high, around 250,368,055 people are now infected, 5,055,944 died worldwide as a result of the worsening of the disease caused by the SARS-CoV-2 coronavirus (Analytics, 2021).

Coronavirus treatment also involves preventing contamination, requiring a set of public health strategies. Many countries have adopted the ban on meetings of more than 1000 people, reducing this number, successively, to 500 and to 50. The closing of cinemas, restaurants, gyms, shopping malls and places of worship was also determined, as well as the use of PPE's and washing of hands. Germany closed most non-essential stores and extended supermarket hours to reduce the number of shoppers at the same time. In some countries, stores have reserved the first hours of the day for older customers at high risk of serious illness. China initiated a form of isolation with hospitalization of all cases (not just those who needed hospital care) and, at the same time, implemented social distancing across the entire population, which resulted in reduced transmission. Several studies have estimated that these interventions have lowered the mean transmission rate of Covid-19 to less than 1, that is, showing an average of one less infected person who can be infected for every infected person in the population, which is needed to obtain the decrease in the incidence of cases (Aquino et al., 2020).

2.2   Criteria for Hospitalization of Patients

Intensive Care Units (ICUs) are complex and have a high financial cost, mainly due to the need for a specific physical structure and high technology. These units are made up of a multidisciplinary team, such as doctors, nurses, physiotherapists, nutritionists, dentists, pharmacists and nursing technicians (Nogueira et al., 2012). The number of critically ill patients admitted to these units has been growing, especially with the COVID-19 pandemic.

In the current scenario, there is a need for resources in intensive care units to support patients who need specific care and treatments (Grasselli et al., 2020). Another determining factor is the number of available places, which is extremely limited in public hospitals in Brazil (Sinuff et al., 2004). In several countries, the classification protocol for admission to the ICU are used. Health professionals working in this area screen patients in a scenario where there are people with more possibilities of benefits in intensive care and few existing vacancies, when these two parameters are related to (Ramos et al., 2017). The crisis caused by COVID-19 highlighted certain problems involving intensive care units, such as the lack of adequate treatment due to the lack of sufficient spaces. The collapse and overload of the Unified Health System became imminent, and physicians had to choose which patients to go to the units or (Grasselli et al., 2020) face their mortality.

The resolution of the Federal Council of Medicine of Brazil (CFM) No. 1805/2006 mentions that: "the physician is allowed to limit or suspend procedures and treatments that prolong the life of the patient, in a terminal phase, with a serious and incurable illness, respecting the will of the person or their legal representative". And the resolution of (CFM) No. 2.156/2016 determines the criteria for admission to the ICU, and among the priorities mentioned, it is observed:

- Priority I: patients who need life support interventions, with a high probability of recovery and without any limitation of therapeutic support.

- Priority II: patients who need intensive monitoring, due to the high risk of needing immediate intervention, and without any limitation of therapeutic support.

- Priority III: patients who need life support interventions, with low probability of recovery or with limited therapeutic intervention.

- Priority IV: patients who need intensive monitoring, due to the high risk of needing immediate intervention, but with limited therapeutic intervention.

- Priority V: terminally ill or dying patients with no possibility of recovery.

It is also recommended that patients with priority 2 or 4 should preferably be allocated to semi-intensive units and patients with priority 5 preferably admitted to palliative care units. The Brazilian Association of Intensive Care Medicine, AMIB, filed the guidelines for allocation of depleted resources during the COVID-19 pandemic period. The screening protocol is based on a scoring system, which varies from two to eleven, in which the lower the score, the higher the priority for admission to the ICU (Siqueira-Batista et al., 2020).

Thus, the screening and admission criteria have as a principle the prioritization of patients with greater and better possibilities of benefits and with higher survival expectations (Kretzer et al., 2020). This protocol has the objectives of:

1. Save as many lives (short-term survival);

2. Save as many years of life (long-term survival);

3. Equalize the opportunity for patients to go through different life cycles.

2.3 Artificial Intelligence and Support for Diagnostics

Technology is an ally in the role of doctors and health policies in combating viruses and one of its main support elements is the communication of information quickly. Currently, society has a set of disruptive technologies that has a master: the AI. These technologies converge, mainly, in the health field, interested in fighting a common enemy, making the way to deal with this virus different from the approach with other causative agents of pandemic diseases in the past Neves (2020). AI is a branch of computer science that aims to develop systems that simulate the human capacity in the perception of a problem, identifying its components and, therefore, solving problems and proposing/making decisions (Lobo, 2018).

Artificial intelligence (AI) systems had detected the outbreak of an unknown type of pneumonia in the People's Republic of China long before the outbreak of the global pandemic. As the outbreak has taken on global proportions, AI tools and technologies can be employed to support the efforts of policy makers, aid diagnoses, treatment and society at large to manage all stages of the crisis and its consequences: detection, prevention, response, recovery and accelerate search by quickly analyzing large volumes of search data (OECD, 2020).

Training and evaluation of systems using ARIMA time series models and other machine learning algorithms for time prediction use correlation such as the Pearson, Spearman and Kendell, and RMSE. In Brazil, the percentage error between predicted values and actual values ranged between 2.56% and 6.50%. The COVID-SGIS model proposed by researchers at the Federal University of Pernambuco is robust, flexible and fast, it is important because it can be used to guide and plan direct interventions in public policies (da Silva et al., 2021a,b; de Lima et al., 2020; Silva et al., 2021).

It is also important to remember that the prototype of the system developed by Silva et al. (2021) can be accessed through the link (https://www.cin.ufpe.br/covidsgis). Spatial predictions are presented on the home screen. In the option "More information", you can access the projections of the accumulated cases of Covid-19, in which the user is directed to the page with the graphics. This screen also presents graphs referring to the daily distribution of cases and deaths in Brazil, in addition to daily and cumulative cases and deaths. And the user can choose the option of state they want to analyze the information and graphics.

Also, as some text and data mining AI tools can unravel the history, transmission, means of virus diagnosis, management measures, prevention, diagnosis, treatment and lessons from previous epidemics. Here are some models according to OECD (2020):

- Deep learning models help predict new and old drugs or treatments that can treat patients infected with COVID-19.

- DeepMind is able to predict the structure of proteins associated with SARS-CoV-2, the virus that causes COVID-19.

- Dedicated platforms or forums allow the consolidation and sharing of multidisciplinary knowledge in AI, including internationally.

- Access to datasets in epidemiology, bioinformatics and molecular modeling is being provided, for example, by the US government and partner organizations through the COVID-19 Open Research Dataset Challenge, which makes more than 29,000 academic research articles available to coronaviruses and COVID-19.

- The computing power for AI is also being made available by technology companies like IBM, Amazon, Google and Microsoft.

- Innovative approaches, including awards, collaborations on open source projects, and hackathons, are helping to accelerate the search for AI-driven solutions for the pandemic.

2.4 Classifiers

Artificial Intelligence (AI) is related to the design of computer systems that manipulate and try to solve problems in an intelligent way. Associated with this, AI increases the capacity of computer programs to handle these specific activities (Li, 1996). Intelligent entities have been the target of great prominence for their ability to adapt to new environments and solve new problems. A computer can be programmed to interpret incoming information, and its performance gradually improves (Pontil and Verri, 1998).

A classification is a process that aims to find functions or models that explain and differentiate concepts. Thus, the model obtained can be used to identify objects that have unknown classes. During this classification process, there are two distinct phases: (a) the learning phase and (b) the testing phase. In the learning phase, some data is known by the data classes that are used to form the model, as well as can be called training set (Cortes and Vapnik, 1995). In the test phase, the model established above is tested with other data, called test sets, in order to determine the accuracy of the model.

AI mechanisms have been of paramount importance for studies related to COVID-19, mainly in the processing of patient data and the development of efficient strategies for the treatment (Iwendi et al., 2020). Manual diagnosis has been commonly used, however it is inefficient due to the rapid spread of this virus. For this reason, COVID-19 automatic detection studies are performed with the support of artificial intelligence algorithms (Ozkaya et al., 2020). In this sense, it is understood that artificial intelligence technologies will make important contributions to the benefits process, accurate diagnoses and fight the COVID-19 pandemic.

2.4.1 Support Vector Machines (SVMs)

The Support Vector Machine (SVM) is a learning system to classify data into two groups, using hypothetical space in the form of linear functions of a high-dimensional resource space.

Recently, SVMs have been considered efficient in several real-world applications, such as pattern recognition activities, in the area of fault diagnosis, among others, obtaining specific and efficient results to those achieved by other learning techniques (Azevedo et al., 2015; Cordeiro et al., 2012, 2013; de Freitas et al., 2019; de Lima et al., 2016; de Vasconcelos et al., 2018; P.Konar and Chattopadhyay, 2011; Santana et al., 2018). SVMs are based on statistical learning theory, developed by Vapnik, and specialize for a smaller number of samples, as it is difficult to obtain sufficient failures in practice, SVMs have been applied to machine failure diagnosis (P.Konar and Chattopadhyay, 2011). Vapnik's theory establishes a series of principles that are directed towards obtaining classifiers, and subsequently predicting the class of new data from the same domain.

Andrew (2000) mentions two problems about the algorithm: (a) the original algorithm had limitations in relation to linearly separable learning problems. (b) the algorithm did not present a specific configuration to analyze isolated data or those that were far from the original pattern. Through discussions and research, the use of Kernel functions solved the limitation regarding linearly separable learning, considering that this function allows the evolution of data from the input space to a space with a specific and superior dimension. Boukir et al. (2021) highlight the important characteristics of SVMs, such as: excellent generalizability, robustness in large dimensions and well-defined theory.

This classifier has been applied to promote benefits in relation to the diagnosis and treatment of COVID-19. The study carried out by Sarhan (2020) demonstrated the possibility of a new technique for the detection of COVID-19 cases through chest radiographs, whose main objective is to find specific and discriminative characteristics on radiographs, as well as the association of images and SVMs to classify the extracted resources, coupled with this, the use of limited resources in the proposed system significantly simplifies the work of the SVM classifier, and consequently increases its accuracy. Other studies have also been carried out to detect COVID-19 cases, such as the use of the A Support Vector Machine (SVM) which can classify computed tomography images, proving that this method is more effective in combating COVID-19 (Özkaya et al., 2020).

2.4.2 Random Forest

Random Forests (RF) have emerged as serious classifiers and competitors to state-of-the-art methods such as SVMs (Amaratunga et al., 2008; Barbosa et al., 2021; de Freitas et al., 2019; de Freitas Barbosa et al., 2021; de Santana et al., 2022; Gomes et al., 2020; Santana et al., 2018). This classification algorithm was initially proposed by Breiman, being a technique for grouping classifiers in the decision tree modality, so its structure is randomly constituted. One of the features of this method is the combination of the result of several decision trees through a (Genuer et al., 2010) voting mechanism. The RF can provide the reader with practical guidance, as well as an understanding of the method, linked to it, has important characteristics compared to other algorithms and a competitive performance. There are two types of random processes in RF, the first is aimed at creating data sets that focus on a data sampling technique, while the second type of procedure is called a random subset of attributes, which directly modifies the training of a decision tree. In such a way, that a new node in the tree is formed (Hothorn et al., 2006).

Specifically for the COVID-19 pandemic in Brazil, Lima et al. (2021) studied the applications of the RF classifier in an attempt to predict deaths, and the RF algorithm classified the elderly as a group at higher risk for the negative evolution of the disease, including the highest incidence of deaths in this group. Regarding associated diseases, cardiovascular diseases can be mentioned, as well as oxygen saturation lower than or equal to 95%.

In contrast, Iwendi et al. (2020) investigated the geographic, travel and health data of patients affected with COVID-19 using an RF model in an attempt to predict the severity of the case and the outcome of the clinical picture (recovery or death), in addition, male patients had a higher mortality rate compared to females, and those aged between 20 and 70 years. Researchers have intensified studies in the implementation of a model based on Convolutional Neural Network to detect patients with COVID-19 using X-ray images of the patients' thoracic region. To do so, they used a pre-trained image and trained the model on an open source dataset (Wang et al., 2020b). Note that this method has been shown to be effective in mapping COVID-19, especially in treatment, as well as in the groups most affected by the aforementioned disease.

2.4.3 Bayesian Network

Bayesian networks (BNs) are increasingly being used to model environmental systems, with the objective of integrating various problems and system components, as well as using information from different sources and handling the missing data and uncertainties (Chen and Pollino, 2012). The GNs embody and represent the uncertain information that is expressed in the model outputs. BNs are based on a relatively simple graphical structure, so they can be built without (Voinov and Bousquet, 2010) modeling skills.

The high efficiency and advantages provided by the graphical representation of BNs networks. This approach is based on data that are able to determine the core structure of a system with a limited number of (Sun and Erath, 2015) samples. Through efficiencies, BNs networks can be used to create strategies to combat COVID-19. Neil et al. (2020) applied a BNs model to estimate the prevalence of COVID-19 infection and mortality, and the main highlight of this model is the combinations of multiple data sources in a single model that provide statistical estimates that better reflect the mechanisms of available data, quantity and types of data (Neil et al., 2020). A similar study was carried out by Butcher and Fenton indicates that the BN network can predict the probability of COVID-19 infection based on the profile of each patient, considering behaviors and symptoms, and thus mathematically applying the multivariate combinations, which results in a quick diagnosis.

Thrombosis and thrombocytopenia syndrome (TTS) has been associated with the AstraZeneca vaccine that fights COVID-19. Risk-benefit analyzes of vaccination have been the subject of several studies, mainly due to the rapid evolution of data, increase in transmission levels and variations in COVID-19 mortality rates. A Bayesian network was used to integrate local and international data, government reports, published literature and expert opinion, among others. The probability of dying from severe blood clots related to complications by COVID-19 is extremely higher than by TTS, which demonstrates that the use of BN nets can demonstrate the effectiveness of the AstraZeneca vaccine (Lau et al., 2021).

2.4.4 Naive Bayes

Naive Bayes (NB) is a statistical classifier of a supervised machine learning technique. The algorithm is based on Bayes' theorem, which has the function of determining classification results in which there is no dependence between the variables of a system. Although the hypothesis is inconsistent in some cases, the NB classifier provides satisfactory results (de Moraes et al., 2020).

One of the main benefits of the NB approach is that this classifier has the ability to evaluate data that it has never been trained on before. It is widely used in data mining, data classification and images, being essential in decision-making, medical diagnoses, real-time forecasts (Moraes and Machado, 2009).

In a study carried out by Mansour et al. (2021) with the objective of accurately detecting patients infected with COVID-19, using classification attributes correlated to NB, as well as the creation of a strategy to detect the diagnosis of COVID-19, called Feature. The strategy has four phases: (a) resource selection phase, (b) grouping phase, (c) resource weighting phase and (d) Naive Bayes resource correlation phase, showing that this method outperforms competitive techniques, as that through this it is possible to reach a maximum detection accuracy of 99%

for COVID-19, thus enabling early diagnosis and accurate and immediate treatment, with positive repercussions on health services. The study of Awwalu et al. (2020) and with the same perspective as the study of Mansour et al. (2021) seeking the early detection of COVID-19, both use interactive artificial intelligence, which used the Naive Bayes Multinomial algorithm with the objective to accurately and early detect COVID-19, thus preventing further contagion and spread of the virus. The results were satisfactory, as the Multinomial Naïve Bayes has demonstrated an excellent method for high-precision detection, thus being a reliable method to identify COVID-19 warning symptoms.

3   Related Works

The work from Luo et al. (2021) aims to establish an efficient method to identify key indicators from initial blood routine test results for COVID-19 severity prediction. With an accuracy of 0.77 and an AUC of 0.92, the first key indicator for severity predicting of COVID-19 found was the patient's age. Also, to improve the accuracy of prediction, they proposed the Multiple Criteria Decision Making (MCDM) algorithm, which combines the Technique for Order of Preference by Similarity to Ideal Solution (TOPSIS) and Naïve Bayes (NB) classifier. Thus, the optimized prediction model can achieve an accuracy of 0.82 and an AUC of 0.93. In addition to age, the results indicate that White Blood Cell Count (WBC), Lymphocyte Count (LYMC), and Neutrophil Count (NEUT) were the key factors for COVID-19 severity prediction.

The main objective of the work done by Hany et al. (2021) is detecting COVID-19 in its early stages to minimize the number of deaths caused by the disease. They analyzed 134 cases of different sexes, different ages and separated between positive and negative cases. The database contains blood tests which are Complete Blood Count (CBC), C-reactive Protein (CRP), D-dimer, S-ferritin, Alanine Aminotransferase (ALT), Lactate Dehydrogenase (LDH). They obtained the following accuracy results with the chosen classifiers: 0.76 for Random Forest (RF), 0.88 for Support Vector Machine (SVM), and 0.85 for Naive Bayes. Finally, they point out that the best result obtained in this work performs better than PCR (the accuracy of PCR is 0.8 according to the American Center for Disease Control and Prevention) and costs less.

The authors de Freitas Barbosa et al. (2021) proposed an intelligent system whose function is to support the Covid-19 diagnosis, based on machine learning techniques (Machine Learning). The system employs blood tests as inputs to an expert system to aid in the diagnosis of Covid-19. The database of the Hospital Israelita Albert Einstein, São Paulo, Brazil, which incorporates data from inpatients, was used. The Heg.IA classification seeks to distinguish between patients with and without Covid-19, although they may be affected by other general respiratory and viral diseases.

de Freitas Barbosa et al. (2020) proposed a Covid-19 web diagnostic support system based on machine learning techniques. This system uses blood test results to diagnose Covid-19. The machine learning method was training using the database provided by Hospital Israelita Albert Einstein located in São Paulo, Brazil. For each patient, the database has more than one hundred laboratory tests, such as blood count and urine. From this database, a new database was created that contains only 41 blood tests recommended by the Ministry of Health of Brazil for patients with Covid-19. The project's objective is to provide a web tool that performs an accurate Covid-19 diagnosis with a user-friendly interface and low computational cost.

Henry et al. (2020) have identified several biomarkers that could potentially help in risk stratification models to predict severe and fatal COVID-19. In hospitalized patients with respiratory distress, it is recommended that clinicians closely monitor white blood cell count, lymphocyte count, platelet count, IL-6, and serum ferritin as markers of potential progression to critical illness.

In the work of Shamsi et al. (2021), a learning process similar to ours was carried out, where, through computed tomography images, a system was trained to recognize the diagnosis of covid-19 and carry out the separation of patients. Although the system seems to do much better with CTs, it also works on x-rays. It is important to note that all data was acquired through simulation.

The study by Pathak et al. (2021) proposed a long-term memory network model for the study of COVID-19, with a density network mixture (DBM) using the MADE algorithm. Comparative chest computed tomography analyzes performed showed that the proposed model outperformed several metrics, being a new real-time classification system for COVID-19.

4   Methodology

The diagram in Fig. 1 shows how the diagnostic support system works. The user (health care professional) enters the patient's data (the results of hematological and biochemical tests) into the system. Then, the system performs the pre-processing of these data, in order to organize the information that is input to the system. Then performs the extraction of attributes. After this step, the smart classifiers perform a test and define what type of care is recommended for the patient. Care can be: regular care, semi-intensive care or intensive care. The system returns to the user what type of care the patient should receive, in order to support the medical decision, but it is up to the health professional to make the final decision.

4.1   Database

According to the WHO, until November 10, 2021, Brazil is the second country with the highest number of deaths by Covid-19, surpassing the mark of 610 thousand deaths, and as the third country with the highest number of cases confirmed (last update 11/11/2021, 10:55am CET).

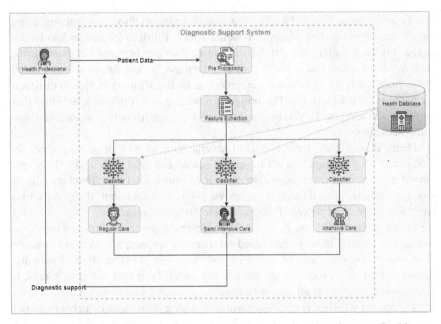

Figure 1: System Use-Case Diagram. According to the diagram, the user (health care professional) enters the patient's data into the system. Then, the system performs the pre-processing of these data, and then performs the attribute extraction. After this step, the smart classifier defines what kind of care the patient should receive.

The city of Paudalho is located in the State of Pernambuco, in the Northeast region of Brazil, the second region with the highest number of cases and deaths. According to IBGE (2010), the municipality has an area of 269,651 km² and a population of 51,357 in 2010 (last census conducted in Brazil). In 2021, the population is estimated at 57,346. It is among the 40 most populous municipalities in the state. In terms of health, the city of Paudalho has 21 SUS establishments. SUS stands for Unique Public Health System and refers to the Brazilian public health system.

The database used in this study consists of 6215 patient records provided by the Health Department of the city of Paudalho. These are records obtained from SUS units that contain hematological parameters and age of men and women, recorded between November 2019 and August 2020. During this period, patients were referred to (i) intensive care unit, (ii) semi-intensive care unit or (iii) regular service. Table 1 shows how the data is distributed according to age and type of service required.

It is important to emphasize that the medical records that served as the basis for this work were organized into three different databases, where each one refers to one of the three types of care. Therefore, each of these databases has 6215 examples and 2 classes (whether or not the patient was referred for that type of care). The distribution is shown in Fig. 2.

Table 1: Distribution of the original database, showing the number of patients who required regular, semi-intensive and intensive care, according to age.

Age	Regular care	Semi-intensive care	Intensive care	Total
0 to 10	85 (14.0%)	494 (81.7%)	26 (4.3%)	605 (100%)
10 to 20	156 (33.5%)	288 (61.8%)	22 (4.7%)	466 (100%)
20 to 30	362 (37.7%)	495 (51.5%)	104 (10.8%)	961 (100%)
30 to 40	409 (45.6%)	400 (44.6%)	87 (9.7%)	896 (100%)
40 to 50	486 (43.5%)	503 (45.1%)	127 (11.4%)	1116 (100%)
50 to 60	278 (36.3%)	393 (51.3%)	95 (12.4%)	766 (100%)
60 to 70	157 (26.7%)	346 (58.9%)	84 (14.3%)	587 (100%)
70 to 80	132 (24.6%)	355 (66.2%)	49 (9.1%)	536 (100%)
80 to 90	34 (17.8%)	138 (72.3%)	19 (9.9%)	191 (100%)
>90	6 (6.6%)	75 (82.4%)	10 (11.0%)	91 (100%)
Total	2105 (33.9%)	3487 (56.1%)	623 (10.0%)	6215 (100%)

(a) Regular care	(b) Semi-intensive care	(c) Cuidado intensivo

Figure 2: Distribution of classes from each of the three databases.

4.2 Definitions

In addition to the age of the patients, 43 hematological parameters are considered (see Fig. 3). These parameters correspond to the tests recommended by the Ministry of Health of Brazil as an initial clinical approach and part of the Covid-19 diagnostic process (Brasil, 2020). Of these, 20 are part of the Complete Blood Count (CBC) with differential, 9 of the arterial blood gas analysis, and the remaining 14 exams are those of total, indirect and direct Bilirubin; Serum Glucose; Lipase dosage; Urea; D-Dimer; Lactic Dehydrogenase; Partial thromboplastin time (PTT); Prothrombin time Activity; C-Reactive Protein (CRP); Creatinine; Ferritin, and Troponin.

It is essential to understand the concepts of the hematological parameters involved in this work. In this way, it is possible to understand the results obtained by the classifiers for each type of care. The following is a brief description of these.

- Complete Blood Count: test used to screen, diagnose or monitor any variety of diseases or conditions that affect blood cells.

  - Red Blood Cells: cells responsible for transporting oxygen from the lungs or gills to all body tissues and transporting carbon dioxide to the lungs, where it is excreted;

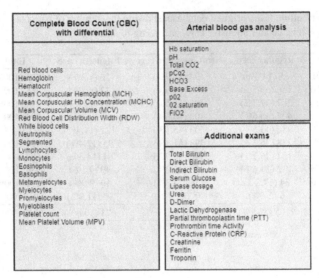

Complete Blood Count (CBC) with differential	Arterial blood gas analysis
Red blood cells Hemoglobin Hematocrit Mean Corpuscular Hemoglobin (MCH) Mean Corpuscular Hb Concentration (MCHC) Mean Corpuscular Volume (MCV) Red Blood Cell Distribution Width (RDW) White blood cells Neutrophils Segmented Lymphocytes Monocytes Eosinophils Basophils Metamyelocytes Myelocytes Promyelocytes Myeloblasts Platelet count Mean Platelet Volume (MPV)	Hb saturation pH Total CO2 pCo2 HCO3 Base Excess p02 02 saturation FiO2

	Additional exams
	Total Bilirubin Direct Bilirubin Indirect Bilirubin Serum Glucose Lipase dosage Urea D-Dimer Lactic Dehydrogenase Partial thromboplastin time (PTT) Prothrombin time Activity C-Reactive Protein (CRP) Creatinine Ferritin Troponin

Figure 3: List of hematological parameters considered in this work.

- Hemoglobin: A protein molecule in red blood cells that transports oxygen from the lungs to the body's tissues and returns carbon dioxide from the tissues to the lungs;

- Hematocrit: proportion, by volume, of blood that consists of red blood cells;

- Mean Corpuscular Hemoglobin (MCH): refers to the average amount of hemoglobin present in a single red blood cell;

- Mean Corpuscular Hemoglobin Concentration (MCHC): describes the mean concentration of hemoglobin in a given volume of red blood cells;

- Mean Corpuscular Volume (MCV): measures the average size of red blood cells;

- Red Blood Cell Distribution Amplitude (RDW): measures the amount of variation of red blood cells in volume and size;

- White Blood Cells: Blood cells produced in the bone marrow, found in the blood and lymph tissue. They are part of the body's immune system;

- Neutrophils: they are part of the immune system, having the ability to phagocytosis. They are mainly responsible for the primary defense against bacteria and fungi, constituting about 60 to 70% of circulating leukocytes;

- Segmented: these are immune system defense cells known as leukocytes. In the case of segmented ones, they are mature neutrophils. The immature ones are called rods.

- Lymphocytes: belong to the group of leukocytes, therefore, they are cells responsible for the defense of the body. They are produced in bone marrow and found in blood and lymph tissue;

- Monocytes: they are part of the immune system and have the function of defending the organism against foreign bodies such as bacteria or viruses, in addition to removing foreign particles and destroying tumor cells;

- Eosinophils: type of white blood cell that helps fight disease. Their exact role is unclear, but they are usually related to allergic diseases and certain infections. They are produced in the bone marrow and then travel to different tissues;

- Basophils: is one of the types of white blood cells and constitutes less than 1 percent of all circulating white blood cells. Basophils are part of the immune system and are created within the bone marrow;

- Metamyelocytes: are precursors of neutrophils, the largest class of leukocytes. They are not normally present in peripheral blood but can be seen in infectious or inflammatory states and in other reactive and neoplastic conditions;

- Myelocytes: together with metamyelocytes and promyelocytes, they are the most frequently observed. These immature neutrophils are normally found only in the bone marrow;

- Promyelocytes: cell in the bone marrow that is at an intermediate stage of development between a myeloblast and a myelocyte and has the characteristic granulations but does not have the specific staining reactions of a mature blood granulocyte;

- Myeloblasts: large non-granular mononuclear cell of the bone marrow and precursor of a myelocyte;

- Platelet Count: measures the average level of platelets in a person's blood. Platelets are fragments of larger cells produced in the bone marrow called megakaryocytes. These fragments are crucial to wound healing;

- Mean Platelet Volume (MPV): measure of mean platelet size;

• Arterial Blood Gas: measures the acidity (pH) and the levels of oxygen and carbon dioxide in the blood of an artery.

- Hemoglobin Saturation: represents the amount of oxygen circulating in the blood. The value is obtained by comparing the amount of hemoglobin that is or is not bound to oxygen;

- pH: specifies the acidity or basicity of the water;

- Total CO2: Carbon dioxide (CO_2) is a waste produced by the body. Blood carries CO_2 to the lungs. A CO_2 blood test measures the amount of carbon dioxide in the blood;

- pCO2: means carbon dioxide partial pressure and reflects the amount of carbon dioxide gas dissolved in the blood;
- HCO3: also called bicarbonate, it is a by-product of the body's metabolism. Blood carries bicarbonate to the lungs and then it is exhaled as carbon dioxide. The kidneys also help regulate bicarbonate by excreting and reabsorbing it;
- Base Excess: value that represents how much the sum of the bases present in the organism differs from the reference value (Base Buffer). Reflects the metabolic component of the blood's acid-base balance;
- pO2: means partial pressure of oxygen and reflects the amount of dissolved oxygen gas in the blood. It primarily measures the effectiveness of the lungs in pulling oxygen from the atmosphere into the bloodstream;
- O2 saturation: is attributed to the amount of O2 that is in the bloodstream;
- FiO2: the inspired oxygen fraction is the percentage of oxygen concentration participating in gas exchange in the alveoli.

• Additional Tests: sometimes requested in order to exclude the possibility of other diseases with similar symptoms.
- Total Bilirubin: Bilirubin is a substance that results from the breakdown of red blood cells. Until cleared from the body, it circulates in the blood as direct bilirubin and indirect bilirubin;
- Direct Bilirubin: corresponds to the conjugation between bilirubin and glucoronic acid in the liver. Its altered concentration is associated with liver damage or biliary obstruction;
- Indirect Bilirubin: corresponds to the substance that is formed at the time of destruction of red blood cells that will later be transported to the liver. Its altered concentration may be associated with some pathological condition involving red blood cells;
- Serum Glucose: allows you to check the amount of sugar in your blood and is considered the main test for diagnosing diabetes;
- Lipase Dosage: Lipase is a digestive enzyme produced in the pancreas. It is usually required in tests to assess pancreatic function;
- Urea: substance produced mainly by the liver, and after metabolized it is filtered by the kidneys. It is generally used to analyze kidney function;
- D-Dimer: one of the products of fibrin degradation. When there are changes in the coagulation process, it is possible that there is an increase in this product;
- Lactic Dehydrogenase: enzyme present inside cells responsible for the metabolism of glucose in the body;

- Partial Thromboplastin Time (PTT): serves to assess whether the patient's blood clotting is normal and whether the clotting time is normal. It usually measures the functionality of the intrinsic coagulation pathway and coagulation factors;

- Prothrombin Activity Time: blood test that assesses the blood's ability to clot;

- C-Reactive Protein (CRP): it is a protein produced by the liver, alterations in the levels of this protein are indicative of inflammatory or infectious processes;

- Creatinine: used to assess kidney function. Creatinine is a waste product produced by the breakdown of a protein called creatine phosphate;

- Ferritin: protein produced by the liver, responsible for storing iron in the body;

- Troponin: the proteins troponin T and troponin I are markers of cardiac damage.

4.3 Pre-Processing

As shown in Fig. 2, it is possible to observe that the three databases are unbalanced, that is, one class has a lower incidence (minority class) than the other (majority class). The first step in pre-processing was to ensure that the databases were balanced. This is done so as not to allow one class, being more frequent than the other, to impair the construction of models and their respective predictions.

In a classic oversampling technique, the number of data from the minority class increases, but it usually does not provide any new information or variation to the machine learning model. The approach proposed by Chawla et al. (2002) is to oversample the minority class by creating synthetic examples. Synthetic Minority Oversampling Technique (SMOTE) joins minority class points with line segments and then adds artificial points on those lines. Hence, synthetic data are created between minority class points and randomly selected nearest neighbors k. The procedure is repeated several times until the minority class has the same proportion as the majority class. That is, the synthetic data generator creates data that resembles the shape or values of existing data, rather than simply copying it. In this work, the databases were balanced using SMOTE with $k = 2$.

To contribute to the performance of the algorithms and obtain a better understanding of the variables involved in the process, we performed feature selection in each of the balanced databases. In this way, it is possible to eliminate highly correlated attributes which do not provide information for the construction of the model and eliminate irrelevant attributes that do not contain useful information for the process. Thus, we obtain a reduced representation of the database in terms of variables but with equivalent results.

The balanced databases were submitted to the selection of attributes from the Particle Swarm Optimization (PSO) (Kennedy and Eberhart, 1995). PSO is a population-based iterative algorithm. The population consists of several randomly generated particles. These particles move in a search space where all possible solutions to the problem are found. Therefore, each particle is associated with a velocity and a position. At each iteration, the particles move in order to reach the optimal solution. From an objective function, the particles are guided by their own result and are also influenced by the result of the others. In this work, the position vector for each particle is composed of 0's and 1's that correspond to the presence or not of each of the 44 attributes of the databases. The output obtained from the objective function refers to the classification performance (accuracy) of a given combination of parameters. In the end, by analyzing all the outputs, it is possible to determine which parameters best represent the complete set. The settings used for the PSO were as follows: population of 50 individuals, 50 generations, individual weight of 0.34, social weight of 0.33, inertia weight of 0.33 and mutation probability of 0.01.

As objective function, we employed a simple decision tree to guide the optimization process. For each particle, each position vector is binary: 1's and 0's correspond to the presence or the absence of one of the 43 features in the process of training and testing the decision tree classifier associated to the objective function. The output of the objective function is the overall accuracy of a 10-fold cross validation training process.

After data balancing and feature selection, we have finally arrived at the databases used in this work. Their characteristics are shown in Table 2.

Table 2: The characteristics of the databases used in this work. They result from balancing (by SMOTE) and feature selection (by PSO) in the original databases.

	Number of patients admitted to		Parameters identified as most relevant	
Regular care	4110 0 = no	4110 1 = yes	age basophils eosinophils lymphocytes	d-dimer troponin creatinine serum glucose c-reactive protein
Semi-intensive care	3486 0 = no	3487 1 = yes	serum glucose metamyelocytes	
Intensive care	5592 0 = no	5591 1 = yes	lactic dehydrogenase prothrombin time activity partial thromboplastin time red blood cell distribution width mean corpuscular Hb concentration	urea ferritin basophils creatinine eosinophils direct bilirubin

4.4 Classification and Metrics

The experiments were performed using the Weka 3.8 (Frank et al., 2016) software in 30 runs and 10-fold cross-validation. The chosen classifiers and their respective configurations were:

- **Support Vector Machine (SVM):** parameter C equals 0.1 and Linear Kernel and Polynomial Kernel (degree 2 and 3);

- **Random Forest:** 10, 50, 100, 150, 200, 250 and 300 trees;

- **Bayesian network**;

- **Naive Bayes**.

The following metrics were selected to evaluate the performance of the classifiers. The mathematical expressions for each of them can be seen in Table 3. As for the predictions of the methods, TN is the number of negative examples that were correctly classified (True Negatives), FP is the number of negative examples that were incorrectly classified as positive (False Positives), FN is the number of positive examples that were incorrectly classified as negative (False Negatives), and TP is the number of positive examples that were correctly classified (True Positives).

- **Accuracy:** the fraction of predictions the model got right. Of all the predictions made by a method, how many of these were classified as True Positive (TP) and True Negative (TN);

- **Sensitivity:** True Positive (TP) rate among all those that should be classified as true. Indicates the ability of the method to correctly identify what is positive;

- **Specificity:** True Negative (TN) rate among all those that should be classified as negative. Indicates the ability of the method to correctly identify what is negative;

- **Area Under the ROC Curve:** discriminative capacity of a method. Given two classes, the area under the ROC curve measures the ability of a test to correctly classify between the two classes. If this value is close to 1, it means that the classifier is able to discriminate between these two cases. If the classifier can not distinguish between these two separately, the area under a curve is equal to 0.5.

5 Results and Discussion

The results were divided into four parts. The first corresponds to the metrics of cases of regular admissions. The second corresponds to the case metrics for semi-intensive admissions. The third deals with intensive inpatient case metrics. Finally, the last one discusses the attributes that were considered relevant according to the system.

Table 3: Mathematical expressions of the metrics chosen to evaluate the performance of the classifiers. The predictions can be classified as TP (True Positive), TN (True Negative), FP (False Positive), or FN (False Negative).

Metric	Mathematical Expression
Accuracy	$\frac{TP+TN}{TP+TN+FP+FN}$
Sensitivity	$\frac{TP}{TP+FN}$
Specificity	$\frac{TN}{TN+FP}$
Area Under the ROC Curve	$AUC = \int TPR\, d(FPR)$

5.1   Intensive Care

In this section, the results for intensive care treatments will be treated. In Table 4, we can see the results of all configurations of all classifiers. The best and worst results are highlighted. The classifier with the best results was Random Forest with 300 trees, obtaining 80.87% ± 0.98% accuracy. But in general, all Random Forest settings had good and similar results (above 80%). The classifier with the lowest accuracy value was the Linear SVM, with 65.70% ± 0.95%.

Figure 4 shows the histogram relating the experiments with the accuracy obtained in percentage. The histogram in question illustrates that the experiments are more concentrated at approximately 65%, and around 80%. Note that matches the results shown in Table 4.

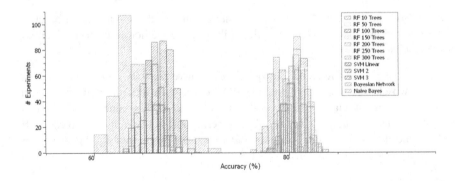

Figure 4: Accuracy for all classifiers and configurations for intensive care. The histogram illustrates that the experiments are more concentrated at approximately 65%, and around 80%. Naive Bayes, SVM Linear, SVM 2, SVM 3 were the classifiers that obtained accuracy close to 65%. All other classifiers were around 80% accuracy, a result that matches the Table 4.

Table 4: Results of all metrics for Random Forest, SVM, Bayesian Network and Naive Bayes, for intensive care. The Table highlights the best and worst results among the configurations of the classifiers. For the best result, we have Random Forest with 300 trees, getting 80.87% ± 0.98% accuracy. But in general, all Random Forest settings obtained similar good results (above 80%). The classifier with the lowest accuracy was the Linear SVM, with 65.70% ± 0.95%.

		INTENSIVE CARE							
		METRICS							
		ACCURACY		AREA UNDER ROC CURVE		SPECIFICITY		SENSITIVITY	
CLASSIFIER	CONFIGURATION	Media	Standard deviation	Media	Standard deviation	Media	Standard deviation	Media	Standard deviation
Random Forest	10 trees	80.29	1.01	0.9011	0.0073	0.9315	0.0113	0.6743	0.0179
	50 trees	80.77	1.01	0.9055	0.0069	0.9415	0.0098	0.6740	0.0180
	100 trees	80.83	1.01	0.9063	0.0071	0.9426	0.0098	0.6741	0.0181
	150 trees	80.85	0.99	0.9064	0.0070	0.9430	0.0098	0.6741	0.0180
	200 trees	80.86	0.97	0.9065	0.0070	0.9431	0.0096	0.6741	0.0179
	250 trees	80.87	0.98	0.9066	0.0070	0.9433	0.0097	0.6740	0.0179
	300 trees	80.87	0.98	0.9067	0.0070	0.9433	0.0097	0.6741	0.0180
SVM	Linear	65.70	0.95	0.6570	0.0095	0.3304	0.0188	0.9835	0.0052
	Polynomial 2	66.24	0.96	0.6624	0.0096	0.3419	0.0190	0.9829	0.0054
	Polynomial 3	67.55	0.97	0.6754	0.0097	0.3701	0.0185	0.9808	0.0057
Bayesian Network		78.82	0.95	0.9145	0.0067	0.5921	0.0183	0.9643	0.0051
Naive Bayes		64.20	2.41	0.7859	0.0125	0.9181	0.0310	0.3659	0.0737

In Fig. 5, we can see that all values were above 0.6. In addition, all Random Forest settings were close to 1. Indicating once again that all Random Forest settings had good results for the ROC curve area metric.

The histogram in Fig. 6 shows that the values for sensitivity of the classifiers vary somewhat. We draw attention to the Bayesian Network, which concentrated the largest number of experiments close to 1. This is the classifier with the best result for the sensitivity metric.

We can observe the specificity results of the classifiers in the histogram of Fig. 7. The configuration of grade 3 polynomial SVM, the Random Forest with 300 trees and the Naive Bayes had the best results, with the highest number of experiments close to 1.

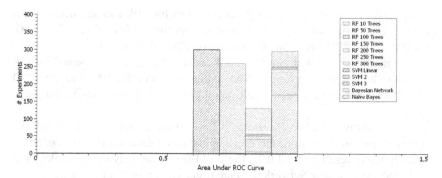

Figure 5: Area Under ROC Curve for all classifiers and configurations for intensive care. Looking at the histogram, we can see that all values were above 0.6. We draw attention to the Random Forest settings, which obtained values close to 1.

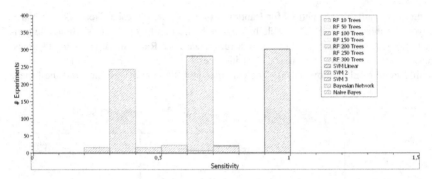

Figure 6: Sensitivity for all classifiers and configurations for intensive care. In general, values for sensitivity of classifiers vary somewhat. But we draw attention to the Bayesian Network, which concentrated the largest number of experiments close to 1.

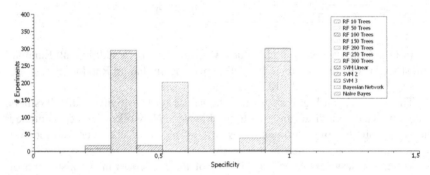

Figure 7: Specificity for all classifiers and configurations for intensive care. The configuration of the grade 3 polynomial SVM, the Random Forest with 300 trees and the Naive Bayes had better results.

Figure 8 shows the boxplot for the accuracy metric. We can see that Random Forest in all configurations got good results. But the configurations of 50, 100, 150, 200, 250 and 300 trees, showed similar results and above 80%.

The graph in Fig. 9 shows that the Random Forest and Bayesian Network classifiers showed the best results. The configurations of 50, 100, 150, 200, 250 and 300 trees presented similar results among themselves and with the Bayesian Network.

In the sensitivity metric, the graph in Fig. 10 shows that the behavior of the classifiers was different from the previous metrics. Random Forest obtained a relatively lower result, around 0.7. The SVM (in linear, polynomial of degree 2 and 3) and the Bayesian Network presented very good results, close to 1.

For the specificity metric, the Random Forest in all configurations showed good results, close to 1, as shown in Fig. 11. With the exception of the 10-tree configuration, the other Random Forest configurations showed very similar results. Naive Bayes also showed a good result, but with more dispersion in the block than Random Forest.

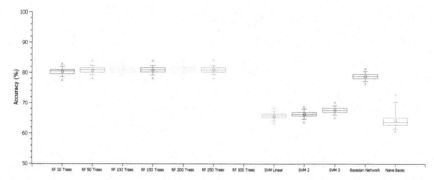

Figure 8: Accuracy for all classifiers and configurations for intensive care. For the Random Forest classifier, the configurations of 50, 100, 150, 200, 250 and 300 trees presented good and similar results.

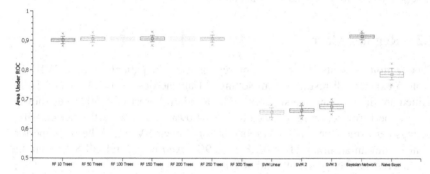

Figure 9: Area Under ROC Curve for all classifiers and configurations for intensive care. The Random Forest and Bayesian Network classifiers showed the best results.

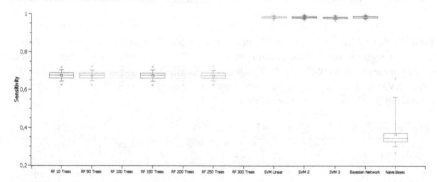

Figure 10: Sensitivity for all classifiers and configurations for intensive care. Random Forest obtained a relatively lower result, compared to the previous metrics, around 0.7. The SVM (in linear, polynomial of degree 2 and 3) and the Bayesian Network presented very good results, close to 1.

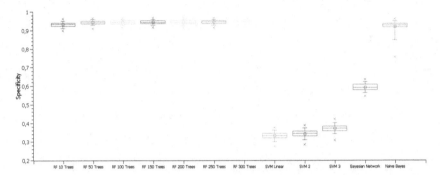

Figure 11: Specificity for all classifiers and configurations for intensive care. With the exception of the 10-tree configuration, the other Random Forest configurations showed results very similar and close to 1. The Naive Bayes also showed a good result, but with more dispersion in the block than the Random Forest ones.

5.2   Regular Care

This section presents the results for regular care in patients with COVID-19. Table 5 exposes all results for all settings of all metrics for regular care. Highlighted are the best and worst results. The Random Forest with 300 trees showed the best performance, with an accuracy of 84.09% ± 1.27%. All other classifier settings performed well as well (above 80%). Linear SVM had the worst performance, with an accuracy of 55.32% ± 4.09%. And in general, all SVM settings had low results (between 55% and 56%).

The histogram in Fig. 12 shows the results for accuracy in regular care. The SVM classifiers in all configurations (linear, polynomial degree 2 and 3) concentrated most of the experiments, and with an accuracy value around 55%. The Ran-

Table 5: Results of all metrics for Random Forest, SVM, Bayesian Network and Naive Bayes, for regular care. The Random Forest with 300 trees showed the best performance, with an accuracy of 84.09% ± 1.27%. All other classifier settings performed well as well. Linear SVM had the worst performance, with an accuracy of 55.32% ± 4.09%. And in general, all SVM settings had low results.

REGULAR CARE									
		METRICS							
		ACCURACY		AREA UNDER ROC CURVE		SPECIFICITY		SENSITIVITY	
CLASSIFIER	CONFIGURATION	Media	Standard deviation	Media	Standard deviation	Media	Standard deviation	Media	Standard deviation
Random Forest	10 trees	83.45	1.23	0.8856	0.0117	0.8360	0.0178	0.8330	0.0189
	50 trees	83.97	1.26	0.8927	0.0112	0.8492	0.0173	0.8302	0.0185
	100 trees	84.02	1.26	0.8935	0.0113	0.8512	0.0172	0.8292	0.0186
	150 trees	84.05	1.27	0.8937	0.0113	0.8521	0.0173	0.8290	0.0191
	200 trees	84.06	1.27	0.8938	0.0113	0.8525	0.0172	0.8287	0.0189
	250 trees	84.08	1.27	0.8939	0.0113	0.8530	0.0171	0.8286	0.0191
	300 trees	84.09	1.27	0.8940	0.0113	0.8533	0.0172	0.8285	0.0190
SVM	Linear	55.32	4.09	0.5533	0.0409	0.9452	0.0639	0.1613	0.1213
	Polynomial 2	56.68	3.94	0.5668	0.0394	0.8774	0.0195	0.2562	0.0748
	Polynomial 3	55.65	2.04	0.5565	0.0204	0.9264	0.0212	0.1867	0.0291
Bayesian Network		81.73	1.38	0.8827	0.0113	0.8892	0.0150	0.7454	0.0234
Naive Bayes		59.41	1.27	0.7737	0.0156	0.9610	0.0092	0.2272	0.0252

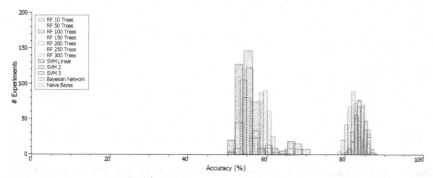

Figure 12: Accuracy for all classifiers and configurations for regular care. The SVM classifiers in all configurations (linear, polynomial degree 2 and 3) concentrated most of the experiments, and with an accuracy value around 55%. All the Random Forest settings (10, 50, 100, 150, 200, 250 and 300 trees) and the Bayesian Network had the highest accuracy values, between 80% and 85%.

dom Forest and Bayesian Network configurations had the highest accuracy values, between 80% and 85%.

For the area under the ROC curve metric, the histogram in Fig. 13 we can highlight the Bayesian Network, which concentrated a large number of experiments (between 250 and 300) with a metric value above 0.8. Naive Bayes also concentrated a large number of experiments, in the range of 300. It obtained a result between 0.7 and 0.8 for the metric.

Evaluating the sensitivity metric, in Fig. 14, we can see that the Linear SVM obtained a considerably low result, with experiments below 0.4. Random Forest with 300 trees and Bayesian Network performed well in the evaluated metric. The first concentrates a remarkable number of experiments (around 300) with sensitivity values between 0.8 and 0.9, and the second (with about 300 experiments as well) with sensitivity values between 0.7 and 0.8.

By observing Fig. 15, which corresponds to the histogram of the specificity metric, we can see that some classifiers concentrated most experiments between 0.8 and 1.0, with experiments above 300. Among these are: Naive Bayes, SVM Polynomial 2, SVM Polynomial 3, Bayesian Network.

Figure 16 shows the boxplots for the accuracy, and Fig. 17 shows the boxplots for the area under the ROC curve, both for regular care. Analyzing statistically, the Random forest with 50, 100, 150, 200, 250 and 300 trees are equivalent for both metrics (accuracy and area of the ROC curve). This means that they obtained similar accuracy values. Linear SVM and Polynomial SVM 2 were the ones with the greatest dispersion of values and the worst performance in both cases.

The boxplot in Fig. 18, shows us that the Random Forest in settings of 50, 100, 150, 200, 250 and 300 are statistically equivalent, and obtained the best results. Both because they were very close to 1, and because they have low dispersion. Linear SVM presented, in addition to a low performance, a considerable dispersion.

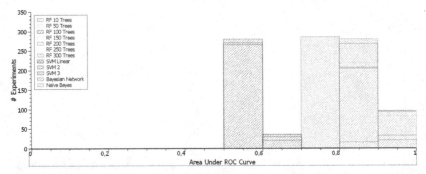

Figure 13: Area Under ROC Curve for all classifiers and configurations for regular care. The Bayesian Network, and the Naive Bayes showed good results. The first concentrated a large number of experiments (between 250 and 300) with a metric value above 0.8. Naive Bayes also concentrated a large number of experiments, in the range of 300. It obtained a result between 0.7 and 0.8 for the ROC curve area metric.

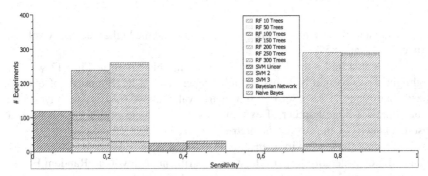

Figure 14: Sensitivity for all classifiers and configurations for regular care. We can observe that the Linear SVM obtained a considerably low result, with experiments below 0.4. Random Forest with 300 trees and Bayesian Network performed well in the evaluated metric.

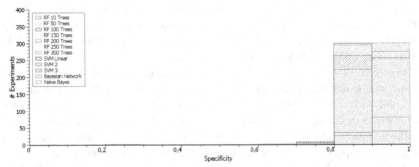

Figure 15: Specificity for all classifiers and configurations for regular care. We can see that Naive Bayes, SVM Polynomial 2, SVM Polynomial 3 and Bayesian Network concentrated most of the experiments between 0.8 and 1.0, with experiments above 300.

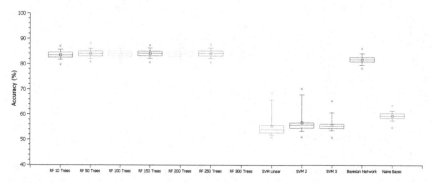

Figure 16: Accuracy for all classifiers and configurations for regular care. As we can see in the graph, Random forest with settings of 50, 100, 150, 200, 250 and 300 trees are statistically equivalent, and show the best result.

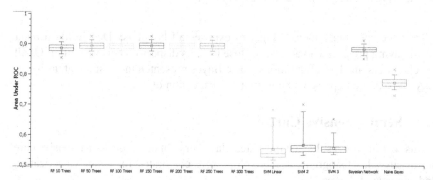

Figure 17: Area Under ROC Curve for all classifiers and configurations for regular care. As we can see in the graph, Random forest with settings of 50, 100, 150, 200, 250 and 300 trees are statistically equivalent, and show the best result.

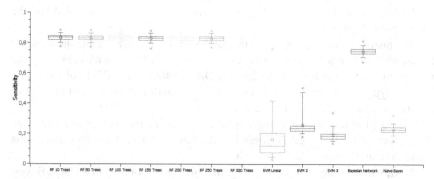

Figure 18: Sensitivity for all classifiers and configurations for regular care. As we can see in the graph, Random forest with settings of 50, 100, 150, 200, 250 and 300 trees are statistically equivalent, and show the best result.

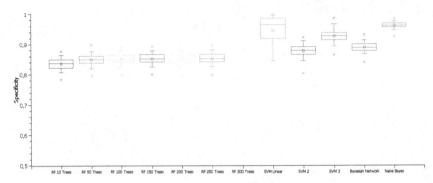

Figure 19: Specificity for all classifiers and configurations for regular care. Of all the classifiers, in all configurations, Nave Bayes presented the best result, as it was very close to 1 and presented the smallest dispersion of all. Despite the Linear SVM having presented a value very close to 1, its dispersion was very high.

For the specificity metric, Fig. 19 exposes all boxplots. Despite the Linear SVM having presented a value very close to 1, its dispersion was very high. Of all the classifiers, in all configurations, Nave Bayes presented the best result, as it was very close to 1 and presented the smallest dispersion of all.

5.3   Semi-Intensive Care

In this section, the results that the tested classifiers obtained for semi-intensive care are discussed. Histograms and boxplots were elaborated for better visualization and analysis of the results.

The Table 6 exposes all the results for all the configurations of the studied classifiers. Results are separated by metric. We can see highlighted in bold the best and the worst result. The Random Forest with a configuration of 300 trees had the best result (with 81.34% ± 1.28% accuracy), while the Linear SVM had the worst result (with 50.05% ± 1.44%).

The histogram in Fig. 20, shows us that the Bayesian Network and the Random Forest with 300 trees obtained the best results, between 75% and 85%, but they did not obtain a large number of experiments. On the other hand, SVM Polynomial 2, SVM Polynomial 3 and Random Forest with 100 trees had the highest number of experiments (above 250), but had an accuracy result close to 50%.

Figure 21 shows us the histogram of the results of the area metric under the ROC curve. As we can see, Bayesan had the best performance, with experiments above 300, and metric value above 0.8.

Next, we have the histogram of Fig. 6. This chart shows us that Naive Bayes, Random Forest with 10 trees, Random Forest with 300 trees, and Bayesian Network had the best results, close to 1.

The histogram of Fig. 23 shows that Naive Bayes obtained the best result of all. With experiments above 300 and values very close to 1. The Polynomial SVM grade 2 and 3 also obtained good results, but with a low number of experiments.

Table 6: Results of all metrics for Random Forest, SVM, Bayesian Network and Naive Bayes, for semi-intensive care. The Random Forest with a configuration of 300 trees had the best result (with 81.34% ± 1.28% accuracy), while the Linear SVM had the worst result (with 50.05% ± 1.44%).

		SEMI INTENSIVE CARE							
		METRICS							
		ACCURACY		AREA UNDER ROC CURVE		SPECIFICITY		SENSITIVITY	
CLASSIFIER	CONFIGURATION	Media	Standard deviation	Media	Standard deviation	Media	Standard deviation	Media	Standard deviation
Random Forest	10 trees	81.33	1.29	0.8562	0.0120	0.7207	0.0210	0.9058	0.0151
	50 trees	81.32	1.29	0.8570	0.0119	0.7208	0.0210	0.9056	0.0151
	100 trees	81.32	1.29	0.8571	0.0119	0.7209	0.0209	0.9056	0.0152
	150 trees	81.33	1.29	0.8572	0.0118	0.7209	0.0209	0.9058	0.0151
	200 trees	81.33	1.28	0.8572	0.0118	0.7208	0.0209	0.9059	0.0151
	250 trees	81.34	1.28	0.8573	0.0118	0.7209	0.0210	0.9060	0.0151
	300 trees	81.34	1.28	0.8573	0.0118	0.7208	0.0209	0.9060	0.0152
SVM	Linear	50.05	1.44	0.5007	0.0143	0.7822	0.4112	0.2192	0.4050
	Polynomial 2	50.10	1.50	0.5013	0.0149	0.6946	0.4595	0.3061	0.4600
	Polynomial 3	51.06	4.54	0.5108	0.0453	0.8215	0.3742	0.2000	0.3775
Bayesian Network		80.67	1.38	0.8592	0.0116	0.7365	0.0225	0.8768	0.0265
Naive Bayes		55.69	1.63	0.6809	0.0137	0.9646	0.0095	0.1492	0.0353

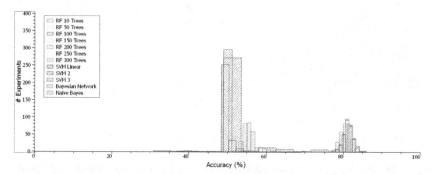

Figure 20: Accuracy for for all classifiers and configurations for semi-intensive care. Bayesian Network and Random Forest with 300 trees had the best results, between 75% and 85%.

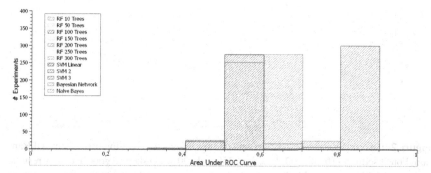

Figure 21: Area Under ROC Curve for for all classifiers and configurations for semi-intensive care. Bayesian had the best performance, with experiments above 300, and metric value above 0.8.

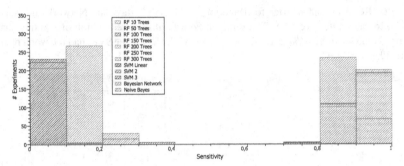

Figure 22: Sensitivity for all classifiers and configurations for semi-intensive care. Naive Bayes, Random Forest with 10 trees, Random Forest with 300 trees and Bayesian Network had the best results, close to 1.

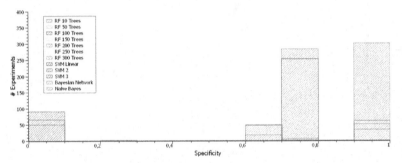

Figure 23: Specificity for all classifiers and configurations for semi-intensive care. Naive Bayes had the best result of all, with experiments above 300 and values very close to 1.

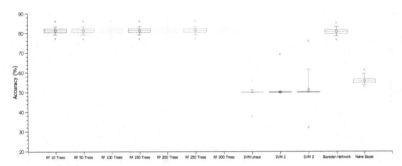

Figure 24: Accuracy for all classifiers and configurations for semi-intensive care. All Random Forest settings (10, 50, 100, 150, 200, 250 and 300 trees) showed good accuracy results, with values above 80% and little dispersion in the boxes. In addition to these, the Bayesian Network also showed a similar result.

The graph in Fig. 24, shows us the boxplot of the results for the accuracy metric. All Random Forest settings (10, 50, 100, 150, 200, 250 and 300 trees)

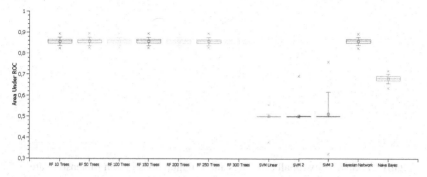

Figure 25: Area Under ROC Curve for all classifiers and configurations for semi-intensive care. All the Random Forest configurations (10, 50, 100, 150, 200, 250 and 300 trees) and the Bayesian Network showed good results for the area under the ROC curve, being statistically equivalent.

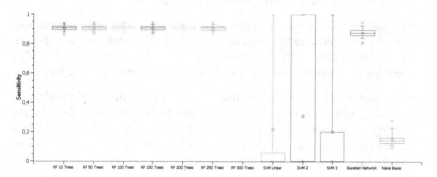

Figure 26: Sensitivity for all classifiers and configurations for semi-intensive care.

showed good accuracy results, with values above 80% and little dispersion in the boxes. In addition to these, the Bayesian Network also showed a similar result.

For the boxplot in Fig. 25, we have the values for the area metric under the ROC curve. As the graph in Fig. 24, all the Random Forest configurations (10, 50, 100, 150, 200, 250 and 300 trees) and the Bayesian Network showed good results for the area under the ROC curve, being equivalent statistically. In Fig. 26, the boxplots for the sensitivity metric can be seen.

5.4 Feature Extraction

In this section we present the parameters we consider most relevant for the attribute selection process with PSO. Here, we seek to explain from a biomedical point of view the clinical reasons for these attributes to be considered more relevant for decision making.

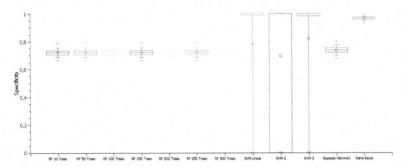

Figure 27: Specificity for all classifiers and configurations for semi-intensive care.

- Age: Age is an important parameter in regular care, probably because of the risks associated with old age. With advancing age, health tends to be more fragile with the natural decrease in immunity. In addition, different comorbidities that may affect the body of the elderly.

- Basophiles: They were considered statistically relevant both in predicting regular care and care in an intensive care unit. Basophils are an important part of the immune system. Basophils are normally in low quantity. A high number of basophils can be a sign of chronic inflammation in the lungs.

- Eosinophils: They were considered relevant for predicting regular and intensive care unit care. The change in eosinophils can represent infections and allergies. Our system may have identified the parameter as important for its role in the prognosis of Covid-19. Eosinophils can also provide an overview of the state of the patient's immune system.

- Lymphocytes: They were highlighted as relevant in predicting regular attendance. Covid-19 has caused lymphopenia in infected patients, so the amount of lymphocytes is a good way to assess the prognosis of the disease when correlated with other tests.

- D-Dimer: It was highlighted as relevant for predicting regular attendance. The increased amount of D-dimer is a common laboratory finding in Covid-19 cases. The increase in the levels of this marker in the blood may be indicative of infection, and may be suggestive of a greater or lesser severity of the disease, including risks of thrombosis and intravascular coagulation.

- Troponin: It was highlighted as relevant to regular care. There are reports of a worse evolution of COVID-19 in patients with heart disease, with cardiac complications in more severe forms. Troponin has been identified as a good prognostic marker for Covid-19, given that high-sensitivity troponin I can predict cardiac injuries caused by SARS-CoV-2.

- Creatinine: It was considered statistically relevant for predicting regular and intensive care unit care. Creatinine is used as a marker of kidney function, but it can also be used to indicate infection.

- Serum Glucose: It was highlighted as relevant for the prediction of regular care and in a semi-intensive care unit. Glucose is the most common test used to diagnose diabetes. In the scenario of Covid-19, diabetics are in a risk group. Probably, our system designated glucose as a priority parameter due to its ability to separate risk groups.

- C-Reactive Protein: CRP was highlighted in predicting regular care. C-Reactive Protein is a marker of inflammatory and infectious processes, and may also act as an early predictor of Covid-19. The identification by the system as a parameter of interest can be given by the association of amounts of CRP with a better or worse prognosis.

- Metamyelocytes: Metamyelocytes were highlighted in the prediction of semi-intensive care. Identification by the system as a parameter of interest can be associated with the function of a marker of infectious, inflammatory and re-active or neoplasic conditions. Its marker function makes metamyelocytes an important prognostic parameter and observation of other neoplasic co-morbidities in the patient.

- Lactic Dehydrogenase (DHL): It was highlighted in the prediction of inten-sive care. It is closely associated with a poor prognosis in Covid-19, as it can be used as a marker of tissue destruction. Therefore, with greater dis-ease severity and lung tissue destruction, there is an increase in LDH.

- Prothrombin Activity Time (PT) and Partial Thromboplastin Time (TTP): Both were highlighted in the prediction of intensive care. PT and TTP play a role as a coagulation marker. In severe Covid-19 patients, the possibility of venous thromboembolism has already been reported, which would increase such markers, justifying their position in intensive care by representing a poor prognosis.

- Red cell width distribution (RDW): It was highlighted in the prediction of intensive care. RDW is currently being used as a marker for a poor prog-nosis of Covid-19: the appearance of a great variety of width distribution, accompanied by a greater amount of erythroblasts, can mean a hasty attempt of the organism to supply an internal lesion, such as lung tissue injury by Covid-19, representing a poor prognosis.

- Mean corpuscular hemoglobin concentration (MCHC): It was highlighted in the prediction of intensive care. Recent studies have pointed to the role of iron in metabolism when related to multiple organ dysfunction syndrome in the most severe cases of COVID-19. Probably for this reason, our system defined the MCHC as an important parameter for intensive care.

- Urea: It was highlighted as statistically relevant in the prediction of intensive care. When related to multiple organ dysfunction syndrome, this marker of renal function fits the parameters for a poor prognosis.

- Ferritin: It was highlighted as statistically relevant in intensive care. Ferritin is a marker of liver damage and general inflammatory processes. Thus, high values are related to poor prognosis.

- Direct Bilirubin: It was highlighted as relevant for the prediction of intensive care. It is among the markers associated with multiple organ dysfunction syndrome, being a marker for liver damage or a sign of biliary obstruction.

6 Conclusion

Considering the whole context of COVID-19, and its consequences worldwide, it is very important to take an accurate decision when it comes to the hospitalization of a patient. Given this situation, knowing the best type of care that a patient affected by the disease should receive can be important in terms of patient costs, bed occupancy rates, and even the risk to life that the patient is subjected to.

Through this perspective, this work was proposed to serve as a tool for professionals in decision making regarding the types of care that the patient should receive.

According to the results obtained for intensive care, we can conclude that the Random Forest classifier in all configurations (10, 50, 100, 150, 200, 250 and 300 trees) obtained the best result overall, and with accuracy above the 80%. This shows us that for this classifier, the problem is not highly complex.

The results for regular care show that again Random Forest performed better. The configurations of 50, 100, 150, 200, 250 and 300 trees showed good results in general, with an average accuracy of 84%. Showing that the problem presents a little more complexity, if compared to intensive care, since the configuration with 10 trees presented a slightly inferior performance.

Finally, for semi-intensive care, once again Random Forest showed the best performance, and this time, all the configurations presented similar accuracy values (around 81%), and very good. This behavior is similar to that of intensive care, where all settings obtained similar results.

Regarding the parameters that were considered most relevant after the selection of attributes, we can say that in regular care there should be a separation of risk groups and prediction of disease severity in patients. In Semi-Intensive Care, it should be related to possible existing comorbidities. And for intensive care, poor prognosis can be associated with markers of damage to different organs, leading to multiple dysfunction.

References

Amaratunga, D., J. Cabrera and Y.-S. Lee. Enriched random forests. Bioinformatics, 24(18): 2010–2014, 2008.

Analytics, D. Dados Covid-19, 2021, 2021.

Andrew, A.M. An introduction to support vector machines and other kernel-based learning methods by nello christianini and john shawe-taylor, Cambridge University Press, Cambridge, 2000, xiii+189 pp., ISBN 0-521-78019-5 (hbk,£ 27.50). Robotica, 18(6): 687–689, 2000.

Aquino, E.M., I.H. Silveira, J.M. Pescarini, R. Aquino, J.A.d. Souza-Filho, A.d.S. Rocha, A. Ferreira, A. Victor, C. Teixeira, D.B. Machado, E. Paixão, F.J.O. Alves, F. Pilecco, G. Menezes, L. Gabrielli, L. Leite, M.C.C. de Almeida, N. Ortelan, Q.H.R.F. Fernandes, R.J.F. Ortiz, R.N. Palmeira, E.P. Pinto Junior, E. Aragão, L.E.P.F. de Souza, M.B. Netto, M.G. Teixeira, M.L. Barreto, M.Y. Ichihara and R.T.R.S. Lima. Medidas de distanciamento social no controle da pandemia de covid-19: Potenciais impactos e desafios no brasil. Ciência & Saúde Coletiva, 25: 2423–2446, 2020.

Awwalu, J., N. A. Umar, M. S. Ibrahim and O. F. Nonyelum. A multinomial naïve bayes decision support system for covid-19 detection. FUDMA Journal of Sciences, 4(2): 704–711, 2020.

Azevedo, W.W., S.M. Lima, I.M. Fernandes, A.D. Rocha, F.R. Cordeiro, A.G. da Silva-Filho and W.P. dos Santos. Fuzzy morphological extreme learning machines to detect and classify masses in mammograms. In 2015 IEEE International Conference on Fuzzy Systems (fuzz-IEEE), pp. 1–8. IEEE, 2015.

Barbosa, V.A.d.F., J.C. Gomes, M.A. de Santana, C.L. de Lima, R.B. Calado, C.R. Bertoldo Junior, J.E.d.A. Albuquerque, R.G. de Souza, R.J.E. de Araújo, L.A.R. Mattos Junior, R.E. de Souza and W.P. dos Santos. Covid-19 rapid test by combining a random forest-based web system and blood tests. Journal of Biomolecular Structure and Dynamics, pp. 1–20, 2021.

Boncristiani, H., M. Criado, E. Arruda and M. Schaechter. Encyclopedia of microbiology, 2009.

Boukir, S., L. Guo and N. Chehata. Improving remote sensing multiple classification by data and ensemble selection. Photogrammetric Engineering & Remote Sensing, 87(11): 841–852, 2021.

Brasil, M.d.S. Diretrizes para diagnóstico e tratamento da covid-19. sociedade brasileira de análises clínicas. Available: http://www.sbac.org.br/blog/2020/04/09/diretrizespara-diagnostico-e-tratamento-da-covid-19/, 2020. Accessed: 202107-20.

Chakraborty, C., A. Sharma, G. Sharma, M. Bhattacharya and S. Lee. Sars-cov-2 causing pneumonia associated respiratory disorder (covid-19): Diagnostic and proposed therapeutic options. Eur. Rev. Med. Pharmacol. Sci., 24(7): 4016–4026, 2020.

Chawla, N., K. Bowyer, L. Hall and W. Kegelmeyer. Smote: Synthetic minority over-sampling technique. J. Artif. Intell. Res. (JAIR), 16: 321–357, 06 2002.

Chen, S.H. and C.A. Pollino. Good practice in Bayesian network modelling. Environmental Modelling & Software, 37: 134–145, 2012.

Cordeiro, F.R., S.M. Lima, A.G. Silva-Filho and W. Santos. Segmentation of mammography by applying extreme learning machine in tumor detection. In International Conference on Intelligent Data Engineering and Automated Learning, pp. 92–100. Springer, 2012.

Cordeiro, F.R., W.P. Santos and A.G. Silva-Filhoa. Segmentation of mammography by applying growcut for mass detection. In MEDINFO 2013, pp. 87–91. IOS Press, 2013.

Cortes, C. and V. Vapnik. Support-vector networks. Machine Learning, 20(3): 273–297, 1995.

da Silva, A.C.G., C.L. de Lima, C.C. da Silva, G.M.M. Moreno, E.L. Silva, G.S. Marques, L.J.B. de Araújo, L.A.A. Júnior, S.B.J. de Souza, M.A. de Santana, J.C. Gomes, V.A. de Freitas Barbosa, A. Musah, P. Kostkova, A.G. da Silva Filho and W.P. dos Santos. Machine learning approaches for temporal and spatio-temporal covid-19 forecasting: A brief review and a contribution. In Assessing COVID-19 and other Pandemics and Epidemics using Computational Modelling and Data Analysis, pp. 333–357. Springer, 2021a.

da Silva, C.C., C.L. de Lima, A.C.G. da Silva, E.L. Silva, G.S. Marques, L.J.B. de Araújo, L.A.A. Júnior, S.B.J. de Souza, M.A. de Santana, J.C. Gomes, V.A. de Freitas Barbosa, A. Musah, P. Kostkova, W.P. dos Santos and A.G. da Silva Filho. Covid-19 dynamic monitoring and real-time spatio-temporal forecasting. Frontiers in Public Health, 9, 2021b.

de Freitas, R.C., R. Alves, A.G. da Silva Filho, R.E. de Souza, B.L. Bezerra and W.P. dos Santos. Electromyography-controlled car: A proof of concept based on surface electromyography, extreme learning machines and low-cost open hardware. Computers & Electrical Engineering, 73: 167–179, 2019.

de Freitas Barbosa, V.A., J.C. Gomes, M.A. de Santana, C.L. de Lima, R.B. Calado, C.R.B. Junior, J.E. de Almeida Albuquerque, R.G. de Souza, R.J.E. de Araujo, R.E. de Souza and W.P. dos Santos. Covid-19 rapid test by combining a random forest based web system and blood tests. medRxiv, 2020.

de Freitas Barbosa, V.A., J.C. Gomes, M.A. de Santana, E.d.A. Jeniffer, R.G. de Souza, R.E. de Souza and W.P. dos Santos. Heg.ia: An intelligent system to support diagnosis of covid-19 based on blood tests. Research on Biomedical Engineering, pp. 1–18, 2021.

de Lima, C.L., C.C. da Silva, A.C.G. da Silva, E. Luiz Silva, G.S. Marques, L.J.B. de Araújo, L.A. Albuquerque Júnior, S.B.J. de Souza, M.A. de Santana, J.C. Gomes, V.A. de Freitas Barbosa, A. Musah, P. Kostkova, W.P. dos Santos and A.G. da Silva Filho. Covid-sgis: A smart tool for dynamic monitoring and temporal forecasting of covid-19. Frontiers in Public Health, 8: 761, 2020.

de Lima, S.M., A.G. da Silva-Filho and W.P. Dos Santos. Detection and classification of masses in mammographic images in a multi-kernel approach. Computer Methods and Programs in Biomedicine, 134: 11–29, 2016.

de Moraes, R.M., I.L.A. da Silva and L. dos Santos Machado. Online skills assessment in training based on virtual reality using a novel fuzzy triangular naive bayes network. In Developments of Artificial Intelligence Technologies in Computation and Robotics: Proceedings of the 14th International FLINS Conference (FLINS 2020), pp. 446–454. World Scientific, 2020.

de Santana, M.A., J.C. Gomes, V.A. de Freitas Barbosa, C.L. de Lima, J. Bandeira, M.J.S. Valença, R.E. de Souza, A.I. Masood and W.P. dos Santos. An intelligent tool to support diagnosis of covid-19 by texture analysis of computerized tomography x-ray images and machine learning. In Assessing COVID-19 and other Pandemics and Epidemics using Computational Modelling and Data Analysis, pp. 259–282. Springer, 2022.

de Vasconcelos, J., W. dos Santos and R.d.C.F. de Lima. Analysis of methods of classification of breast thermographic images to determine their viability in the early breast cancer detection. IEEE Latin America Transactions, 16(6): 1631–1637, 2018.

Frank, E., M.A. Hall and I.H. Witten. The WEKA workbench. Online Appendix for Data Mining: Practical Machine Learning Tools and Techniques. Morgan Kaufmann, Fourth Edition, 2016.

Genuer, R., J.-M. Poggi and C. Tuleau-Malot. Variable selection using random forests. Pattern Recognition Letters, 31(14): 2225–2236, 2010.

Gomes, J.C., V.A.d.F. Barbosa, M.A. Santana, J. Bandeira, M.J.S. Valença, R.E. de Souza, A.M. Ismael and W.P. dos Santos. Ikonos: An intelligent tool to support diagnosis of covid-19 by texture analysis of x-ray images. Research on Biomedical Engineering, pp. 1–14, 2020.

Gralinski, L. and V. Menachery. Return of the coronavirus: 2019-ncov. Viruses, 12(2): 135, 2020.

Grasselli, G., A. Pesenti and M. Cecconi. Critical care utilization for the covid-19 outbreak in lombardy, Italy: Early experience and forecast during an emergency response. Jama, 323(16): 1545–1546, 2020.

Hany, N., N. Atef, N. Mostafa, S. Mohamed, M. ElSahhar and A. AbdelRaouf. Detection covid-19 using machine learning from blood tests. In 2021 International Mobile, Intelligent, and Ubiquitous Computing Conference (MIUCC), pp. 229–234, 2021.

Henry, B.M., M.H.S. de Oliveira, S. Benoit, M. Plebani and G. Lippi. Hematologic, biochemical and immune biomarker abnormalities associated with severe illness and mortality in coronavirus disease 2019 (covid-19): A meta-analysis. Clinical Chemistry and Laboratory Medicine (CCLM), 58(7): 1021–1028, 2020. URL https://doi.org/10.1515/cclm-2020-0369.

Hothorn, T., K. Hornik and A. Zeileis. Unbiased recursive partitioning: A conditional inference framework. Journal of Computational and Graphical Statistics, 15(3): 651–674, 2006.

IBGE, I.B.d.G.e.E. Censo brasileiro de 2010. Available: https://censo2010.ibge.gov.br/, 2010. Accessed: 202111-09.

Iwendi, C., A.K. Bashir, A. Peshkar, R. Sujatha, J.M. Chatterjee, S. Pasupuleti, R. Mishra, S. Pillai and O. Jo. Covid-19 patient health prediction using boosted random forest algorithm. Frontiers in Public Health, 8: 357, 2020.

Jin, Y., L. Cai, Z. Cheng, H. Cheng, T. Deng, Y. Fan, C. Fang, D. Huang, L. Huang, Q. Huang, Y. Han, B. Hu, F. Hu, B.H. Li, Y.R. Li, K. Liang, L.K. Lin, L.S. Luo, J. Ma, L.L. Ma, Z.Y. Peng, Y.B. Pan, Z.Y. Pan, X.Q. Ren, H.M. Sun, Y. Wang, Y.Y. Wang, H. Weng, C.J. Wei, D.F. Wu, J. Xia, Y. Xiong, H.B. Xu, X.M. Yao, Y.F. Yuan, T.S. Ye, X.C. Zhang, Y.W. Zhang, Y.G. Zhang, H.M. Zhang, Y. Zhao, M.J. Zhao, H. Zi, X.T. Zeng, Y.Y. Wang and X.H. Wang. A rapid advice guideline for the diagnosis and treatment of 2019 novel coronavirus (2019-ncov) infected pneumonia (standard version). Military Medical Research, 7(1): 4. Retrieved May 20, 2020, 2020.

Johns Hopkins University. Covid-19 Dashboard by the Center for Systems Science and Engineering (CSSE) at Johns Hopkins University (JHU). Avaliable: https://https://coronavirus.jhu.edu/map.html. Access in: 03h December 2021, 2021.

Kennedy, J. and R. Eberhart. Particle swarm optimization. In Proceedings of ICNN'95—International Conference on Neural Networks, volume 4, pp. 1942–1948 vol. 4, 1995.

Klopfenstein, T., N. Kadiane-Oussou, L. Toko, P.-Y. Royer, Q. Lepiller, V. Gendrin and S. Zayet. Features of anosmia in covid-19. Médecine et Maladies Infectieuses, 50(5): 436–439, 2020.

Konar, P. and P. Chattopadhyay. Bearing fault detection of induction motor using wavelet and support vector machines (SVMs). Applied Soft Computing, 11(6): 4203–4211, 2011.

Kretzer, L., E. Berbigier, R. Lisboa, A.C. Grumann and J. Andrade. Protocolo amib de alocação de recursos em esgotamento durante a pandemia por covid-19. Associação de Medicina Intensiva Brasileira.[Versão eletrônica]. Obtido em, 28, 2020.

Lau, C.L., H.J. Mayfield, J.E. Sinclair, S.J. Brown, M. Waller, A.K. Enjeti, A. Baird, K. Short, K. Mengersen and J. Litt. Risk-benefit analysis of the astrazeneca covid-19 vaccine in Australia using a Bayesian network modelling framework. Vaccine, 2021.

Levi, M., M. Nieuwdorp, T. van der Poll and E. Stroes. Metabolic modulation of inflammation-induced activation of coagulation. In Seminars in Thrombosis and Hemostasis, volume 34, pp. 026–032. Thieme Medical Publishers, 2008.

Li, H. Case-based reasoning for intelligent support of construction negotiation. Information & Management, 30(5): 231–238, 1996.

Lima, T.P.F., G.R. Sena, C.S. Neves, S.A. Vidal, J.T.O. Lima, M.J.G. Mello and F.A.d.O.L.d.F. Silva. Previsão de óbito e importância de características clínicas em idosos com covid-19 utilizando o algoritmo random forest. Revista Brasileira de Saúde Materno Infantil, 21: 445–451, 2021.

Lins de Lima, C., A. Silva, C. Silva, E. Silva, G. Marques, L. Araujo, L. Junior, S. Souza, M. Santana, J. Gomes, V. Barbosa, A. Musah, P. Kostkova, W. dos Santos and A.G. da Silva-Filho. Monitoramento dinâmico e predição espaço-temporal da covid-19 usando aprendizagem de máquina. In Anais do IV Simpósio de Inovação em Engenharia Biomédica - SABIO 2020, 01 2021.

Lobo, L.C. Artificial intelligence, the future of medicine and medical education. Revista Brasileira de Educação Médica, 42(3): 3–8, 2018.

Luo, J., L. Zhou, Y. Feng, B. Li and S. Guo. The selection of indicators from initial blood routine test results to improve the accuracy of early prediction of covid-19 severity. PLOS ONE, 16(6): e0253329, 2021.

Mansour, N.A., A.I. Saleh, M. Badawy and H.A. Ali. Accurate detection of covid-19 patients based on feature correlated naïve bayes (fcnb) classification strategy. Journal of Ambient Intelligence and Humanized Computing, pp. 1–33, 2021.

Mizrahi, B., S. Shilo, H. Rossman, N. Kalkstein, K. Marcus, Y. Barer, A. Keshet, N. Shamir-Stein, V. Shalev, A.E. Zohar, G. Chodick and E. Segal. Longitudinal symptom dynamics of covid-19 infection. Nature Communications, 11(1): 1–10, 2020.

Moraes, R.M. and L.S. Machado. Gaussian naive bayes for online training assessment in virtual reality-based simulators. Mathware & Soft Computing, 16(2): 123–132, 2009.

Moreira, R.d.S. Covid-19: Unidades de terapia intensiva, ventiladores mecânicos e perfis latentes de mortalidade associados à letalidade no brasil. Cadernos de Saúde Pública, 36: e00080020, 2020.

Neil, M., N. Fenton, M. Osman and S. McLachlan. Bayesian network analysis of covid-19 data reveals higher infection prevalence rates and lower fatality rates than widely reported. Journal of Risk Research, 23(7-8): 866–879, 2020.

Neves, B.C. Metodologias, ferramentas e aplicações da inteligência artificial nas diferentes linhas do combate a covid-19. Folha de Rosto, 6(2): 44–57, 2020.

Nogueira, L.d.S., R.M.C.d. Sousa, K.G. Padilha and K.M. Koike. Características clínicas e gravidade de pacientes internados em utis públicas e privadas. Texto & Contexto-Enfermagem, 21: 59–67, 2012.

OECD, O. Using artificial intelligence to help combat covid-19, 2020.

Ozkaya, E., F.E. Topal, T. Bulut, M. Gursoy, M. Ozuysal and Z. Karakaya. Evaluation of an artificial intelligence system for diagnosing scaphoid fracture on direct radiography. European Journal of Trauma and Emergency Surgery, pp. 1–8, 2020.

Özkaya, U., Ş. Öztürk, S. Budak, F. Melgani and K. Polat. Classification of covid-19 in chest CT images using convolutional support vector machines. arXiv preprint arXiv:2011.05746, 2020.

Pathak, Y., P.K. Shukla and K.V. Arya. Deep bidirectional classification model for covid-19 disease infected patients. IEEE/ACM Transactions on Computational Biology and Bioinformatics, 18(4): 1234–1241, 2021.

Pontil, M. and A. Verri. Support vector machines for 3d object recognition. IEEE Transactions on Pattern Analysis and Machine Intelligence, 20(6): 637–646, 1998.

Ramos, J.G.R., R.d.H. Passos, P.B.P. Baptista and D.N. Forte. Fatores potencialmente associados à decisão de admissão à unidade de terapia intensiva em um país em desenvolvimento: um levantamento de médicos brasileiros. Revista Brasileira de Terapia Intensiva, 29: 154–162, 2017.

Santana, M.A.d., J.M.S. Pereira, F.L.d. Silva, N.M.d. Lima, F.N.d. Sousa, G.M.S.d. Arruda, R.d.C.F.d. Lima, W.W.A. d. Silva and W.P.d. Santos. Breast cancer diagnosis based on mammary thermography and extreme learning machines. Research on Biomedical Engineering, 34: 45–53, 2018.

Sarhan, A.M. Detection of covid-19 cases in chest x-ray images using wavelets and support vector machines. Research Square, 2020, 2020.

Shamsi, A., H. Asgharnezhad, S.S. Jokandan, A. Khosravi, P.M. Kebria, D. Nahavandi, S. Nahavandi and D. Srinivasan. An uncertainty-aware transfer learning-based framework for covid-19 diagnosis. IEEE Transactions on Neural Networks and Learning Systems, 32(4): 1408–1417, 2021.

Silva, A., C. Lins de Lima, C. Silva, E. Silva, G. Marques, L. Araujo, L. Junior, S. Souza, M. Santana, J. Gomes, V. Barbosa, A. Musah, P. Kostkova, W. dos Santos and A.G. da Silva-Filho. Covid-sgis: Uma ferramenta inteligente para monitoramento dinâmico previsão temporal da covid-19. In Anais do IV Simpósio de Inovação em Engenharia Biomédica-SABIO 2020, 01 2021.

Sinuff, T., K. Kahnamoui, D.J. Cook, J.M. Luce and M.M. Levy. Rationing critical care beds: A systematic review. Critical Care Medicine, 32(7): 1588–1597, 2004.

Siqueira-Batista, R., A.P. Gomes, L.M. Braga, A.d.S. Costa, B. Thomé, F.R. Schramm, J.A.L. Sales Júnior, P. Fortes, S. Rego and S. Santos. Covid-19 e o fim da vida: quem será admitido na unidade de terapia intensiva? Observatório Covid-19: Informação para ação, 2020.

Su, S., G. Wong, W. Shi, J. Liu, A.C. Lai, J. Zhou, W. Liu, Y. Bi and G.F. Gao. Epidemiology, genetic recombination, and pathogenesis of coronaviruses. Trends in Microbiology, 24(6): 490–502, 2016.

Sun, L. and A. Erath. A Bayesian network approach for population synthesis. Transportation Research Part C: Emerging Technologies, 61: 49–62, 2015.

Thachil, J., N. Tang, S. Gando, A. Falanga, M. Cattaneo, M. Levi, C. Clark and T. Iba. Isth interim guidance on recognition and management of coagulopathy in covid-19. Journal of Thrombosis and Haemostasis, 18(5): 1023–1026, 2020.

Torcate, A.S., F.S. Fonseca, A.R.T. Lima, F.P. Santos, T.D.M.S. Oliveira, M.A.d. Santana, J.C. Gomes, C.L.d. Lima, V.A.d. Freitas Barbosa, R.E.d. Souza and W.P. dos Santos. Prediction of care for patients in a covid-19 pandemic situation based on hematological parameters. In Assessing COVID-19 and other Pandemics and Epidemics using Computational Modelling and Data Analysis, pp. 169–196. Springer, 2022.

Voinov, A. and F. Bousquet. Modelling with stakeholders. Environmetal Modelling and Software, 25: 1268–1281. Refereed Journal Papers, 2010.

Wang, C., P.W. Horby, F.G. Hayden and G.F. Gao. A novel coronavirus outbreak of global health concern. The Lancet, 395(10223): 470–473, 2020a.

Wang, L., Z.Q. Lin and A. Wong. Covid-net: A tailored deep convolutional neural network design for detection of covid-19 cases from chest x-ray images. Scientific Reports, 10(1): 1–12, 2020b.

Werneck, G.L. and M.S. Carvalho. A pandemia de covid-19 no brasil: Crônica de uma crise sanitária anunciada, 2020.

Xiang-Hua, Y., W. Le-Min, L. Ai-Bin, G. Zhu, L. Riquan, Z. Xu-You, R. Wei-Wei and W. Ye-Nan. Severe acute respiratory syndrome and venous thromboembolism in multiple organs. American Journal of Respiratory and Critical Care Medicine, 182(3): 436–437, 2010.

Chapter 9

The Sound of the Mind: Detection of Common Mental Disorders Using Vocal Acoustic Analysis and Machine Learning

Caroline Wanderley Espinola,[1,2] *Juliana Carneiro Gomes,*[1]
Jessiane Mônica Silva Pereira[3] and *Wellington Pinheiro
dos Santos*[1,*]

1 Introduction

1.1 Motivation and Problem Outlining

Psychiatry lacks objective measurements and diagnostic tests (Cuthbert and Insel, 2013; Torus et al., 2016; Hirschtritt and Insel, 2018). Unlike other medical fields, psychiatry is a relatively new medical specialty that heavily relies on subjective data and observable signs, from patient reports to clinical assessments (Insel and Cuthbert, 2015). Despite successive improvements in the Diagnostic and Statistical Manual of Mental Disorders (DSM) (Torus et al., 2016), their diagnostic criteria

---

[1] Departamento de Engenharia Biomédica, Universidade Federal de Pernambuco, Recife, Brazil.
[2] Serviço de Emergências Psiquiátricas, Hospital Ulysses Pernambucano, Recife, Brazil.
[3] Núcleo de Engenharia da Computação, Escola Politécnica da Universidade de Pernambuco, Recife, Brazil.
  Emails: caroline.espinola@ufpe.br; {jcg, jmsp}@ecomp.poli.br
* Corresponding author: wellington.santos@ufpe.br

have been criticized due to poor diagnostic stability and lack of neurobiological validity (Bzdok and Meyer-Lindenberg, 2018), which often leads to low clinical predictability and trial-and-error treatments (Bzdok and Meyer-Lindenberg, 2018; Moragdo et al., 2017). The use of psychometric scales may increase inter-rater agreement, but they frequently require special training, and are time-consuming, rely on symptom-based assessments, and still depend on some rater's subjectivity (Moragdo et al., 2017). An alternative to categorical diagnosis Research Domain Criteria (RDoC) (NIMH, 2021), has been proposed by the National Institute of Mental Health as an attempt to enable precision medicine in psychiatry (Torus et al., 2017).

Other equally relevant issues in the field of psychiatry are difficult access to mental health services, lack of specialized mental health professionals, both in developed and in developing countries (Hirschtritt and Insel, 2018). This bottleneck frequently results in the onset of delayed treatment, which leads to prolonged suffering and poor treatment outcomes (Hirschtritt and Insel, 2018). A promising strategy to mitigate low access to mental healthcare is to develop screening and assessment methods that are objective, accessible and can be remotely performed.

The RDoC framework is built upon functional dimensions that aim to characterize human behavior beyond self-report, from low level biological units to observable behaviors (NIMH, 2016). Several units of analysis have been described for each domain (Higuchi et al 2018); among these, vocal parameters appear to be particularly interesting as being non-invasive, cost-effective markers that do not require a trained professional to be collected. In the RDoC framework these are included as objective measures of affective prosody and non-verbal social communication (NIMH, 2021). Several studies have demonstrated the potential of voice-based tools in mental health, including diagnosis (Cummins et al., 2011; Liu et al., 2015; Alghowinem et al., 2012; Low et al., 2011; Sturim et al., 2011; Espinola et al., 2020a; Afshan et al., 2018), symptom severity assessment (Hashim et al., 2017; Mundt et al., 2012; Mundt et al., 2007), identification of specific symptoms (Compton et al., 2018), detection of comorbidities (Wang et al., 2017), and monitoring treatment response (Mundt et al., 2012; Mundt et al., 2007). Given the psychophysiological nature of speech production, vocal feature analysis offers a window into a person's internal affective, cognitive and psychomotor status (van Puyvelde et al., 2018).

Previous work has suggested that translational power of the RDoC framework can be leveraged by computational data-driven approaches (Sanislow et al., 2019). Digital psychiatry applies machine learning (ML) techniques to optimize generalizability at an individual level with the aims of providing clinical applications and enabling personalized treatments (Bzdok and Meyer-Lindenberg, 2018; Petzschner et al., 2017). Instead of current categorical diagnoses, the use of ML in psychiatry may pave the way for precision medicine, enabling the description of symptom domains and disease subtypes, and the discovery objective biomarkers across mental disorders (Insel and Cuthbert, 2015). ML is particularly appropriate to deal with the complexity of multivariate relations and interdependencies related to brain connections, while dealing with high dimensional data to improve diagnosis, individualized treatment selection and prognosis (Dwyer et al., 2018). Examples of successful applications of ML techniques in medicine include multiple sclerosis diagnosis (Commowick et al., 2018), diagnosis of Alzheimer's disease (dos Santos et al., 2009; Bhagya Shree and Sheshadri, 2014; dos Santos et al., 2008), cancer diagnosis and prognosis (Kourou et al., 2015; Corderio et al., 2017; de Santana et al., 2018, Elouedi et al., 2014), and the development of novel pharmacotherapeutics (Carpenter and Huang, 2018; Langdon et al., 2002).

Accumulating evidence supports the use of ML for vocal acoustic analysis in mental health. Changes in speech patterns can be objectively measured using various classes of vocal features, including prosodic, spectral, articulatory, cepstral and voice quality features (Larsen et al., 2015; Hoing et al., 2014; Taguchi et al., 2017). In this context, ML can be applied for a multivariate analysis of speech for a more precise characterization of speech in mental disorders, as opposed to traditional univariate assessments (Parola et al., 2019). This is well supported by a growing body of literature that shows successful applications of ML-based speech analysis in several mental disorders, including major depressive disorder (MDD) (Albuquerque et al., 2021; Alghowinem et al., 2013b; Joshi et al., 2013; Mitra et al., 2015), bipolar disorder (BD) (Faurholt-Jepsen et al., 2016; Maxhuni et al., 2016), schizophrenia (Parola et al., 2019; Chakraborty et al., 2018; Chakraborty et al., 2018), and even suicidal behavior (Cummins et al., 2015).

MDD is a common mental disorder that affects more than 300 million people worldwide and is a leading cause of disability (WHO, 2018). Depressive symptoms include low mood, loss of interest, irritability, fatigue, psychomotor retardation, cognitive impairment (difficulty in decision making, poor concentration) and somatic disturbances (insomnia or hypersomnia, appetite disorders, body weight changes) (APA, 2013). These symptoms are associated with intense suffering and/ or functional impairment and may ultimately lead to suicide (APA, 2013). In MDD, vocal acoustic properties may be affected by persistent changes in affective states and initial depressive symptoms, such as psychomotor retardation and cognitive impairment (Hashim et al., 2017; Mundt et al., 2012). Depressive speech has long ago been described as hesitant, monotonous, uninteresting and lacking energy (Kraepelin, 1921; Darby and Hollien, 1977; Alpert et al., 2001). More recently, speech signal processing has shown quantitative changes in depressed speech, including the following: reduced pitch variability (Mundt et al., 2012; Vanello et al., 2017); increased number and duration of pauses (Low et al., 2011; Mundt et al., 2012); slowed speech rate (Faurholt-Jepsen et al., 2016; Cannizzaro et al., 2004); decreased speech volume (Hoing et al., 2014; Faurholt-Jepsen et al., 2016); reduced articulation rate (Scherer et al., 2013); and atypical voice quality (Low et al., 2011). Consequently, speech acoustic analysis demonstrates great potential as an objective biomarker for MDD (Jiang et al., 2018).

Schizophrenia is a group of severe psychotic disorders with heterogeneous etiologies, clinical presentations and responses to treatment (APA, 2013). With a lifetime prevalence of 1.11% (Simone et al., 2015), schizophrenia is characterized by delusions, hallucinations, thought and behavior disorder, and 'negative symptoms' (APA, 2013). These are defined as an absence of normal function and consists of blunted affect, poverty of speech, avolition, anhedonia, and asociality (Foussias and Remington, 2010). Since the early descriptions of schizophrenia, speech abnormalities have been a hallmark feature of this disorder and are often associated with core negative symptoms and social impairment (Parola et al., 2019). There are several speech-languages which include disorganized speech, derailment, poverty of speech, tangentiality, neologism, incoherence, mutism, perseveration, echolalia, aprosodia (Parola et al., 2019; Chakraborty et al., 2018; Elite et al., 2014), and thought blocking (Mac-Kay et al., 2018). Aprosodia is "a deficit in comprehending or expressing variations in tone of voice used to express both linguistic and emotional information" (Leon and Rodriguez, 2008). It consists of diminished vocal emphasis (Alpert and Anderson, 1977), reduced inflection and fluency (Alpert et al., 2000), and prosody comprehension deficits, such as difficulties in recognizing intonation patterns (Elite et al., 2014). Taken together, these speech symptoms contribute to the frequently severe communication deficits in schizophrenia (Mac-Kay et al., 2018; Kuperberg, 2010) and can be potentially used for the detection and assessment of this disorder (Parola et al., 2019).

Bipolar disorder (BD) is one of the most severe and disabling mental disorders. With a lifetime prevalence of 2.4% for the bipolar spectrum (Merikangas et al., 2011), BD is a worldwide leading cause of disability that is associated with intense psychological suffering and high suicide rates (Sadok et al., 2017; Rowland and Marwaha, 2018). Signs and symptoms of BD consist of cyclic episodes of persistently elevated mood (*i.e.*, expansivity or irritability) and increased energy associated with increased psychomotor activity, cognitive changes (*e.g.*, distractibility, racing thoughts), and neurovegetative dysfunctions (*e.g.*, reduced need for sleep) (APA, 2013). These episodes are known as hypomania or, when severe, known as mania. In manic/hypomanic states, language-speech disorders are frequently present, including increased speech activity (Farhoult-Jepsen et al., 2016) and changes in vocal pitch, intensity/loudness and rhythm that correlate with mood swings (Maxhuni et al., 2016). Most bipolar patients also experience depressive episodes (APA, 2013). Consequently, changes in vocal patterns could be used as a potential marker of affective state change from euthymia to hypomania/mania.

Anxiety disorders comprise a heterogeneous diagnostic group that share dysfunctional behavioral responses to excessive fear and anxious states (APA, 2013). These are the most prevalent mental disorders, with a lifetime prevalence of up to 33.7%, and are associated with significant disability and elevated healthcare costs (Bandelow and Michaelis, 2015). Within this diagnostic group, generalized anxiety disorder (GAD) is a chronic and debilitating disorder characterized by persistent worrying, concentration problems, insomnia, muscular tension, irritability and restlessness (Sadock et al., 2017; Wittchen, 2002). Since vocalization depends on the integration of central and autonomic nervous systems, stress can induce changes in speech patterns, with respiration playing a key role in the relation between speech and stress (van Puyvelde et al., 2018). Several speech parameters are directly affected by the severity of a speaker's anxious states. Specifically, increased subglottic pressure and muscle tension caused by anxious states lead to changes in vocal patterns, with decreased vocalization of vowels (Ozseven et al., 2018) and altered voice quality (Andrea et al., 2017). Other common measures of anxiety include increased pitch or fundamental frequency (F0), higher pitch variability, and increased speech rate, and increased speech rate (Albuquerue et al., 2021). These acoustic differences can even be perceived by a non-trained listener and may be used to objectively detect anxiety through vocal acoustic analysis.

2 Related Work

Speech production is the result of complex interactions between cognitive functions and the musculoskeletal system, and slight physiological and cognitive changes due to intense fluctuations in affective states can yield noticeable acoustic changes (Larsen et al. 2015). Vocal and speech patterns in mental disorders have been reported in studies that date back to 1938, initially within affective disorders such as MDD and BD (Farhoult-Jepsen et al., 2016; Newman and Mather, 1938). In the following decades, speech-language abnormalities have been reported within other mental disorders, including schizophrenia (Compton et al., 2018; Parola et al., 2019; Covington et al., 2012; Zhang et al., 2016; Tahir et al., 2019), autism spectrum disorders (Sharda et al., 2010; Marchi et al., 2015), and anxiety disorders (*e.g.*, social anxiety disorder and post-traumatic stress disorder, PTSD) (Scherer et al., 2013; Laukka et al., 2008a; Weeks et al., 2016).

2.1 Major Depressive Disorder

Previous work on speech patterns of depressed patients described changes in several parameters. For the recognition of changes in mood states using vocal parameters, prosodic, phonetic, spectral, and cepstral components are relevant, particularly pitch (or F0), intensity, rhythm, speed, jitter, shimmer, energy distribution between formants, and mel frequency cepstral coefficients (MFCC). In a sample of depressed patients, Cohn et al., 2009 analyzed prosodic and facial expression cues using the ML classifiers of support vector machines (SVM) and logistic regression (LR). Their reported accuracy for the identification of depression was 79% for prosodic features and ranged between 79–88% for facial expressions.

In a study with adolescents, Ooi et al., 2014 combined glottal, prosodic and spectral features, and the Teager energy operator for the prediction of early symptoms of depression. The authors reported a classification accuracy of 73%, with a sensibility of 79% and specificity of 67%. Similarly, Low et al. 2010 utilized the above features with the addition of cepstral features in a larger sample of adolescents. Using SVM and Gaussian Mixture Models (GMM) classifiers, they reported significant differences in classifier performances for detecting depression based on gender, with an accuracy of 81–87% for males, and 72–79% for females.

In an adult sample, Hönig et al., 2014 applied feature selection algorithms in a large set of vocal features to investigate their association with depressive symptoms. Overall, 34 features were selected among spectral, cepstral, prosodic, and voice quality or phonetic features. Their findings showed that the classification performance of the small subset was similar to that from the larger original feature set. In line with findings from Low et al., 2010, the authors reported a slightly higher correlation between vocal features and depressive symptoms for males (ρ = .39) as opposed to females (ρ = .36). These findings suggest that clinical depression is associated with more significant changes in vocal patterns in men than in women. Similarly, Jiang et al., 2017 reported gender differences in classifier performances, with superior results in males. In a sample of 170 subjects, the authors tested SVM, GMM and k-nearest neighbors (kNN) classifiers for the detection of depression. Best results were achieved by SVM, with an accuracy of 80.30% for males, and 75.96% for females. On the other hand, Higuchi et al., 2018 applied polytomous logistic regression for the classification of depression bipolar disorder and healthy controls based on pitch, spectral centroid and MFCC parameters; no difference between genders was found. An overall accuracy of 90.79% was reported, with 93.33% for the binary classification between depression and healthy controls.

Another aspect that may potentially impact the performance of ML classifiers is the type of speech task used for voice data capture. For example, previous studies have shown that spontaneous speech (e.g., dialogues or interviews) is associated with higher classification rates than using reading tasks. A possible reason for this finding is that spontaneous speech would allow for more acoustic variability, thus improving depression detection when compared to reading tasks (Alghowinem et al., 2013b; Jiang et al., 2017). Another hypothesis is that depressed patients may somewhat suppress negative affective states during reading tasks, because of the irrelevance of the content being read or their concentration on reading, or even both (Mitra et al., 2015).

2.2 Bipolar Disorder

Despite the scarcity of available literature, changes in vocal parameters have also been reported in BD. For example, studies have demonstrated that pitch variations could help discriminate between bipolar patients from healthy controls (Maxhuni et al., 2016). Higuchi et al., 2018 reported different values of cepstral parameters (MFCCs), F0 envelope and spectral centroid parameters between bipolar patients, depressed patients and healthy controls. In the following study (Higuchi, 2019), the same authors used polytomous logistic regression analysis of vocal features to distinguish between healthy and bipolar I (BD I) or II (BD II) disorder. Although their model could not easily distinguish between BD I and BD II, they reported an overall accuracy of 66.7% for the classification of bipolar patients.

In order to monitor long-term mood states of patients with BD, Karam et al., 2014 performed a pilot longitudinal study where they recorded real-life mobile phone conversations from six participants for up to one year. Using two SVM kernels and feature selection techniques, they reported an average AUC 0.63 ± 0.04 for detecting hypomania in three subjects, and an AUC of 0.64 ± 0.16 for depression in four individuals. However, a critical limitation to this study is its small sample size. Faurholt-Jepsen et al., 2016 monitored illness activity in BD through phone calls. They assessed vocal features with and without phone data on social interaction (*i.e.*, number of text messages and phone calls), motor activity (*i.e.*, accelerometer data), and self-monitored data on mood of 28 bipolar outpatients for 12 weeks. Increased speech rate was reported to predict a mood switch to hypomania, while reduced speech activity and changes in pitch indicated prodromal symptoms of depression and response to treatment. The authors concluded that the combination of vocal features with smartphone and self-monitored data slightly improved the classification accuracy of affective states in BD when compared to vocal features alone, with 73–77% for manic or mixed states, and 63–66% for depressive states. Similarly, Maxhuni et al., 2016 investigated the use of prosodic and spectral audio features, mobile accelerometer signals and self-assessment data from five bipolar patients during routine activities over a period of 12 weeks. After testing several classifiers, the best results were achieved by bagging using a combination of accelerometer frequency-domain features and all audio features, with an accuracy of 85.57% for the classification of mood states or relapse.

In a sample of bipolar inpatients in a manic episode, Ringeval et al., 2018 applied low-level descriptors (LLDs) from audio and video data to classify patients into mania, hypomania, and remission. Audio data included spectral, cepstral and voice quality features, while video data consisted of appearance and geometrical information. Features were analyzed using supervised, semi-supervised and unsupervised computational methods. A better performance for the unsupervised deep convolutional neural networks (CNN) was reported, as opposed to supervised and semi-supervised ML algorithms. Their results highlight the potential of unsupervised ML models, such as deep learning, for the representation of high dimensional speech data in bipolar disorder.

2.3 Schizophrenia

Speech-language abnormalities are core features of schizophrenia. Patients frequently present with slowed speech, reduced pitch variability, significantly increased number of pauses, and decreased variability in syllable timing than healthy individuals. These characteristics were observed by Martínez-sánchez et al., 2015 in a semi-automatic analysis of pitch during an emotionally neutral reading task. A discrimination accuracy of 93.8% was reported between patients with schizophrenia and healthy controls with audio signal processing algorithms. Notably, the authors also observed significant intergroup differences, with patients showing slower speech, with low volume and many pauses.

Vocal acoustic analysis can also measure the severity of negative symptoms such as aprosodia. Covington et al., 2012 analyzed pitch (F0), first (F1) and second (F2) formants of video-recorded interviews from schizophrenic patients. They investigated tongue movement as an indicator of negative symptom severity in first-episode schizophrenia-spectrum patients. Their study concluded that F2, a measure of variability of tongue anterior or posterior position, was significantly correlated with the severity of negative symptoms. In a following study, the same group (Compton et al., 2018) compared audio recordings from patients with aprosodia, patients without aprosodia, and healthy controls using as parameters a variability in F0, F1 and F2, and intensity/loudness. Their results showed significant differences for the group with aprosodia, with reduced variation in pitch, F2 and intensity/loudness than patients without aprosodia and healthy controls.

In a meta-analysis on vocal patterns in schizophrenia, Parola et al., 2020 compared three categories of study design: qualitative ratings, quantitative univariate analyses, and multivariate ML studies. Machine learning studies provided superior results, with overall out-of-sample accuracy of 76.5–87.5%. The authors also identified remarkable differences in acoustic patterns between patients with schizophrenia and healthy controls, with the former showing decreased proportion of spoken time, reduced speech rate and increased duration of pauses, all of which were related to flat affect and alogia. In addition, they observed that studies with dialogical and free speech provided the greatest differences between groups, in contrast with ones with constrained monologues. These findings were well aligned with the literature for depression studies, as described above.

Chakraborty et al., 2018 analyzed LLDs alone and combined with body movements to predict negative symptoms of schizophrenia using SVM. The authors reported a classification accuracy of 79.49% using only speech LLDs, and of 86.36% for their combination with body movements. Similarly, Tahir et al., 2019 examined negative symptoms in schizophrenia using conversational, prosodic and statistical features. Features included speaking duration, speaking turns, interruptions and interjections, F0, MFCCs, amplitude (entropy, minimum, maximum and mean volume) and formants F1, F2, and F3. Four ML algorithms were tested for the classification of patients and healthy controls: SVM, Multilayer Perceptron (MLP), random forest, and ensemble (bagging). Best classification results were achieved by MLP, which provided an accuracy of 81.3%, with speaking rate, frequency and volume entropy showing significant differences between groups.

2.4 Generalized Anxiety Disorder

Regarding vocal patterns across different anxiety disorders, there are several studies exploring vocal acoustic measures of stress or specific disorders, such as social anxiety disorder (SAD or social phobia) and PTSD. However, no previous study about vocal patterns of GAD was found, even though it is a chronic, debilitating and common disorder with persistent anxiety symptoms.

In the context of SAD, Laukka et al., 2008b compared acoustic parameters of audio samples from patients with SAD before and after pharmacotherapy. They reported that a reduction in experienced anxiety states following treatment was accompanied by a reduction in these parameters (mean and maximum pitch, high frequency components in energy spectrum, and proportion of silent pauses). A decrease in listeners' perceived level of anxiety was also reported. Similarly, Weeks et al., 2012 analyzed pitch parameter of SAD individuals during a social engagement task and found a positive correlation between increased mean F0 and the severity of SAD symptoms. This finding was replicated in a subsequent study by the same authors in a sample of men with SAD (Weeks et al., 2016).

Scherer et al. (Scherer et al., 2013) investigated voice quality features as indicators of PTSD and depression using SVM radial basis function (RBF) kernel classifier during interactions with a virtual human. Their classification accuracy for PTSD varied according to emotional polarity, from 52.38% for speech passages with negative affective polarity to 72.09% for passages with neutral polarity; no significant difference between genders was reported.

The related works outlined here demonstrate the potential of vocal parameters to support the diagnosis of various mental disorders using ML classifiers. Many cited works use characteristics that are already well established to represent the patients' audio samples in speech studies, while others employed LLDs to characterize speech signals. However, we believe that, despite the use of well-established attributes, classical features for audio representation in phonological studies might not be sufficient to support the diagnosis. In our study, we added statistical, temporal and time-frequency features that are frequently used for the analysis of other biomedical signals. In addition, it is important to highlight that the results presented in all related works were obtained in a highly controlled laboratory environment, where full control over noise and interference on a patient's speech is possible. Despite controlling for undesired interferences, such an approach seriously hampers the scalability and adaptability of previous in-lab solutions to real-world scenarios, where noise is a common issue. In the present study, data were obtained both in inpatient and outpatient environments at two public hospitals in Brazil. Therefore, we collected audio from real clinical visits under real conditions, with exposure to noise and interference that are typical of the context of psychiatric care.

2.5 Objective

In previous work, we used ML classifiers and vocal features to detect depression and schizophrenia with high accuracy (87.6% and 91.8%, respectively) (Espinola et al., 2020a; Espinola et al., 2020b). We expand on our previous findings to propose a methodology to support the diagnosis of major depressive disorder, bipolar disorder, schizophrenia, and generalized anxiety disorder using vocal acoustic analysis and machine learning. We hypothesized that ML models could be successfully used in more complex (*i.e.*, non-binary) classification tasks of several mental disorders.

3 Methods

3.1 Participant Selection

This study was approved by the Research Ethics Board of the Hospital das Clínicas, Federal University of Pernambuco, Recife, Pernambuco, Brazil, under registration number 19422619.2.0000.8807, report 3.565.104. Informed consent was obtained for all participants. For inpatients from psychiatric wards, family consent was also obtained.

Seventy-eight volunteers aged 18 years or older from both genders were recruited into one of the five following diagnostic groups:

- Control group: 12 healthy participants (7 males) were selected through the Self-Reporting Questionnaire (SRQ-20), a screening tool for common mental disorders (Ozseven et al., 2018);
- Depression group: 28 patients with major depressive disorder (17 males), according to the Hamilton Depression Rating Scale (HAM-D 17) (Andrea et al., 2016);
- Schizophrenia group: 21 patients with diagnosis of schizophrenia (12 males) were assessed through the Brief Psychiatric Rating Scale (BPRS), an established symptom severity scale for schizophrenia (Newman and Mather, 1938; Covington et al., 2012);
- Bipolar disorder group: 14 patients with bipolar disorder, in current manic or hypomanic episode diagnosed by an independent clinician, with symptom severity assessed by the Portuguese version of Young Mania Rating Scale

(YMRS) (Zang et al., 2016; Tahir et al., 2019; Young et al., 1978; Vilela et al., 2005);

• Generalized anxiety disorder group: four patients diagnosed with GAD, with symptoms assessed by GAD-7 Scale (Sharda et al., 2010; Marchi et al., 2015).

All individuals from the disease groups fulfilled DSM-5 diagnostic criteria for their respective disorders and were diagnosed by an independent clinician prior to this study. Data for these groups were collected in an outpatient and in inpatient psychiatric wards in two public hospitals in Recife, Brazil. Exclusion criteria consisted of: (1) comorbid neurological disorders; (2) professional use of voices; and (3) transgender participants (to avoid confusion sex- and gender-based analyses). Validated psychometric scales were used to verify previous diagnostic consistency and assess symptom severity. The diagnoses were considered ground-truth due to the large clinical experience of the specialists that performed clinical assessment. However, there is still some uncertainty due to the diagnosis by a human specialist that could not be measured in this cross-sectional study. This study was conducted only after approval of a local Research Ethical Board, and all participants have given written consent. Table 1 summarizes mean age and mean scale scores for all groups.

For the control group the SRQ-20 cutoff score was 6/7 (Laukka et al., 2008b), and for the depression group the eligibility criterion was HAM-D 17 score above 7. Consequently, patients suffering from mild to severe depression were selected, and a mean HAM-D 17 score of 19.32 indicates moderate depression (Weeks et al., 2016). For schizophrenia group, participants with prior diagnosis were included, irrespective of their score in the BPRS; an average score of 45.16 found in this group corresponds to moderate illness severity (Newman and Mather, 1938). Likewise, patients from BD group were selected regardless of their YMRS score; their average YMRS score was 23.00, which corresponds to 'severely ill' (Cohn et al., 2009). Unfortunately, during the data acquisition phase we were able to recruit only four patients with GAD; their mean GAD-7 score was 13.75,

Table 1: Mean age and rating scale scores for all groups.

Group	Age (years) (SD)	Rating scale	Avg. score (SD)
Control	29.2 (± 12.4)	SRQ-20	3.00 (± 1.86)
Major depressive disorder	42.0 (± 12.4)	HAM-D 17	19.32 (± 7.36)
Schizophrenia	36.0 (± 11.3)	BPRS	45.16 (± 11.25)
Bipolar disorder	40.5 (± 8.0)	YMRS	23.00 (± 11.95)
Generalized anxiety disorder	25.8 (± 8.5)	GAD-7	13.75 (± 2.22)

Notes: BPRS: Brief Psychiatric Rating Scale; YMRS: Young Mania Rating Scale; GAD-7: Generalized Anxiety Disorder-7 Scale; HAM-D 17: Hamilton Depression Scale; SD: standard deviation; SRQ-20: Self-Reporting Questionnaire.

which corresponds to moderate disease (Marchi et al., 2015). Table 1 provides a summary of mean age and scale scores for each group.

3.2   Voice Data Collection

Audio recordings were made with a Tascam™ 16-bit linear PCM recorder, at 44.1 KHz sampling rate, in WAV format, without compressions, using environment noise cancellation. No time limit was set for any recording. Voice acquisitions were made during an interview with a psychiatrist in naturalistic settings, *i.e.*, patients from the disease groups were recorded during a routine medical evaluation in an outpatient office or a hospital ward. After each interview, the interviewer applied an appropriate rating scale to assess symptom severity. Exceptions were GAD and control groups, since GAD-7 scale and SRQ-20 are self-applied; consequently, participants from these groups were required to answer it after the interview. Recordings for the control group were acquired in different environments, specifically an office, a classroom, and a gym, but using the same recorder's noise cancellation function. Therefore, the acquired signals in all environments are similar regarding environment noise cancellation residuals. As conversations were thoroughly recorded, clinician's and potential third parties' speech were also acquired and needed to be further removed. We obtained one record per subject. The total duration of recordings for all groups was 980.3 minutes (16.3 hours).

It is important to notice that, in order to acquire data in accordance with the clinical practice and differently from the works of the state-of-the-art, all audio data was recorded in a naturalistic environment: the psychiatric emergency care services of Hospital Ulysses Pernambucano and Hospital das Clínicas. All data were recorded under similar real conditions, including interferences and noise. We considered the background noise in these non-clinical environments slightly similar to the one present at the psychiatric emergency health service, with the sounds of corridors (human steps and voices, for instance) and air-conditioning noise as the most common noise present at the recordings. However, these types of noise were minimized by the use of a professional audio recorder with environment noise cancellation hardware provided by the device arrangement based on a pair of unidirectional microphones positioned in opposition, with a 90 degrees angle between them. This arrangement is able to cancel or, at least, minimize the environment noise, common to both audio sources, while the main information of the two audio sources slightly out of phase is emphasized. Therefore, no additional audio preprocessing by software was performed to minimize this background noise. The set of all participants with a positive diagnosis for a mental disorder seen in the emergency condition is approximately equally distributed between the two health services. This was done so that there would be no classification bias due to different signal acquisition environments, despite the minimization of ambient noise performed by the digital audio recorder.

3.3 Audio Editing

After voice acquisition, Audacity™ audio software was used to remove recorded audio from the interviewer and any potential companion. The edition process was manually made, and yielded 591 minutes (9.85 hours) of recorded audio from participants as follows: 100.7 minutes for control group; 222.6 minutes for MDD group; 125.7 minutes for schizophrenia group, 102 minutes for BD group, and 40 minutes for GAD group. Table 2 provides detailed information about recording duration for all groups.

Table 2: Recording duration after audio editing.

Group	Number of participants	Total recording duration	Avg. recording duration (SD)
Control	12	6039s (100.7 min)	503.3s (8.4 min) ± 159.0s
Major depressive disorder	28	13355s (222.6 min)	477.0s ($\cong$ 8.0 min) ± 203.0s
Schizophrenia	20	7541s (125.7 min)	377.1s (6.3 min) ± 270.4s
Bipolar disorder	14	6122s (102.0 min)	437.3s (7.3 min) ± 253.9s
Generalized anxiety disorder	4	2401 s (40.0 min)	600.3s (10.0 min) ± 194.8s

3.4 Feature Extraction

Edited audio recordings were submitted to vocal feature extraction on GNU Octave™, a free open-source signal-processing software. Windowing was made with rectangular windows and frame length of 10s with 50% overlap. As raw audio data was used, no filtering process was applied. Consequently, background noise was captured as well. However, with the selected attributes, we believe this noise is not able to interfere significantly due to its homogeneous spectral behavior. At this phase, the following 33 features were extracted: skewness; kurtosis; zero crossing rates; slope sign changes; variance; standard deviation; mean absolute value; logarithm detector; root mean square; average amplitude change; difference absolute deviation; integrated absolute value; mean logarithm kernel; simple square integral; mean value; third, fourth and fifth moments; maximum amplitude; power spectrum ratio; peak frequency; mean power; mean frequency; median frequency; total power; variance of central frequency; first, second and third spectral moments; Hjorth parameter activity, mobility and complexity; and waveform length.

The duration of the 10s-windows was defined by the research team empirically, considering a scenario for the use of a future application to support the clinical diagnosis of mental disorders in a psychiatric emergency context. A window of only 10s would allow the specialist to obtain diagnostic indications during the patient's interview, and then make the decision based on the most frequent indication, also considering the discourse analysis and the anamnesis process as a whole. The choice of the above features relies on their accurate representation of input signals to computational models, because decision making process in machine learning does not depend on human interpretation. Furthermore, these features have already been successfully used for representing other signal types, such as electroencephalography in rectangular windows, which comprises much more spectral complexity than audio signals.

3.5   Classification

To investigate the best machine learning model, all classes were balanced through the addition of synthetic instances by using the algorithm SMOTE, Synthetic Minority Oversampling Technique (Ooi et al., 2013; Jiang et al., 2017). SMOTE is an oversampling technique where random synthetic feature vectors are generated for the minority class, overcoming the overfitting problem (Ooi et al., 2013; Jiang et al., 2017). Using the k-nearest neighbors algorithm, for a randomly selected instance in a given class, the k nearest neighbors are selected. Then, a synthetic instance is generated by the interpolation among these k selected instances (Ooi et al., 2013; Jiang et al., 2017). The original dataset was composed by 1175 windows instances for control, 2640 instances for major depressive disorder, 1483 instances for schizophrenia, 1206 instances for bipolar disorder, and 475 instances for generalized anxiety disorder. The SMOTE algorithm was applied to an unbalanced dataset selected as a 10% sample of the 6979 instances original dataset, generating a dataset with 1320 instances, 264 instances for each class. This sample was obtained preserving the statistical behavior of the original dataset, evaluated by the similarities between feature statistics (mean and standard deviation) and histograms in each class compared to its previous descriptive statistics in the original dataset.

Class balancing was crucial to prevent computational biases towards the classes with more representativeness, in this case depression and schizophrenia classes. Experiments were performed using the following ML algorithms on Weka™: multilayer perceptron (MLP), logistic regression, random forest (RF), decision trees, Bayes net, Naïve Bayes, and SVM with different kernels (linear, polynomial kernel, radial basis function or RBF, PUK, and normalized polynomial kernel). Investigation experiments were performed using 30-run 10-fold cross-validation. In the distribution of instances in folds for cross validation, it is guaranteed that there is no repetition of instances in the training and test sets, given that the distribution in folds is without instance replacement. Figure 1 summarizes the steps of data collection and our proposed solution.

Afterwards, considering the best machine learning model found with the oversampled balanced dataset, we created two balanced, disjointed and statistically similar sets, to be used as a training and test set at the validation stage. In each set, we selected 300 instances for each class, trying to preserve the statistical behavior for each feature in each class regarding the original dataset.

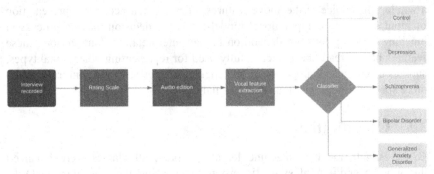

Figure 1: Block diagram of data collection and proposed solution.

4　Results

In this section, we outline the results for the three stages of our research: (a) investigation of the best machine learning model based on a 10% sample of the dataset. This sample was balanced by oversampling, inserting synthetic instances generated by the SMOTE method, in order to optimize the training conditions for all evaluated models. (b) feature selection by evolutionary computing and bioinspired meta-heuristic optimization methods, showing that just one feature is redundant. (c) validation: the best machine learning model found in stage (a) is evaluated considering balanced training and test sets constructed by undersampling, by randomly selecting 300 instances in each class, for each set, trying to get two statistically similar sets. These results are presented as quality metrics and a confusion matrix corresponding to a one-shot learning.

4.1　Investigation of Best Performing Model

Experiments were initially performed under default settings on Weka™. Subsequently, different setups for all algorithms with adjustable settings were tested (MLP; polynomial kernel and normalized polynomial kernel SVM, SVM PUK kernel, and random forest). Table 3 describes in detail our best results for each machine learning model. These results are highlighted. We tested the following configurations:

- Decision Tree (J48);
- Random Tree;
- Random Forests, for 50, 100, 200, and 300 trees;
- Bayesian Networks;
- Naïve Bayes classifier;

Table 3: Mean classification performance for machine learning algorithms for all groups.

Classifier	Accuracy (%)	Kappa	Sensitivity	Specificity
Decision Tree J48	78.37 ± 3.26	0.7296 ± 0.0408	0.6767 ± 0.0912	0.9166 ± 0.0275
Random Tree	71.20 ± 4.11	0.6400 ± 0.0514	0.6286 ± 0.1020	0.8980 ± 0.0301
Bayes Net	91.29 ± 2.38	0.8911 ± 0.0298	0.8566 ± 0.0694	0.9616 ± 0.0185
Naïve Bayes	92.12 ± 2.12	0.9014 ± 0.0265	0.8777 ± 0.0607	0.9754 ± 0.0138
Random Forest, 50 trees	88.91 ± 2.63	0.8613 ± 0.0329	0.8422 ± 0.0690	0.9524 ± 0.0203
Random Forest, 100 trees	89.51 ± 2.60	0.8688 ± 0.0325	0.8514 ± 0.0668	0.9539 ± 0.0198
Random Forest, 200 trees	89.90 ± 2.48	0.8738 ± 0.0310	0.8619 ± 0.0636	0.9547 ± 0.0202
Random Forest, 300 trees	90.01 ± 2.42	0.8751 ± 0.0303	0.8630 ± 0.0627	0.9561 ± 0.0193
MLP, 20 neurons	77.55 ± 3.51	0.7193 ± 0.0439	0.6481 ± 0.1113	0.9139 ± 0.0369
MLP, 50 neurons	78.89 ± 3.58	0.7361 ± 0.0447	0.6744 ± 0.1082	0.9210 ± 0.0361
MLP, 100 neurons	79.38 ± 3.48	0.7422 ± 0.0435	0.6905 ± 0.1013	0.9211 ± 0.0338
MLP, 150 neurons	79.81 ± 3.47	0.7476 ± 0.0434	0.6970 ± 0.0992	0.9237 ± 0.0346
MLP, 200 neurons	79.81 ± 3.58	0.7476 ± 0.0448	0.6939 ± 0.1020	0.9223 ± 0.0348
SVM, linear, C = 0.1	68.83 ± 3.50	0.6103 ± 0.0437	0.4796 ± 0.0935	0.9158 ± 0.0236
SVM, linear, C = 1.0	80.02 ± 3.27	0.7502 ± 0.0408	0.6866 ± 0.0818	0.9287 ± 0.0252
SVM, linear, C = 10.0	82.06 ± 3.36	0.7757 ± 0.0420	0.7166 ± 0.0865	0.9327 ± 0.0258
SVM, polynomial, p = 2, C = 0.1	76.71 ± 3.42	0.7089 ± 0.0428	0.6551 ± 0.0866	0.9146 ± 0.0279
SVM, polynomial, p = 2, C = 1.0	82.51 ± 3.24	0.7814 ± 0.0405	0.7166 ± 0.0838	0.9384 ± 0.0236
SVM, polynomial, p = 2, C = 10.0	83.97 ± 3.31	0.7997 ± 0.0413	0.7638 ± 0.0771	0.9418 ± 0.0246
SVM, polynomial, p = 3, C = 0.1	80.04 ± 3.34	0.7505 ± 0.0417	0.6937 ± 0.0808	0.9269 ± 0.0254
SVM, polynomial, p = 3, C = 1.0	83.53 ± 3.24	0.7941 ± 0.0405	0.7549 ± 0.0798	0.9364 ± 0.0248
SVM, polynomial, p = 3, C = 10.0	82.83 ± 3.26	0.7854 ± 0.0408	0.7721 ± 0.0767	0.9366 ± 0.0257
SVM, PUK, C = 0.1	76.78 ± 3.39	0.7097 ± 0.0424	0.5676 ± 0.0916	0.9408 ± 0.0229
SVM, PUK, C = 1.0	83.28 ± 3.20	0.7910 ± 0.0400	0.7369 ± 0.0837	0.9384 ± 0.0240
SVM, PUK, C = 10.0	83.79 ± 3.15	0.7973 ± 0.0394	0.7720 ± 0.0814	0.9388 ± 0.0232

Table 3 contd. ...

...Table 3 contd.

Classifier	Accuracy (%)	Kappa	Sensitivity	Specificity
SVM, RBF, G = 0.01, C = 0.1	33.96 ± 8.31	0.1776 ± 0.1035	0.3622 ± 0.3710	0.7859 ± 0.2773
SVM, RBF, G = 0.01, C = 1.0	45.62 ± 5.09	0.3222 ± 0.0634	0.4040 ± 0.4240	0.7516 ± 0.2924
SVM, RBF, G = 0.01, C = 10.0	73.15 ± 3.65	0.6643 ± 0.0456	0.5877 ± 0.0878	0.9147 ± 0.0262
SVM, RBF, G = 0.25, C = 0.1	60.25 ± 4.46	0.5039 ± 0.0554	0.4396 ± 0.3101	0.8504 ± 0.1335
SVM, RBF, G = 0.25, C = 1.0	79.04 ± 3.29	0.7380 ± 0.0411	0.6610 ± 0.0849	0.9292 ± 0.0243
SVM, RBF, G = 0.25, C = 10.0	83.17 ± 3.23	0.7964 ± 0.0404	0.7296 ± 0.0808	0.9430 ± 0.0234
SVM, RBF, G = 0.5, C = 0.1	69.66 ± 3.60	0.6207 ± 0.0450	0.4817 ± 0.0929	0.9123 ± 0.0245
SVM, RBF, G = 0.5, C = 1.0	81.30 ± 3.34	0.7662 ± 0.0417	0.6960 ± 0.0862	0.9357 ± 0.0229
SVM, RBF, G = 0.5, C = 10.0	84.50 ± 3.11	0.8062 ± 0.0388	0.7719 ± 0.0772	0.9423 ± 0.0240

Notes: MLP: Multilayer Perceptron; PUK: Pearson Universal VII Kernel; RBF: Radial Basis Function; SVM: Support Vector Machines.

- Multi-layer Perceptron (MLP): one hidden layer with 20, 50, 100, 150, and 200 neurons;
- Support Vector Machine (SVM): linear kernel; 2- and 3-degree polynomial kernels (p = 2, 3); Pearson Universal VII (PUK) kernel; Radial Basis Function (RBF) kernel, (G = 0.01, 0.25 and 0.50). All SVM configurations were evaluated for C = 0.1, 1.0 and 10.0.

The results above show that classification performances varied significantly according to the ML algorithm used, with Bayesian Network, Naïve Bayes and Random Forest (300 trees) achieving the highest discrimination accuracy of 91.29% ± 2.38, 92.12% ± 2.12 and 90.01% ± 2.42 (sensitivity: 0.8566 ± 0.0694, 0.8777 ± 0.0607 and 0.8630 ± 0.0627; specificity: 0.9616 ± 0.0185, 0.9754 ± 0.0138 and 0.9561 ± 0.0193), and kappa coefficient of 0.8911 ± 0.0298, 0.9014 ± 0.0265 and 0.8751 ± 0.0303, respectively. The best MLP configuration employed 200 neurons in the hidden layer, obtaining the following metrics for accuracy, kappa, sensitivity, and specificity: 79.81% ± 3.58, 0.7476 ± 0.0448, 0.6939 ± 0.1020, and 0.9223 ± 0.0348, in this order. The best SVM configuration was the RBF kernel, with G = 0.5 and C = 10.0, with the following results for accuracy, kappa, sensitivity, and specificity: 84.50% ± 3.11, 0.8062 ± 0.0388, 0.7719 ± 0.0772, and 0.9423 ± 0.0240, respectively. Since the best results, *i.e.*, Bayesian Networks, Naïve Bayes and 300-tree Random Forest, are statistically similar for the three best models, we have chosen the 300-tree Random Forest. This decision was supported by the fact that Random Forests do not assume normality over the data. Furthermore, since Random Forests are based on committees of decision trees, they tend to be more robust to noise and other outliers. Random Forest also tend to present larger generalization capacity. The confusion matrix for a random iteration of this model is shown in Table 4 below.

Table 4: Confusion matrix for the model with the highest performance, Random Forest with 300 trees, considering the balanced oversampled dataset.

	Classified as control	Classified as major depressive disorder	Classified as schizophrenia	Classified as bipolar disorder	Classified as generalized anxiety disorder
Control	**2361 (89.43%)**	25 (0.95%)	74 (2.80%)	0 (0.00%)	180 (6.82%)
Major depressive disorder	58 (2.20%)	**2342 (88.71%)**	222 (8.41%)	0 (0.00%)	18 (0.68%)
Schizophrenia	146 (5.53%)	67 (2.54%)	**2362 (89.47%)**	1 (0.04%)	64 (2.42%)
Bipolar disorder	0 (0.00%)	0 (0.00%)	0 (0.00%)	**2640 (100%)**	0 (0.00%)
Generalized anxiety disorder	138 (5.23%)	2 (0.08%)	45 (1.70%)	0 (0.00%)	**2455 (92.99%)**

Our best Random Forest model correctly classified 88.71% of time-windows related to depressed patients, and 89.43% of time-windows of healthy controls; discrimination rates between schizophrenia and GAD groups were high, with accuracies of 89.47% and 92.99%, respectively. The highest performance was achieved in BD group, with 100% classification accuracy. Higher confusion rates were observed between depression and schizophrenia, with 8.41% time-samples of depressed patients classified as schizophrenia; and between GAD and control, with 5.23% GAD time-samples classified as control and 6.82% control time-samples classified as GAD.

4.2 Feature Ranking

To evaluate the relevance of the features selected to represent the 10s-window samples, we used meta-heuristic optimization methods. Artificial populations of 50 individuals were used, evolving in 50 generations. As an objective function, we used a decision tree, trained and tested using 10-fold cross-validation. Each individual represents the attributes used in the classification by means of a binary vector, where "1" models the presence of that attribute, whilst "0" represents its opposite. We employed meta-heuristic libraries developed in Java for Weka data mining platform ((Higuchi et al., 2019). We adopted the following feature selection methods:

1. Evolutionary Search, with crossover probability of 0.6, mutation probability of 0.1, bit-flip mutation, random initialization, generational replacement operator, report frequency of 20, survivor selection by tournament (Karam et al., 2014, Ringeval et al., 2018);

2. Particle Swarm Optimization, individual weight of 0.34, inertia weight of 0.33, mutation probability of 0.01, report frequency of 20, social weight of 0.33 (Martinez-Sanchez et al., 2015; Tahir et al., 2019; Laukka et al., 2008a);

3. Ant Colony Search, with chaotic coefficient of 4.0, chaotic type of logistic map, evaporation of 0.9, heuristic of 0.7, bit-flip mutation, mutation probability of 0.01 (Weeks et al., 2012; Espinola et al., 2020b).

4.3 Generalization Evaluation

In this stage, we evaluated the generalization capacity of the best model found in the model investigation stage. In Table 5 we present the validation results, considering training and test sets with a total of 1500 instances, *i.e.*, 300 instances for each class. We achieved a validation accuracy of 75.2667% and a kappa index of 0.6908, which corresponds to substantial agreement between iterations (Viera and Garrett, 2005). Although this result was inferior to the one obtained in the context of the oversampled dataset, it is realistic and can be considered clinically relevant to our scope. For the control group, we obtained 0.713 for sensitivity, 0.925 for specificity, and 0.940 AUC. For major depressive disorder, we obtained 0.600 for sensitivity, 0.957 for specificity, and 0.905 AUC. For schizophrenia, we got 0.700 for sensitivity, 0.913 for specificity, and 0.929 AUC. For bipolar disorder, we have 0.830 for sensitivity, 0.952 for specificity, and

Table 5: Confusion matrix for the Random Forest with 300 trees, considering the balanced under-sampled validation dataset.

	Classified as control	Classified as major depressive disorder	Classified as schizophrenia	Classified as bipolar disorder	Classified as generalized anxiety disorder
Control	**214 (71.33%)**	16 (5.33%)	32 (10.67%)	9 (3.00%)	29 (9.67%)
Major depressive disorder	42 (14.00%)	**180 (60.00%)**	42 (14.00%)	14 (4.67%)	22 (7.33%)
Schizophrenia	29 (9.67%)	23 (7.67%)	**210 (70.00%)**	30 (10.00%)	8 (2.67%)
Bipolar disorder	6 (2.00%)	10 (3.33%)	26 (8.67%)	**249 (83.00%)**	9 (3.00%)
Generalized anxiety disorder	13 (4.33%)	3 (1.00%)	4 (1.33%)	4 (1.33%)	**276 (92.00%)**

0.966 AUC. As for GAD, we achieved 0.920 for sensitivity, 0.943 for specificity, and 0.985 AUC. Considering the control group and all mental disorders investigated in this work, we have weighted sensitivity of 0.753, weighted specificity of 0.938, and weighted AUC of 0.945.

5 Discussion

Despite recent improvements in current diagnostic manuals, psychiatry still lacks objective markers. This study proposed a ML framework based on vocal parameters for the detection of four mental disorders. As shown in the confusion matrix above, classification accuracies showed considerable variability among groups, from 60% to MDD to 92% for GAD. However, even the lowest accuracy of 60% and 70% can be considered satisfactory in the context of clinical diagnosis, given that: (1) current psychiatric diagnosis suffers from poor temporal consistency, which can be as low as 29% (Bzdok and Meyer-Lindenberg, 2018); and (2) only 33 audio features were considered in the analysis. On the other hand, discrimination rates for BD and GAD were considerably higher. For GAD, the reduced sample size may have caused classifier to over fit the data, thus artificially increasing classification performance for this group. For BD, we hypothesize that higher discrimination rates were due to the fact that BD patients in our sample had more severe symptoms and, therefore, more significant changes in vocal patterns. Patients from other diagnostic groups were moderately ill, and hence might have shown less severe vocal abnormalities. Another hypothesis is that the changes in vocal parameters associated with manic/hypomanic episodes in BD, such as increased pitch variability and increased intensity/volume, might be a 'fingerprint' of this group and, consequently, could be more easily distinguishable. In contrast, vocal characteristics that are shared by other diagnostic groups, such as reduced pitch range in depression and schizophrenia, may be a confounding factor for automated classifiers between these classes.

Greater confusion rates were observed between MDD vs. control and MDD vs. schizophrenia. For the former, we believe that higher error rates were a result of the MDD group having more individuals with mild symptoms than other groups and, therefore, less severe changes in vocal features. For the latter, as noted above, MDD and schizophrenia share vocal changes that may have increased confusion rates between both groups.

This study has several limitations. Firstly, it is a pilot study with small sample sizes for each of the five groups, particularly GAD with only four participants. Therefore, results should be interpreted with caution and should not be generalized to other samples. Second, given the small sample size demographic variables were not controlled for; this represents another important limitation, as variables such as age and educational background may influence speech style and vocal acoustic properties. Third, smoking history, which is known to impact voice, and pharmacotherapy were not controlled and represent a limitation to our findings.

Regarding feature selection using evolutionary search, ant colony search and particle swarm optimization, these three meta-heuristics based feature selection methods agreed that 32 of the employed 33 features were statistically relevant for the classification: the Average Amplitude Change (AAC) returned a probability of relevance of 80%; to the Integrated Absolute Value (IAV) was associated a relevance of 90%; the Simple Square Integral (SSI), however, was considered absolutely irrelevant: 0%; all other features returned a relevance of 100%. After removing SSI, classification results remained the same. This indicates that not just SSI is not relevant to the classification, but using additional features not usually adopted as audio features contributes to get good classification results.

Since most previous studies were only built on binary classification experiments (disease vs. control), we extend the current literature by being the first to pilot a 5-class classification with four mental disorders and a control group. To our knowledge, this study was also the first to assess the classification of GAD using vocal parameters. As we simultaneously performed the detection of various mental disorders with high accuracy rates, we extend the findings from this study to demonstrate the feasibility our framework as a screening tool for mental disorders. Future studies including larger samples, additional mental disorders and controlling for co-variables should be performed to assess the effectiveness of this framework as a screening tool in psychiatry. We assume that a larger number of categories increased data complexity, which tends to decrease classification performances. Even in this scenario, our results outperformed most previous studies, which were carried out using simple binary classification and in a controlled environment. These findings underscore the potential of our proposed solution for the identification of several mental disorders. To the best of our knowledge, the relevance of this work is unprecedented, as no previous study has used automated classifiers for the simultaneous classification of several mental disorders, and no other study has encompassed several disorders before. The use of vocal parameters in this study are also in line with the proposed RDoC framework for assessing mental disorders through behavioral units of analysis. Therefore, our high discrimination power supports a future use of ML models as diagnostic (and even screening) tools for mental disorders.

6 Conclusion

Current psychiatric diagnosis still lacks objective biomarkers and relies mostly on subjective diagnostic criteria. These show no correlation with neurobiology and etiopathogenesis of mental disorders, leading to trial-and-error treatments and increasing patient suffering and disability. Despite the prevalence and relevance of mental disorders, access to mental health services is problematic due to lack of professionals, difficulty in seeking help, and the stigma of mental disorders. A potential solution to address current limitations in psychiatric diagnosis is the RDoC framework with the development and implementation of its units of analysis as functional biomarkers. Within this framework, vocal features have demonstrated to be potential biomarkers that can be remotely collected and assessed. As changes in vocal patterns have been reported in several mental disorders and appear to correlate with illness severity, vocal features have shown to be promising biomarkers, with the advantages of being abundant, inexpensive, non-invasive. In this study, we performed classification experiments in an unprecedented manner using machine learning algorithms with four mental disorders and a healthy control group. The results provided by our solution are very promising and outperform most from previous studies using binary classification. In addition, it supports the use of vocal features as a feasible biomarker within the RDoC framework. This evidence supports the feasibility of a ML-based method using vocal parameters to assist clinicians in patient screening and psychiatric diagnosis.

Acknowledgements

The authors are grateful to Conselho Nacional de Desenvolvimento Científico e Tecnológico, CNPq-Brazil, for the partial support of this research.

Compliance with Ethical Standards

This study was funded by the Brazilian research agency CNPq (grant 314896/ 2018-0).

Ethical Approval

All procedures performed in studies involving human participants were in accordance with the ethical standards of the institutional and/or national research committee and with the 1964 Helsinki Declaration and its later amendments or comparable ethical standards. The study was approved by the Research Ethics Committee of the Hospital das Clínicas, Federal University of Pernambuco, Recife, Pernambuco, Brazil, under registration 19422619.2.0000.8807, report 3.565.104.

Conflict of Interest

All authors declare they have no conflicts of interest.

References

Afshan, A., J. Guo, S.J. Park, V. Ravi, J. Flint and A. Alwan. Effectiveness of voice quality features in detecting depression. Proceedings of the Annual Conference of the International Speech Communication Association, INTERSPEECH, 2018-Septe(September): 1676–1680, 2018. doi:10.21437/Interspeech.2018-1399.

Albuquerque, L., A.R.S. Valente, A. Teixeira, D. Figueiredo, P. Sa-Couto and C. Oliveira. Association between acoustic speech features and non-severe levels of anxiety and depression symptoms across lifespan. PLoS ONE, 16(4): e0248842, 2021. doi:10.1371/journal.pone.0248842.

Alghowinem, S., R. Goecke, M. Wagner, J. Epps, M. Breakspear and G. Parker. From joyous to clinically depressed: Mood detection using spontaneous speech. In: Proceedings of the 25th International Florida Artificial Intelligence Research Society Conference, FLAIRS-25, 2012: 141–146, 2012.

Alghowinem, S., R. Goecke, M. Wagner, J. Epps, T. Gedeon, M. Breakspear and G. Parker. A comparative study of different classifiers for detecting depression from spontaneous speech. In: ICASSP, IEEE International Conference on Acoustics, Speech and Signal Processing— Proceedings, 2013: 8022–8026, 2013a. doi:10.1109/ICASSP.2013.6639227.

Alghowinem, S., R. Goecke, M. Wagner and J. Epps. Detecting depression: A comparison between spontaneous and read speech. In: 2013 IEEE International Conference on Acoustics, Speech and Signal Processing, 7547–7551, 2013b. doi:10.1109/ICASSP.2013.6639130.

Alpert, M. and L.T. Anderson. Imagery mediation of vocal emphasis in flat affect. Archives of General Psychiatry, 34(2): 208–212, 1977.

Alpert, M., S.D. Rosenberg, E.R. Pouget and R.J. Shaw. Prosody and lexical accuracy in flat affect schizophrenia. Psychiatry Research, 97: 107–118, 2000.

Alpert, M., E.R. Pouget and R.R. Silva. Reflections of depression in acoustic measures of the patient's speech. Journal of Affective Disorders, 66: 59–69, 2001.

Andrea, M., O. Dias, M. Andrea and M.L. Figueira. Functional voice disorders: The importance of the psychologist in clinical voice assessment. Journal of Voice, 31(4): 507.e13–507.e22, 2017. doi:10.1016/j.jvoice.2016.10.013.

APA (American Psychiatric Association). Diagnostic and Statistical Manual of Mental Disorders: DSM-5TM (5th Ed.), 2013. doi:https://doi.org/10.1176/appi.books.9780890425596.

Baca-Garcia, E., M.M. Perez-Rodriguez, I. Basurte-Villamor, A.L.F. Del Moral, M.A. Jimenez-Arriero, J.L.G. De Rivera, J. Saiz-Ruiz and Maria A. Oquendo. Diagnostic stability of psychiatric disorders in clinical practice. British Journal of Psychiatry, 190(MAR.): 210–216, 2007. doi:10.1192/bjp.bp.106.024026.

Bandelow, B. and S. Michaelis. Epidemiology of anxiety disorders in the 21st century. Dialogues in Clinical Neuroscience, 17(3): 327–335, 2015.

Bhagya Shree, S.R. and H.S. Sheshadri. An initial investigation in the diagnosis of Alzheimer's disease using various classification techniques. In: 2014 IEEE International Conference on Computational Intelligence and Computing Research, 2014: 1–5, 2015. doi:10.1109/ICCIC.2014.7238300.

Bzdok, D. and A. Meyer-Lindenberg. Machine learning for precision psychiatry: Opportunities and challenges. Biological Psychiatry: Cognitive Neuroscience and Neuroimaging, 3: 223–230, 2018. doi:10.1016/j.bpsc.2017.11.007.

Cannizzaro, M., B. Harel, N. Reilly, P. Chappell and P.J. Snyder. Voice acoustical measurement of the severity of major depression. Brain and Cognition, 56: 30–35, 2004. doi:10.1016/j.bandc.2004.05.003.

Carpenter, K.A. and X. Huang. Machine learning-based virtual screening and its applications to Alzheimer's drug discovery: A review. Current Pharmaceutical Design, 24(28): 3347–3358, 2018. doi:10.2174/1381612824666180607124038.

Chakraborty, D., S. Xu, Z. Yang, Y.H.V. Chua, Y. Tahir, J. Dauwels, N.M. Thalmann, B.L. Tan and J.L.C. Keong. Prediction of negative symptoms of schizophrenia from objective linguistic, acoustic and non-verbal conversational cues. IEEE 2018 International Conference on Cyberworlds Prediction. Published Online, 2018: 280–283, 2018. doi:10.1109/CW.2018.00057.

Chakraborty, D., Z. Yang, Y. Tahir, T. Maszczyk, J. Dauwels, N. Thalmann, J. Zheng, Y. Maniam, N. Amirah, B.L. Tan and J. Lee. Prediction of negative symptoms of schizophrenia from emotion related low-level speech signals. IEEE. Published Online, 2018: 6024–6028, 2018.

Cohn, J.F., T.S. Kruez and I. Matthews. Detecting depression from facial actions and vocal prosody. Proceedings—2009 3rd International Conference on Affective Computing and Intelligent Interaction and Workshops, ACII, 2009(October). doi:10.1109/ACII.2009.5349358.

Commowick, O., A. Istace, M. Kain, B. Laurent, F. Leray, M. Simon, S.C. Pop, P. Girard, R. Améli, J.C. Ferré, A. Kerbrat, T. Tourdias, F. Cervenansky, T. Glatard, J. Beaumont, S. Doyle, F. Forbes, J. Knight, A. Khademi, A. Mahbod, C. Wang, R. McKinley, F. Wagner, J. Muschelli, E. Sweeney, E. Roura, X. Lladó, M.M. Santos, W.P. Santos, A.G. Silva-Filho, X. Tomas-Fernandez, H. Urien, I. Bloch, S. Valverde, M. Cabezas, F.J. Vera-Olmos, N. Malpica, C. Guttmann, S. Vukusic, G. Edan, M. Dojat, M. Styner, S.K. Warfield, F. Cotton and C. Barillot. Objective evaluation of multiple sclerosis lesion segmentation using a data management and processing infrastructure. Scientific Reports, 8(13650): 1–17, 2018.

Compton, M.T., A. Lunden, S.D. Cleary, L. Pauselli, Y. Alolayan, B. Halpern, B. Broussard, A. Crisafio, L. Capulong, P.M. Balducci, F. Bernardini and M.A. Covington. The aprosody of schizophrenia: Computationally derived acoustic phonetic underpinnings of monotone speech. Schizophrenia Research. Published Online, 2018: 1–8, 2018. doi:10.1016/j.schres.2018.01.007.

Cordeiro, F.R., W.P.D. Santos and A.G. Silva-Filho. Analysis of supervised and semi-supervised GrowCut applied to segmentation of masses in mammography images. Biomechanics and Biomedical Engineering: Imaging & Visualization, 5(4): 297–315, 2017.

Covingto, M.A., S.L.A. Lunden, S.L. Cristofaro, C.R. Wan, C.T. Bailey, B. Broussard, R. Fogarty, S. Johnson, S. Zhang and M.T. Compton. Phonetic measures of reduced tongue movement correlate with negative symptom severity in hospitalized patients with first-episode schizophrenia-spectrum disorders. Schizophrenia Research, 142: 93–95, 2012.

Cummins, N., J. Epps, M. Breakspear and R. Goecke. An investigation of depressed speech detection: Features and normalization. In: 2011.

Cummins, N., S. Scherer, J. Krajewski, S. Schnieder, J. Epps and T.F. Quatieri. A review of depression and suicide risk assessment using speech analysis. Speech Communication, 71(April): 10–49, 2015. doi:10.1016/j.specom.2015.03.004.

Cuthbert, B.N. and T.R. Insel. Toward the future of psychiatric diagnosis: The seven pillars of RDoC. BMC Medicine, 11(1): 126, 2013. doi:10.1186/1741-7015-11-126.

Darby, J.K. and H. Hollien. Vocal and speech patterns of depressive patients. Folia Phoniatrica, 29: 279–291, 1977.

de Santana, M.A., J.M.S. Pereira, F.L. da Silva, N.M. de Lima, F.N. de Sousa, G.M.S. de Arruda and W.P. dos Santos. Breast cancer diagnosis based on mammary thermography and extreme learning machines. Research on Biomedical Engineering, 34(1): 45–53, 2018.

dos Santos, W.P., F.M. de Assis, R.E. de Souza, D. Santos and P.B. Filho. Evaluation of Alzheimer's disease by analysis of MR images using objective dialectical classifiers as an alternative to ADC maps. In: 2008 30th Annual International Conference of the IEEE Engineering in Medicine and Biology Society, 2008: 5506–5509, 2008.

dos Santos, W.P., F.M. de Assis, R.E. de Souza, P.B. Mendes, H.S. de Souza Monteiro and H.D. Alves. A dialectical method to classify Alzheimer's magnetic resonance images. Evolutionary Computation. Published Online, 2009: 473, 2009.

Dwyer, D., P. Falkai and N. Koutsouleris. Machine learning approaches for clinical psychology and psychiatry. Annu. Rev. Clin. Psychol., 14(January): 1–28, 2018.

Elite, A., L.J. Pedrão, N.E. Zamberlan-Amorim, A.M.P. Carvalho and A.M. Bárbaro. Comportamento comunicativo de indivíduos com esquizofrenia. Rev. CEFAC, 16(4): 1283–1293, 2014.

Elouedi, H., W. Meliani, Z. Elouedi and N. Ben Amor. A hybrid approach based on decision trees and clustering for breast cancer classification. In: 2014 6th International Conference of Soft Computing and Pattern Recognition (SoCPaR), 2014: 226–231, 2014. doi:10.1109/SOCPAR.2014.7008010.

Espinola, C.W., J.C. Gomes, J.M.S. Pereira and W.P. dos Santos. Detection of major depressive disorder using vocal acoustic analysis and machine learning—An exploratory study. Research on Biomedical Engineering. Published Online, 2020a. doi:10.1007/s42600-020-00100-9.

Espinola, C.W., J.C. Gomes, J.M.S. Pereira and W.P. dos Santos. Vocal acoustic analysis and machine learning for the identification of schizophrenia. Research on Biomedical Engineering. Published Online, 2020b. doi:10.1007/s42600-020-00097-1.

Faurholt-Jepsen, M., J. Busk, M. Frost, M. Vinberg, E.M. Christensen, O. Winther, J.E. Bardram and L.V. Kessing. Voice analysis as an objective state marker in bipolar disorder. Transl Psychiatry, 6(7): e856–8, 2016. doi:10.1038/tp.2016.123.

Foussias, G. and G. Remington. Negative symptoms in Schizophrenia: Avolition and Occam's razor. Schizophrenia Bulletin, 36(2): 359–369, 2010. doi:10.1093/schbul/sbn094.

Hashim, N.W., M. Wilkes, R. Salomon, J. Meggs and D.J. France. Evaluation of voice acoustics as predictors of clinical depression scores. Journal of Voice, 31(2): 256.e1–256.e6, 2017. doi:10.1016/j.jvoice.2016.06.006.

Higuchi, M., S. Tokuno, M. Nakamura and S. Shinohara. Classification of bipolar disorder, major depressive disorder, and healthy state using voice. Asian Journal of Pharmaceutical and Clinical Research, 11(3): 89–93, 2018. doi:10.22159/ajpcr.2018.v11s3.30042.

Higuchi, M., M. Nakamura, S. Shinohara, Y. Omiya, T. Takano, H. Toda, T. Saito, A. Yoshino, S. Mitsuyoshi and S. Tokuno. Discrimination of bipolar disorders using voice. MindCare, 1: 199–207, 2019. doi:10.1007/978-3-030-25872-6.

Hirschtritt, M. and T. Insel. Digital technologies in Psychiatry: Present and future. Focus, 16(3): 251–258, 2018. doi:10.1176/appi.focus.20180001.

Hönig, F., A. Batliner, E. Nöth, S. Schnieder and J. Krajewski. Automatic modelling of depressed speech: Relevant features and relevance of gender. Proceedings of the Annual Conference of the International Speech Communication Association, INTERSPEECH, 2014(444): 1248–1252, 2014.

Insel, T.R. and B.N. Cuthbert. Brain disorders? Precisely: Precision medicine comes to psychiatry. Science, 348(6234): 499–500, 2015. doi:10.1126/science.aaa9102.

Karam, Z.N., E.M. Provost, S. Singh, J. Montgomery, C. Archer, G. Harrington and M.G. Mcinnis. Ecologically valid long-term mood monitoring of individuals with bipolar disorder using speech. 2014 IEEE International Conference on Acoustic, Speech and Signal Processing (ICASSP). Published Online, 2014: 4858–4862, 2014.

Kraepelin, E. Manic-Depressive Insanity and Paranoia. Livingstone, 1921.

Kourou, K., T.P. Exarchos, K.P. Exarchos, M.V. Karamouzis and D.I. Fotiadis. Machine learning applications in cancer prognosis and prediction. Computational and Structural Biotechnology Journal, 13: 8–17, 2015. doi:https://doi.org/10.1016/j.csbj.2014.11.005.

Kuperberg, G.R. Language in schizophrenia Part 1: An introduction. Lang Linguist Compass, 4(8): 576–589, 2010. doi:10.1111/j.1749-818X.2010.00216.x.Language.

Jiang, H., B. Hu, Z. Liu, L. Yan, T. Wang, F. Liu, H. Kang and X. Li. Investigation of different speech types and emotions for detecting depression using different classifiers. Speech Communication, 90: 39–46, 2017. doi:10.1016/j.specom.2017.04.001.

Jiang, H., B. Hu, Z. Liu, G. Wang, L. Zhang, X. Li and H. Kang. Detecting depression using an ensemble logistic regression model based on multiple speech features. Computational and Mathematical Methods in Medicine, 2018. doi:10.1155/2018/6508319.

Joshi, J., R. Goecke, S. Alghowinem, A. Dhall, M. Wagner, J. Epps, G. Parker and M. Breakspear. Multimodal assistive technologies for depression diagnosis and monitoring. Journal on Multimodal User Interfaces, 7(3): 217–228, 2013. doi:10.1007/s12193-013-0123-2.

Langdon, W.B., S.J. Barrett and B.F. Buxton. Combining decision trees and neural networks for drug discovery. In: European Conference on Genetic Programming. Springer. Springer, 2002: 60–70, 2002. doi:10.1007/3-540-45984-7_6.

Larsen, M.E., N. Cummins, T.W. Boonstra, B. O'Dea, J. Tighe, J. Nicholas, F. Shand, J. Epps and H. Christensen. The use of technology in Suicide Prevention. In: Proceedings of the Annual International Conference of the IEEE Engineering in Medicine and Biology Society, EMBS, 2015: 7316–7319, 2015. doi:10.1109/EMBC.2015.7320081.

Laukka, P., K. Elenius, M. Fredrikson, T. Furmark and D. Neiberg. Vocal expression in spontaneous and experimentally induced affective speech: Acoustic correlates of anxiety, irritation and resignation. Published Online, 2008a.

Laukka, P., C. Linnman, F. Åhs, A. Pissiota, O. Frans, V. Faria, A. Michelgård, L. Appel, M. Fredrikson and T. Furmark. In a nervous voice: Acoustic analysis and perception of anxiety in social phobics' speech. J. Nonverbal. Behav., 32: 195–214, 2008b. doi:10.1007/s10919-008-0055-9.

Leon, S.A. and A.D. Rodriguez. Aprosodia and its treatment. Perspectives on Neurophysiology and Neurogenic Speech and Language Disorders, 18(2): 66–72, 2008. doi:10.1044/nnsld18.2.66.

Liu, Z., B. Hu, L. Yan, T. Wang, F. Liu, X. Li and H. Kang. Detection of depression in speech. In: 2015 International Conference on Affective Computing and Intelligent Interaction (ACII), 2015: 743–747, 2015.

Low, L.S.A., N.C. Maddage, M. Lech, L.B. Sheeber and N.B. Allen. Detection of clinical depression in adolescents' speech during family interactions. IEEE Transactions on Biomedical Engineering, 58(3 PART 1): 574–586, 2011. doi:10.1109/TBME.2010.2091640.

Mac-Kay, A., I. Jerez and P. Pesenti. Speech-language intervention in schizophrenia: An integrative review. Rev. CEFAC, 20(2): 238–246, 2018. doi:10.1590/1982-0216201820219317.

Marchi, E., B. Schuller, S. Baron-Cohen, O. Golan, S. Bölte, P. Arora and R. Häb-Umbach. Typicality and Emotion in the Voice of Children with Autism Spectrum Condition: Evidence Across Three Languages Machine Intelligence & Signal Processing Group, MMK, Technische Universit Chair of Complex & Intelligent Systems, University of Passau, G. In: INTERSPEECH, 2015: 115–119, 2015.

Martínez-Sánchez, F., J.A. Muela-Martínez, P. Cortés-soto, J.J.G. Meilán, J.A.V. Ferrándiz, A.E. Caparrós and I.M.P. Valverde. Can the acoustic analysis of expressive prosody discriminate schizophrenia? The Spanish Journal of Psychology, 18(86): 1–9, 2015. doi:10.1017/sjp.2015.85.

Maxhuni, A., A. Muñoz-Meléndez, V. Osmani, H. Perez, O. Mayora and E.F. Morales. Classification of bipolar disorder episodes based on analysis of voice and motor activity of patients. Pervasive and Mobile Computing, 31(1): 50–66, 2016. doi:10.1016/j.pmcj.2016.01.008.

Merikangas, K.R., R. Jin, J.P. He, R.C. Kessler, S. Lee, N.A. Sampson, M.C. Viana, L.H. Andrade, C. Hu, E.G. Karam, M. Ladea, M.E. Medina-Mora, Y. Ono, J. Posada-Villa, R. Sagar, J.E. Wells and Z. Zarkov. Prevalence and correlates of bipolar spectrum disorder in the World Mental Health Survey initiative. Archives of General Psychiatry, 68(3): 241–251, 2011. doi:10.1001/archgenpsychiatry.2011.12.

Mitra, V. and E. Shriberg. Effects of feature type, learning algorithm and speaking style for depression detection from speech. In: 2015 IEEE International Conference on Acoustics, Speech and Signal Processing (ICASSP), 2015: 4774–4778, 2015. doi:10.1109/ICASSP.2015.7178877.

Morgado, F.F.R., J.F.F. Meireles, C.M. Neves, A.C.S. Amaral and M.E.C. Ferreira. Scale development: Ten main limitations and recommendations to improve future research practices. Psicologia: Reflexao e Critica, 30(3), 2017. doi:10.1186/s41155-016-0057-1.

Mundt, J.C., P.J. Snyde, M.S. Cannizzaro, K. Chappie and D.S. Geralts. Voice acoustic measures of depression severity and treatment response collected via interactive voice response (IVR) technology. Journal of Neurolinguistics, 20: 50–64, 2007. doi:10.1016/j.jneuroling.2006.04.001.

Mundt, J.C., A.P. Vogel, D.E. Feltner and W.R. Lenderking. Vocal acoustic biomarkers of depression severity and treatment response. Biological Psychiatry, 72(7): 580–587, 2012. doi:10.1016/j. biopsych.2012.03.015.

Newman, S. and V.G. Mather. Analysis of spoken language of patients with affective disorders. American Journal of Psychiatry, 94: 913–942, 1938.

The National Institute of Mental Health (NIMH). Behavioral Assessment Methods for RDoC Constructs, 2016.

The National Institute of Mental Health (NIMH). About RDoC. Accessed February 18, 2021. https:// www.nimh.nih.gov/research/research-funded-by-nimh/rdoc/about-rdoc.shtml.

Ooi, K.E.B., M. Lech and N.B. Allen. Multichannel weighted speech classification system for prediction of major depression in adolescents. IEEE Transactions on Biomedical Engineering, 60(2): 497–506, 2013. doi:10.1016/j.bspc.2014.08.006.

Özseven, T., M. Dügenci, A. Doruk and H.I. Kahraman. Voice traces of anxiety: Acoustic parameters affected by anxiety disorder. Archives of Acoustics, 43(4): 625–636, 2018. doi:10.24425/ aoa.2018.125156.

Parola, A., A. Simonsen, V. Bliksted and R. Fusaroli. Voice patterns in schizophrenia: A systematic review and Bayesian meta-analysis. Schizophrenia Research, 216: 24–40, 2020. doi:10.1016/j. schres.2019.11.031.

Petzschner, F.H., L.A.E. Weber, T. Gard and K.E. Stephan. Review computational psychosomatics and computational psychiatry: Toward a joint framework for differential diagnosis. Biological Psychiatry. Published Online, 2017: 1–10, 2017. doi:10.1016/j.biopsych.2017.05.012.

Ringeval, F., M. Valstar, R. Cowie, H. Kaya, M. Schmitt, S. Amiriparian, N. Cummins, D. Lalanne, A. Michaud, E. Ciftçi, H. Güleç, A.A. Salah and M. Pantic. AVEC 2018 Workshop and Challenge: Bipolar Disorder and Cross-Cultural Affect Recognition. AVEC'18. Published Online, 2018: 3–13, 2018.

Rowland, T.A. and S. Marwaha. Epidemiology and risk factors for bipolar disorder. Therapeutic Advances in Psychopharmacology, 8(9): 251–269, 2018. doi:10.1177/https.

Sadock, B., V. Sadock and P. Rui. Compêndio de Psiquiatria: Ciência Do Comportamento e Psiquiatria Clínica. 11. Artmed, 2017.

Sanislow, C.A., M. Ferrante, J. Pacheco, M.V. Rudorfer and S.E. Morris. Advancing translational research using NIMH research domain criteria and computational methods. Neuron, 101(5): 779–782, 2019. doi:10.1016/j.neuron.2019.02.024.

Scherer, S., G. Stratou, J. Gratch and L.P. Morency. Investigating voice quality as a speaker-independent indicator of depression and PTSD. Proceedings of the Annual Conference of the International Speech Communication Association, INTERSPEECH, 2013(August): 847–851, 2013.

Sharda, M., T.P. Subhadra, S. Sahay, C. Nagaraja, L. Singh, R. Mishra, A. Sen, N. Singhal, D. Erickson and N.C. Singh. Sounds of melody—Pitch patterns of speech in autism. Neuroscience Letters, 478(1): 42–45, 2010. doi:https://doi.org/10.1016/j.neulet.2010.04.066.

Simeone, J.C., A.J. Ward, P. Rotella, J. Collins and R. Windisch. An evaluation of variation in published estimates of schizophrenia prevalence from 1990–2013: A systematic literature review. BMC Psychiatry, 15(193), 2015. doi:10.1186/s12888-015-0578-7.

Sturim, D., P. Torres-Carrasquillo, T.F. Quatieri, N. Malyska and A. McCree. Automatic detection of depression in speech using Gaussian mixture modeling with factor analysis. Proceedings of the Annual Conference of the International Speech Communication Association, INTERSPEECH. Published Online, 2011: 2981–2984, 2011.

Taguchi, T., H. Tachikawa, K. Nemoto, M. Suzuki, T. Nagano, R. Tachibana, M. Nishimura and T. Arai. Major depressive disorder discrimination using vocal acoustic features. Journal of Affective Disorders, 225: 214–220, 2018. doi:10.1016/j.jad.2017.08.038.

Tahir, Y., Z. Yang, D. Chakraborty, N. Thalmann, D. Thalmann, Y. Maniam, N.A.b.A. Rashid, B.L. Tan, J.L.C. Keong and J. Dauwels. Non-verbal speech cues as objective measures for negative symptoms in patients with schizophrenia. PLOS ONE. Published Online, 2019: 1–17, 2019. doi:10.1371/journal.pone.0214314, 2019.

Torous, J., M.V. Kiang, J. Lorme and J.P. Onnela. New tools for new research in psychiatry: A scalable and customizable platform to empower data driven smartphone research. JMIR Mental Health, 3(2): e16, 2016. doi:10.2196/mental.5165.

Torous, J., J.P. Onnela and M. Keshavan. New dimensions and new tools to realize the potential of RDoC: Digital phenotyping via smartphones and connected devices. Translational Psychiatry, 7(3): 2–4, 2017. doi:10.1038/tp.2017.25.

Vanello, N., A. Guidi, C. Gentili, S. Werner, G. Bertschy, G. Valenza, A. Lanatá and E.P. Scilingo. Speech analysis for mood state characterization in bipolar patients. In: 34th Annual International Conference of the IEEE EMBS, 2012: 2104–2107, 2012.

van Puyvelde, M., X. Neyt, F. McGlone and N. Pattyn. Voice stress analysis: A new framework for voice and effort in human performance. Frontiers in Psychology, 9(NOV): 1–25, 2018. doi:10.3389/fpsyg.2018.01994.

Viera, A.J. and J.M. Garrett. Understanding interobserver agreement: the kappa statistic. Family Medicine, 37(5): 360–363, 2005. http://www1.cs.columbia.edu/~julia/courses/CS6998/Interrater_agreement.Kappa_statistic.pdf.

Vilela, J.A.A., J.A.S. Crippa, C.M. Del-Ben and S.R. Loureiro. Reliability and validity of a Portuguese version of the Young Mania Rating Scale. Brazilian Journal of Medical and Biological Research, 38(9): 1429–1439, 2005. doi:10.1590/S0100-879X2005000900019.

Wang, J., X. Sui, T. Zhu and J. Flint. Identifying comorbidities from depressed people via voice analysis. In: IEEE International Conference on Bioinformatics and Biomedicine (BIBM), 2017: 986–991, 2017.

Weeks, J.W., C.Y. Lee, A.R. Reilly, A.N. Howell, C. France, J.M. Kowalsky and A. Bush. The sound of fear: Assessing vocal fundamental frequency as a physiological indicator of social anxiety disorder. Journal of Anxiety Disorders, 26(8): 811–822, 2012. doi:10.1016/j.janxdis.2012.07.005.

Weeks, J.W., A. Srivastav, A.N. Howell and A.R. Menatti. Speaking more than words: Classifying men with social anxiety disorder via vocal acoustic analyses of diagnostic interviews. J. Psychopathol. Behav. Assess., 38: 30–41, 2016. doi:10.1007/s10862-015-9495-9.

WHO (World Health Organization). Depression. Published 2018. Accessed November 10, 2019. https://www.who.int/en/news-room/fact-sheets/detail/depression.

Wittchen, H-U. Generalized Anxiety disorder: Prevalence, burden, and cost to society. Depression and Anxiety, 6: 162–171, 2002. doi:10.1002/da.10065.

Young, R.C., J.T. Biggs, V.E. Ziegler and D.A. Meyer. A rating scale for mania. British Journal of Psychiatry, 133: 429–435, 1975. doi:10.1192/bjp.133.5.429.

Zhang, J., Z. Pan, C. Gui, J. Zhu and D. Cui. Clinical investigation of speech signal features among patients with schizophrenia. Shanghai Archives of Psychiatry, 28(2): 95–102, 2016. doi:10.11919/j.issn.1002-0829.216025.

Index

Printed in the United States
by Baker & Taylor Publisher Services